# Growing Up with SCIENCE®

## Third Edition

## 17

### Index

Marshall Cavendish
Reference
New York

Marshall Cavendish
99 White Plains Road
Tarrytown, NY 10591

www.marshallcavendish.us

**Library of Congress Cataloging-in-Publication Data**

Growing up with science.— 3rd ed.
    p.  cm.
  Includes index.
  Contents: v. 1. Abrasive-Astronomy — v. 2. Atmosphere-Cable television —
v. 3. Cable travel-Cotton — v. 4. Crane-Electricity — v. 5 Electric motor-
Friction — v. 6. Fuel cell-Immune system — v. 7. Induction-Magnetism —
v. 8. Mapmaking-Mining and quarrying — v. 9. Missile and torpedo-Oil
exploration and refining — v. 10. Optics-Plant kingdom — v. 11. Plasma
physics-Radiotherapy — v. 12. Railroad system-Seismology — v. 13.
Semiconductor-Sports — v. 14. Spring-Thermography — v. 15. Thermometer-
Virus, biological — v. 16. Virus, computer-Zoology — v. 17. Index.
  ISBN 0-7614-7505-2 (set)
  ISBN 0-7614-7522-2 (vol. 17)
  1. Science—Encyclopedias.

Q121.G764 2006
503—dc22

                                                    2004049962
                                  09 08 07 06 05 6 5 4 3 2 1
Printed in China

CONSULTANT

Donald R. Franceschetti, Ph.D.

Dunavant Professor at the University of Memphis

Donald R. Franceschetti is a member of the American
Chemical Society, the American Physical Society, the
Cognitive Science Society, the History of Science Society,
and the Society for Neuroscience.

**Marshall Cavendish**

Editors: Peter Mavrikis and Susan Rescigno

Editorial Director: Paul Bernabeo

Production Manager: Alan Tsai


**The Brown Reference Group**

Editors: Leon Gray and Simon Hall

Designer: Sarah Williams

Picture Researchers: Becky Cox, Susy Forbes, Clare
    Newman, Helen Simm, and Laila Torsun

Indexer: Kay Ollerenshaw

Illustrators: Darren Awuah and Mark Walker

Managing Editor: Bridget Giles

Art Director: Dave Goodman

# CONTENTS

**Periodic table** . . . . . . . . . . . . . . . . . . . . . . . . . . .2052

**Weights and measures** . . . . . . . . . . . . . . . . . .2054

**Further study**

Books . . . . . . . . . . . . . . . . . . . . . . . . . . . . .2056

Magazines . . . . . . . . . . . . . . . . . . . . . . . . . .2059

Web sites . . . . . . . . . . . . . . . . . . . . . . . . . .2060

Museums . . . . . . . . . . . . . . . . . . . . . . . . . .2061

**Time line**

Inventions and discoveries . . . . . . . . . . . . . . .2062

Geologic time line . . . . . . . . . . . . . . . . . . . . .2065

**Glossary** . . . . . . . . . . . . . . . . . . . . . . . . . . . . .2066

**Thematic indexes**

Earth, space, and environmental sciences . . . . .2082

Life sciences . . . . . . . . . . . . . . . . . . . . . . . . .2090

Mathematics . . . . . . . . . . . . . . . . . . . . . . . . .2098

Physics and chemistry . . . . . . . . . . . . . . . . . .2098

Technology . . . . . . . . . . . . . . . . . . . . . . . . . .2109

People . . . . . . . . . . . . . . . . . . . . . . . . . . . . .2121

**General index** . . . . . . . . . . . . . . . . . . . . . . . . .2126

# Periodic table

The periodic table of chemical elements was devised by Russian chemist Dmitry Ivanovich Mendeleyev (1834–1907) in 1869. Mendeleyev discovered a repeating pattern to the elements. The columns in the periodic table show groups of elements with similar chemical properties. The rows represent the periods. Each period begins with a reactive metal and ends with an inert (nonreactive) gas. The elements between follow a periodic pattern.

| 1* Ia** | 2 IIa | 3 IIIb | 4 IVb | 5 Vb | 6 VIb | 7 VIIb | 8 VIIIb | 9 VIIIb | 10 |
|---|---|---|---|---|---|---|---|---|---|
| 1 H | | | | | | | | | |
| 3 Li | 4 Be | | | | | | | | |
| 11 Na | 12 Mg | | | | | | | | |
| 19 K | 20 Ca | 21 Sc | 22 Ti | 23 V | 24 Cr | 25 Mn | 26 Fe | 27 Co | 28 Ni |
| 37 Rb | 38 Sr | 39 Y | 40 Zr | 41 Nb | 42 Mo | 43 Tc | 44 Ru | 45 Rh | 46 Pd |
| 55 Cs | 56 Ba | 57* La | 72 Hf | 73 Ta | 74 W | 75 Re | 76 Os | 77 Ir | 78 Pt |
| 87 Fr | 88 Ra | 89+ Ac | 104 Rf | 105 Db | 106 Sg | 107 Bh | 108 Hs | 109 Mt | 110 Ds |

GROUP

PERIOD

* Column numbering system recommended by the International Union of Pure and Applied Chemistry (IUPAC)
** Column numbering system recommended by the Chemical Abstracts Service

| *58 Ce | 59 Pr | 60 Nd | 61 Pm | 62 Sm |
|---|---|---|---|---|
| +90 Th | 91 Pa | 92 U | 93 Np | 94 Pu |

## A–Z LIST OF THE ELEMENTS

| | | | | | | | |
|---|---|---|---|---|---|---|---|
| Actinium (89) | Ac | Boron (5) | B | Curium (96) | Cm | Germanium (32) | Ge |
| Aluminum (13) | Al | Bromine (35) | Br | Darmstadtium (110) | Ds | Gold (79) | Au |
| Americium (95) | Am | Cadmium (48) | Cd | Dubnium (105) | Db | Hafnium (72) | Hf |
| Antimony (51) | Sb | Calcium (20) | Ca | Dysprosium (66) | Dy | Hassium (108) | Hs |
| Argon (18) | Ar | Californium (98) | Cf | Einsteinium (99) | Es | Helium (2) | He |
| Arsenic (33) | As | Carbon (6) | C | Erbium (68) | Er | Holmium (67) | Ho |
| Astatine (85) | At | Cerium (58) | Ce | Europium (63) | Eu | Hydrogen (1) | H |
| Barium (56) | Ba | Cesium (55) | Cs | Fermium (100) | Fm | Indium (49) | In |
| Berkelium (97) | Bk | Chlorine (17) | Cl | Fluorine (9) | F | Iodine (53) | I |
| Beryllium (4) | Be | Chromium (24) | Cr | Francium (87) | Fr | Iridium (77) | Ir |
| Bismuth (83) | Bi | Cobalt (27) | Co | Gadolinium (64) | Gd | Iron (26) | Fe |
| Bohrium (107) | Bh | Copper (29) | Cu | Gallium (31) | Ga | Krypton (36) | Kr |

| | |
|---|---|
| Lanthanum (57) | La |
| Lawrencium (103) | Lr |
| Lead (82) | Pb |
| Lithium (3) | Li |
| Lutetium (71) | Lu |
| Magnesium (12) | Mg |
| Manganese (25) | Mn |
| Meitnerium (109) | Mt |
| Mendelevium (101) | Md |
| Mercury (80) | Hg |
| Molybdenum (42) | Mo |
| Neodymium (60) | Nd |

**18**
**O**

**2**
**He**

**13**
**IIIa**

**14**
**IVa**

**15**
**Va**

**16**
**VIa**

**17**
**VIIa**

| Hydrogen |
| Metals |
| Metaolids |
| Nonmetals |
| Inert gases |

| 5 B | 6 C | 7 N | 8 O | 9 F | 10 Ne |
| 13 Al | 14 Si | 15 P | 16 S | 17 Cl | 18 Ar |

**11**
**Ib**

**12**
**IIb**

| 29 Cu | 30 Zn | 31 Ga | 32 Ge | 33 As | 34 Se | 35 Br | 36 Kr |
| 47 Ag | 48 Cd | 49 In | 50 Sn | 51 Sb | 52 Te | 53 I | 54 Xe |
| 79 Au | 80 Hg | 81 Tl | 82 Pb | 83 Bi | 84 Po | 85 At | 86 Rn |
| 111 Rg | 112 Uub |

| 63 Eu | 64 Gd | 65 Tb | 66 Dy | 67 Ho | 68 Er | 69 Tm | 70 Yb | 71 Lu |
| 95 Am | 96 Cm | 97 Bk | 98 Cf | 99 Es | 100 Fm | 101 Md | 102 No | 103 Lr |

| | | | | | |
|---|---|---|---|---|---|
| Neon (10) | Ne | Potassium (19) | K | Scandium (21) | Sc | Thorium (90) | Th |
| Neptunium (93) | Np | Praseodymium (59) | Pr | Seaborgium (106) | Sg | Thulium (69) | Tm |
| Nickel (28) | Ni | Promethium (61) | Pm | Selenium (34) | Se | Tin (50) | Sn |
| Niobium (41) | Nb | Protactinium (91) | Pa | Silicon (14) | Si | Titanium (22) | Ti |
| Nitrogen (7) | N | Radium (88) | Ra | Silver (47) | Ag | Tungsten (74) | W |
| Nobelium (102) | No | Radon (86) | Rn | Sodium (11) | Na | Ununbium (112) | Uub |
| Osmium (76) | Os | Rhenium (75) | Re | Strontium (38) | Sr | Uranium (92) | U |
| Oxygen (8) | O | Rhodium (45) | Rh | Sulfur (16) | S | Vanadium (23) | V |
| Palladium (46) | Pd | Roentgenium (111) | Rg | Tantalum (73) | Ta | Xenon (54) | Xe |
| Phosphorus (15) | P | Rubidium (37) | Rb | Technetium (43) | Tc | Ytterbium (70) | Yb |
| Platinum (78) | Pt | Ruthenium (44) | Ru | Tellurium (52) | Te | Yttrium (39) | Y |
| Plutonium (94) | Pu | Rutherfordium (104) | Rf | Terbium (65) | Tb | Zinc (30) | Zn |
| Polonium (84) | Po | Samarium (62) | Sm | Thallium (81) | Tl | Zirconium (40) | Zr |

# Weights and measures

Standard weights and measures are needed to measure everyday quantities such as ingredients for recipes or the temperature of a room. Scientists need more complex systems of weights and measures so that they can do their experiments.

There are two main systems. The imperial system uses the foot, pound, gallon, and degree Fahrenheit. The metric system uses the meter, kilogram, liter, and degree Celsius. There are many other weights and measures that do not fit into these two groups.

## CONVERSION CHART

### LENGTH

| | |
|---|---|
| 1 inch (in) | = 2.54 cm |
| 1 foot (ft) | = 0.3048 m |
| 1 yard | = 0.9144 m |
| 1 mile | = 1.6093 km |
| 1 millimeter (mm) | = 0.0394 in |
| 1 centimeter (cm) | = 0.3937 in |
| 1 meter (m) | = 3.2808 ft |
| 1 kilometer (km) | = 0.62137 mile |
| 1 angstrom (Å) | = $10^{-10}$ m |
| 1 astronomical unit (AU) | = $1.4965 \times 10^{11}$ m |
| | = $92.96 \times 10^{9}$ miles |
| 1 parsec (pc) | = $3.0845 \times 10^{16}$ m |
| 1 light-year (ly) | = $9.4605 \times 10^{15}$ m |

### AREA

| | |
|---|---|
| 1 acre | = 0.4047 ha |
| 1 square mile | = 2.59 km$^2$ |
| 1 hectare (ha) | = 2.4711 acres |
| 1 km$^2$ | = 0.3861 square miles |

### VOLUME

| | |
|---|---|
| 1 gallon (gal) | = 3.7854 liters |
| 1 liter | = 0.2642 gal |
| 1 cubic foot | = 0.028 m$^3$ |
| 1 m$^3$ | = 35.314 cubic feet |
| 1 cubic inch | = 16.38 cm$^3$ |
| 1 cm$^3$ | = 0.061 cubic inches |

### WEIGHT

| | |
|---|---|
| 1 ounce (oz) | = 28.35 g |
| 1 pound (lb) | = 0.4536 kg |
| 1 ton | = 0.907 tonnes |
| 1 gram (g) | = 0.0353 oz |
| 1 kilogram (kg) | = 2.2046 lb |
| 1 tonne | = 1.1025 tons |

### TEMPERATURE

| | |
|---|---|
| Fahrenheit to Celsius: | °C = (°F − 32) × ⅝ |
| Celsius to Fahrenheit: | °F = °C + 32 × ⅝ |

## SI PREFIXES

| Multiple | Prefix | Symbol | Example |
|---|---|---|---|
| 1,000,000,000,000,000,000 ($10^{18}$) | exa- | E | Eg (exagram) |
| 1,000,000,000,000,000 ($10^{15}$) | peta- | P | PJ (petajoule) |
| 1,000,000,000,000 ($10^{12}$) | tera- | T | TV (teravolt) |
| 1,000,000,000 ($10^{9}$) | giga- | G | GW (gigawatt) |
| 1,000,000 ($10^{6}$) | mega- | M | Mhz (megahertz) |
| 1,000 ($10^{3}$) | kilo- | k | kg (kilogram) |
| 100 ($10^{2}$) | hecto- | h | hm (hectometer) |
| 10 | deca- | da | daN (decanewton) |
| 1/10 ($10^{-1}$) | deci- | d | dC (decicoulomb) |
| 1/100 ($10^{-2}$) | centi- | c | cm (centimeter) |
| 1/1,000 ($10^{-3}$) | milli- | m | mA (milliampere) |
| 1/1,000,000 ($10^{-6}$) | micro- | μ | μF (microfarad) |
| 1/1,000,000,000 ($10^{-9}$) | nano- | n | nm (nanometer) |
| 1/1,000,000,000,000 ($10^{-12}$) | pico- | p | ps (picosecond) |
| 1/1,000,000,000,000,000 ($10^{-15}$) | femto- | f | frad (femtoradian) |
| 1/1,000,000,000,000,000,000 ($10^{-18}$) | atto- | a | aT (attotesla) |

## PHYSICAL CONSTANTS

| Quantity | Symbol | Value | SI Unit |
|---|---|---|---|
| Avogadro's number | $N_A$ | $6.023 \times 10^{23}$ | $mol^{-1}$ |
| Boltzmann's constant | $k$ | $1.381 \times 10^{-23}$ | $JK^{-1}$ |
| Elementary charge | $e$ | $1.602 \times 10^{-19}$ | $C$ |
| Gravitational constant | $G$ | $6.673 \times 10^{-11}$ | $m^3kg^{-1}s^{-2}$ |
| Lunar mass | $M_m$ | $7.35 \times 10^{22}$ | $kg$ |
| Lunar radius (mean) | $R_m$ | $1.74 \times 10^6$ | $m$ |
| Mass of Earth | — | $5.98 \times 10^{24}$ | $kg$ |
| Rest mass of electron | $m_e$ | $9.109 \times 10^{-31}$ | $kg$ |
| Rest mass of neutron | $m_n$ | $1.675 \times 10^{-27}$ | $kg$ |
| Rest mass of proton | $m_p$ | $1.673 \times 10^{-27}$ | $kg$ |
| Molar gas constant | $R$ | $8.314$ | $J(mol\ K)^{-1}$ |
| Permeability of vacuum | $\mu_o$ | $4\pi \times 10^{-7}$ | $TmA^{-1}$ |
| Permittivity of vacuum | $\varepsilon_0$ | $8.854 \times 10^{-12}$ | $Fm^{-1}$ |
| Planck's constant | $h$ | $6.626 \times 10^{-34}$ | $Js$ |
| Radius of Earth (at equator) | — | $6.34 \times 10^6$ | $m$ |
| Solar mass | $M_\odot$ | $1.989 \times 10^{30}$ | $kg$ |
| Solar radius (mean) | $R_\odot$ | $6.960 \times 10^9$ | $m$ |
| Speed of light in vacuum | $c$ | $2.998 \times 10^8$ | $ms^{-1}$ |
| Standard gravity | $g$ | $9.80665$ | $ms^{-2}$ |

## SI BASE UNITS

| Quantity | Unit | Symbol |
|---|---|---|
| Length | meter | m |
| Mass | kilogram | kg |
| Time | second | s |
| Electrical current | ampere | A |
| Thermodynamic temperature | kelvin | K |
| Amount of substance | mole | mol |
| Luminous intensity | candela | cd |

## SI DERIVED UNITS

| Quantity | Unit | Symbol | Equivalent Units |
|---|---|---|---|
| Absorbed dose | gray | Gy | $Jkg^{-1}$ |
| Activity (of radionuclides) | becquerel | Bq | $s^{-1}$ |
| Capacitance | farad | F | $CV^{-1}$ |
| Electric charge | coulomb | C | $A.s$ |
| Electric potential | volt | V | $JC^{-1}$ |
| Electric resistance | ohm | $\Omega$ | $VA^{-1}$ |
| Energy | joule | J | $Nm$ |
| Force | newton | N | $kg.ms^{-2}$ |
| Frequency | hertz | hz | $s^{-1}$ |
| Magnetic flux density | tesla | T | $kg.A^{-1}s^{-2}$ |
| Power | watt | W | $Js^{-1}$ |
| Pressure | pascal | Pa | $Nm^{-2}$ |

*Note:* SI refers to Système International d'Unités, or International System of Units, commonly called the metric system.

# Further study

## BOOKS

### EARTH, SPACE, AND ENVIRONMENTAL SCIENCES

#### Agriculture

Halvorsen, L. *George Washington Carver: Innovator in Agriculture (Giants of Science)*. Woodbridge, Connecticut: Blackbirch Press, 2002. ISBN: 1567116574.

Hansen, D., and E. Hanson. *Agriculture (Yesterday and Today)*. Woodbridge, Connecticut: Blackbirch Press, 2005. ISBN: 1567118275.

Woods, M., and B. Woods. *Ancient Agriculture: From Foraging to Farming (Ancient Technology)*. Minneapolis: Runestone Press, 2000. ISBN: 0822529955.

*World Agriculture (Creative Discoveries)*. Edited by D. Bour and L. Ottenheimer. New York: Creative Education Foundation, 1998. ISBN: 0886829526.

#### Astronomy

Becan, J. *Astronomy for Beginners*. New York: Writers and Readers Publishing, 2004. ISBN: 0863169996.

Coles, P. *Cosmology: A Very Short Introduction*. New York: Oxford Paperbacks (Oxford University Press), 2001. ISBN: 019285416X.

Dickinson, T., and A. Dyer. *The Backyard Astronomer's Guide*. Ontario, Canada: Firefly Books Ltd., 2002. ISBN: 155209507X.

Kerrod, R. *Universe (DK EYEWITNESS BOOKS)*. London, England: DK Children, 2003. ISBN: 0789492385.

Koppes, S. *Killer Rocks from Outer Space: Asteroids, Comets, and Meteors (Discovery)*. Minneapolis: Carolrhoda Books, 2003. ISBN: 0822528614.

Ride, S., and T. O'Shaughnessy. *Exploring Our Solar System*. New York: Crown Books for Young Readers Publishing, 2003. ISBN: 0375812040.

Ridpath, I. *The Monthly Sky Guide*. New York: Cambridge University Press, 2003. ISBN: 0521533066.

Ryden, B. *Introduction to Cosmology*. New York: Addison-Wesley (Pearson Education), 2002. ISBN: 0805389121.

#### Geography

Armstrong, A., et al. *Geography: The World and Its People*. New York: Glencoe/McGraw-Hill, 2000. ISBN: 0028214854.

Bednarz, S. *World Cultures and Geography*. Boston, Massachusetts: Houghton Mifflin School Division, 2003. ISBN: 0618377492.

*Brief Review: History and Geography*. New York: Prentice Hall (Pearson Education), 2004. ISBN: 0131309919.

Claybourne, A., S. Davidson, and G. Doherty. *The Usborne Internet-Linked Encyclopedia of World Geography with Complete World Atlas (Geography)*. London, England: Usborne Publishing, 2004. ISBN: 0794508057.

De Blij, H. D., and P. Muller. *Geography: Realms, Regions and Concepts*. Hoboken, New Jersey: Wiley, 2001. ISBN: 0471407755.

*DK Geography of the World*. London, England: DK Publishing, 2003. ISBN: 078948594X.

Gifford, C. *The Kingfisher Geography Encyclopedia (Kingfisher Family of Encyclopedias)*. New York: Kingfisher Books, 2003. ISBN: 0753455919.

Rayburn, R. *World Geography (Teacher Created Materials)*. 2nd edition. Westminster, California: Teacher Created Resources, 2004. ISBN: 0743937996.

#### Meteorology

Ackerman, S., and J. Knox. *Meteorology: Understanding the Atmosphere*. Pacific Grove, California: Brooks/Cole, 2002. ISBN: 053437199X.

Allaby, M. *Droughts (Facts on File Dangerous Weather Series)*. New York: Facts on File, 2003. ISBN: 0816047936.

Barry, R., and R. J. Chorley. *Atmosphere, Weather and Climate*. 8th edition. New York: Routledge, 2003. ISBN: 0415271711.

Burnett, R., P. Lehr, and H. Zim. *Weather: Air Masses, Clouds, Rainfall, Storms, Weather Maps, Climate*. Racine, Wisconsin: Golden Books Publishing Company, 1987. ISBN: 0307240517.

*Climate: Into the 21st Century*. Edited by W. Burroughs. New York: Cambridge University Press, 2003. ISBN: 0521792029.

Gallant, R. *Resources: Nature's Riches (Earthworks)*. New York: Benchmark Books, 2002. ISBN: 0761413693.

Godrej, D. *The No-Nonsense Guide to Climate Change*. New York: Verso Books, 2001. ISBN: 1859843352.

Gribbin, J., and M. Gribbin. *FitzRoy: The Remarkable Story of Darwin's Captain and the Invention of the Weather Forecast*. London, England: Hodder Headline, 2004. ISBN: 0755311825.

Haley, J. *Global Warming: Opposing Viewpoints*. San Diego: Greenhaven Press, 2001. ISBN: 0737709081.

Houghton, J. *Global Warming: The Complete Briefing*. New York: Cambridge University Press, 2004. ISBN: 0521528747.

Howell, L. *Introduction to Weather and Climate Change*. London, England: Usborne Publishing, 2003. ISBN: 0794506291.

Kling, A. *Tornadoes (Natural Disasters)*. San Diego: Greenhaven Press, 2002. ISBN: 1560069775.

Maslin, M. *Global Warming*. Grantown-on-Spey, Scotland: Colin Baxter Photography Ltd., 2002. ISBN: 184107120X.

Motavelli, J. *Feeling the Heat*. New York: Routledge, 2004. ISBN: 0415946565.

Naylor, J. *Out of the Blue: A 24-Hour Skywatcher's Guide*. New York: Cambridge University Press, 2002. ISBN: 0521809258.

Reid, S. *Ozone and Climate Change: A Beginner's Guide*. London, England: Taylor and Francis, 2000. ISBN: 184107120X.

Runkle, B. *World Physical Geography.* Norman, Oklahoma: Runkle Publishers, Inc., 2000. ISBN: 0970111207.

Verkaik, J., and A. Verkaik. *Under the Whirlwind: Everything You Need to Ask About Tornadoes But Didn't Know Who To Ask.* Chicago: Independent Publishers Group, 2001. ISBN: 0968153747.

Watts, A. *The Weather Handbook.* London, England: Adlard Coles Nautical, 2004. ISBN: 0713669381.

# LIFE SCIENCES AND MEDICINE

## Biochemistry

Berg, J., L. Stryer, and J. Tymoczko. *Biochemistry.* New York: W. H. Freeman, 2002. ISBN: 0716730510.

Champe, P., and R. Harvey. *Lippincott's Illustrated Reviews: Biochemistry.* 2nd edition. Philadelphia: Lippincott Williams & Wilkins, 1994. ISBN: 0397510918.

Cox, M., and D. Nelson. *Lehninger Principles of Biochemistry.* 4th edition. New York: W. H. Freeman, 2004. ISBN: 0716743396.

## Biology

Ardley, B., and N. Ardley. *Oxford Children's A to Z to the Human Body.* New York: Oxford University Press, 2003. ISBN: 0199109907.

Biggs, A. *Biology: The Dynamics of Life.* New York: Glencoe/McGraw-Hill, 2000. ISBN: 0028282426.

Givens, P., and M. Reiss. *Human Biology and Health Studies.* Cheltenham, England: Nelson Thornes, 2004. ISBN: 0174900600.

Krogh, D. *Biology: A Guide to the Natural World.* 3rd edition. Englewood Cliffs, New Jersey: Prentice Hall, 2000. ISBN: 0131414496.

Levine, J., and K. Miller. *Prentice Hall Biology.* New York: Prentice Hall (Pearson Education), 2003. ISBN: 0131811126.

Staff, R. *High School Biology Tutor.* New Jersey: Research and Education Association, 1992. ISBN: 0878919074.

Strauss, E., and M. Lisowski. *Biology: The Web of Life.* Englewood Cliffs, New Jersey: Prentice Hall, 2000. ISBN: 0201334402.

Towle, A. *Modern Biology.* 9th edition. Austin, Texas: Holt, Rinehart and Winston, 2000. ISBN: 0030177448.

Tudge, C. *The Variety of Life: A Survey and Celebration of All the Creatures That Have Ever Lived.* New York: Oxford University Press, 2002. ISBN: 0198604262.

## Botany

Elpel, T. *Botany in a Day: The Patterns Method of Plant Identification.* Pony, Montana: HOPS Press, 2004. ISBN: 1892784157.

Graham, L., and L. Wilcox. *Algae.* Englewood Cliffs, New Jersey: Prentice Hall, 1999. ISBN: 0136603335.

Harris, J., and M. Harris. *Plant Identification Terminology: An Illustrated Glossary.* Spring Lake, Utah: Spring Lake Publications, 2001. ISBN: 0964022168.

Mauseth, J. *Botany: An Introduction to Plant Biology.* Sudbury, Massachusetts: Jones and Bartlett Publishers, Inc., 2003. ISBN: 0763721344.

Nabors, M. *Introduction to Botany.* New York: Benjamin Cummings (Pearson Education), 2003. ISBN: 0805344160.

Patent, D. *Plants on the Trail with Lewis and Clark.* New York: Clarion Books, 2003. ISBN: 0618067760.

Ray, D. *The Flower Hunter: William Bartram, America's First Naturalist.* New York: Farrar, Straus and Giroux, 2004. ISBN: 0374345899.

Spilsbury, L., and R. Spilsbury. *Plant Classification.* Chicago: Heinemann Library, 2003. ISBN: 1403402930.

Thomas, P. *Trees: Their Natural History.* New York: Cambridge University Press, 2001. ISBN: 052145963X.

## Ecology

Benz, R. *Ecology and Evolution: Island of Change.* Arlington, Virginia: National Science Teachers Association, 2000. ISBN: 0873551834.

*Ecology (Discovery Channel School Science).* Edited by J. Ball and A. Prokos. Milwaukee, Wisconsin: Gareth Stevens Publishing, 2004. ISBN: 0836833805.

*Ecology.* Editors of *National Geographic.* New York: Glencoe/McGraw-Hill, 2002. ISBN: 0078255880.

Heller, C. *Ecology (Human Biology).* New York: Glencoe/McGraw-Hill, 2002. ISBN: 1570396752.

Leuzzi, L. *Life Connections: Pioneers in Ecology (Lives in Science).* London, England: Franklin Watts, 2000. ISBN: 0531115666.

Pollock, S. *Ecology (DK EYEWITNESS BOOKS).* London, England: DK Children, 2000. ISBN: 0789455811.

## Medicine

Aeseng, N. *Disease Fighters: The Nobel Prize in Medicine.* School and Library Binding edition. Minneapolis: Lerner Publishing Group, 2001. ISBN: 0613277937.

Bendick, J. *Galen and the Gateway to Medicine (Living History Library).* Bathgate, North Dakota: Bethlehem Books, 2002. ISBN: 1883937752.

Fradin, D. B. *Medicine: Yesterday, Today, and Tomorrow (Twentieth Century Science and Beyond).* Danbury, Connecticut: Children's Press, 1989. ISBN: 0516005383.

Dawson, I. *Prehistoric and Egyptian Medicine (History of Medicine).* New York: Enchanted Lion Books, 2005. ISBN: 1592700357.

Gates, P. *History News: Medicine.* Cambridge, Massachusetts: Candlewick Press, 1997. ISBN: 0763603163.

Orr, T. *Native American Medicine (Native American Life).* Broomall, Pennsylvania: Mason Crest Publishers, 2003. ISBN: 1590841190.

*Medicine: Opposing Viewpoints (Opposing Viewpoints).* Edited by L. Egendorf. San Diego: Greenhaven Press, 2002. ISBN: 0737712333.

Miller, B. *Just What the Doctor Ordered: The History of American Medicine (People's History Series).* Minneapolis: Lerner Publishing Group, 1997. ISBN: 082251737X.

Parker, S. *Medicine (DK EYEWITNESS BOOKS).* London, England: DK Children, 2000. ISBN: 0789455803.

## Microbiology

Black, J. *Microbiology: Principles and Explorations.* Hoboken, New Jersey: Wiley, 2001. ISBN: 0471387290.

Breidahl, H. *The Zoo on You: Life on Human Skin (Life in Strange Places).* Langhorne, Pennsylvania: Chelsea House Publications, 2001. ISBN: 0791066193.

Case, C., B. Funke, and G. Tortora. *Microbiology: An Introduction.* New York: Benjamin Cummings (Pearson Education), 2003. ISBN: 0805376143.

Claybourne, A. *Microlife: From Amoebas to Viruses (Science Answers).* Chicago: Heinemann Library, 2004. ISBN: 1403447683.

Farrell, J. *Invisible Allies: Microbes That Shape Our Lives.* New York: Farrar, Straus and Giroux, 2005. ISBN: 0374336083.

Gladwin, M., and B. Trattler. *Clinical Microbiology Made Ridiculously Simple.* Miami: MedMaster, Inc. 2001. ISBN: 0940780496.

Grady, S., and J. Tabek. *Biohazards: Humanity's Battle With Infectious Disease (Science and Technology in Focus).* New York: Facts on File, 2005. ISBN: 0816046875.

Loewer, P., and J. Jenkins. *Pond Water Zoo: An Introduction to Microscopic Life.* New York: Atheneum Publishers, 1996. ISBN: 0689317360.

Solway, A. *What's Living Inside Your Body? (Hidden Life).* Chicago: Heinemann-Raintree, 2004. ISBN: 1403454868.

Sneddon, R. *The Benefits of Bacteria (Microlife).* Chicago: Heinemann Library, 2004. ISBN: 1575722429.

Sneddon, R. *Scientists and Discoveries (Microlife).* Chicago: Heinemann Library, 2000. ISBN: 1575722445.

## Zoology

Attenborough, D. *Life of Mammals.* London, England: BBC Books, 2002. ISBN: 0563534230.

Attenborough, D. *The Life of Birds.* London, England: BBC Books, 1998. ISBN: 0563387920.

Bateman, R. *Safari.* New York: Little, Brown and Company, 1998. ISBN: 0316082651.

Carde, R., and V. Resh. *Encyclopedia of Insects.* San Diego: Academic Press, 2003. ISBN: 0125869908.

*Encyclopaedia of Marine Mammals.* Edited by W. Perrin, J. Thewissen, and B. Wursig. San Diego: Academic Press, 2002. ISBN: 0125513404.

Hare, T. *Animal Habitats: How Animals Live in the World.* New York: Facts on File, 2001. ISBN: 0816045941.

*Into Wild California.* Edited by J. Corwin and E. Pascoe. Woodbridge, Connecticut: Blackbirch Press, 2004. ISBN: 1410301788.

Mara, W. *Dian Fossey: Among the Gorillas (Great Life Stories).* London, England: Franklin Watts, 2004. ISBN: 0531120597.

Taylor, B., and S. Pollock. *Discovery Plus: Animal Kingdom.* San Diego: Silver Dolphin Books, 2000. ISBN: 1571454446.

Turner, A. *National Geographic Prehistoric Mammals.* Washington, D.C.: National Geographic Library, 2004. ISBN: 0792269977

## MATHEMATICS

*Everyday Mathematics: Student Reference Book Level 5.* Edited by University of Chicago School Mathematics Project. Everyday Learning Corp., 2002. ISBN: 1570399190.

Larson, R. *Passport to Mathematics: Book 1.* Evanston, Illinois: McDougal Littell/ Houghton Mifflin, 1999. ISBN: 0395879825.

*Mathematics: Applications and Connections, Course 1, Student Edition.* New York: Glencoe/McGraw-Hill, 2000. ISBN: 0078228662.

*Say It With Symbols (Prentice Hall Connected Mathematics).* New York: Prentice Hall (Pearson Education), 2000. ISBN: 0130530816.

University of Chicago School of Mathematics. *Transition Mathematics.* Oakland, New Jersey: Scott Foresman, 1998. ISBN: 067345939X.

## PHYSICS AND CHEMISTRY

## Chemistry

Bendick, J., and B. Wiker. *The Mystery of the Periodic Table (Living History Library).*

Bathgate, North Dakota: Bethlehem Books, 2003. ISBN: 188393771X.

Brown, T., J. Burdge, B. Burnsten, and E. LeMay. *Chemistry: The Central Science.* Englewood Cliffs, New Jersey: Prentice Hall, 2003. ISBN: 0130669970.

*Chemistry in the Community (Student Edition): Chemcom.* Edited by American Chemical Society Staff. New York: W. H. Freeman, 2000. ISBN: 0716735512.

*Chemistry Laboratory Student Notebook.* New York: W. H. Freeman, 2000. ISBN: 0716739003.

Davis, M. *Modern Chemistry.* New York: Henry Holt, 2000. ISBN: 0030511224.

Gunter, V., and J. Rhatigan. *Cool Chemistry Concoctions: 50 Formulas that Fizz, Foam, Splatter and Ooze.* Asheville, North Carolina: Lark, 2005. ISBN: 1579906206.

Kavanah, P. *Chemistry: The Physical Setting: Brief Review for New York 2005.* New York: Prentice Hall (Pearson Education), 2004. ISBN: 0131260936.

LeMay, E. *Chemistry: Connections to Our Changing World.* New York: Prentice Hall (Pearson Education), 2000. ISBN: 0134347765.

*Modern Chemistry.* Austin, Texas: Holt, Rinehart and Winston, 2002. ISBN: 0030565375.

*Prentice Hall Science Explorer: Chemical Building Blocks.* New York: Prentice Hall (Pearson Education), 2004. ISBN: 0131150960.

*Science Smart Junior : Discovering the Secrets of Science (Princeton Review Series).* Edited by D. Linker. Princeton, New Jersey: Princeton Review, 2002. ISBN: 0375762620.

Stwertka, A. *A Guide to the Elements.* New York: Oxford University Press, 2002. ISBN: 0195150279.

Tiner, J. H. *Exploring the World of Chemistry: From Ancient Metals to High-Speed Computers.* Green Forest, Arizona: Master Books, 2000. ISBN: 0890512957.

Wertheim, J. *Illustrated Dictionary of Chemistry (Usborne Illustrated Dictionaries).* London, England: Usborne Publishing, 2000. ISBN: 0746037945.

Wilbraham, A., et al. *Chemistry*. New York: Prentice Hall (Pearson Education), 2000. ISBN: 0201321424.

## Physics

Ade, C., and J. Wertheim. *The Usborne Illustrated Dictionary of Physics (Usborne Illustrated Dictionaries)*. London, England: Usborne Publishing, 2002. ISBN: 0746037961.

Cook, B. *Physics: The Physical Setting (Brief Review for New York)*. New York: Prentice Hall (Pearson Education), 2004. ISBN: 0131260928.

Fleisher, P. *Relativity and Quantum Mechanics: Principles of Modern Physics (Secrets of the Universe)*. Minneapolis: Lerner Publishing Group, 2001. ISBN: 0822529890.

Friedhoffer, B., and R. Friedhoffer. *Physics Lab in a Housewares Store (Physical Science Labs)*. London, England: Franklin Watts, 1996. ISBN: 0531112934.

Gardner, R. *Bicycle Science Projects: Physics on Wheels (Science Fair Success)*. Berkeley Heights, New Jersey: Enslow Publishers, Inc., 2004. ISBN: 0766016307.

Goodwin, P., and R. Goodwin. *Physics Projects for Young Scientists (Projects for Young Scientists)*. London, England: Franklin Watts, 2000. ISBN: 0531116670.

Hewitt, P. *Conceptual Physics: With Expanded Technology: The High School Physics Program*. New York: Addison-Wesley (Pearson Education), 1999. ISBN: 0201332876.

Hickman, J. B. *Problem-Solving Exercises in Physics*. New York: Prentice Hall (Pearson Education), 2002. ISBN: 013054275X.

Knight, J., and N. Schlager. *Science of Everyday Things: Real-Life Physics (Science of Everyday Things)*. Farmington Hills, Michigan: Thomson Gale, 2001. ISBN: 078765633X.

Kuhn, K. *Basic Physics : A Self-Teaching Guide (Wiley Self-Teaching Guides)*. Hoboken, New Jersey: Wiley, 1996. ISBN: 0471134473.

Landa, J. *Physics: A Contemporary Approach*. New York: Amsco School Publications, Inc., 2002. ISBN: 0877201706.

Seiden, A. *Particle Physics : A Comprehensive Introduction*. New York: Addison-Wesley (Pearson Education), 2004. ISBN: 0805387366.

## TECHNOLOGY

Abernathy, F., J. Dunlop, J. Hammond, and D. Weil. *A Stitch in Time: Lean Retailing and the Transformation of Manufacturing: Lessons from the Apparel and Textile Industries*. New York: Oxford University Press, 1999. ISBN: 0195126157.

Bull, S. *Encyclopedia of Military Technology and Innovation*. Westport, Connecticut: Greenwood Publishing Group, 2004. ISBN: 1573565571.

Collier, B., and P. Tortora. *Understanding Textiles*. Englewood Cliffs, New Jersey, Prentice Hall, 2000. ISBN: 0130219517

Gifford, C. *How The Future Began: Everyday Life (How The Future Began)*. New York: Kingfisher Books, 2000. ISBN: 0753452685.

Kadolph, S., and A. Langford. *Textiles*. Englewood Cliffs, New Jersey: Prentice Hall, 2001. ISBN: 0130254436.

MacAulay, D. *Way Things Work*. La Vergne, Tennessee: Publisher Resources Inc., 1998. ISBN: 0395428572.

Pacey, A. *Technology in World Civilization: A Thousand-Year History*. Cambridge, Massachusetts: MIT Press, 1991. ISBN: 0262660725.

Scott, P., and F. Vizard. *21st Century Soldier: The Weaponry, Gear, and Technology of the Military in the New Century*. New York: Time Inc. Home Entertainment, 2002. ISBN: 1931933162.

Stone, R. *Introduction to Internal Combustion Engines*. Warrendale, Pennsylvania: SAE International, Inc., 1999. ISBN: 0768004950.

Woods, M. *Ancient Warfare: From Clubs to Catapults (Ancient Technology)*. Minneapolis: Runestone Press, 2000. ISBN: 0822529998.

Yafa, S. *Big Cotton: How A Humble Fiber Created Fortunes, Wrecked Civilizations, and Put America on the Map*. New York: Viking, 2005. ISBN: 0670033677.

## PEOPLE

Aeseng, N. *Twentieth-Century Inventors (American Profiles)*. New York: Facts on File, 1991. ISBN: 0816024855.

*Albert Einstein (People Who Made History)*. Edited by C. Swisher. San Diego: Greenhaven Press, 2001. ISBN: 0737708921.

Bowler, P. *Charles Darwin: The Man and His Influence (Cambridge Science Biographies)*. New York: Cambridge University Press, 1996. ISBN: 0521566681.

Frank, P. *Einstein: His Life and Times*. Cambridge, Massachusetts: Da Capo Press, 2002. ISBN: 030681109X.

Gleick, J. *Isaac Newton*. New York: Pantheon Books, 2003. ISBN: 1400032954.

Kjelle, M. M. *Antoine Lavoisier: Father of Chemistry (Uncharted, Unexplored, and Unexplained)*. Hockessin, Delaware: Mitchell Lane Publishers, Inc., 2004. ISBN: 1584153091.

MacFarlane, G. *Alexander Fleming: The Man and the Myth*. Cambridge, Massachusetts: Harvard University Press, 1984. ISBN: 0674014901.

MacLeod, E. *Marie Curie: A Brilliant Life (Snapshots: Images of People and Places in History.)* New York: Kids Can Press, 2004. ISBN: 1553375718.

Russell, C. *Michael Faraday: Physics and Faith*. New York: Oxford University Press, 2000. ISBN: 0195117638.

Smith, L. W. *Louis Pasteur: Disease Fighter (Great Minds of Science)*. Berkeley Heights, New Jersey: Enslow Publishers, Inc., 2001. ISBN: 0766018741.

Westfall, R. *The Life of Isaac Newton*. New York: Cambridge University Press, 1994. ISBN: 0521477379.

## MAGAZINES

*Astronomy*
P. O. Box 1612
Waukesha
WI 53186-4055
(800) 446 5489
www.astronomy.com

*American Scientist*
Sigma Xi
P. O. Box 13975
3106 East NC Highway 54
Research Triangle Park
NC 27709
(919) 549 0097
www.americanscientist.org

*Discover*
114 Fifth Avenue
NYC 10011
(212) 633 4400
www.discover.com

*National Geographic*
National Geographic Society
P. O. Box 98199
Washington, D.C. 20090-8199
(800) 647 5463
800 548 9797 (TDD)

*New Scientist*
New Scientist Customer Services
6277 Sea Harbor Drive
Orlando
FL 32887
(888) 822 3242
www.newscientist.com

*Popular Mechanics*
810 Seventh Avenue
NYC 10019
Fax: (212) 586 5562
www.popularmechanics.com

*Popular Science Magazine*
P. O. Box 60001
Tampa
FL 33660-0001
(800) 289 9399
www.popsci.com

*Science Magazine*
Member Services
Danbury
CT 1-800-731-4939
(202) 326 6417
www.sciencemag.org

*Science News*
Science Service Incorporated
1719 N Street NW
Washington, D.C. 20036-2888
(202) 785 2255
www.sciencenews.org

*Science Now*
American Association for the
    Advancement of Science
1200 New York Ave. NW
Washington, D.C. 20005
(202) 326 6417
www.sciencenow.org

*Scientific American*
ScientificAmerican.com
415 Madison Avenue
NYC 10017
(212) 451 8202
www.sciam.com

*Sky and Telescope*
Sky Publishing Corporation
49 Bay State Road
Cambridge
MA 02138-1200
(800) 253 0245
www.skyandtelescope.com

# WEB SITES

**AIDS:** News, factsheets, and FAQs.
www.aids.org

**Anatomy:** Online edition of *Gray's Anatomy of the Human Body,* featuring more than one thousand illustrations.
www.bartleby.com/107/

**Anatomy:** Illustrated guide to the human body.
www.innerbody.com

**Air Travel:** Guide to history of air travel, decade by decade.
http://airlines.afriqonline.com/

**Astronomy:** Describes the development of modern astronomy and provides an overview of the solar system.
www.csep10.phys.utk.edu/astr161/lect/

**Astronomy:** A comprehensive online resource about space and astronomy for all levels of comprehension. Includes tutorials and interactive puzzles.
www.enchantedlearning.com/subjects/astronomy/

**Bicycle History:** Web page charting the development of the bicycle.
www.inventors.about.com/library/inventors/blbicycle.htm

**Biology, General:** Covers a range of material with links to relevant Web sites. Also offers a biology dictionary.
www.biology-online.org

**Biology, General:** News, homework help, and articles from publications and resources, covering the full spectrum of biology topics.
www.biologyabout.com

**Biology, General:** A membership-only site promising coverage of biological concepts for high-school and college, with tutorials, demonstrations, and animations.
www.biology.com

**Biology, General:** Recent articles available in summarized version following registration or in-full to subscribers.
www.current-biology.com

**Biology, General:** Introductory and up-to-date biology text adapted from print version by Dr. Kimball, retired from Harvard University.
http://users.rcn.com/jkimball.ma.ultranet/BiologyPages/

**Botany:** The Plants National Database. Provides online database for plants and relevant factsheets.
http://plants.usda.gov/

**Botany:** Botanical Society of America. Includes introductory articles, latest news, and a library of images.
www.botany.org

**Chemistry, General.** Provides answers to users' questions and offers archive containing more than four hundred previous answers.
http://antoine.frostburg.edu/chem/senese/101/just-ask-antoine.shtml

**Chemistry, General:** The Amercian Chemical Society's Kids' page. Offers experiments for users to follow, with explanations.
www.chemistry.org/kids

**Chemistry:** The periodic table online.
www.webelements.com

**Ecology:** Nuclear accidents. Information on the long-term consequences of the Chernobyl disaster.
www.chernobyl.info

**Ecology:** Web site for the Ecology Center. Working for a cleaner environment. Information on activities, recycling, and sustainable land use.
www.ecocenter.org

**Ecology:** Official Web site of the U.S. Environmental Protection Agency. News and information about a range of environmental issues.
www.epa.gov

**Ecology:** Renewable Resource Data Centre. Information on alternative forms of energy.
http://rredc.nrel.gov

**Encyclopedia:** *Britannica.* The online version of one of the world's most highly regarded encylopedias. Includes a younger readers' version available on a subscription service.
www.britannica.com

**Encyclopedia:** Encyclopedia.com. Free resource with more than five thousand concise articles. Includes a dictionary and thesaurus.
www.encyclopedia.com

**Encyclopedia:** Wikipedia. A free enclyopedia covering topics including mathematics, science, and technology. Unlike most encyclopedias, it also includes current events and may be edited by readers. www.en.wikipedia.org/wiki/Wikipedia

**General:** About.com. Covers one hundred topics and offers advice and solutions. www.about.com

**General:** High School Hub. Free and comprehensive homework help, including mathematics and science. www.highschoolhub.org

**General:** How Stuff Works. Providing a wealth of information, this Web site covers diverse topics from human biology to the workings of household appliances. www.howstuffworks.com

**General:** Fun home science experiments. http://scifun.chem.wisc.edu/HomeExpts/ HOMEEXPTS.HTML

**Geology:** Comprehensive guide to wide spectrum of relevant issues. www.geology.about.com

**Geology:** Topics include tsunamis, earthquakes, minerals, and rocks. www.geology.com

**Geology:** The United States Geological Survey (USGS) Web site. The USGS provides reliable scientific information to describe and understand the Earth; to minimize loss of life and property from natural disasters; to manage resources; and to protect our quality of life. Includes a state-by-state analysis. www.usgs.gov

**Inventors:** Information about key U.S. inventors and their achievements. www.northstar.k12.ak.us/schools/ryn/ projects/inventors/

**Inventions:** Describes great inventions of the twentieth century, including a timeline charting the development of the Internet. www.greatinventions.com

**Medicine, History of:** Concise details about wide range of inventions and inventors. http://inventors.about.com/library/inventors/ blmedical.htm

**Medicine, History of:** Information and interactive quiz for young readers. http://www.schoolscience.co.uk/content/4/ biology/abpi/history/history15.html

**Medicine:** The discovery of penicillin. http://nobelprize.org/medicine/educational/ penicillin/readmore.html

**Meteorology:** American Meteorological Society. This Web site includes the latest meteorological news and information. http://Ametsoc.org

**National Aeronautics and Space Administration:** The official Web site offers information about space travel and exploring the universe. www.nasa.gov

**National Oceanic and Atmospheric Administration:** Information about topics including oceans, weather, and coasts. www.noaa.gov

**Nobel Foundation:** The Nobel Prize is the first international award given yearly since 1901 for achievements in physics, chemistry, physiology or medicine, literature, and peace. This official Web site includes articles by Nobel laureates and details of prizes awarded. www.nobelprize.org

**Physics:** The Amercian Physical Society. Resources for students, with links to further information. www.physicscentral.com

**Physics and Astronomy Online:** Up-to-date news available free. Links to further physics and astronomy resources. Glossary of physics terms. Also offers a discussion forum and an "ask the experts" section. www.physlink.com

**The Physics Classroom:** Online interactive tutorial covering the basic physics concepts discussed in a first-year high school course. Physicsclassroom.com

**Physics Web:** Free physics news. www.physicsweb.org

**Prehistoric Life:** Information about cavemen and dinosaurs. http://www.bbc.co.uk/sn/prehistoriclife/

# MUSEUMS

**Women of Science**
Marine Biological Laboratory
7 MBL Street
Woods Hole, MA 02543
(508) 548 3705
www.mbl.edu

**Museums of Science**
Science Park
Boston, MA 02114
(617) 723 2500
www.mos.org

**Kennedy Space Center (NASA)**
Merritt Island, FL 32899
(321) 449 4444
www.kennedySpaceCenter.com

**National Air and Space Museum**
Independence Ave at 4th Street, SW
Washington, D.C., 20560
(202) 633 1000
www.nasm.si/edu

**National Air and Space Museum**
14390 Air and Space Museum Parkway
Chantilly, VA 20151
(202) 633 1000
www.nasm.si/edu

**Museum of Science and Industry**
57th Street and Lake Shore Drive
Chicago, IL 60637
(773) 684 1414
www.msichicago.org

**National Inventors Hall of Fame
Inventure Place**
221 South Broadway Street
Akron, OH 44308-1505
(330) 762 4463
www.invent.org

**International Space Hall of Fame
The Space Center**
2000 Scenic Drive
Alamogordo, NM 88311-0533
(505) 437 2840
www.spacefame.org

**National Museum of Nuclear Science
and History**
1905 Mountain Road NW
Albuquerque, NM
(505) 245 2137
www.atomicmuseum.com

**The Exploratorium**
3601 Lyon Street
San Francisco, CA 94123
(415) 563 7337
www.exploratorium.edu/

**Lawrence Hall of Science**
University of California at Berkeley
Centennial Drive
Berkeley, CA 94720
(510) 642 5132
www.lhs.berkeley.edu/

# Time line

| | |
|---|---|
| **1452** | German inventor Johannes Gutenberg (1400–1468) develops printing by movable type |
| **1569** | Publication of a map projection that displays the spherical shape of Earth |
| **1608** | Dutch spectacle maker Hans Lippershey (1570–1619) invents the telescope |
| **1621** | Dutch scientist Willebrord Snell (1580–1626) discovers the law of light refraction |
| **1647** | French scientist Blaise Pascal (1623–1662) devises the basic laws of hydraulic systems |
| **1655** | Dutch scientist Christiaan Huygens (1629–1695) discovers Saturn's ring system and its fourth satellite, Titan |
| **1662** | Irish scientist Robert Boyle (1627–1691) discovers that the volume and pressure of a gas are inversely proportional |
| **1665** | The word *cell* is used for the first time |
| **1668** | English physicist and mathematician Isaac Newton (1642–1727) invents the reflecting telescope |
| **1678** | Huygens proposes the wave theory of light |
| **1687** | Newton proposes three laws of motion and a law of gravity |
| **1691** | English naturalist John Ray (1627–1705) suggests that fossils are the remains of animals from the distant past |
| **1704** | Newton demonstrates that white light consists of different colors |
| **1714** | German physicist Daniel Fahrenheit (1686–1736) invents an accurate mercury thermometer |
| **1735** | Swedish botanist Carl Linnaeus (1707–1778) publishes *Systema Natura,* in which he presents the modern system of classification |
| **1738** | Swiss mathematician Daniel Bernoulli (1700–1782) discovers the principle of fluid flow |
| **1742** | Swedish astronomer Anders Celsius (1701–1744) devises the Celsius temperature scale |
| **1752** | U.S. politician and scientist Benjamin Franklin (1706–1790) performs the famous kite experiment to show that lightning is a form of electricity |
| **1765** | Scottish engineer and inventor James Watt (1736–1819) develops an efficient steam engine |
| **1771** | Italian physicist Luigi Galvani (1737–1798) discovers the electrical nature of nerve impulses |
| **1788** | French chemist Antoine-Laurent Lavoisier (1734–1794) shows that combustion occurs as a result of reactions with oxygen in air |
| **1793** | German botanist Christian Sprengel (1750–1816) publishes his discoveries on plant fertilization |
| **1796** | English physician Edward Jenner (1749–1823) develops the first successful vaccine (for smallpox) |
| **1800** | Italian physicist Alessandro Volta (1745–1827) invents the first electrical battery (the voltaic pile) |
| **1812** | German mineralogist Friedrich Mohs (1773–1839) proposes the Mohs scale of mineral hardness |
| **1816** | French physician René Théophile Laënnec (1781–1826) invents the stethoscope |
| **1820** | Danish physicist Hans Ørsted (1777–1851) discovers a link between electricity and magnetism |
| **1821** | English physicist and chemist Michael Faraday (1791–1867) invents an early electric motor |
| **1822** | English geologist Gideon Mantell (1790–1852) discovers the first dinosaur fossils |
| **1830** | Scottish geologist Charles Lyell (1797–1875) offers evidence that Earth is at least several hundred million years old |
| **1834** | English mathematician and inventor Charles Babbage (1792–1871) builds the analytical engine, a forerunner of the modern computer |
| **1837** | French painter Louis-Jacque-Mandé Daguerre (1789–1851) invents the first photographic process |

**1841** Augusta Ada King, Countess of Lovelace (1815–1852), invents the first computer program

**1849** French scientists make the first measurements of the speed of light

**1852** Canadian geologist Abraham Gesner (1797–1864) makes kerosene by distilling crude oil

**1856** English engineer Henry Bessemer (1813–1898) invents the Bessemer steelmaking process

**1856** French scientist Louis Pasteur (1822–1895) demonstrates that living organisms cause fermentation

**1857** Austrian botanist Gregor Mendel (1822–1884) proposes the laws of heredity using pea plants

**1859** Belgian inventor Étienne Lenoir (1822–1900) invents a practical internal combustion engine

**1859** English naturalist Charles Darwin (1809–1882) publishes *On the Origin of Species,* a book describing the theories of natural selection and evolution

**1864** Pasteur demonstrates that microorganisms in some foods are destroyed by heating

**1865** German botanist Julius von Sachs (1832–1897) discovers the role of chlorophyll in photosynthesis

**1871** Russian chemist Dmitry Mendeleyev (1834–1907) explains that the gaps in his periodic table represent undiscovered elements

**1875** Scottish-born U.S. inventor Alexander Graham Bell (1847–1922) invents the telephone

**1876** Pasteur announces his discovery of anaerobic organisms (those that live without oxygen)

**1877** U.S. inventor Thomas Edison (1847–1931) invents the phonograph

**1884** German-born U.S. inventor Ottmar Mergenthaler (1854–1899) invents the Linotype machine

**1884** Irish engineer Charles Parsons (1854–1931) invents the steam turbine

**1885** German engineer Carl Benz (1844–1929) designs and builds the first practical automobile

**1887** U.S. architect Martin Roche (1853–1927) designs the first skyscraper

**1888** German physicist Heinrich Hertz (1857–1894) transmits and receives radio waves for the first time

**1893** German engineer Rudolf Diesel (1858–1913) invents the compression ignition (diesel) engine

**1895** German physicist Wilhelm Röntgen (1845–1923) discovers X-rays

**1896** French physicist Antoine-Henri Becquerel (1852–1908) detects radioactivity for the first time

**1897** English physicist Joseph Thomson (1856–1940) discovers the electron

**1898** French chemists Pierre Curie (1859–1906) and Marie Curie (1867–1934) discover the radioactive elements radium and polonium

**1900** German physicist Max Planck (1858–1947) discovers photons and devises quantum theory

**1903** U.S. aviation pioneers Wilbur Wright (1867–1912) and Orville Wright (1871–1948) build the first powered airplane

**1905** German-born U.S. physicist Albert Einstein (1879–1955) proposes the special theory of relativity and explains the photoelectric effect

**1907** U.S. chemist and inventor Leo Baekeland (1863–1944) invents Bakelite, the first synthetic plastic

**1909** The word *gene* is first used to describe a unit of inheritance

**1911** Dutch physicist Heike Kamerlingh Onnes (1853–1926) discovers superconductivity

**1911** New Zealand–born British physicist Ernest Rutherford (1871–1937) figures out that an atom consists of a positive nucleus surrounded by negative electrons

**1912** German geophysicist Alfred Wegener (1880–1930) proposes his theory of continental drift

**1916** Einstein publishes his general theory of relativity

**1920** Rutherford discovers the proton

**1927** Belgian astronomer Georges-Henri Lemaître (1894–1966) proposes the big bang theory for the origin of the universe

**1928** Scottish physician Alexander Fleming (1881–1955) discovers the antibiotic penicillin

**1931** German electrical engineer Ernst Ruska (1906–1988) invents the electron microscope

**1932** English engineer Francis Thomas Bacon (1904–1992) develops the first practical fuel cell

**1934** Rutherford creates the hydrogen isotope tritium in the first nuclear fusion reaction

**1935** U.S. chemist Wallace Carothers (1896–1937) invents nylon

**1937** English mathematician Alan Turing (1912–1954) publishes a paper describing a machine that processes symbols according to a set of rules

**1938** German chemists Otto Hahn (1879–1968) and Fritz Strassmann (1902–1980) and Austrian physicist Lise Meitner (1878–1968) discover nuclear fission

**1944** International Business Machines (IBM) use punched paper tape to program a computer

**1947** U.S. physicists John Bardeen (1908–1991), Walter Brattain (1902–1987), and William Shockley (1910–1989) invent the transistor

**1953** English scientist Francis Crick (1916–2004) and U.S. biologist James Watson (1928– ) discover the helical structure of deoxyribonucleic acid (DNA)

**1956** German engineer Felix Wankel (1902–1988) invents the rotary engine

**1957** The former Soviet Union launches the first artificial satellite into Earth orbit

**1961** Soviet cosmonaut Yuri Gagarin (1934–1968) is the first person in space

**1962** U.S. biologist Rachel Carson (1907–1964) publishes *Silent Spring*

**1964** U.S. physicist Charles H. Townes (1915– ) and Soviet physicists Nicolay G. Basov (1922–2001) and Alexander M. Prochorov (1916–2002) receive Nobel prize for work in quantum electronics, leading to construction of instruments based on maser-laser principles

**1965** Hungarian-born U.S. computer scientist John Kemeny (1926–1992) and U.S. computer scientist Thomas Kurtz (1928– ) develop the BASIC computer language

**1967** South African surgeon Christiaan Barnard (1922–2001) performs the first human heart transplant

**1969** U.S. astronaut Neil Armstrong (1930– ) takes the first steps on the Moon

**1973** Herbert Boyer (1936– ) and Stanley Cohen (1922) perform the first recombinant DNA cloning experiment using restriction enzymes

**1974** U.S. anthropologist Donald Johanson (1943– ) discovers three-million-year-old skeleton of an early human ancestor, named Lucy

**1983** U.S. scientist Kary Mullis (1944– ) invents the polymerase chain reaction (PCR) to amplify minute amounts of DNA

**1985** A hole in the ozone layer is detected over Antarctica

**1987** Genetic fingerprinting is first used to convict a criminal in England

**1990** English computer scientist Tim Berners-Lee (1955– ) invents the World Wide Web

**1992** Earth Summit talks take place to discuss environmental problems such as global warming

**1997** Scottish embryologist Ian Wilmut (1944– ) heads a team that produces Dolly the sheep, the first successful clone from an adult mammal

**2003** Scientists in the United States and Britain independently complete the map of the human genome as part of the Human Genome Project

**2003** Two NASA spacecraft land on Mars

# Geologic timescale

The geologic timescale provides a chronological arrangement of geologic events over the last 4.6 billion years. Divisions in the geologic timescale are linked to systems of layered rock, called strata, deposited during those periods. Radioactive isotopes are used to obtain absolute ages of the rock, but fossils are also used to date and correlate sedimentary strata. The boundaries between the divisions generally correspond to major geological events in Earth's history.

The geologic timescale is divided into four major eons. There are three eons before the Cambrian period begins. These are called the Pre-Archean, the Archean, and the Proterozoic eons, which are collectively known as the Precambrian. The fourth, and most recent eon, is the Phanerozoic, which includes the Paleozoic, the Mesozoic, and the Cenozoic eras. The eras of the Phanerozoic eon are divided into periods, and these periods are further divided into epochs.

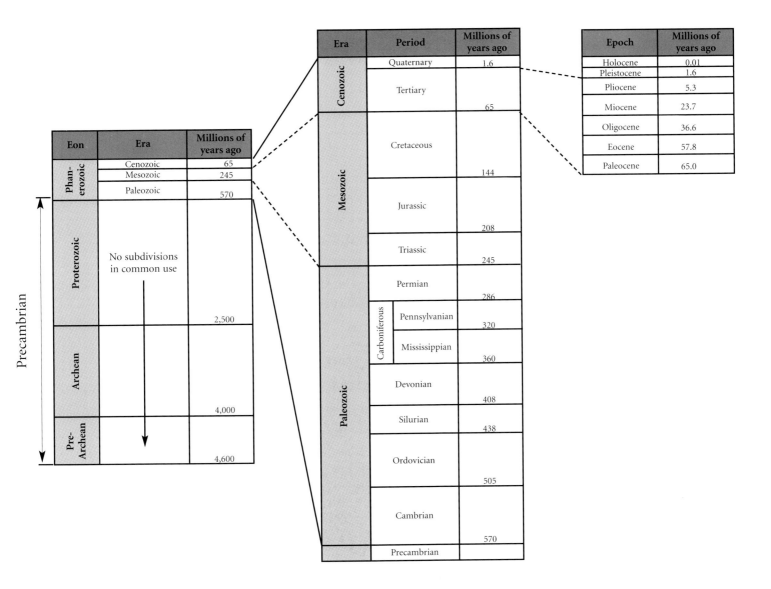

# Glossary

**Aberration** In optical lenses, a fault in an image that occurs because of the shape of the lens (spherical aberration) or because of an alteration in color (chromatic aberration).

**Abrasive** A hard substance, often used for cleaning or sharpening by rubbing against another object.

**Absolute zero** The lowest possible theoretical temperature limit, measured on the Kelvin scale as 0K (−459.67°F or −273.15°C).

**Absorb** To take in a substance as, for example, a sponge absorbs water. A substance that does this is said to be absorbent. Also, to reduce the effect of a force, as a beach absorbs the energy of waves.

**Absorption spectrum** A type of spectrum that contains dark bands where an absorbing substance has removed some of the frequencies (colors).

**Acceleration** The increase in velocity of an object.

**Accelerometer** An instrument used for measuring the rate at which a vehicle gathers velocity.

**Acid** One of a class of substances that react with and dissolve certain metals to form salts.

**Acoustic** Related to sound. An acoustic mine has a microphone that can pick up propeller noise.

**Additive** A substance that is added to another substance to improve, strengthen, or otherwise change that substance.

**Adhere** To stick to the surface of another substance by suction or by the use of a gluing agent called an adhesive.

**Adsorption** The taking up of one substance at the surface of another but not going inside it.

**Aerodynamics** The study of the way in which air moves around objects. An aerodynamic object is one with a shape that minimizes disturbance of air flowing around it.

**Afterburn** The injection of fuel into the hot exhaust gases of a jet engine to improve performance. Used in takeoff of jet airplanes with small engines.

**Air pressure** The force that air puts on an object, especially when it is in motion.

**Alkali** One of a class of substances that form chemical salts when combined with acids and that can corrode or burn when mixed with water.

**Allergy** A biological reaction (such as a rash) to an otherwise harmless substance (the antigen).

**Allotrope** One or more forms of an element that differ in physical, and often chemical, properties.

**Alloys** Mixtures of metals with other elements, often other metals or carbon, to make them stronger or give them certain qualities.

**Alpha rays** A stream of high-speed alpha particles emitted during the energetic radioactive decay of certain atoms. Alpha particles consist of two protons and two neutrons, forming a helium nucleus.

**Alternating current (AC)** An electrical current that reverses periodically. Domestic electricity supplies use alternating current.

**Alternator** A type of generator that produces an alternating electrical current.

**Altimeter** An instrument that measures height above the ground.

**Altitude** The height of an object above sea level.

**Alveoli** The small sacs in the lungs where gaseous exchange takes place.

**Amino acids** Organic molecules consisting of a central carbon atom, a carboxyl group (−COOH), and a side chain (−R). Amino acids are the building blocks of proteins.

**Ammeter** An instrument for measuring either direct (DC) or alternating (AC) electrical current, in amperes.

**Amorphous** Having no distinct shape—in particular, lacking the structure characteristic of living bodies or without apparent crystalline form.

**Ampere** The SI base unit used to measure a quantity of electricity flowing past a point.

**Amplification** Increasing the strength of an electrical current by applying a low, alternating voltage to one or a series of electron tubes or transistors.

**Amplitude** The "height" of a wave; more accurately, half the distance between a peak and a trough.

**Amplitude modulation (AM)** A radio broadcasting technique in which the radio signal is always of the same frequency, but its amplitude varies.

**Anabolism** Chemical reaction in which a complex substance is made from simpler ones. This leads to the storage of energy.

**Analog** Of a computer, describing the way scientific and technical information is held and displayed by means of physical quantities (weight or length) that are similar (analogous) to the actual reality.

**Anechoic chamber** An "echoless" room designed to absorb all sound within it without reflections from the walls, roof, or floor.

**Anemometer** An instrument used to measure the speed of a flowing fluid, including gases.

**Anhydrous** Without water.

**Anion** A negatively charged ion, showing an excess of electrons. An anion is attracted to the positive electrode (anode) in an electrochemical cell.

**Anneal** To heat metal or glass and then to cool it gradually to make it stronger.

**Anode** The positive electrode in an electrochemical cell; the electrode toward which anions (negatively charged ions) migrate.

**Anodization** A way of providing light metals, such as aluminum, with a protection against corrosion by covering the metal with a thin oxide film.

**Antenna** A device used for transmitting and receiving electromagnetic waves.

**Antibiotic** An organic compound that inhibits the growth of, or destroys, bacteria. Antibiotics are used to treat a range of infectious diseases, from cholera and syphilis to meningitis and pneumonia.

**Antibodies** Protective proteins produced by the body's immune system in response to the presence of foreign substances, called antigens.

**Antigen** A foreign substance in the body that stimulates an immune response.

**Antimatter** Each fundamental particle has an antimatter equivalent, which has the same mass but opposite charge. If the two particles meet, they annihilate each other with the release of energy.

**Aperture** A circular opening through which light passes, for example, in a camera or telescope.

**Aqua regia** A strong acid composed of concentrated hydrochloric and nitric acids. Aqua regia can dissolve gold and platinum.

**Aqueduct** A bridge or canal that carries a water supply across a distance.

**Aquifer** A layer of water-saturated permeable rock. Groundwater is obtained from an aquifer.

**Archimedean screw** An ancient device used to raise water by means of a spiral enclosed in a tube.

**Artery** A blood vessel carrying oxygenated blood away from the heart.

**Asteroid** Small rocky body that orbits the Sun between Mars and Jupiter and forms what is known as the asteroid belt.

**Atmosphere** The layer of gaseous chemicals surrounding Earth. The atmosphere provides oxygen and contains water vapor, which falls as precipitation. It also protects Earth from radiation and meteors.

**Atom** The smallest particle of an element that has all the properties of that element.

**Atomic number** The number of protons in the nucleus of an atom. The atomic number determines the position of elements in the periodic table.

**Auroras** The dramatic visual displays seen in the sky at the North and South poles, which are caused by the interaction of the solar wind with Earth's magnetic field.

**Axis** The central line, usually an imaginary one, around which a body such as Earth turns.

**Bacteria** Single-celled organisms most of which are decomposers, but many of which are responsible for infectious diseases in plants, animals, and people.

**Baffle** A structure used to control or change the flow of gases, sounds, liquids, and other materials.

**Ballast** Heavy materials, such as stones or lead, put in the holds of ships to keep them stable. In balloons or airships, ballast is carried and then thrown overboard so the craft can go higher.

**Barometer** An instrument used to measure air pressure. A mercury column is a simple barometer.

**Bergschrund** Large ice crevasse that occurs at the highest point of a glacier.

**Big bang theory** Theory that the universe began with a cosmic explosion from a single point around 10 to 15 billion years ago.

**Biodegradable** Capable of being decomposed by biological agents, especially bacteria.

**Bioluminescence** The production of light without heat by biological means.

**Biome** Any of Earth's major ecosystems that extend over large areas and are characterized by a distinctive climate and vegetation, such as deserts or rain forests.

**Biorhythms** The variations in the biological clock of an organism.

**Biotechnology** The use of microorganisms, such as bacteria, or biological substances, such as enzymes, to produce useful products, such as antibiotics.

**Bit** An abbreviation for binary digit, a bit is the smallest unit of information, represented by the binary numbers 0 and 1. Digital information, as used by computers, is always stored in bits.

**Black hole** Region of space in which the pull of gravity is so strong that nothing, not even light, can escape from it.

**Boiler** A tank in which water is heated before being circulated as hot water or steam for heating or power.

**Boolean algebra** A system of algebra in which there are two elements of sets that can be combined or shown in a relationship.

**Boyle's law** For a given mass of gas at constant temperature, the volume of the gas varies inversely with its pressure.

**Buttress** A brick or stone support built against a wall to help it resist outward pressure.

**Calculus** The branch of mathematics that deals with rates of change in systems.

**Cam** A machine component that either rotates or reciprocates (moves back and forth) to create a set motion in a contacting element known as a follower.

**Capacitance** The ability of a capacitor to store electrical current or charges. A capacitor is a device that controls the supply of electricity by means of two plates—separated by insulating material—that hold the positive and negative charges.

**Capillary action** The force that causes a liquid to rise up a narrow tube.

**Carbohydrates** Large organic molecules, such as sugars or starch, which can be used by organisms to produce energy.

**Carburetor** A device used in older internal combustion engines to produce an explosive mixture of fuel vapor (mist) and air.

**Carcinogen** Any substance or agent that causes a normal cell to become cancerous.

**Catabolism** All the enzymatic breakdown processes in an organism, such as digestion and respiration.

**Catalysts** Substances that initiate or speed up chemical reactions without themselves being altered during the reaction.

**Catheter** A narrow tube used to drain or inject fluids through a body passage such as the nose or a vein.

**Cathode** The negative electrode in an electrochemical cell; the electrode toward which cations (positively charged ions) migrate.

**Cation** A positively charged ion, showing a depletion of electrons. A cation is attracted to the negative electrode (cathode) of an electrochemical cell.

**Cavitation** The process by which an object is worn away by bubbles created as the object moves through a liquid, such as a ship's propeller through water.

**Cell** The basic unit of life, which consists of genetic material, cytoplasm, a cell membrane, and (in plants and bacteria) a cell wall. Also, a type of electric battery that works by chemical reaction.

**Cell membrane** A thin, flexible layer covering the surface of a cell.

**Cellulose** A tough, structural protein that strengthens the cell walls of plants.

**Centrifuge** An apparatus that spins liquids or solids at high speeds, forcing the heavier parts out to the edge and keeping the lighter parts nearer the center, thus separating them.

**Ceramics** Certain types of hard, nonmetallic, crystalline solids. China and silicon are ceramics.

**Cerebellum** The part of the brain that controls and coordinates the movement of muscles.

**Cerebrum** The largest part of the brain; it controls the senses and provides people with the power of speech and understanding.

**Chemical bond** The electrical forces linking atoms in molecules.

**Chromosome** A threadlike strand of coiled deoxyribonucleic acid (DNA) composed of genes.

**Chronometer** An accurate mechanical timekeeping device. Can also be used as a ship's clock, unlike the pendulum clock.

**Cilium** A small hairlike projection of the surface of some cells, often responsible for movement.

**Circadian rhythm** The cycle of approximately 24 hours in which plants, animals, and people operate and that makes them sleep or wake at certain times.

**Circuit** The completed path around which an electrical current passes, usually made up of a positive (live) path and a negative (neutral) path.

**Clutch** A mechanical device in an automobile that disengages the engine from the driveshaft while the gears in the transmission are being shifted.

**Coaxial** In transmitting signals, a coaxial cable has an outer tubular electrical conductor separated from an inner electrical conductor by insulating material. This improves the efficiency of the signal.

**Codon** Group of three messenger ribonucleic acid (mRNA) bases that specify an amino acid or polypeptide chain.

**Coherent** In physics, describing pure light that has only one wavelength, traveling in one direction, and that is in phase (or step) and so does not fan out.

**Combustion** The process of burning in which a substance is mixed with oxygen and then lit, producing heat and light as a result.

**Comet** Small body of ice and dust in orbit around the Sun. As a comet passes by the Sun, a glowing tail may form as dust and ionized gases trail behind it.

**Commutator** The part of an electric motor consisting of two metal half-rings that reverse the direction of the flow of an electrical current.

**Composite** A material that is strengthened by the addition of other materials.

**Compound** A pure substance consisting of atoms or ions of two or more different chemical elements in definite proportions that cannot be separated by physical means.

**Concave** Having a surface that is curved inward, as in a concave lens or mirror that causes light rays to move in different directions.

**Condensation** A change of physical state from a gas to a liquid, or from a liquid to a solid.

**Conduction** The transfer of heat from warmer to cooler regions through a medium or from one substance to another.

**Conductor** A substance or medium (such as liquid or gas) that conducts heat, light, sound, or especially an electrical charge.

**Constellation** Group of stars that can be seen in a particular part of the night sky.

**Contamination** The process of making a substance or a body impure or diseased by its contact with something unclean or harmful.

**Convection** The transfer of heat from one part of a fluid (liquid or gas) to another.

**Converge** To come together, as, for example, in the converging lens of a camera or magnifying glass that bends light rays so that they focus on one place. Also, in mathematics, a series of infinite numbers added together to come gradually nearer to a total without ever actually reaching it.

**Coordinates** In mathematics, the measurements that find the position of a point, using its distance from perpendicular lines called axes.

**Corona** Outermost layer of the Sun's atmosphere that becomes visible only during total solar eclipses.

**Corrosion** Oxidation of metals or alloys on exposure to air, moisture, or acids.

**Covalent compound** A compound formed when two atoms attract and share the same pair of electrons. A covalent bond affects only two atoms, but most atoms can form more than one covalent bond at a time, with many elements involved in the compound.

**Cracking** The breaking of large hydrocarbons, such as crude oil, into smaller ones, such as gasoline, by means of either heat or a catalyst.

**Crank** A device for transmitting rotary motion, consisting of a handle or arm attached at right angles to a driveshaft.

**Critical mass** The mass of an unstable element, such as uranium-235, required to start spontaneous nuclear fission.

**Critical temperature** The temperature above which a gas cannot be liquefied by increasing pressure.

**Cryolite** A mineral substance containing sodium and aluminum fluoride that is used in the process of purifying aluminum.

**Cryosurgery** The destruction of harmful tissue by the application of extreme cold.

**Crystal** Any solid object in which an orderly three-dimensional arrangement of the atoms, ions, or molecules is repeated throughout the entire volume.

**Current** In a wire, a measure of the quantity of electrons passing any point of the wire per unit of time. Current is usually measured in amperes.

**Cyclotron** A type of particle accelerator that forces particles into a spiral path.

**Cylinder** In automotive engineering, a round chamber in which a piston moves in an engine.

**Cytoplasm** The colorless, semifluid substance of a living cell (excluding the central nucleus).

**Damping** Progressive decrease in the amplitude of an oscillation or vibration due to the expenditure of energy by friction, viscosity, or other means.

**Deceleration** The decrease in velocity of an object.

**Decibel** A measure of the loudness of sound starting with 0, the faintest sound heard by the human ear, and increasing without limit.

**Decompose** To break up into simpler parts as a molecule does into atoms. Also, the decay of organic material, such as dead animals and plants. This process is called decomposition. A decomposer is an organism, such as a bacterium or fungus, that breaks down plant and animal remains into carbon, nitrogen, and other elements.

**Deformation** The permanent change in shape that occurs when a substance is subjected to a force beyond its elastic limit.

**Density** Quantity representing the mass of a substance, distribution of a quantity, or the number of individuals per unit of volume, area, or length.

**Detritus** The dead plant and animal remains and dung that form the beginnings of the food chain.

**Deuterium** An isotope of hydrogen with one proton and one neutron in the nucleus.

**Dew point** The temperature at which moist air becomes saturated (full of water) and produces droplets in the form of dew on the ground.

**Dialysis** The separation of substances in a liquid by means of the ability of some of them to pass through a cell wall while others cannot.

**Diamagnetism** The ability of an atom, ion, or molecule to align along a magnetic field.

**Diameter** A straight line passing from one side to the other side and through the center of a circle or other curved shape.

**Die** A block of metal made in a mold that is used to form other materials when in contact with them under heavy pressure.

**Dielectric** A substance put between the plates of a capacitor so as to increase its capacitance.

**Differentiation** In a branch of mathematics called calculus, the calculation of rates of change and maximum and minimum values of one quantity with respect to another.

**Diffraction** The spreading of waves around obstacles. Diffraction takes place with sound, electromagnetic radiation (such as light, X-rays, and gamma rays), and very small moving particles that show wavelike properties (such as atoms, neutrons, and electrons).

**Diffuse** For particles in liquids and gases to move from areas of high concentration to areas of lower concentration so that the particles become more evenly distributed.

**Digital** In communication, the representation of information as numbers. In computer technology, the representation of numbers as discrete units.

**Diode** An electrical device that allows current to flow in one direction only.

**Direct current (DC)** An electrical current that flows continuously in one direction. The current from a battery is an example of direct current.

**Dispersion** The splitting of light into its various colors when passed through certain objects.

**Displacement** The weight or volume of a fluid pushed aside by a floating body (used as a measurement of the weight or bulk of ships). Also, the distance moved by a particle or body in a specific direction.

**Distillation** Process involving the conversion of a liquid into vapor and then condensing it back to liquid form. Distillation is used to refine and separate mixtures of different liquids.

**Doppler effect** Apparent change in the wavelength of sound or electromagnetic radiation due to the relative motion between the source and the observer.

**Drag** The resistance of a fluid (a liquid or gas) to the movement of a body through it, measured as drag coefficient ($C_D$).

**Dynamics** The study of the motion of particles with mass.

**Eclipse** Complete or partial blocking of light from one celestial body by another. An eclipse occurs when three celestial bodies become aligned.

**Ecosystem** An interdependent community of living organisms functioning together within its nonliving environment as a unit.

**Electrode** Solid plate, grid, or wire for emitting, collecting, or deflecting charged particles.

**Electrolysis** The process by which the passage of an electrical current through a solution or a molten ionic compound brings about a chemical change.

**Electrolyte** Solution or pure liquid that contains anions and cations. The passage of an electrical current can cause an electrolyte to decompose.

**Electromagnet** An iron core with wires wound around it that operates as a magnet only when an electrical current is passed through the wire.

**Electrons** Subatomic particles (particles smaller than atoms) that have a negative electrical charge.

**Electroplating** Process of coating with metal by means of an electrical current. Plating metal may be transferred to nonconductive surfaces by first coating them with a conductive base layer.

**Electrostatic field** An electrical force surrounding objects that have a static (unmoving) electrical charge.

**Element** Any one of the fundamental chemical substances of which all matter is composed. At present, 112 elements are known. Elements are made up of atoms that contain the same number of protons and cannot be decomposed into simpler substances by ordinary chemical processes.

**Ellipse** The curve that is seen when looking at an oval shape sideways. An elliptical orbit is one in which satellites move from a lower position to a higher one and back again as they revolve around Earth.

**E-mail** An abbreviation of electronic mail, e-mail is a system for sending and receiving messages electronically over a computer network.

**Emission spectrum** A type of spectrum that is caused by a direct source, broken into strong individual frequencies (colors).

**Emulsion** A mixture of two or more liquids in which one liquid is present as droplets of microscopic size distributed throughout the other.

**Endoscopy** An examination technique in medicine using fiber-optic instruments that can be inserted into the body.

**Enzymes** Proteins that catalyze chemical reactions in biological systems.

**Epicenter** The point on the surface of Earth lying immediately above where an earthquake occurs.

**Equator** The imaginary circle around Earth's surface equidistant from the poles. It divides Earth into the Northern Hemisphere and the Southern Hemisphere.

**Equilibrium** The state of a body or physical system at rest or in unaccelerated motion in which all acting influences are canceled by others, resulting in a stable, balanced, or unchanging system.

**Escapement** A mechanism in a clock or watch that transfers power from the weight or spring to maintain the vibration of the pendulum or balance.

**Estuary** A wide inlet at the mouth of a river into which the sea enters at high tide.

**Eukaryotes** Organisms composed of one or more cells containing distinct nuclei and organelles.

**Eutrophication** Rapid increase in the nutrients contained in a body of water; it may occur naturally or as a consequence of human activities, such as the overuse of fertilizers in agriculture.

**Evaporate** Of liquids, to change into steam or vapor. The process is called evaporation.

**Evolution** The gradual development in plant and animal life from simpler to more complex structures over a long period.

**Excretion** The process by which animals rid themselves of waste products and the by-products of metabolism. Processes of excretion in humans include exhalation, urination, sweating, and egestion (discharge) from the digestive system.

**Exposure** The length of time a photographic film must be open to the light to make a photograph.

**Extrusion** A molding process whereby a viscous molten substance is forced through a small hole.

**Fats** Organic molecules made from fatty acids and glycerol. They are a major source of food to animals.

**Fault** Fracture in rock along which the rocks on either side have been displaced relative to one another.

**Feldspar** A group of red or white crystalline minerals based on aluminum silicate.

**Fermentation** Anaerobic (in the absence of oxygen) breakdown of organic substances, usually sugars or fats, to give simpler organic products.

**Fetus** Unborn offspring after it has completed most of its development; in humans, the term applies from the second or third month of pregnancy to birth.

**Fiber optics** The transmission of light signals through glass fibers.

**Filament** A thin thread made of wire through which an electrical current passes to give off light or heat.

**Filter** A material that separates liquids from solids. Also, a colored glass plate in a camera or viewing instrument that keeps some types of light from passing through.

**Fission, nuclear** The splitting of large nuclei, such as uranium-235, accompanied by the release of vast amounts of energy.

**Fixing** In photography, the process by which a photographic film is made insensitive to light while preserving any image already present.

**Flagellum** A long, hairlike projection on a bacterium that is responsible for movement.

**Fluid** Any substance that flows, such as a liquid or gas.

**Fluorescent** The emission of electromagnetic radiation, especially of visible light, given off by certain substances when they are irradiated by ultraviolet rays.

**Focal length** The distance from the surface of a lens or mirror to its focal point (the point at which a subject is in focus). Also called focal distance.

**Focus** The point to which light rays come together through a lens or by means of a mirror in a camera or telescope.

**Forensics** The use of scientific methods to help police fight crime.

**Fossil** Naturally preserved remains or other trace of a once-living organism.

**Fossil fuels** Fuels, such as coal, natural gas, or oil, formed from the remains of organisms that lived millions of years ago.

**Free fall** Acceleration of a body under the sole influence of a gravitational field; that is, there is no air resistance or buoyancy.

**Frequency** The rate at which something occurs or is repeated, as in the number of pulses in radio waves or the number of times an alternating current flows back and forth in an electric circuit.

**Frequency modulation (FM)** A radio broadcasting technique for improving the quality of sound in which the radio signal is always the same strength but comes at varying times per second.

**Friction** The resistance encountered when one body is moved in contact with another.

**Fusion, nuclear** The joining together of atomic nuclei to form heavier nuclei, accompanied by the release of vast amounts of energy.

# Geologic timescale

The geologic timescale provides a chronological arrangement of geologic events over the last 4.6 billion years. Divisions in the geologic timescale are linked to systems of layered rock, called strata, deposited during those periods. Radioactive isotopes are used to obtain absolute ages of the rock, but fossils are also used to date and correlate sedimentary strata. The boundaries between the divisions generally correspond to major geological events in Earth's history.

The geologic timescale is divided into four major eons. There are three eons before the Cambrian period begins. These are called the Pre-Archean, the Archean, and the Proterozoic eons, which are collectively known as the Precambrian. The fourth, and most recent eon, is the Phanerozoic, which includes the Paleozoic, the Mesozoic, and the Cenozoic eras. The eras of the Phanerozoic eon are divided into periods, and these periods are further divided into epochs.

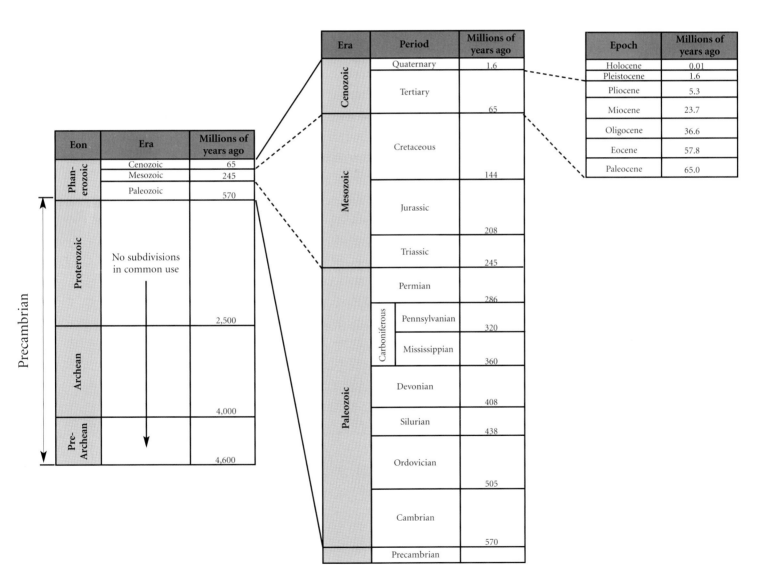

| Eon | Era | Millions of years ago |
|-----|-----|-----------------------|
| Phanerozoic | Cenozoic | 65 |
| | Mesozoic | 245 |
| | Paleozoic | 570 |
| Proterozoic | No subdivisions in common use | 2,500 |
| Archean | | 4,000 |
| Pre-Archean | | 4,600 |

| Era | Period | | Millions of years ago |
|-----|--------|--|-----------------------|
| Cenozoic | Quaternary | | 1.6 |
| | Tertiary | | 65 |
| Mesozoic | Cretaceous | | 144 |
| | Jurassic | | 208 |
| | Triassic | | 245 |
| Paleozoic | Permian | | 286 |
| | Carboniferous | Pennsylvanian | 320 |
| | | Mississippian | 360 |
| | Devonian | | 408 |
| | Silurian | | 438 |
| | Ordovician | | 505 |
| | Cambrian | | 570 |
| | Precambrian | | |

| Epoch | Millions of years ago |
|-------|-----------------------|
| Holocene | 0.01 |
| Pleistocene | 1.6 |
| Pliocene | 5.3 |
| Miocene | 23.7 |
| Oligocene | 36.6 |
| Eocene | 57.8 |
| Paleocene | 65.0 |

Precambrian

# Glossary

**Aberration** In optical lenses, a fault in an image that occurs because of the shape of the lens (spherical aberration) or because of an alteration in color (chromatic aberration).

**Abrasive** A hard substance, often used for cleaning or sharpening by rubbing against another object.

**Absolute zero** The lowest possible theoretical temperature limit, measured on the Kelvin scale as 0K (−459.67°F or −273.15°C).

**Absorb** To take in a substance as, for example, a sponge absorbs water. A substance that does this is said to be absorbent. Also, to reduce the effect of a force, as a beach absorbs the energy of waves.

**Absorption spectrum** A type of spectrum that contains dark bands where an absorbing substance has removed some of the frequencies (colors).

**Acceleration** The increase in velocity of an object.

**Accelerometer** An instrument used for measuring the rate at which a vehicle gathers velocity.

**Acid** One of a class of substances that react with and dissolve certain metals to form salts.

**Acoustic** Related to sound. An acoustic mine has a microphone that can pick up propeller noise.

**Additive** A substance that is added to another substance to improve, strengthen, or otherwise change that substance.

**Adhere** To stick to the surface of another substance by suction or by the use of a gluing agent called an adhesive.

**Adsorption** The taking up of one substance at the surface of another but not going inside it.

**Aerodynamics** The study of the way in which air moves around objects. An aerodynamic object is one with a shape that minimizes disturbance of air flowing around it.

**Afterburn** The injection of fuel into the hot exhaust gases of a jet engine to improve performance. Used in takeoff of jet airplanes with small engines.

**Air pressure** The force that air puts on an object, especially when it is in motion.

**Alkali** One of a class of substances that form chemical salts when combined with acids and that can corrode or burn when mixed with water.

**Allergy** A biological reaction (such as a rash) to an otherwise harmless substance (the antigen).

**Allotrope** One or more forms of an element that differ in physical, and often chemical, properties.

**Alloys** Mixtures of metals with other elements, often other metals or carbon, to make them stronger or give them certain qualities.

**Alpha rays** A stream of high-speed alpha particles emitted during the energetic radioactive decay of certain atoms. Alpha particles consist of two protons and two neutrons, forming a helium nucleus.

**Alternating current (AC)** An electrical current that reverses periodically. Domestic electricity supplies use alternating current.

**Alternator** A type of generator that produces an alternating electrical current.

**Altimeter** An instrument that measures height above the ground.

**Altitude** The height of an object above sea level.

**Alveoli** The small sacs in the lungs where gaseous exchange takes place.

**Amino acids** Organic molecules consisting of a central carbon atom, a carboxyl group (−COOH), and a side chain (−R). Amino acids are the building blocks of proteins.

**Ammeter** An instrument for measuring either direct (DC) or alternating (AC) electrical current, in amperes.

**Amorphous** Having no distinct shape—in particular, lacking the structure characteristic of living bodies or without apparent crystalline form.

**Ampere** The SI base unit used to measure a quantity of electricity flowing past a point.

**Amplification** Increasing the strength of an electrical current by applying a low, alternating voltage to one or a series of electron tubes or transistors.

**Amplitude** The "height" of a wave; more accurately, half the distance between a peak and a trough.

**Amplitude modulation (AM)** A radio broadcasting technique in which the radio signal is always of the same frequency, but its amplitude varies.

**Anabolism** Chemical reaction in which a complex substance is made from simpler ones. This leads to the storage of energy.

**Analog** Of a computer, describing the way scientific and technical information is held and displayed by means of physical quantities (weight or length) that are similar (analogous) to the actual reality.

**Anechoic chamber** An "echoless" room designed to absorb all sound within it without reflections from the walls, roof, or floor.

**Anemometer** An instrument used to measure the speed of a flowing fluid, including gases.

**Anhydrous** Without water.

**Anion** A negatively charged ion, showing an excess of electrons. An anion is attracted to the positive electrode (anode) in an electrochemical cell.

**Anneal** To heat metal or glass and then to cool it gradually to make it stronger.

**Anode** The positive electrode in an electrochemical cell; the electrode toward which anions (negatively charged ions) migrate.

**Anodization** A way of providing light metals, such as aluminum, with a protection against corrosion by covering the metal with a thin oxide film.

**Antenna** A device used for transmitting and receiving electromagnetic waves.

**Antibiotic** An organic compound that inhibits the growth of, or destroys, bacteria. Antibiotics are used to treat a range of infectious diseases, from cholera and syphilis to meningitis and pneumonia.

**Antibodies** Protective proteins produced by the body's immune system in response to the presence of foreign substances, called antigens.

**Antigen** A foreign substance in the body that stimulates an immune response.

**Antimatter** Each fundamental particle has an antimatter equivalent, which has the same mass but opposite charge. If the two particles meet, they annihilate each other with the release of energy.

**Aperture** A circular opening through which light passes, for example, in a camera or telescope.

**Aqua regia** A strong acid composed of concentrated hydrochloric and nitric acids. Aqua regia can dissolve gold and platinum.

**Aqueduct** A bridge or canal that carries a water supply across a distance.

**Aquifer** A layer of water-saturated permeable rock. Groundwater is obtained from an aquifer.

**Archimedean screw** An ancient device used to raise water by means of a spiral enclosed in a tube.

**Artery** A blood vessel carrying oxygenated blood away from the heart.

**Asteroid** Small rocky body that orbits the Sun between Mars and Jupiter and forms what is known as the asteroid belt.

**Atmosphere** The layer of gaseous chemicals surrounding Earth. The atmosphere provides oxygen and contains water vapor, which falls as precipitation. It also protects Earth from radiation and meteors.

**Atom** The smallest particle of an element that has all the properties of that element.

**Atomic number** The number of protons in the nucleus of an atom. The atomic number determines the position of elements in the periodic table.

**Auroras** The dramatic visual displays seen in the sky at the North and South poles, which are caused by the interaction of the solar wind with Earth's magnetic field.

**Axis** The central line, usually an imaginary one, around which a body such as Earth turns.

**Bacteria** Single-celled organisms most of which are decomposers, but many of which are responsible for infectious diseases in plants, animals, and people.

**Baffle** A structure used to control or change the flow of gases, sounds, liquids, and other materials.

**Ballast** Heavy materials, such as stones or lead, put in the holds of ships to keep them stable. In balloons or airships, ballast is carried and then thrown overboard so the craft can go higher.

**Barometer** An instrument used to measure air pressure. A mercury column is a simple barometer.

**Bergschrund** Large ice crevasse that occurs at the highest point of a glacier.

**Big bang theory** Theory that the universe began with a cosmic explosion from a single point around 10 to 15 billion years ago.

**Biodegradable** Capable of being decomposed by biological agents, especially bacteria.

**Bioluminescence** The production of light without heat by biological means.

**Biome** Any of Earth's major ecosystems that extend over large areas and are characterized by a distinctive climate and vegetation, such as deserts or rain forests.

**Biorhythms** The variations in the biological clock of an organism.

**Biotechnology** The use of microorganisms, such as bacteria, or biological substances, such as enzymes, to produce useful products, such as antibiotics.

**Bit** An abbreviation for binary digit, a bit is the smallest unit of information, represented by the binary numbers 0 and 1. Digital information, as used by computers, is always stored in bits.

**Black hole** Region of space in which the pull of gravity is so strong that nothing, not even light, can escape from it.

**Boiler** A tank in which water is heated before being circulated as hot water or steam for heating or power.

**Boolean algebra** A system of algebra in which there are two elements of sets that can be combined or shown in a relationship.

**Boyle's law** For a given mass of gas at constant temperature, the volume of the gas varies inversely with its pressure.

**Buttress** A brick or stone support built against a wall to help it resist outward pressure.

**Calculus** The branch of mathematics that deals with rates of change in systems.

**Cam** A machine component that either rotates or reciprocates (moves back and forth) to create a set motion in a contacting element known as a follower.

**Capacitance** The ability of a capacitor to store electrical current or charges. A capacitor is a device that controls the supply of electricity by means of two plates—separated by insulating material—that hold the positive and negative charges.

**Capillary action** The force that causes a liquid to rise up a narrow tube.

**Carbohydrates** Large organic molecules, such as sugars or starch, which can be used by organisms to produce energy.

**Carburetor** A device used in older internal combustion engines to produce an explosive mixture of fuel vapor (mist) and air.

**Carcinogen** Any substance or agent that causes a normal cell to become cancerous.

**Catabolism** All the enzymatic breakdown processes in an organism, such as digestion and respiration.

**Catalysts** Substances that initiate or speed up chemical reactions without themselves being altered during the reaction.

**Catheter** A narrow tube used to drain or inject fluids through a body passage such as the nose or a vein.

**Cathode** The negative electrode in an electrochemical cell; the electrode toward which cations (positively charged ions) migrate.

**Cation** A positively charged ion, showing a depletion of electrons. A cation is attracted to the negative electrode (cathode) of an electrochemical cell.

**Cavitation** The process by which an object is worn away by bubbles created as the object moves through a liquid, such as a ship's propeller through water.

**Cell** The basic unit of life, which consists of genetic material, cytoplasm, a cell membrane, and (in plants and bacteria) a cell wall. Also, a type of electric battery that works by chemical reaction.

**Cell membrane** A thin, flexible layer covering the surface of a cell.

**Cellulose** A tough, structural protein that strengthens the cell walls of plants.

**Centrifuge** An apparatus that spins liquids or solids at high speeds, forcing the heavier parts out to the edge and keeping the lighter parts nearer the center, thus separating them.

**Ceramics** Certain types of hard, nonmetallic, crystalline solids. China and silicon are ceramics.

**Cerebellum** The part of the brain that controls and coordinates the movement of muscles.

**Cerebrum** The largest part of the brain; it controls the senses and provides people with the power of speech and understanding.

**Chemical bond** The electrical forces linking atoms in molecules.

**Chromosome** A threadlike strand of coiled deoxyribonucleic acid (DNA) composed of genes.

**Chronometer** An accurate mechanical timekeeping device. Can also be used as a ship's clock, unlike the pendulum clock.

**Cilium** A small hairlike projection of the surface of some cells, often responsible for movement.

**Circadian rhythm** The cycle of approximately 24 hours in which plants, animals, and people operate and that makes them sleep or wake at certain times.

**Circuit** The completed path around which an electrical current passes, usually made up of a positive (live) path and a negative (neutral) path.

**Clutch** A mechanical device in an automobile that disengages the engine from the driveshaft while the gears in the transmission are being shifted.

**Coaxial** In transmitting signals, a coaxial cable has an outer tubular electrical conductor separated from an inner electrical conductor by insulating material. This improves the efficiency of the signal.

**Codon** Group of three messenger ribonucleic acid (mRNA) bases that specify an amino acid or polypeptide chain.

**Coherent** In physics, describing pure light that has only one wavelength, traveling in one direction, and that is in phase (or step) and so does not fan out.

**Combustion** The process of burning in which a substance is mixed with oxygen and then lit, producing heat and light as a result.

**Comet** Small body of ice and dust in orbit around the Sun. As a comet passes by the Sun, a glowing tail may form as dust and ionized gases trail behind it.

**Commutator** The part of an electric motor consisting of two metal half-rings that reverse the direction of the flow of an electrical current.

**Composite** A material that is strengthened by the addition of other materials.

**Compound** A pure substance consisting of atoms or ions of two or more different chemical elements in definite proportions that cannot be separated by physical means.

**Concave** Having a surface that is curved inward, as in a concave lens or mirror that causes light rays to move in different directions.

**Condensation** A change of physical state from a gas to a liquid, or from a liquid to a solid.

**Conduction** The transfer of heat from warmer to cooler regions through a medium or from one substance to another.

**Conductor** A substance or medium (such as liquid or gas) that conducts heat, light, sound, or especially an electrical charge.

**Constellation** Group of stars that can be seen in a particular part of the night sky.

**Contamination** The process of making a substance or a body impure or diseased by its contact with something unclean or harmful.

**Convection** The transfer of heat from one part of a fluid (liquid or gas) to another.

**Converge** To come together, as, for example, in the converging lens of a camera or magnifying glass that bends light rays so that they focus on one place. Also, in mathematics, a series of infinite numbers added together to come gradually nearer to a total without ever actually reaching it.

**Coordinates** In mathematics, the measurements that find the position of a point, using its distance from perpendicular lines called axes.

**Corona** Outermost layer of the Sun's atmosphere that becomes visible only during total solar eclipses.

**Corrosion** Oxidation of metals or alloys on exposure to air, moisture, or acids.

**Covalent compound** A compound formed when two atoms attract and share the same pair of electrons. A covalent bond affects only two atoms, but most atoms can form more than one covalent bond at a time, with many elements involved in the compound.

**Cracking** The breaking of large hydrocarbons, such as crude oil, into smaller ones, such as gasoline, by means of either heat or a catalyst.

**Crank** A device for transmitting rotary motion, consisting of a handle or arm attached at right angles to a driveshaft.

**Critical mass** The mass of an unstable element, such as uranium-235, required to start spontaneous nuclear fission.

**Critical temperature** The temperature above which a gas cannot be liquefied by increasing pressure.

**Cryolite** A mineral substance containing sodium and aluminum fluoride that is used in the process of purifying aluminum.

**Cryosurgery** The destruction of harmful tissue by the application of extreme cold.

**Crystal** Any solid object in which an orderly three-dimensional arrangement of the atoms, ions, or molecules is repeated throughout the entire volume.

**Current** In a wire, a measure of the quantity of electrons passing any point of the wire per unit of time. Current is usually measured in amperes.

**Cyclotron** A type of particle accelerator that forces particles into a spiral path.

**Cylinder** In automotive engineering, a round chamber in which a piston moves in an engine.

**Cytoplasm** The colorless, semifluid substance of a living cell (excluding the central nucleus).

**Damping** Progressive decrease in the amplitude of an oscillation or vibration due to the expenditure of energy by friction, viscosity, or other means.

**Deceleration** The decrease in velocity of an object.

**Decibel** A measure of the loudness of sound starting with 0, the faintest sound heard by the human ear, and increasing without limit.

**Decompose** To break up into simpler parts as a molecule does into atoms. Also, the decay of organic material, such as dead animals and plants. This process is called decomposition. A decomposer is an organism, such as a bacterium or fungus, that breaks down plant and animal remains into carbon, nitrogen, and other elements.

**Deformation** The permanent change in shape that occurs when a substance is subjected to a force beyond its elastic limit.

**Density** Quantity representing the mass of a substance, distribution of a quantity, or the number of individuals per unit of volume, area, or length.

**Detritus** The dead plant and animal remains and dung that form the beginnings of the food chain.

**Deuterium** An isotope of hydrogen with one proton and one neutron in the nucleus.

**Dew point** The temperature at which moist air becomes saturated (full of water) and produces droplets in the form of dew on the ground.

**Dialysis** The separation of substances in a liquid by means of the ability of some of them to pass through a cell wall while others cannot.

**Diamagnetism** The ability of an atom, ion, or molecule to align along a magnetic field.

**Diameter** A straight line passing from one side to the other side and through the center of a circle or other curved shape.

**Die** A block of metal made in a mold that is used to form other materials when in contact with them under heavy pressure.

**Dielectric** A substance put between the plates of a capacitor so as to increase its capacitance.

**Differentiation** In a branch of mathematics called calculus, the calculation of rates of change and maximum and minimum values of one quantity with respect to another.

**Diffraction** The spreading of waves around obstacles. Diffraction takes place with sound, electromagnetic radiation (such as light, X-rays, and gamma rays), and very small moving particles that show wavelike properties (such as atoms, neutrons, and electrons).

**Diffuse** For particles in liquids and gases to move from areas of high concentration to areas of lower concentration so that the particles become more evenly distributed.

**Digital** In communication, the representation of information as numbers. In computer technology, the representation of numbers as discrete units.

**Diode** An electrical device that allows current to flow in one direction only.

**Direct current (DC)** An electrical current that flows continuously in one direction. The current from a battery is an example of direct current.

**Dispersion** The splitting of light into its various colors when passed through certain objects.

**Displacement** The weight or volume of a fluid pushed aside by a floating body (used as a measurement of the weight or bulk of ships). Also, the distance moved by a particle or body in a specific direction.

**Distillation** Process involving the conversion of a liquid into vapor and then condensing it back to liquid form. Distillation is used to refine and separate mixtures of different liquids.

**Doppler effect** Apparent change in the wavelength of sound or electromagnetic radiation due to the relative motion between the source and the observer.

**Drag** The resistance of a fluid (a liquid or gas) to the movement of a body through it, measured as drag coefficient ($C_D$).

**Dynamics** The study of the motion of particles with mass.

**Eclipse** Complete or partial blocking of light from one celestial body by another. An eclipse occurs when three celestial bodies become aligned.

**Ecosystem** An interdependent community of living organisms functioning together within its nonliving environment as a unit.

**Electrode** Solid plate, grid, or wire for emitting, collecting, or deflecting charged particles.

**Electrolysis** The process by which the passage of an electrical current through a solution or a molten ionic compound brings about a chemical change.

**Electrolyte** Solution or pure liquid that contains anions and cations. The passage of an electrical current can cause an electrolyte to decompose.

**Electromagnet** An iron core with wires wound around it that operates as a magnet only when an electrical current is passed through the wire.

**Electrons** Subatomic particles (particles smaller than atoms) that have a negative electrical charge.

**Electroplating** Process of coating with metal by means of an electrical current. Plating metal may be transferred to nonconductive surfaces by first coating them with a conductive base layer.

**Electrostatic field** An electrical force surrounding objects that have a static (unmoving) electrical charge.

**Element** Any one of the fundamental chemical substances of which all matter is composed. At present, 112 elements are known. Elements are made up of atoms that contain the same number of protons and cannot be decomposed into simpler substances by ordinary chemical processes.

**Ellipse** The curve that is seen when looking at an oval shape sideways. An elliptical orbit is one in which satellites move from a lower position to a higher one and back again as they revolve around Earth.

**E-mail** An abbreviation of electronic mail, e-mail is a system for sending and receiving messages electronically over a computer network.

**Emission spectrum** A type of spectrum that is caused by a direct source, broken into strong individual frequencies (colors).

**Emulsion** A mixture of two or more liquids in which one liquid is present as droplets of microscopic size distributed throughout the other.

**Endoscopy** An examination technique in medicine using fiber-optic instruments that can be inserted into the body.

**Enzymes** Proteins that catalyze chemical reactions in biological systems.

**Epicenter** The point on the surface of Earth lying immediately above where an earthquake occurs.

**Equator** The imaginary circle around Earth's surface equidistant from the poles. It divides Earth into the Northern Hemisphere and the Southern Hemisphere.

**Equilibrium** The state of a body or physical system at rest or in unaccelerated motion in which all acting influences are canceled by others, resulting in a stable, balanced, or unchanging system.

**Escapement** A mechanism in a clock or watch that transfers power from the weight or spring to maintain the vibration of the pendulum or balance.

**Estuary** A wide inlet at the mouth of a river into which the sea enters at high tide.

**Eukaryotes** Organisms composed of one or more cells containing distinct nuclei and organelles.

**Eutrophication** Rapid increase in the nutrients contained in a body of water; it may occur naturally or as a consequence of human activities, such as the overuse of fertilizers in agriculture.

**Evaporate** Of liquids, to change into steam or vapor. The process is called evaporation.

**Evolution** The gradual development in plant and animal life from simpler to more complex structures over a long period.

**Excretion** The process by which animals rid themselves of waste products and the by-products of metabolism. Processes of excretion in humans include exhalation, urination, sweating, and egestion (discharge) from the digestive system.

**Exposure** The length of time a photographic film must be open to the light to make a photograph.

**Extrusion** A molding process whereby a viscous molten substance is forced through a small hole.

**Fats** Organic molecules made from fatty acids and glycerol. They are a major source of food to animals.

**Fault** Fracture in rock along which the rocks on either side have been displaced relative to one another.

**Feldspar** A group of red or white crystalline minerals based on aluminum silicate.

**Fermentation** Anaerobic (in the absence of oxygen) breakdown of organic substances, usually sugars or fats, to give simpler organic products.

**Fetus** Unborn offspring after it has completed most of its development; in humans, the term applies from the second or third month of pregnancy to birth.

**Fiber optics** The transmission of light signals through glass fibers.

**Filament** A thin thread made of wire through which an electrical current passes to give off light or heat.

**Filter** A material that separates liquids from solids. Also, a colored glass plate in a camera or viewing instrument that keeps some types of light from passing through.

**Fission, nuclear** The splitting of large nuclei, such as uranium-235, accompanied by the release of vast amounts of energy.

**Fixing** In photography, the process by which a photographic film is made insensitive to light while preserving any image already present.

**Flagellum** A long, hairlike projection on a bacterium that is responsible for movement.

**Fluid** Any substance that flows, such as a liquid or gas.

**Fluorescent** The emission of electromagnetic radiation, especially of visible light, given off by certain substances when they are irradiated by ultraviolet rays.

**Focal length** The distance from the surface of a lens or mirror to its focal point (the point at which a subject is in focus). Also called focal distance.

**Focus** The point to which light rays come together through a lens or by means of a mirror in a camera or telescope.

**Forensics** The use of scientific methods to help police fight crime.

**Fossil** Naturally preserved remains or other trace of a once-living organism.

**Fossil fuels** Fuels, such as coal, natural gas, or oil, formed from the remains of organisms that lived millions of years ago.

**Free fall** Acceleration of a body under the sole influence of a gravitational field; that is, there is no air resistance or buoyancy.

**Frequency** The rate at which something occurs or is repeated, as in the number of pulses in radio waves or the number of times an alternating current flows back and forth in an electric circuit.

**Frequency modulation (FM)** A radio broadcasting technique for improving the quality of sound in which the radio signal is always the same strength but comes at varying times per second.

**Friction** The resistance encountered when one body is moved in contact with another.

**Fusion, nuclear** The joining together of atomic nuclei to form heavier nuclei, accompanied by the release of vast amounts of energy.

**Galaxy** The group of stars seen in the heavens as a milky band—the Milky Way. Also, any other group of stars, gas, and dust outside the solar system.

**Galvanize** To coat steel and iron with zinc to protect the metals from corrosion from the air or other sources. The process is called galvanization.

**Gametes** Cells used in sexual reproduction, also called germ cells. In plants and animals, the female gamete is the egg and the male gamete is the sperm.

**Gamma radiation** Rays with very short wavelengths and no electrical charge that are sent out by radioactive substances.

**Gasoline** A volatile, flammable mixture derived from petroleum. Used mainly as a fuel.

**Gas turbine** A rotary engine that uses pressurized, burning gases to rotate (turn) sets of blades (turbines), producing continuous turning power.

**Gear** Toothed wheel used to transmit motion from one moving part of a machine to another. The teeth of one gear mesh with the teeth of another gear.

**Gene** A hereditary unit consisting of a segment of deoxyribonucleic acid (DNA). Each gene occupies a specific location on a chromosome (a threadlike body made of DNA in the cell nucleus) and determines a particular characteristic in an organism.

**Generator** A machine that converts mechanical energy into electrical energy.

**Genetic engineering** The joining together of genetic material, especially DNA, from one or more species of organism, and the introduction of the result into an organism to change one or more of its characteristics.

**Genetic fingerprinting** Method of isolating and making images of sequences of deoxyribonucleic acid (DNA). Also called DNA fingerprinting.

**Genus** Classification of a group of organisms that are closely related in their form and structure. Genera are subdivided into groups of species.

**Geometric** A shape conforming to the mathematical properties of lines, angles, and curves.

**Geometry** The mathematics of the properties, measurement, and relationships of angles, lines, points, solids, and surfaces.

**Glacier** Large body of ice formed in mountainous regions from compacted snow. The movement of glaciers down river valleys gives rise to many geographical features.

**Golgi apparatus** A fine network in cells that takes certain chemicals through cell walls to other cells.

**Gravity** The natural force of attraction exerted by a massive body, such as Earth, upon objects at or near its surface, tending to draw the objects toward the center of the body.

**Gyroscope** A mechanical device with a rapidly rotating wheel that stays pointing in the same direction in space even if its support frame is moved.

**Habitat** The area in which an organism normally lives.

**Hardware** In technology, the mechanical and electronic parts of a computer.

**Harmonic** A frequency (pitch) that is a multiple of some fundamental frequency.

**Hereditary** Biological characteristics transmitted from one generation to the next.

**Hertz** Unit of frequency, abbreviated Hz. The number of hertz equals the number of cycles per second. Hertz are most often used to express electrical current alternations, electromagnetic waves (such as light), and sound.

**Histamine** Substance release in response to the presence of a particular antigen; it makes blood vessels dilate and causes the symptoms of allergic and inflammatory reactions.

**Holography** The production of three-dimensional images using laser light.

**Homeostasis** Body processes that help maintain a relatively constant internal environment despite fluctuations in the external environment.

**Hormones** Chemicals secreted into the blood by ductless glands and carried to specific cells, organs, or tissues to stimulate chemical activity.

**Horsepower** A unit of power equal to 745.7 watts or 33,000 foot-pounds per minute. Used, in particular, to rate the power of engines.

**Hydraulics** The science and technology of the static and dynamic behavior of fluids, especially in relation

to the control and management of water and the use of fluids to operate machines.

**Hydrocarbons** Organic compounds that contain the elements carbon and hydrogen. Hydrocarbons are present in fossil fuels such as crude oil.

**Hydrodynamics** The branch of physics that deals with the motion of fluids and the forces acting on solid bodies immersed in fluids.

**Hydroelectricity** The electricity generated when using water to drive a turbine.

**Hydrofoil** An airfoil for use in the water. The passage of water causes a lift to be given to the hydrofoil.

**Hydrostatics** The branch of physics that deals with fluids at rest and the pressures they exert or transmit under pressure.

**Igneous** Of rocks such as granite, formed from magma (molten rock) that has cooled and hardened.

**Impulse** A force acting for a short time in one direction along a nerve, muscle fiber, or wire.

**Incandescent** Giving off visible light because of being heated, as with the filament of an electric lightbulb.

**Induction** The process by which an electrical current is made to flow in a wire by means of the wire's proximity to a magnet or magnetic field and to another current-carrying wire.

**Inert** An element that is not readily reactive with other elements and forms few or no chemical compounds.

**Inertia** The state of matter that prevents it from moving when it is at rest or from stopping or changing course when it is moving in a straight line, unless an outside force is applied.

**Infinite** In mathematics, describing numbers that may be continued indefinitely and without any limit.

**Infrared** Of light rays, invisible but giving off heat that can be detected by instruments.

**Insulator** Object or medium (such as a liquid or gas) with an unusually low capacity to conduct electrical current, heat, or sound.

**Integrated circuit** An assembly of microscopic electronic components built as a single unit with no connecting wires.

**Integration** In a branch of mathematics called calculus, the method of calculating the areas, surfaces, and volumes of various shapes.

**Interference** The combined effect of the intersection (crossing) or coinciding of two or more waves. The effect is that of the addition of the amplitudes (wave heights) of the individual waves.

**Internal combustion engine** A heat engine in which the combustion that generates the heat takes place inside the engine itself.

**Internet** Large, international computer network linking millions of users worldwide. The Internet is used for communication and for obtaining information on almost any subject.

**Infection** The invasion of the body by any of various infectious agents—including bacteria, viruses, fungi, protozoans, and worms—and the reaction of the body to them or their toxins.

**Invertebrates** Animals without backbones.

**Ion** An atom or group of atoms that has acquired an overall electric charge by gaining or losing one or more electrons.

**Ionic compound** A chemical compound formed by the electrostatic attraction between oppositely charged ions. The overall charge of the entire substance is zero.

**Ionosphere** Region of Earth's upper atmosphere, beginning about 25 miles (40 kilometers) above the planet's surface and extending outward 250 miles (400 kilometers) or more. In this region, ion particles and free electrons exist as a result of radiation and cosmic rays.

**Isomer** One of two or more substances that have molecules with the same atoms but differently arranged and therefore showing different properties.

**Isotope** Any of two or more forms of a chemical element with the same atomic number but different nuclear masses.

**Jet engine** A gas turbine engine in which some of the hot, pressurized gases produced are ejected at high speed through a narrow nozzle at the rear of the engine to provide thrust.

**Kelly** A square or hexagonal pipe at the top of a drilling rig that controls the string of pipes and the drilling tool.

**Kinetic energy** Energy possessed by a moving object or a particle. Kinetic energy depends not only on the motion of an object or particle, but also on its mass.

**Kinetic theory** The mathematical description of the behavior of gases.

**Kuiper belt** A ring of large bodies of rock and ice that lies far beyond the orbit of Pluto.

**Laminar** Referring to a thin layer. Laminar flow is the smooth stream of air that flows over the wings of an aircraft or other kinds of airfoils.

**Laser** A device that generates an intense beam of pure electromagnetic radiation, which can, among other things, be used to cut through metal, perform eye surgery, and carry telephone conversations.

**Latitude** Part of the grid system used to locate points on Earth's surface. Lines of latitude form parallel circles around Earth, concentric to the Poles.

**Lava** The hot liquid rock that flows from a volcano and cools to a solid substance.

**Leaching** The removal of essential nutrients from the soil by their dissolving in rain.

**Light-year** The distance that light travels in a vacuum in one year—approximately 5.88 trillion miles or 9.46 trillion kilometers.

**Liquid** One of the four states of matter (the others are solid, gas, and plasma). Liquids have no fixed shape but take the shape of their containers; however, liquids do have a fixed volume.

**Liquid crystals** Liquids possessing directional physical properties, for example, viscosity.

**Lithosphere** Outer layer of Earth, composed of hard, rigid crustal rocks.

**Litmus paper** Uncoated paper treated with litmus, a powder from lichens, and used to test for acids and alkalis in substances. Litmus paper turns red in acids and blue in alkalis.

**Longitude** Part of the grid system used to locate points on Earth's surface. Lines of longitude form semicircles joining the Poles.

**Lubricate** To use an oily liquid or solid to make machine parts move more smoothly and with less wear. The substance used is called a lubricant and the process is lubrication.

**Mach number** The ratio of an object's velocity to the speed of sound. Velocities below the speed of sound (Mach 1) are called subsonic; velocities above Mach 1 are supersonic.

**Magazine** In gunnery, a container holding bullets that are fed into the firing chamber.

**Magma** Hot, molten rock material within Earth's crust and upper mantle.

**Magnet** A body that attracts iron and certain other materials. A magnetized needle in a compass points approximately north and south.

**Magnetism** An invisible force that draws together some metals, such as iron, or pushes them apart. Magnetism is one of the basic forces of nature, and it is closely related to electricity.

**Mantle** Thick middle layer of Earth (or other rocky planet) between the crust and the core, composed of dense, rocky matter.

**Mass** Amount of matter in a body, which is measured as the body's inertia or resistance to being moved and is distinct from its weight.

**Mass number** The total number of protons and neutrons in the nucleus of an atom.

**Matter** The general term for the substances that make up the physical universe.

**Mean** An average value of a set of values, which is expressed as the sum total of the set of values divided by the number of values.

**Mechanics** The study of how forces act on bodies, and their subsequent motion.

**Median** A value in an ordered set of values above and below which there is an equal number of values; also, the arithmetic mean of the two middle values when there is no middle number.

**Membrane** A thin tissue that lines or connects areas, structures, or organs of plants and animals.

**Meniscus** The curved upper surface of a column of liquid.

**Menstrual cycle** The monthly intervals of discharging blood and dead cells from the nonpregnant uterus by females, starting at puberty and ending with the menopause.

**Metabolism** Simultaneous and interrelated chemical reactions taking place in a cell at any one time.

**Metamorphic rock** Minerals that have been rearranged or recrystallized by great heat and pressure exerted by Earth on existing rocks.

**Metamorphosis** The complete change in form that occurs in some animals when the young mature, for example, from a tadpole into a frog.

**Meteorite** A piece of rock or metal that comes from space and falls to the surface of Earth or other planets.

**Meteorology** The study of Earth's atmosphere, in particular weather forecasting.

**Mica** The name given to a group of silicate minerals that contain atoms of aluminum, oxygen, and silicon bonded into flat layers that split cleanly into thin sheets.

**Microchip** A tiny silicon wafer containing millions of microscopic electronic components in an integrated circuit. Microchips or microprocessors are the "brains" of computers.

**Microorganism** An organism, such as a bacterium, that is too small to be seen by the naked eye.

**Microphone** A device for converting sound into an electrical impulse.

**Microprocessor** A tiny silicon wafer containing millions of microscopic electronic components in an integrated circuit. Microprocessors, or microchips, are the "brains" of computers.

**Microwave** One of a group of radio waves with short wavelengths and extremely high frequencies, used especially in radar systems.

**Minerals** Naturally formed solids with specific crystal structures and definite chemical compositions.

**Mitochondrion** Spherical or elongated structure in a cell in which aerobic respiration occurs.

**Mode** The most frequent value in a set of values.

**Molecule** The smallest chemical unit that makes up a compound. Molecules are composed of more than one atom.

**Momentum** A property of moving matter that is defined as the product of its mass and velocity.

**Mordants** Chemicals (such as tannic acid combined with various metal salts or, sometimes, the salts alone) used to fix dyes in or on a substance by combining with the dye to form an insoluble compound.

**MP3** Short for MPEG-1, Layer 3. MP3 is a popular compressed digital music-file format.

**MPEG** Short for Moving Pictures Experts Group, MPEG was created by the International Standards Organization as a standard for compressing sound and movie files.

**Mycelium** Tangled mass of hyphae (threadlike structures) that form the vegetative body of a fungus.

**Mycoprotein** Artificial meat substitute made from the fermented fungus *Fusarium gramineurum*, usually with colorings and flavorings added.

**Nanotechnology** The manipulation of matter, such as individual molecules, on the nanometer scale. One nanometer is one-billionth of one meter, or $10^{-9}$ meters.

**Nebula** A gas cloud in space generally composed of hydrogen and organic molecules. Star formation occurs in nebulas when the gas conglomerates.

**Nerve** Any of the cordlike bundles of fibers made up of neurons through which sensory stimuli and motor (movement) impulses pass between the brain or other parts of the central nervous system and the body.

**Neurons** Any of the impulse-conducting cells that constitute the brain, spinal column, and nerves.

**Neutron star** Extremely compact, dense star composed almost entirely of neutrons.

**Nova** Stars that suddenly increase in brightness roughly a thousandfold.

**Nucleus** The central part of an atom containing protons and neutrons and surrounded by electrons.

**Nutrients** Substances that are beneficial to the existence and development of living organisms.

**Ohm** A unit of electrical resistance when one ampere is sent through a wire and produces a potential difference of one volt.

**Optics** The study of light and its interactions with matter, such as diffraction and refraction.

**Orbit** The path described by one body, such as Earth, in its revolution around another, such as the Sun, as a result of their mutual gravitational attraction.

**Ores** Minerals from which metals can be extracted.

**Organic** Containing carbon and hydrogen, often in conjunction with other elements, such as nitrogen and sulfur.

**Oscillate** To swing back and forth between alternate extremes with a steady, uninterrupted rhythm, usually within a definable period of time.

**Oscillator** An electronic device that produces alternating electrical current. Oscillators are often stabilized using the vibrations of a piezoelectric crystal, usually quartz.

**Osmosis** The passage of a solvent through a semipermeable membrane from the lower concentration solution to the higher.

**Oxbow lake** A crescent-shaped lake that develops from a mature river.

**Oxidation** The addition of oxygen to a substance, the removal of hydrogen from a substance, or the loss of one or more electrons during a reaction.

**Ozone ($O_3$)** Colorless gas that occurs naturally as a layer in Earth's atmosphere and also concentrates near Earth's surface in polluted air or smog.

**Pangaea** Supercontinent in Earth's history formed of the landmasses Gondwana and Laurasia.

**Parabola** A curve that rises in the middle and drops at the end.

**Parallel** Of two or more lines going in the same direction and remaining at a fixed distance from one another.

**Paramagnetism** Magnetic property of an atom, ion, or molecule that is not affected by a magnetic field.

**Parasite** An organism living on another and deriving nutrition from it, usually harming it.

**Parsec** An astronomical measurement of distance equivalent to 3.5 light-years.

**Pathogen** Any agent that provokes an immune response from an organism. Bacteria are pathogens.

**Patina** A thin greenish layer that forms on the surface of a metal such as copper through oxidation.

**Pendulum** A body suspended from a fixed point so that it can swing back and forth under the influence of gravity. Pendulums are used to regulate the movement of clocks.

**Peristalsis** The contractions of muscle that occur in the walls of hollow organs, such as parts of the digestive system, that move the contents of the organ through the tube.

**Permeable** The property of a material that allows a liquid to pass through it.

**Perpendicular** A line that joins another line at right angles (90 degrees).

**Petrochemicals** Referring to the chemicals obtained from petroleum or natural gas.

**Phagocytosis** The process by which certain cells, such as white blood cells, engulf particles, such as bacteria, from their surroundings.

**Pheromones** Chemicals produced by animals enabling them to communicate by the sense of smell.

**Phosphor** A solid material that emits light, or luminesces, when exposed to radiation such as ultraviolet light or electricity.

**Photoelectric effect** Emission of electrons from the surface of a metal when the metal is hit by electromagnetic radiation at certain frequencies.

**Photon** The smallest unit of light. A photon is a light particle and exhibits the properties of a particle as well as a wave.

**Photosynthesis** The metabolic process by which energy from sunlight is converted into energy stored in chemical compounds. Photosynthesis occurs in plants and some types of bacteria.

**Piezoelectricity** The electricity emitted by certain crystals when placed under mechanical pressure.

**Pigment** A coloring material found naturally or made chemically that is used in paints or dyes.

**Piston** A cylindrical piece of metal inside a cylinder that moves up and down under pressure.

**Pitch** In music, the position of one single sound in the overall sound range. Sounds are higher or lower in pitch according to the frequency of vibration of the sound waves producing them.

**Pitot tube** Device used for the measurement of the flow velocity of a fluid.

**Pivot** A fixed point or pin on which something turns.

**Placebo** In pharmacology, an inert or innocuous substance used as a control in experiments testing the effectiveness of an active substance (such as a drug).

**Plane** In geometry, a flat surface where a straight line joining two points in it lies completely on the surface.

**Plasma** One of the four states of matter, plasma is a collection of charged particles in which the numbers of positive and negative ions are approximately equal.

**Plasmid** In bacteria, a small ring of DNA.

**Plastic** A material that when heated to a liquid or semisolid form can be molded into almost any desired shape, and when cool, hardens into a solid.

**Pneumatic** Run by or using compressed air, or filled with air (especially compressed air).

**Polarity** A positive or negative electrical state, or the alignment of a magnetic field north or south.

**Polarization** In optics, the process of reducing the glare of ordinary light by making the light waves vibrate in one direction only and filtering out the unwanted light.

**Polymer** Molecule that consists of simple, repeating units called monomers.

**Porous** Of a substance such as rock, having tiny openings through which liquids and gases can pass.

**Positron** The antimatter equivalent of an electron, having the same mass but opposite (positive) charge.

**Precession** When a spinning gyroscope starts to move in a circle in addition to its spinning motion.

**Precipitate** A solid formed from a liquid by means of chemical reaction.

**Precipitation** Hail, rain, sleet, or snow that condenses in the atmosphere and falls to Earth's surface.

**Pressure** The force that is exerted on a surface by an object, fluid, or gas in contact with it.

**Prions** Protein particles that are deformed versions of normal brain proteins. Prions attack brain tissue and cause severe mental breakdown and death.

**Prism** In optics, a transparent solid used to produce or analyze a continuous spectrum.

**Program** The step-by-step instructions that control the operation of a computer. Also called software.

**Prokaryotes** Typically single-celled organisms that lack distinct nuclei and organelles.

**Propel** To start off or keep a body in motion.

**Proteins** Large organic molecules containing nitrogen. Proteins are formed from combinations of amino acids.

**Protists** Any of the unicellular (single-celled) plant- and animal-like organisms and their descendant multicellular (many-celled) organisms.

**Proton** An elementary particle in the atomic nucleus with a positive electric charge and a mass about equal to that of a neutron.

**Pseudopod** An extension of an amoeboid cell that is used for feeding and locomotion.

**Pulsar** A source of regular pulses of radio energy. Astronomers think that pulsars are rapidly rotating neutron stars.

**Pyrometer** A thermometer capable of measuring extremely high temperatures.

**Quanta** Discrete natural units, or packets, of energy, charge, angular momentum, or other physical property. Light comprises quanta called photons.

**Quarks** The component parts that make up certain fundamental particles.

**Quasars** Extremely distant cosmic bodies believed to be fundamental to the formation of the universe.

**Radar** Short for "radio detection and ranging." Equipment used to locate the position and velocity of distant objects using narrow beams of high-frequency radio or microwave pulses.

**Radiation** Energy radiated or transmitted as rays, waves, or in the form of particles. Visible light and X-rays are examples of radiation.

**Radioactivity** The spontaneous disintegration of unstable nuclei, which is accompanied by the emission of particles or rays.

**Radiological dating** Method of determining the age of a substance or object by comparing the ratios of a radioactive isotope with that of a stable isotope formed by the decay of the radioactive version.

**Radio waves** The group of electrical impulses with certain frequencies used in the transmission of sound signals, as in broadcasting.

**Radius** The length of the straight line from the center of a circle to any point at the circle's edge.

**Ratio** The relationship between two amounts involving the number of times one amount contains the other. In a ratio of 2:1, for example, there is twice one amount than the other.

**Rational number** In mathematics, a number that can be expressed as a ratio between two numbers.

**Reaction** The chemical process that occurs when one substance produces an effect on another or releases another substance. Substances that take part in a chemical reaction are called reactants.

**Real number** In mathematics, a number that has no imaginary parts, including fractions and decimals.

**Rectifier** In electronics, a device used for converting alternating current (AC) into direct current (DC).

**Red giant** Large, cool star that shines brightly with a reddish light.

**Reduction** In chemistry, a process in which an electron is added to an atom or ion. This happens when oxygen is removed from a molecule, when hydrogen is added to a molecule, and when a metal is extracted from a compound.

**Refining** Any one of a number of processes used to free metals from impurities or unwanted material.

**Reflection** The bouncing of light off a surface in another direction, as can be seen in a mirror.

**Refraction** The bending of light when it travels from one medium to another. The bending is due to the change in velocity that the light undergoes.

**Resistance** The opposition of a body or substance to electrical current passing through it, resulting in a change of electrical energy into heat or another form of energy.

**Resolution** Degree of fineness to which detail can be discerned in an image.

**Resonance** When sympathetic vibrations lengthen and deepen a sound or increase the response of an electrical or mechanical system.

**Respiration** Metabolic process by which cells use oxygen, produce carbon dioxide, and store the energy of food molecules. In living organisms, respiration is the process of gaseous exchange (breathing).

**Rheostat** An adjustable resistor used to adjust current or vary the resistance in electric circuits.

**Ribosomes** Structures within cells that are the sites of protein synthesis.

**Richter scale** Open-ended logarithmic scale used to express the amount of energy released by earthquakes.

**Salt** A crystalline solid, especially sodium chloride (common salt); a compound formed by replacing one or more hydrogen atoms of an acid by metal atoms.

**Saltpeter** A main constituent of gunpowder. Its chemical name is potassium nitrate.

**Saprophyte** An organism that obtains its food from dying or dead organic material.

**Satellite** A body orbiting another, for example, the Moon or a communications satellite.

**Saturated** Full of water or moisture.

**Scalar** Of quantities, having a magnitude or amount but not direction. Time is a scalar quantity.

**Sedimentary rock** Rocks formed by the deposition and compression of sediments that are carried in the waters of rivers, for example.

**Seismology** The science and study of earthquakes and of Earth in general.

**Semiconductor** Any of a class of crystalline solids intermediate in electrical conductivity between a conductor and an insulator. Semiconductors are used to control an electrical current.

**Servomechanism** A system of automatic controls in a device involving the use of small amounts of power to control much larger amounts.

**Software** Instructions that tell a computer what to do, comprising all the programs, procedures, and routines associated with its operation.

**Solar wind** A stream of charged particles flowing from the Sun. The solar wind is responsible for the appearance of auroras at the poles.

**Solenoid** A round coil of wire that behaves like a bar magnet when electrical current passes through it.

**Solution** A mixture of two or more substances in which one substance dissolves the others.

**Solvent** A substance that breaks down or dissolves another substance.

**Sonar** A system for finding the position of an object by sending out sound waves that hit the object and bounce back.

**Species** A classification of organisms that are capable of breeding with one another.

**Specific gravity** The mass per unit volume of a substance, as compared with water.

**Spectroscopy** The study of light rays (spectra), their wavelengths, and properties.

**Stalagmites and stalactites** Columnlike features of limestone caverns caused by seepage of carbon dioxide containing water through the rock.

**Starch** A white energy-producing carbohydrate found in many plants.

**Static electricity** Created when friction transfers electrically charged particles from one body to another.

**Statics** The study of forces acting in equilibrium, such as those on a bridge.

**Stator** The part of an electric motor that does not move.

**Sterilize** To rid of living organisms (especially microorganisms) by treating with heat or chemicals.

**Strain** Deformation or change of volume of a body or part of a body due to an applied stress.

**Stress** System of forces in equilibrium applied to deform a body. Stress is expressed as a ratio of the force divided by the area of the object.

**Striations** In geology, marks on rocks caused by the movement of frozen rocks during the ice ages.

**Sublimation** The conversion of a solid into a gas or a gas into a solid without becoming a liquid.

**Succession** In ecology, the changes that happen to plants over a long period of time in one area.

**Sunspot** Large, cool patch with a strong magnetic field, visible on the surface of the Sun.

**Superconductivity** The virtual disappearance of electric resistance at temperatures close to absolute zero –459.69°F (–273.16°C).

**Supernova** Rare stellar outburst during which a star increases in brightness by roughly a millionfold.

**Supersonic** Moving at a speed great than the speed of sound.

**Surface tension** The force in the thin skinlike surface of a liquid that tends to make the surface take up the smallest possible area.

**Symmetry** The quality that a crystal has of showing an identical and repeating arrangement of facets.

**Synchronous** Moving or operating at the same rate. A synchronous communications satellite has an orbital period the same as that of Earth's rotation, thus the satellite remains above the same point on Earth's surface. A synchronous motor has a speed proportionally equal to the frequency of the current.

**Synchrotron** A large circular machine used to study the behavior of particles in which the particles are accelerated by magnets of varying strengths.

**Synthetic** Of or related to materials manufactured to imitate natural products.

**Temperate** Of climates or land areas, free from very high or very low temperatures.

**Tempering** The process of hardening or strengthening a metal by heating or heating and cooling.

**Tensile** Able to be extended without breaking.

**Terminal** The point in an electrical circuit where a connection can be made.

**Terrestrial** Of, or relating to, Earth.

**Thalamus** The interior part of the brain where nerves controlling the senses originate.

**Theodolite** An instrument used in surveying to measure angles.

**Thermionic emission** Emission of electrons from the surface of a hot metal by virtue of the thermal energy possessed by the electrons.

**Thermistor** A temperature-dependent resistor.

**Thermostat** A device that regulates temperature. Both central-heating and refrigeration systems contain thermostats to keep them at a constant temperature.

**Thrust** The forward-directed force developed in a jet or rocket engine as a reaction to the high-velocity rearward ejection of exhaust gases.

**Galaxy** The group of stars seen in the heavens as a milky band—the Milky Way. Also, any other group of stars, gas, and dust outside the solar system.

**Galvanize** To coat steel and iron with zinc to protect the metals from corrosion from the air or other sources. The process is called galvanization.

**Gametes** Cells used in sexual reproduction, also called germ cells. In plants and animals, the female gamete is the egg and the male gamete is the sperm.

**Gamma radiation** Rays with very short wavelengths and no electrical charge that are sent out by radioactive substances.

**Gasoline** A volatile, flammable mixture derived from petroleum. Used mainly as a fuel.

**Gas turbine** A rotary engine that uses pressurized, burning gases to rotate (turn) sets of blades (turbines), producing continuous turning power.

**Gear** Toothed wheel used to transmit motion from one moving part of a machine to another. The teeth of one gear mesh with the teeth of another gear.

**Gene** A hereditary unit consisting of a segment of deoxyribonucleic acid (DNA). Each gene occupies a specific location on a chromosome (a threadlike body made of DNA in the cell nucleus) and determines a particular characteristic in an organism.

**Generator** A machine that converts mechanical energy into electrical energy.

**Genetic engineering** The joining together of genetic material, especially DNA, from one or more species of organism, and the introduction of the result into an organism to change one or more of its characteristics.

**Genetic fingerprinting** Method of isolating and making images of sequences of deoxyribonucleic acid (DNA). Also called DNA fingerprinting.

**Genus** Classification of a group of organisms that are closely related in their form and structure. Genera are subdivided into groups of species.

**Geometric** A shape conforming to the mathematical properties of lines, angles, and curves.

**Geometry** The mathematics of the properties, measurement, and relationships of angles, lines, points, solids, and surfaces.

**Glacier** Large body of ice formed in mountainous regions from compacted snow. The movement of glaciers down river valleys gives rise to many geographical features.

**Golgi apparatus** A fine network in cells that takes certain chemicals through cell walls to other cells.

**Gravity** The natural force of attraction exerted by a massive body, such as Earth, upon objects at or near its surface, tending to draw the objects toward the center of the body.

**Gyroscope** A mechanical device with a rapidly rotating wheel that stays pointing in the same direction in space even if its support frame is moved.

**Habitat** The area in which an organism normally lives.

**Hardware** In technology, the mechanical and electronic parts of a computer.

**Harmonic** A frequency (pitch) that is a multiple of some fundamental frequency.

**Hereditary** Biological characteristics transmitted from one generation to the next.

**Hertz** Unit of frequency, abbreviated Hz. The number of hertz equals the number of cycles per second. Hertz are most often used to express electrical current alternations, electromagnetic waves (such as light), and sound.

**Histamine** Substance release in response to the presence of a particular antigen; it makes blood vessels dilate and causes the symptoms of allergic and inflammatory reactions.

**Holography** The production of three-dimensional images using laser light.

**Homeostasis** Body processes that help maintain a relatively constant internal environment despite fluctuations in the external environment.

**Hormones** Chemicals secreted into the blood by ductless glands and carried to specific cells, organs, or tissues to stimulate chemical activity.

**Horsepower** A unit of power equal to 745.7 watts or 33,000 foot-pounds per minute. Used, in particular, to rate the power of engines.

**Hydraulics** The science and technology of the static and dynamic behavior of fluids, especially in relation

to the control and management of water and the use of fluids to operate machines.

**Hydrocarbons** Organic compounds that contain the elements carbon and hydrogen. Hydrocarbons are present in fossil fuels such as crude oil.

**Hydrodynamics** The branch of physics that deals with the motion of fluids and the forces acting on solid bodies immersed in fluids.

**Hydroelectricity** The electricity generated when using water to drive a turbine.

**Hydrofoil** An airfoil for use in the water. The passage of water causes a lift to be given to the hydrofoil.

**Hydrostatics** The branch of physics that deals with fluids at rest and the pressures they exert or transmit under pressure.

**Igneous** Of rocks such as granite, formed from magma (molten rock) that has cooled and hardened.

**Impulse** A force acting for a short time in one direction along a nerve, muscle fiber, or wire.

**Incandescent** Giving off visible light because of being heated, as with the filament of an electric lightbulb.

**Induction** The process by which an electrical current is made to flow in a wire by means of the wire's proximity to a magnet or magnetic field and to another current-carrying wire.

**Inert** An element that is not readily reactive with other elements and forms few or no chemical compounds.

**Inertia** The state of matter that prevents it from moving when it is at rest or from stopping or changing course when it is moving in a straight line, unless an outside force is applied.

**Infinite** In mathematics, describing numbers that may be continued indefinitely and without any limit.

**Infrared** Of light rays, invisible but giving off heat that can be detected by instruments.

**Insulator** Object or medium (such as a liquid or gas) with an unusually low capacity to conduct electrical current, heat, or sound.

**Integrated circuit** An assembly of microscopic electronic components built as a single unit with no connecting wires.

**Integration** In a branch of mathematics called calculus, the method of calculating the areas, surfaces, and volumes of various shapes.

**Interference** The combined effect of the intersection (crossing) or coinciding of two or more waves. The effect is that of the addition of the amplitudes (wave heights) of the individual waves.

**Internal combustion engine** A heat engine in which the combustion that generates the heat takes place inside the engine itself.

**Internet** Large, international computer network linking millions of users worldwide. The Internet is used for communication and for obtaining information on almost any subject.

**Infection** The invasion of the body by any of various infectious agents—including bacteria, viruses, fungi, protozoans, and worms—and the reaction of the body to them or their toxins.

**Invertebrates** Animals without backbones.

**Ion** An atom or group of atoms that has acquired an overall electric charge by gaining or losing one or more electrons.

**Ionic compound** A chemical compound formed by the electrostatic attraction between oppositely charged ions. The overall charge of the entire substance is zero.

**Ionosphere** Region of Earth's upper atmosphere, beginning about 25 miles (40 kilometers) above the planet's surface and extending outward 250 miles (400 kilometers) or more. In this region, ion particles and free electrons exist as a result of radiation and cosmic rays.

**Isomer** One of two or more substances that have molecules with the same atoms but differently arranged and therefore showing different properties.

**Isotope** Any of two or more forms of a chemical element with the same atomic number but different nuclear masses.

**Jet engine** A gas turbine engine in which some of the hot, pressurized gases produced are ejected at high speed through a narrow nozzle at the rear of the engine to provide thrust.

**Kelly** A square or hexagonal pipe at the top of a drilling rig that controls the string of pipes and the drilling tool.

**Kinetic energy** Energy possessed by a moving object or a particle. Kinetic energy depends not only on the motion of an object or particle, but also on its mass.

**Kinetic theory** The mathematical description of the behavior of gases.

**Kuiper belt** A ring of large bodies of rock and ice that lies far beyond the orbit of Pluto.

**Laminar** Referring to a thin layer. Laminar flow is the smooth stream of air that flows over the wings of an aircraft or other kinds of airfoils.

**Laser** A device that generates an intense beam of pure electromagnetic radiation, which can, among other things, be used to cut through metal, perform eye surgery, and carry telephone conversations.

**Latitude** Part of the grid system used to locate points on Earth's surface. Lines of latitude form parallel circles around Earth, concentric to the Poles.

**Lava** The hot liquid rock that flows from a volcano and cools to a solid substance.

**Leaching** The removal of essential nutrients from the soil by their dissolving in rain.

**Light-year** The distance that light travels in a vacuum in one year—approximately 5.88 trillion miles or 9.46 trillion kilometers.

**Liquid** One of the four states of matter (the others are solid, gas, and plasma). Liquids have no fixed shape but take the shape of their containers; however, liquids do have a fixed volume.

**Liquid crystals** Liquids possessing directional physical properties, for example, viscosity.

**Lithosphere** Outer layer of Earth, composed of hard, rigid crustal rocks.

**Litmus paper** Uncoated paper treated with litmus, a powder from lichens, and used to test for acids and alkalis in substances. Litmus paper turns red in acids and blue in alkalis.

**Longitude** Part of the grid system used to locate points on Earth's surface. Lines of longitude form semicircles joining the Poles.

**Lubricate** To use an oily liquid or solid to make machine parts move more smoothly and with less wear. The substance used is called a lubricant and the process is lubrication.

**Mach number** The ratio of an object's velocity to the speed of sound. Velocities below the speed of sound (Mach 1) are called subsonic; velocities above Mach 1 are supersonic.

**Magazine** In gunnery, a container holding bullets that are fed into the firing chamber.

**Magma** Hot, molten rock material within Earth's crust and upper mantle.

**Magnet** A body that attracts iron and certain other materials. A magnetized needle in a compass points approximately north and south.

**Magnetism** An invisible force that draws together some metals, such as iron, or pushes them apart. Magnetism is one of the basic forces of nature, and it is closely related to electricity.

**Mantle** Thick middle layer of Earth (or other rocky planet) between the crust and the core, composed of dense, rocky matter.

**Mass** Amount of matter in a body, which is measured as the body's inertia or resistance to being moved and is distinct from its weight.

**Mass number** The total number of protons and neutrons in the nucleus of an atom.

**Matter** The general term for the substances that make up the physical universe.

**Mean** An average value of a set of values, which is expressed as the sum total of the set of values divided by the number of values.

**Mechanics** The study of how forces act on bodies, and their subsequent motion.

**Median** A value in an ordered set of values above and below which there is an equal number of values; also, the arithmetic mean of the two middle values when there is no middle number.

**Membrane** A thin tissue that lines or connects areas, structures, or organs of plants and animals.

**Meniscus** The curved upper surface of a column of liquid.

**Menstrual cycle** The monthly intervals of discharging blood and dead cells from the nonpregnant uterus by females, starting at puberty and ending with the menopause.

**Metabolism** Simultaneous and interrelated chemical reactions taking place in a cell at any one time.

**Metamorphic rock** Minerals that have been rearranged or recrystallized by great heat and pressure exerted by Earth on existing rocks.

**Metamorphosis** The complete change in form that occurs in some animals when the young mature, for example, from a tadpole into a frog.

**Meteorite** A piece of rock or metal that comes from space and falls to the surface of Earth or other planets.

**Meteorology** The study of Earth's atmosphere, in particular weather forecasting.

**Mica** The name given to a group of silicate minerals that contain atoms of aluminum, oxygen, and silicon bonded into flat layers that split cleanly into thin sheets.

**Microchip** A tiny silicon wafer containing millions of microscopic electronic components in an integrated circuit. Microchips or microprocessors are the "brains" of computers.

**Microorganism** An organism, such as a bacterium, that is too small to be seen by the naked eye.

**Microphone** A device for converting sound into an electrical impulse.

**Microprocessor** A tiny silicon wafer containing millions of microscopic electronic components in an integrated circuit. Microprocessors, or microchips, are the "brains" of computers.

**Microwave** One of a group of radio waves with short wavelengths and extremely high frequencies, used especially in radar systems.

**Minerals** Naturally formed solids with specific crystal structures and definite chemical compositions.

**Mitochondrion** Spherical or elongated structure in a cell in which aerobic respiration occurs.

**Mode** The most frequent value in a set of values.

**Molecule** The smallest chemical unit that makes up a compound. Molecules are composed of more than one atom.

**Momentum** A property of moving matter that is defined as the product of its mass and velocity.

**Mordants** Chemicals (such as tannic acid combined with various metal salts or, sometimes, the salts alone) used to fix dyes in or on a substance by combining with the dye to form an insoluble compound.

**MP3** Short for MPEG-1, Layer 3. MP3 is a popular compressed digital music-file format.

**MPEG** Short for Moving Pictures Experts Group, MPEG was created by the International Standards Organization as a standard for compressing sound and movie files.

**Mycelium** Tangled mass of hyphae (threadlike structures) that form the vegetative body of a fungus.

**Mycoprotein** Artificial meat substitute made from the fermented fungus *Fusarium gramineurum*, usually with colorings and flavorings added.

**Nanotechnology** The manipulation of matter, such as individual molecules, on the nanometer scale. One nanometer is one-billionth of one meter, or $10^{-9}$ meters.

**Nebula** A gas cloud in space generally composed of hydrogen and organic molecules. Star formation occurs in nebulas when the gas conglomerates.

**Nerve** Any of the cordlike bundles of fibers made up of neurons through which sensory stimuli and motor (movement) impulses pass between the brain or other parts of the central nervous system and the body.

**Neurons** Any of the impulse-conducting cells that constitute the brain, spinal column, and nerves.

**Neutron star** Extremely compact, dense star composed almost entirely of neutrons.

**Nova** Stars that suddenly increase in brightness roughly a thousandfold.

**Nucleus** The central part of an atom containing protons and neutrons and surrounded by electrons.

**Nutrients** Substances that are beneficial to the existence and development of living organisms.

**Ohm** A unit of electrical resistance when one ampere is sent through a wire and produces a potential difference of one volt.

**Optics** The study of light and its interactions with matter, such as diffraction and refraction.

**Orbit** The path described by one body, such as Earth, in its revolution around another, such as the Sun, as a result of their mutual gravitational attraction.

**Ores** Minerals from which metals can be extracted.

**Organic** Containing carbon and hydrogen, often in conjunction with other elements, such as nitrogen and sulfur.

**Oscillate** To swing back and forth between alternate extremes with a steady, uninterrupted rhythm, usually within a definable period of time.

**Oscillator** An electronic device that produces alternating electrical current. Oscillators are often stabilized using the vibrations of a piezoelectric crystal, usually quartz.

**Osmosis** The passage of a solvent through a semipermeable membrane from the lower concentration solution to the higher.

**Oxbow lake** A crescent-shaped lake that develops from a mature river.

**Oxidation** The addition of oxygen to a substance, the removal of hydrogen from a substance, or the loss of one or more electrons during a reaction.

**Ozone ($O_3$)** Colorless gas that occurs naturally as a layer in Earth's atmosphere and also concentrates near Earth's surface in polluted air or smog.

**Pangaea** Supercontinent in Earth's history formed of the landmasses Gondwana and Laurasia.

**Parabola** A curve that rises in the middle and drops at the end.

**Parallel** Of two or more lines going in the same direction and remaining at a fixed distance from one another.

**Paramagnetism** Magnetic property of an atom, ion, or molecule that is not affected by a magnetic field.

**Parasite** An organism living on another and deriving nutrition from it, usually harming it.

**Parsec** An astronomical measurement of distance equivalent to 3.5 light-years.

**Pathogen** Any agent that provokes an immune response from an organism. Bacteria are pathogens.

**Patina** A thin greenish layer that forms on the surface of a metal such as copper through oxidation.

**Pendulum** A body suspended from a fixed point so that it can swing back and forth under the influence of gravity. Pendulums are used to regulate the movement of clocks.

**Peristalsis** The contractions of muscle that occur in the walls of hollow organs, such as parts of the digestive system, that move the contents of the organ through the tube.

**Permeable** The property of a material that allows a liquid to pass through it.

**Perpendicular** A line that joins another line at right angles (90 degrees).

**Petrochemicals** Referring to the chemicals obtained from petroleum or natural gas.

**Phagocytosis** The process by which certain cells, such as white blood cells, engulf particles, such as bacteria, from their surroundings.

**Pheromones** Chemicals produced by animals enabling them to communicate by the sense of smell.

**Phosphor** A solid material that emits light, or luminesces, when exposed to radiation such as ultraviolet light or electricity.

**Photoelectric effect** Emission of electrons from the surface of a metal when the metal is hit by electromagnetic radiation at certain frequencies.

**Photon** The smallest unit of light. A photon is a light particle and exhibits the properties of a particle as well as a wave.

**Photosynthesis** The metabolic process by which energy from sunlight is converted into energy stored in chemical compounds. Photosynthesis occurs in plants and some types of bacteria.

**Piezoelectricity** The electricity emitted by certain crystals when placed under mechanical pressure.

**Pigment** A coloring material found naturally or made chemically that is used in paints or dyes.

**Piston** A cylindrical piece of metal inside a cylinder that moves up and down under pressure.

**Pitch** In music, the position of one single sound in the overall sound range. Sounds are higher or lower in pitch according to the frequency of vibration of the sound waves producing them.

**Pitot tube** Device used for the measurement of the flow velocity of a fluid.

**Pivot** A fixed point or pin on which something turns.

**Placebo** In pharmacology, an inert or innocuous substance used as a control in experiments testing the effectiveness of an active substance (such as a drug).

**Plane** In geometry, a flat surface where a straight line joining two points in it lies completely on the surface.

**Plasma** One of the four states of matter, plasma is a collection of charged particles in which the numbers of positive and negative ions are approximately equal.

**Plasmid** In bacteria, a small ring of DNA.

**Plastic** A material that when heated to a liquid or semisolid form can be molded into almost any desired shape, and when cool, hardens into a solid.

**Pneumatic** Run by or using compressed air, or filled with air (especially compressed air).

**Polarity** A positive or negative electrical state, or the alignment of a magnetic field north or south.

**Polarization** In optics, the process of reducing the glare of ordinary light by making the light waves vibrate in one direction only and filtering out the unwanted light.

**Polymer** Molecule that consists of simple, repeating units called monomers.

**Porous** Of a substance such as rock, having tiny openings through which liquids and gases can pass.

**Positron** The antimatter equivalent of an electron, having the same mass but opposite (positive) charge.

**Precession** When a spinning gyroscope starts to move in a circle in addition to its spinning motion.

**Precipitate** A solid formed from a liquid by means of chemical reaction.

**Precipitation** Hail, rain, sleet, or snow that condenses in the atmosphere and falls to Earth's surface.

**Pressure** The force that is exerted on a surface by an object, fluid, or gas in contact with it.

**Prions** Protein particles that are deformed versions of normal brain proteins. Prions attack brain tissue and cause severe mental breakdown and death.

**Prism** In optics, a transparent solid used to produce or analyze a continuous spectrum.

**Program** The step-by-step instructions that control the operation of a computer. Also called software.

**Prokaryotes** Typically single-celled organisms that lack distinct nuclei and organelles.

**Propel** To start off or keep a body in motion.

**Proteins** Large organic molecules containing nitrogen. Proteins are formed from combinations of amino acids.

**Protists** Any of the unicellular (single-celled) plant- and animal-like organisms and their descendant multicellular (many-celled) organisms.

**Proton** An elementary particle in the atomic nucleus with a positive electric charge and a mass about equal to that of a neutron.

**Pseudopod** An extension of an amoeboid cell that is used for feeding and locomotion.

**Pulsar** A source of regular pulses of radio energy. Astronomers think that pulsars are rapidly rotating neutron stars.

**Pyrometer** A thermometer capable of measuring extremely high temperatures.

**Quanta** Discrete natural units, or packets, of energy, charge, angular momentum, or other physical property. Light comprises quanta called photons.

**Quarks** The component parts that make up certain fundamental particles.

**Quasars** Extremely distant cosmic bodies believed to be fundamental to the formation of the universe.

**Radar** Short for "radio detection and ranging." Equipment used to locate the position and velocity of distant objects using narrow beams of high-frequency radio or microwave pulses.

**Radiation** Energy radiated or transmitted as rays, waves, or in the form of particles. Visible light and X-rays are examples of radiation.

**Radioactivity** The spontaneous disintegration of unstable nuclei, which is accompanied by the emission of particles or rays.

**Radiological dating** Method of determining the age of a substance or object by comparing the ratios of a radioactive isotope with that of a stable isotope formed by the decay of the radioactive version.

**Radio waves** The group of electrical impulses with certain frequencies used in the transmission of sound signals, as in broadcasting.

**Radius** The length of the straight line from the center of a circle to any point at the circle's edge.

**Ratio** The relationship between two amounts involving the number of times one amount contains the other. In a ratio of 2:1, for example, there is twice one amount than the other.

**Rational number** In mathematics, a number that can be expressed as a ratio between two numbers.

**Reaction** The chemical process that occurs when one substance produces an effect on another or releases another substance. Substances that take part in a chemical reaction are called reactants.

**Real number** In mathematics, a number that has no imaginary parts, including fractions and decimals.

**Rectifier** In electronics, a device used for converting alternating current (AC) into direct current (DC).

**Red giant** Large, cool star that shines brightly with a reddish light.

**Reduction** In chemistry, a process in which an electron is added to an atom or ion. This happens when oxygen is removed from a molecule, when hydrogen is added to a molecule, and when a metal is extracted from a compound.

**Refining** Any one of a number of processes used to free metals from impurities or unwanted material.

**Reflection** The bouncing of light off a surface in another direction, as can be seen in a mirror.

**Refraction** The bending of light when it travels from one medium to another. The bending is due to the change in velocity that the light undergoes.

**Resistance** The opposition of a body or substance to electrical current passing through it, resulting in a change of electrical energy into heat or another form of energy.

**Resolution** Degree of fineness to which detail can be discerned in an image.

**Resonance** When sympathetic vibrations lengthen and deepen a sound or increase the response of an electrical or mechanical system.

**Respiration** Metabolic process by which cells use oxygen, produce carbon dioxide, and store the energy of food molecules. In living organisms, respiration is the process of gaseous exchange (breathing).

**Rheostat** An adjustable resistor used to adjust current or vary the resistance in electric circuits.

**Ribosomes** Structures within cells that are the sites of protein synthesis.

**Richter scale** Open-ended logarithmic scale used to express the amount of energy released by earthquakes.

**Salt** A crystalline solid, especially sodium chloride (common salt); a compound formed by replacing one or more hydrogen atoms of an acid by metal atoms.

**Saltpeter** A main constituent of gunpowder. Its chemical name is potassium nitrate.

**Saprophyte** An organism that obtains its food from dying or dead organic material.

**Satellite** A body orbiting another, for example, the Moon or a communications satellite.

**Saturated** Full of water or moisture.

**Scalar** Of quantities, having a magnitude or amount but not direction. Time is a scalar quantity.

**Sedimentary rock** Rocks formed by the deposition and compression of sediments that are carried in the waters of rivers, for example.

**Seismology** The science and study of earthquakes and of Earth in general.

**Semiconductor** Any of a class of crystalline solids intermediate in electrical conductivity between a conductor and an insulator. Semiconductors are used to control an electrical current.

**Servomechanism** A system of automatic controls in a device involving the use of small amounts of power to control much larger amounts.

**Software** Instructions that tell a computer what to do, comprising all the programs, procedures, and routines associated with its operation.

**Solar wind** A stream of charged particles flowing from the Sun. The solar wind is responsible for the appearance of auroras at the poles.

**Solenoid** A round coil of wire that behaves like a bar magnet when electrical current passes through it.

**Solution** A mixture of two or more substances in which one substance dissolves the others.

**Solvent** A substance that breaks down or dissolves another substance.

**Sonar** A system for finding the position of an object by sending out sound waves that hit the object and bounce back.

**Species** A classification of organisms that are capable of breeding with one another.

**Specific gravity** The mass per unit volume of a substance, as compared with water.

**Spectroscopy** The study of light rays (spectra), their wavelengths, and properties.

**Stalagmites and stalactites** Columnlike features of limestone caverns caused by seepage of carbon dioxide containing water through the rock.

**Starch** A white energy-producing carbohydrate found in many plants.

**Static electricity** Created when friction transfers electrically charged particles from one body to another.

**Statics** The study of forces acting in equilibrium, such as those on a bridge.

**Stator** The part of an electric motor that does not move.

**Sterilize** To rid of living organisms (especially microorganisms) by treating with heat or chemicals.

**Strain** Deformation or change of volume of a body or part of a body due to an applied stress.

**Stress** System of forces in equilibrium applied to deform a body. Stress is expressed as a ratio of the force divided by the area of the object.

**Striations** In geology, marks on rocks caused by the movement of frozen rocks during the ice ages.

**Sublimation** The conversion of a solid into a gas or a gas into a solid without becoming a liquid.

**Succession** In ecology, the changes that happen to plants over a long period of time in one area.

**Sunspot** Large, cool patch with a strong magnetic field, visible on the surface of the Sun.

**Superconductivity** The virtual disappearance of electric resistance at temperatures close to absolute zero –459.69°F (–273.16°C).

**Supernova** Rare stellar outburst during which a star increases in brightness by roughly a millionfold.

**Supersonic** Moving at a speed great than the speed of sound.

**Surface tension** The force in the thin skinlike surface of a liquid that tends to make the surface take up the smallest possible area.

**Symmetry** The quality that a crystal has of showing an identical and repeating arrangement of facets.

**Synchronous** Moving or operating at the same rate. A synchronous communications satellite has an orbital period the same as that of Earth's rotation, thus the satellite remains above the same point on Earth's surface. A synchronous motor has a speed proportionally equal to the frequency of the current.

**Synchrotron** A large circular machine used to study the behavior of particles in which the particles are accelerated by magnets of varying strengths.

**Synthetic** Of or related to materials manufactured to imitate natural products.

**Temperate** Of climates or land areas, free from very high or very low temperatures.

**Tempering** The process of hardening or strengthening a metal by heating or heating and cooling.

**Tensile** Able to be extended without breaking.

**Terminal** The point in an electrical circuit where a connection can be made.

**Terrestrial** Of, or relating to, Earth.

**Thalamus** The interior part of the brain where nerves controlling the senses originate.

**Theodolite** An instrument used in surveying to measure angles.

**Thermionic emission** Emission of electrons from the surface of a hot metal by virtue of the thermal energy possessed by the electrons.

**Thermistor** A temperature-dependent resistor.

**Thermostat** A device that regulates temperature. Both central-heating and refrigeration systems contain thermostats to keep them at a constant temperature.

**Thrust** The forward-directed force developed in a jet or rocket engine as a reaction to the high-velocity rearward ejection of exhaust gases.

**Thryistor** A semiconductor device that acts like a current-controlled switch.

**Tissue** A group of cells that make up a particular part of an animal or plant, such as lung or leaf tissue.

**Torque** Force that tends to produce rotation.

**Toxin** Any substance poisonous to an organism. The term is sometimes restricted to poisons produced by living organisms (biotoxins).

**Transcription** The production of a molecule of ribonucleic acid (RNA) from a DNA template.

**Transducer** Any of various devices for converting nonelectrical information into electrical impulses, for example, microphones and camcorders.

**Transformer** A device that steps up (increases) or steps down (decreases) an electrical force.

**Transistor** An electronic semiconductor device, often used as a current amplifier.

**Translation** Ribosomal stage of protein synthesis when information provided by messenger RNA (mRNA) is translated into a particular sequence of amino acids in a polypeptide chain.

**Triangulation** A method in surveying that enables the accurate measurement of a distance between any two points.

**Trigonometry** The branch of mathematics that deals with the relationships between the sides and the angles of triangles.

**Tsunami** Large ocean wave usually produced by seismic activity on the seafloor.

**Turbine** A wheel driven by moving water, steam, or gas, usually used to work engines and generators.

**Ultrasound** Sound waves that have a frequency beyond the limits of human hearing.

**Ultraviolet** Of light waves, having a wavelength beyond the violet end of the visible light spectrum and before X-rays.

**Vaccine** Therapeutic material containing weakened antigens that, when administered to a patient, stimulates immunity and protects against infection.

**Vacuum** A space entirely devoid of matter, or more generally, a space that has been exhausted to a high degree by an air pump or other artificial means.

**Valency** The power of atoms to combine with each other in terms of the numbers of electrons in the outer shell.

**Vapor** The gaseous form of matter under certain conditions of heat and pressure so that it exists both as a liquid and/or a solid.

**Vaporization** A change of physical state from a liquid to a gas.

**Vector** In mathematics, a quantity that possesses both size and direction. Velocity is a vector quantity.

**Velocity** Rate and direction of the change of location of matter, measured in meters per second (m/s).

**Vitamins** Substances that are needed in minute quantities by the body to function properly.

**Volt** A unit of measurement of electric force. One volt is the amount of force needed to produce one ampere of electric current when the resistance of the material carrying the current is one ohm.

**Voltmeter** A device for measuring volts.

**Vulcanization** The process of treating crude or synthetic rubber with chemicals, such as sulfur, to give it useful properties, such as elasticity.

**Wave** A progressive transfer of energy from one point to another in a medium, for example, air or water.

**Waveband** A range of wavelengths occupied by transmissions of a particular type, for example, broadcasting transmissions.

**Wavelength** The distance between one point on a wave to exactly the same point on the next wave cycle.

**Weight** The force with which a body is attracted to Earth or another celestial body, equal to the product of the object's mass and the acceleration of gravity.

**White dwarf** Dense, hot star that has exhausted nearly all its available energy and has shrunk to a size roughly equal to that of Earth.

**X-ray** Short-wave electromagnetic radiation produced when speeding electrons hit a solid target.

**Yeast** Any one of a number of single-celled fungi that multiply by a budding process. Some yeasts produce enzymes that convert sugar into alcohol and carbon dioxide and so are important in the brewing and baking industries.

# Thematic indexes

Numbers in **bold** refer to volume; page numbers in **bold** refer to main articles; page numbers in *italics* refer to illustrations.

## EARTH, SPACE, AND ENVIRONMENTAL SCIENCES

### A

*aa* (lava) **16:***1940*
accretion disks **13:**1604
acid rain **2:***135*; **3:***339*; **4:**490; **5:***564*; **10:**1178; **11:***1316, 1318*
agriculture **1:23–30**
  antibiotics in **1:**92
  breeding livestock **1:**25–26, 28
  breeding plants **1:**29
  crop rotation **1:**25; **10:**1222
  genetically engineered plants **1:**29–30
  history **1:***23–26*
  intensive farming **1:**27–28
  irrigation **1:**27
  machinery **1:***25*, 26, 30
  organic farming **1:**26
  plows **1:***23, 24*; **11:1300–1301**
  slash and burn **4:**489
  water and **16:**1974
  *see also* crops; pest control
air **1:33**
  air pressure **1:***33*; **16:**1989–1990, *1991*, 1992–1993
  fractional distillation **9:**1104; **10:**1179
  freezing constituents of **13:**1610
  liquid **4:**393; **9:**1104
  *see also* atmosphere
air masses **16:**1990, 1991
alluvial deposits, gold **6:**713
alluvium **13:**1596
Alpha Centauri **14:**1677
Alps **6:***688*
altitude
  and mountain habitats **9:**1065
  climate and **3:***336–337*
anemometers **8:**980
anglesite **7:**836
Antarctica
  a polar desert **4:**415
  hole in ozone layer **2:***135*
  ice shelves **6:***697*
anticlines **6:**692; **12:**1488
  oil reservoirs **9:***1145*
anticyclones (highs) **16:**1993–1994
aphids, pest control **10:**1224, *1226*
Apollo space missions **9:**1042, *1043*, 1045

aquifers **16:**1970
Aral Sea, pollution **11:**1314–1315
arches
  rock **6:***689*
  sea **5:**563
Arctic, global warming and **6:**711–712
Arecibo, radio telescope **9:**1135; **14:**1765
argentine **13:**1558
Ariel (moon) **15:***1886*, 1888
armalcolite **9:**1043
arroyos (wadis) **4:**414
ash, volcanic **16:***1940*
asteroids, comets, and meteors **1:116–119**
  asteroids **1:**116, *117*–118; **6:**687–688; **13:**1603
  comets **1:**116, *117*, 119; **13:**1606; **14:**1696
  meteorites **1:**116, *118, 119*; **4:**437; **9:**1139
  meteoroids **1:**116, 118
  meteors (shooting stars) **1:**116, *117*, 118
  space probes sent to **13:**1630
asthenosphere **11:**1294
astronauts, and weightlessness **8:**918, *919*; **12:***1435*; **16:***1997, 1998*
astronomy **1:120–125**
  Copernicus **1:**120; **3:372–373**; **14:**1711
  development of **1:**120
  Galileo and **6:**655–656
  Herschel (William) and **6:***743–744*; **15:**1885
  radar astronomy **9:**1135; **11:***1396*
  radio astronomy **1:***124–125*; **9:**1134–1135; **14:***1763–1765*
  *see also* black holes; planets; solar system; stars; universe
astrophysics **1:**123–124; **10:**1258
Atacama Desert **4:**416
Atlantic Ocean **9:**1137
*Atlantis* (space shuttle) **13:**1624, *1634–1635, 1636*
atmosphere **2:132–135**; **4:**473
  and radio **11:***1398*
  gases in the **1:**33; **6:**661; **9:**1104
  in the past **2:**132; **6:**710
  water vapor in **15:**1901
  *see also* air
attrition **12:**1465
auroras **3:**313; **7:***795*; **11:**1284–1285
auxin herbicides **10:**1226

### B

Bailey's Beads **4:**488
barometers **1:**33; **2:167–168**; **8:**951, *981*
  aneroid **2:**168; **11:**1349
barycenter **10:**1163
basalt **8:***1012*; **12:**1484
basins **7:**824
bauxite **1:***64–65*; **8:***963*, 965; **13:**1595
bays **9:**1138
beaches **5:**564
Beaufort scale **16:**2009, 2010
*bergschrunds* **6:***699*
beryl **8:***1009*
Bhopal, Union Carbide disaster **11:***1308*
big bang **1:**123; **2:**198; **5:***538*; **12:**1438; **15:***1877, 1879*
big crunch **15:**1881
biogeography **6:**682
biomes and habitats **2:188–193**
  biomes **2:**188–*193*; **4:**490
  cave life **3:**298–299
  mountain habitats **9:***1065*
  *see also* food webs
black holes **1:**122, 124; **2:197–199**; **6:**718; **9:**1109; **12:***1438*; **14:**1676; **15:***1881*
black smokers **9:***1143*
blizzards **13:**1579
blowholes **5:**563
boat lifts **3:**275
boreholes **6:**693
bores, river **15:**1810
boulder clay **6:**700
Burgess Shale **6:**685, 686
buttes **7:**824

### C

calcite **12:**1488
Cambrian period **6:**686
  Cambrian explosion **1:**81
canals **3:273–276**
canyons **7:**824
carbon, cycle **4:**492
carbonates, mineral **8:**1012
Carboniferous period **6:**686
*Cassini* (space probe) **13:***1625*, 1626, 1630; **14:***1787*
Cassiopeia A (supernova remnant) **15:***1882*
cassiterite **15:***1826*
Castor **14:**1677
caves **3:297–299**

celestial sphere **14**:1670, *1671*
Cenozoic era **6**:688
Cepheids (variable stars) **14**:1676;
  **15**:1880
Ceres (asteroid) **1**:117
cerussite **7**:836
cesspools **13**:1549
CFCs *see* chlorofluorocarbons
chalcedony **8**:1010; **15**:1830
chalk **12**:*1485*
*Challenger* (space shuttle) **13**:1631, 1632
Chandra (satellite) **9**:1136
Charon (moon) **11**:*1305*
chernozems **13**:1596
Chicxulub impact crater **1**:118; **6**:688
china clay (kaolin) **11**:1329, *1330*
chlorofluorocarbons (CFCs) **2**:135;
  **6**:711; **10**:1179; **12**:1434
chromosphere **14**:1715
cinnabar **8**:950, *951*
cirques **6**:699
cliffs **7**:825
  chalk **12**:*1485*
climate **3**:336–339; **6**:681
  change **3**:338–339; **8**:*984*–985;
    **11**:1316–1318
  effect of ocean currents on **9**:1139
  effect on soils **13**:1594–1596
  *see also* weather
*Climate Orbiter* (space probe) **13**:1592
climax communities **4**:491
clouds **2**:*132*; **3**:344–345; **12**:1419;
  **15**:*1900*, 1901; **16**:1967, 1990
  altocumulus **3**:*344*, 345
  altostratus **3**:345; **16**:1993
  and cyclones (depressions) **4**:400,
    401; **16**:1993
  cirrocumulus **3**:345
  cirrostratus **3**:345; **16**:1993
  cirrus **3**:*344*, 345; **16**:1993
  cumulonimbus (thunderstorm) **3**:*344*,
    345; **7**:856; **15**:*1801*, 1802, 1836, 1837
  cumulus **3**:*344*
  mammatus **16**:*1989*
  nimbostratus **3**:345; **16**:1993
  nimbus **3**:345
  stratus **16**:1993
coal **5**:550; **12**:1485
  formation **3**:*347*
Coalsack Nebula **9**:1091
coasts
  coastal deserts **4**:416–417
  erosion **5**:*561*, *562*–564; **7**:825
  landforms **7**:825
  colonization **4**:491
Colorado River **12**:*1465*, *1468*
*Columbia* (space shuttle) **13**:*1631*, 1632
comets *see* asteroids, comets, and
  meteors

communications satellites **3**:352–355;
  **9**:*1035*, 1037; **10**:1163; **12**:1518, *1520*,
  1521–1522; **14**:*1756*
  and radio **11**:*1398*
  and television **2**:237, 252–253; **3**:352
  and videophones **15**:1908–1909
companion stars **14**:1676–1677
Compton Gamma Ray Observatory
  (CGRO) **9**:1136; **14**:1766
conglomerates **12**:1484
conservation **3**:343; **4**:492; **16**:2044–2045
constellations **1**:*120*, 121; **14**:1670–1671
continental drift **4**:474–475, 484;
  **6**:690–691, 694; **7**:893; **11**:*1293*–*1294*;
  **16**:*1995*–1996
  *see also* plate tectonics
continental shelves **9**:1140
continental slopes **9**:1140
conveyor belt, global **9**:1139
cooperite **11**:1297
core, study of Earth's **6**:693–694
Corinth Canal **3**:*275*
corona, solar **14**:1715–1716
corundum **8**:1013
cosmic background explorer (COBE)
  satellite **9**:1135; **15**:1881
cosmic rays **6**:670; **10**:1207
  detection **10**:1202
Crab Nebula **9**:*1090*, 1091, 1110
Crater Lake **12**:*1469*
craters, impact **1**:118; **6**:*688*; **7**:821
Cretaceous period **6**:687
crops
  rotation **1**:25; **10**:1222
  *see also* agriculture; pest control
crude oil *see* oil, crude
crust, Earth's **9**:1063; **11**:1294
  rock cycle and **12**:*1487*
currents (oceanic) **9**:*1138*–1139
  and coastal erosion **5**:563–564
  effect on climate **9**:1139
  global warming and **6**:712; **9**:1139
cyclones (depressions; lows) *see*
  depressions
cyclones (hurricanes; typhoons)
  **4**:400–401; **8**:*980*, 985; **15**:1836;
  **16**:*1992*, 1993, 1994, *2007*
  *see also* tornadoes
Cygnus X-1 **2**:199

**D**
dams **2**:*193*; **4**:404–407; **5**:*549*; **6**:*754*,
  *757*; **12**:1470; **16**:*1973*
days **4**:475, 477
  sidereal and solar **15**:1816
DDT *see* dichlorodiphenyltrichloroethane
*Deep Space 1* (space probe) **13**:1626,
  1630

deforestation **15**:1814
  and global warming **6**:711
Deimos (moon) **8**:913
deltas **7**:*824*; **12**:*1467*
depressions (cyclones; lows) **12**:1419,
  1470; **16**:1992–1993
desertification **4**:416
deserts **2**:191; **4**:414–417, *475*; **7**:*822*;
  **12**:1419
  polar **12**:1419
Devonian period **6**:686
dew **15**:*1901*
dew point **3**:344; **12**:1418; **13**:1578;
  **15**:1901
diamond-ring effect **4**:*487*, 488
dichlorodiphenyltrichloroethane (DDT)
  **4**:492; **10**:1223; **11**:1313
dikes **9**:1138
dimension stones **8**:1019, 1020, *1021*
dioxin **10**:1225
*Discovery* (space shuttle) **13**:*1634*
doldrums **16**:2007
drift (glaciofluvial deposits) **6**:700
drift, longshore **5**:564
drought **3**:*337*
drumlins **6**:700; **7**:824
dunes **7**:*822*, 825
  coastal **7**:825

**E**
Earth **4**:473–478; **13**:1604
  age **4**:473; **5**:566; **6**:689
  circumference **8**:902, 929
  history compressed into a year **6**:687
  layers **4**:473–474, *475*
  magnetic field **7**:890, 891
  movements **4**:475–476
  solar heating **4**:476–477
  solar year **4**:477–*478*
  temperature **2**:133; **4**:474
  vegetation cover **7**:*777*
  *see also* atmosphere; plate tectonics
earthquakes **4**:483–486
  causes **4**:483–484; **11**:*1294*, 1295
  causing tsunamis **15**:1859–*1860*, *1861*
  epicenter **12**:1531
  focus **12**:1531
  prediction **4**:485; **12**:1533
  scales used to measure **4**:486; **12**:1530
  seismic waves (shockwaves) **4**:486;
    **6**:693–694; **12**:1531
  skyscrapers built to withstand **13**:1571
  *see also* seismology
eclipses **4**:487–488; **9**:1044–*1045*; **14**:1715
ecology **4**:489–492
ecosystems **4**:489–490
  changing **4**:491
El Niño Southern Oscillation (ENSO)
  **8**:985

emerald 8:*1013*; 15:*1854*
end moraine 6:700
*Envisat* (satellite) 12:*1521*
eons, geological 6:*683*
epochs, geological 6:688
equator 4:476–477
equinoxes 4:477, 478
eras, geological 6:*683*
erosion 5:559–564; 7:820, 824; 13:*1595*;
   16:1983–1984
  average rate 16:1987
  by rivers 5:561–562; 12:1465–1466,
    1467–1468
  cycles of 6:690
  glacial 5:564; 6:699; 7:*821*; 12:1468
  soil 5:560–561, *563*; 13:*1595*
  *see also* weathering
erratics 6:700
eskers 6:700; 7:824
Etna, Mount 16:1940
eutrophication 11:1313–1314
Everest, Mount 7:821; 9:*1063*
  height calculated 9:1064
Everglades 2:*192*
exfoliation (weathering) 16:1987
Exosat 14:1766
exosphere 2:*133*, 135; 11:*1398*
*Explorer 1* (satellite) 12:1518
Exxon *Valdez* oil spill 2:152; 11:1314;
  14:*1748*

**F**
farming *see* agriculture
faults 4:*485*; 6:692
  and earthquakes 4:484
  and oil reservoirs 9:*1145*
  and tsunamis 15:1859–1860
  transform 11:1295
fires, forest 15:1812
fjords 6:699
flooding 8:*984*; 12:1469–1470
  flood barriers 4:*406*, 407; 12:*1470*
  tidal 12:*1470*
floodplains 12:1466
fluorite 8:1011
food chains 5:624, *625*
  poisons and pesticides in 11:1313,
    1314
food webs 5:624–625
forests
  forestry 15:1814
  helping forests regrow 15:*1814*
  temperate 2:190–191, 193
  tropical 2:192
  *see also* rain forests
fossil fuels 5:550; 10:1165
  and climate change 3:339;
    11:1316–*1317*
  underwater 9:1143

fossils 6:685–687, 689–690, 692
  dinosaur 2:*186*; 6:*686*
  fish 5:*565*
  *Hylonomus* 6:*684*
  index (zone) 6:684, *685*, 690
  skulls 13:1563
fronts, weather 12:1419; 16:1990–1991,
    1992–1993
frost 13:1579
frost shattering 16:1987
fumaroles 16:1941

**G**
galaxies 1:122–123; 9:*1135*; 14:*1670*
  and black holes 2:198
  clusters 14:1677
  nearest 15:1878
  receding 1:123; 15:1878
  *see also* Milky Way galaxy
galena (lead sulfide) 7:*836*; 8:964, *1009*
Galileo (Global Positioning System)
  6:705, *707*
*Galileo* (space probe) 7:814; 13:1626,
  1630
*Galileo Orbiter* (spacecraft) 9:1046
garbage 6:*712*
garnet 8:*1009*, 1013
gemstones 8:1013
*Genesis* (space probe) 14:*1715*
Geographical Information Systems
  (GISs) 6:682
geography 6:681–682
  biogeography 6:682
  human 6:681, *682*
  physical 6:681
geologic timescale 6:683–688
geology 6:689–692
  geological remote sensors 12:1448
geomorphology 6:691; 7:820
  geomorphic cycle 7:821–822
geophysics 6:692, 693–696; 10:1258
geysers 16:*1970*
*Giotto* (space probe) 13:1626, 1630
glaciation 6:697–700; 16:*1966*,
  1968–1969
  creation of landforms 7:*821*, 824
  glacial erosion 5:564; 6:699; 7:*821*;
    12:1468
global conveyor belt 9:1139
global warming 3:*339*; 6:709–712;
  11:*1317*–1318
GLONASS 6:705
Gobi Desert 4:416
gorges 7:824, 825
Grand Canyon 12:1468
Grand Teton National Park, Wyoming
  4:*491*
granite 8:1019; 12:1483–1484
  energy from 6:696

graphite 8:*1010*
grasslands
  temperate 2:191
  tropical 2:*191*
Great Barrier Reef 7:*825*; 9:1141–1142
Great Basin 6:696
Great Lakes 12:1468
greenhouse effect 6:709–710
  greenhouse gases 2:135; 3:339; 6:710,
    *712*; 8:984; 11:1317
groins 5:*562*, 564
groundwater 16:*1969*, 1970, 1974
gulfs 9:1138
Gulf Stream 9:1139
gullies 5:561
gummite 15:*1883*
gypsum 8:1013; 16:1985

**H**
hail 3:345; 12:1419
hailstones 7:856; 13:1579
Halley, Comet 1:119
halons 2:135
Hawaiian Islands 9:1063
hematite 7:*796*, 797; 8:967
herbicides 10:1226–1227
Hertzsprung-Russell diagrams
  14:1674–1675
highs *see* anticyclones
Himalayas, formation 9:*1063*,
  1064–1065; 11:1295; 12:1488
Holocene epoch 6:688
Hooker Telescope 15:1878
Horsehead Nebula 9:1090; 14:*1675*
horse latitudes 16:2007
Hubble constant 15:1880
Hubble Space Telescope (HST) 1:124;
  5:*538*; 9:*1136*; 11:*1304*; 13:*1602*;
  14:*1766*–1767
humidity, relative 15:1901
hurricanes *see* cyclones
*Huygens* (space probe) 12:1524, 1526;
  13:1630
hydrological cycle *see* water cycle
hydrothermal vents 9:1143
hygrometers 1:35; 8:980; 15:1901

**I**
ice
  global warming and polar ice
    6:711–712
  melting 6:*736*
ice ages 8:984–985
  mountain formation after 9:1065
  Pleistocene 6:697
icebergs 6:*697*; 16:1968
Iceland 9:1140
Iceland spar 8:1011
ice sheets 6:697, 698

ice shelves **6:***697*
ilmenite **15:**1829
incineration, waste **11:**1319
Indian Ocean **9:**1137
Infrared Astronomical Satellite (IRAS)
    **9:***1136*; **14:**1766
insecticides *see* pesticides and
    insecticides
*Intelsat VI* (satellite) **12:***1520*
*Intelsat IX* (satellite) **12:**1520
interglacial periods **6:**697
International Gamma-Ray Astrophysics
    Laboratory **10:***1259*
International Space Station **10:***1163*;
    **13:***1621*, 1624, *1637*
International Ultraviolet Explorer (IUE)
    **9:**1136; **14:**1766
ionosphere *see* thermosphere
islands **7:**825
    barrier **7:**825
    formation **16:**1941
    speciation on **2:**182
isobars **16:**1992, 1993, 2010
isostasy **9:**1065

**J**
James Webb Telescope **1:**124; **14:**1767
jet streams **16:**1991, 2010
Jupiter **7:**811–814; **10:***1162*; **13:**1604
    Great Red Spot **7:***812*
    missions to **13:**1629–1630
    moons **6:***656*; **7:***813*
Jurassic period **6:**687

**K**
kames **6:**700; **7:**824
kaolin (china clay) **11:**1329, *1330*
kaolinite **11:**1329
Keck II Telescope **1:***123*, 124
kimberlite **4:**418
Kitt Peak National Observatory (KPNO)
    **9:***1134*
Koeppen classification **3:**337–338
Krakatoa, volcanic eruption **15:**1860;
    **16:**1939
K-T boundary, extinctions at **6:**687–688
Kuiper belt **1:**119, 125; **13:**1606
Kyoto Protocol **6:**712

**L**
laccoliths **16:**1938
lahars **16:**1939
lakes **2:**192; **6:**700; **12:***1468–1469*
    oxbow **12:**1467, 1469
landfills **11:**1319
landforms **7:820–825**
    biogenic **7:**825
    coastal and ocean **7:**825

continental **7:**822–825
    streamlined **6:**699; **7:**824
    structural **7:**820
landslides, causing tsunamis **15:**1860
lapilli **16:**1938
Large Magellanic Cloud, Tarantula
    Nebula **9:**1089
laterites **13:**1595
latitude **8:**901–902
    climate and **3:**336
    measuring **9:**1084
latosols **13:**1595–*1596*
lava **12:***1483*, 1484; **16:**1938, *1940*
    pillow **16:**1941
lava caves **3:**297–298
leaching **13:**1594
Leonid meteor shower **9:**1093
levees **12:**1466, 1470
lightning **4:***504*; **7:856–857**;
    **15:***1801–1802*
light-years **1:***122*; **14:**1672
limestone **7:**821, 825; **8:***1019*; **12:**1485
    caves **3:**297; **7:**825; **16:***1985*, 1986
    scenery **12:**1488
limonite **8:**964
lithosphere **11:**1294
locks (on canals) **3:***274–275*, *276*
locusts **10:***1225*
loess **12:**1484–1485
longitude **8:**901, 902
    and time zones **15:**1818
    measuring **9:**1084–1085; **15:***1816*, 1821
Love Canal **11:**1319
lows *see* depressions
*Lunar Orbiter 2* (space probe) **9:***1046*
*Lunar Prospector* (space probe) **9:***1042*
Luna space probes **9:**1044; **13:**1626

**M**
*Magellan* (space probe) **1:**125; **13:***1558*,
    *1605*; **15:**1905
magma **8:***1012*; **16:**1938, 1939
magnetite **7:**797; **8:**964
malachite **8:***1011*
Mammoth Cave, Kentucky **3:**299
mantle, study of **6:**693–694
mapmaking **8:900–905**
    distortions **8:**902–903
    from photographs **14:***1735*
    latitude and longitude **8:**901–902
    printing techniques **8:**905
    projections **8:**904–905
    scales **8:**901
    symbols **8:**902
marble **8:**1019; **12:***1486*
Mariana Trench **9:**1141
Mariner space probes **13:**1626
    *Mariner 2* **13:**1626, 1627; **15:***1905*
    *Mariner 4* **13:**1626, 1628

*Mariner 9* **13:***1628*
*Mariner 10* **8:***952*, 953, *955*; **13:**1626
Mars **1:***124*; **8:913–916**; **13:**1604
    life on **8:**915; **13:***1628–1629*
    missions to **1:**125; **8:**915, *916*; **12:***1445*;
        **13:***1628–1629*, *1630*
    moons **8:**913, *914*
    poles **8:***913*, 914
    seismology **12:**1532
    surface **8:***913*, 914–*915*
    water on **8:**916
    weather **8:**913–914
Mars Exploration Rovers **13:***1629*, *1630*
*Mars Express* (space probe) **13:**1629
Mars Global Surveyor, images from
    **8:***915*
*Mars Observer* (space probe) **13:**1628
*Mars Pathfinder* (space probe) **13:**1628
*Mars Rovers* (robotic vehicles) **13:**1626
Mauna Kea Observatory **9:***1133*, 1134,
    1135–1136; **12:***1430*; **14:**1762
Mead, Lake **4:***406*
meanders, river **12:**1467, 1468
Mediterranean Sea **9:**1138
    pollution **15:**1810
    Trans-Mediterranean pipeline
        **10:**1269–1270
Mercalli scale **12:**1530
Mercury, planet **8:952–955**; **10:**1162;
    **13:**1604
    missions to **8:**952, 953, *955*; **13:**1627
meridian, prime **8:**902
mesas **7:***823*, 824
mesopause **2:***133*, 134
mesosphere **2:***133*, 134
*Messenger* (space probe) **8:***954*
Meteor Crater, Arizona **1:***119*
meteorites **1:**116, *118*, *119*; **9:**1139
    and dinosaur extinction **4:**437
meteoroids **1:**116, 118
meteorology **8:980–985**
    Dalton (John) and **4:**402
    radiosondes and **15:**1845
    *see also* barometers; weather;
        weather systems
meteors *see* asteroids, comets, and
    meteors
microbursts **16:**2010
mid-Atlantic ridge **6:**694; **11:**1295
Milky Way galaxy **1:**122–123; **6:**744;
    **14:**1713; **15:**1878
mineralogy **6:**692
minerals **6:**692; **8:1008–1013**
    breaking and cleavage **8:**1011
    color and streak **8:**1011
    crystals **8:***1009*, *1010*
    formation **8:**1008
    gemstones **8:**1013
    groups **8:**1011–1012

minerals (*continued*)
  hardness **8:**1010
  identification **8:**1008
  in rocks **8:**1012–1013
  light effects **8:**1011
  resources **8:**1013
  weight **8:**1010
*Mir* (space station) **13:***1622*, 1624,
  1634–*1635*
Mississippian period **6:**686
Mohs' scale **8:**1010
monsoon winds **16:**2008–2009
Monument Valley **7:***823*; **14:***1776*
Moon **9:1042–1047**
  and eclipses **4:***487–488*; **9:***1044–1045*
  and lunar months **9:**1044
  and tides **15:**1807, 1808, *1809*
  dust **9:**1046
  first television pictures from the
    **14:**1770
  Galileo and the **6:**656
  librations **9:**1044
  missions to **9:**1042, *1043, 1044*
  movements **9:**1043–1044
  origin **9:**1047
  phases **9:**1044
  probes to **13:**1626
  rocks **9:**1046–*1047*
  size **9:***1043*
  surface **9:***1042*, 1045–*1047*
  temperature **9:***1043*
moraine **6:**699–700; **7:**824
moths, peppered **5:***570*
mountains **2:***192–193*; **7:***820*;
    **9:1063–1066**
  animals **9:***1065–1066*
  climate **3:***336–337*
  dome **9:***1065*
  fault-block mountains **9:***1064*, 1065;
    **12:**1488
  fold mountains **9:***1064*
  formation **7:**822–824; **9:***1063–1065*
  habitats **9:***1065*
  height calculated **9:***1064*; **14:***1734*
  railroads **3:**260–261, *350, 351*
  rain shadows **4:**416–417
  rise and fall **9:**1065
  underwater **9:**1065
  volcanic **9:***1064*
*MSG-I* satellite **3:***355*
mudstones **12:**1485

## N

National Radio Astronomy Observatory
  (NRAO) **15:***1878*
Navstar **6:**705–*706*, 707, *708*
Nazca Plate **11:**1295
*Near Earth Asteroid Rendezvous (NEAR)*
  (space probe) **13:**1626, 1630

nebulas **9:1089–1091**; **14:***1675*; **15:**1878
  bright **9:**1089
  dark **9:**1089, 1091
  emission nebulas **9:**1089–1090, 1091
  planetary **9:**1090–*1091*; **14:**1673
  reflection nebulas **9:**1090
  supernova remnants and **9:***1090*, 1091
  the birthplace of stars **9:**1089–1090;
    **13:**1603; **14:***1673*, 1675
Neptune **9:1092–1095**; **13:**1605
  missions to **9:***1094–1095*; **13:***1628*, 1630
  moons **9:***1095*
Nereid (moon) **9:***1095*
Next Generation Space Telescope
  (NGST) **14:**1767
niches **4:**491
nodules, polymetallic **8:**1021
northern lights **2:***134*
novas and supernovas **9:1107–1110**
  novas **9:**1107, 1109; **14:***1676*
  supernova remnants **9:**1091,
    1109–*1110*; **14:***1767*; **15:***1882*
  supernovas **1:**121, 123; **9:***1090*, 1091,
    1107–*1109*; **14:***1675, 1676, *1677*;
    **15:**1880
nuée ardente **16:***1939–1940*
Nyos, Lake **6:***693*

## O

Oberon (moon) **15:***1886, 1888*
observatories **9:1133–1136**
occlusions, warm and cold **16:***1991*
ocean basin **9:***1139*
ocean ridges **9:**1065, 1140, *1143*;
    **11:**1294–1295; **16:***1996*
  mid-Atlantic ridge **6:**694; **11:**1295
oceans **2:***192*; **9:1137–1143**
  and climate **3:***337*; **9:***1139*
  area, volume, and depth **9:***1137*
  creation **9:**1139
  exploitation of **9:**1143
  floor (seabed) **8:**1021; **9:***1139*, 1140
  landforms **7:**825
  life in **2:***183*; **9:***1141*–1142, 1143
  surface temperatures **7:***777*
  *see also* currents; tides
oil, crude (petroleum) **5:**550
  composition **9:**1144
  formation **9:**1144
  from coal using bacteria **2:**152–153
  geology **9:***1145*
  pipelines **10:***1266–1267*
  spills **2:**152; **11:***1314*; **13:***1583*;
    **14:**1747, *1748*
  world's supply **9:**1145–1146; **14:**1749
  *see also* oil exploration and refining
oil exploration and refining **9:1144–1149**
  drilling operations **4:***460–461*; **6:***662*;
    **9:***1144, 1147*

exploration **6:**695–*696*; **9:***1146*–1147
  history **9:**1145
  petroleum production and refining
    **4:***444*; **9:***1147–1149*
Oort cloud **1:**119; **13:**1606
opal **8:***1010*; **13:**1556
*Opportunity* (robot vehicle) **8:***916*
orange giants **14:**1673
orbit **10:1162–1163**
  objects in **6:***718*
Orbiting Astronomical Observatories
    **14:**1766
Ordovician period **6:**686
ores **8:***963*, 964–965, *1016*
  extraction of metals from **8:***967–968*
Orion
  Horsehead Nebula **9:**1090
  Orion Nebula **9:***1089*–1090
orthoclase **8:***1009*; **16:**1985–1986
orthophotomaps **8:**905
*OTS2* (orbital test satellite) **3:**354
overfishing **4:**489–*490*; **9:**1143
oxbow lakes **12:**1467, 1469
oxides, mineral **8:**1012
ozone layer **2:***134*; **10:**1179
  development **2:**132
  hole and depletion of ozone **2:***135*;
    **6:**711

## P

Pacific Ocean **9:**1137
  "ring of fire" **15:**1861
  seafloor trenches **9:***1140*, 1141
*pahoehoe* **16:**1940
paleoclimatology **6:**691
paleogeography **6:**691
paleomagnetism **11:**1293
paleontology **6:**691
Panama Canal **3:***276*
Pangaea **4:**433; **6:**686, 690;
    **11:**1292–1293; **16:**1996
parallax method **14:**1672
paraquat **10:**1227
parsecs **14:**1672
peat, humans preserved in **1:**100–101
peneplains **6:**690; **7:**822; **12:**1467
Pennsylvanian period **6:**686
periods, geological **6:***683*
Permian period **6:**686
Peru-Chile Trench **11:**1295
pest control **10:1222–1227**
  direct and indirect **10:**1222–1223
  pesticides and insecticides **1:***29*; **4:**492;
    **10:***1222, 1223*, 1224–1227;
    **11:**1312–1313
  using parasites **10:**1197
pesticides and insecticides **1:***29*; **4:**492;
    **10:***1222, 1223*, 1224–1227;
    **11:**1312–1313

petroleum *see* oil, crude
petrology 6:692
Phanerozoic eon 6:685
Phobos (moon) 8:913, *914*
*Pioneer 10* (space probe) 13:1626, 1629
*Pioneer 11* (space probe) 12:1524;
  13:1626, 1629
*Pioneer Venus Orbiter* (space probe)
  13:1627
pitchblende 4:399
placer deposits 6:713; 8:1019
plagioclase, in Moon rock 9:1047
planetesimals 13:1604–1605, 1606
planetoids 1:117
planets 13:1604–1605
  atmospheres 2:134
  formation 7:812; 9:1110; 13:1604–1605
  orbits round the Sun 10:1162; 13:*1605*
  terrestrial and giant 13:1603
  *see also* solar system; and *names of individual planets*
Planet X 11:1302
plateaus 7:822, 823
plate tectonics 6:694; 11:**1292–1295**;
  16:1996
  and earthquakes 4:483–484
  and mountain formation 9:1063,
    1064–1065; 12:1486
  evidence for 11:1292, 1293–1294
  mechanisms 11:*1293*
  *see also* continental drift
platforms, wave-cut 5:563; 7:825
Pleiades 9:1090; 14:1677
Pleistocene epoch 6:688
  Ice Age 6:697
Pluto 1:119, 125; 10:1162;
  11:**1302–1305**; 13:1605
podsols 13:*1595*
polar deserts 2:*190*; 4:*415*
polar easterlies 16:2008
polar front 16:2008
*Polar Lander* (space probe) 13:1592
pollution 11:**1312–1319**
  acid rain 2:135; 3:339; 5:*564*;
    10:1178; 11:*1316, 1318*
  and global warming 6:*709*
  atmospheric 2:135; 3:286; 6:*709*;
    11:*1315*–1316
  climate change and global warming
    6:*709*; 11:*1317*–1318
  light 11:1312
  nuclear (radioactive) 5:551;
    9:1116–*1117*; 11:1318; 12:1521
  pesticides as 11:1312–1313
  sound 11:1312
  toxic waste 11:1318–1319
  water 1:30; 4:492; 5:595; 11:*1313*–1315,
    *1319*; 13:1583; 14:*1748*, 1749
  *see also* global warming

population growth 11:**1324–1327**
  modeling 3:266
Powell, Lake 12:*1468*
Precambrian period 6:*683*, 685
precipitation 3:345; 16:1967–1968
  *see also* rain and rainfall; snow and frost
prickly pears 10:1227
prime meridian 8:902
projections, map 8:904–905
Proxima Centauri 15:1878
pulsars 1:122; 14:1676, 1677
  and time measurement 15:1824
pumice 12:1484
pyrethroids 10:1225
pyrite 8:*1013*
pyroclasts 16:1938

Q
quartz 8:*1008, 1009*; 16:1984
  a piezoelectric crystal 13:1557; 15:1817,
    1822, 1871
  in quartz watches and clocks 10:*1264*;
    15:1817
  specific gravity 8:1010
quasars 1:124; 15:1878, 1879
Quaternary period 6:688

R
radiation, Hawking 2:199
radiosondes (weather balloons) 8:982,
  *983*
rain and rainfall 3:344; 12:**1418–1419**;
  16:1966
  acid rain 2:*135*; 3:339; 5:*564*; 10:1178;
    11:*1316, 1318*
  and erosion 5:559–560
  and weathering 16:*1984*, 1986, *1987*,
    1988
  areas with highest and lowest 4:474
  how raindrops form 12:1418–1419;
    13:1578
  kinds 12:1419
  rainfall distribution 12:1419
  water cycle and 12:1418
rain forests, tropical 2:*180*; 16:2045
  slash and burn agriculture 4:*489*
rain gauges 8:980–981
rain shadows 4:416–417
Rance River, tidal power 6:757;
  15:*1803*, 1804, 1810
recycling 1:67; 12:**1426–1429**
  glass 12:1427–1428, *1429*
  plastics 11:*1291*; 12:1428
  silver 13:1560
red giants 1:121; 9:1109; 14:1675
rejuvenation 12:1467, 1468
Remotely Operated Vehicles (ROVs)
  14:*1706*

reservoirs 12:1470; 16:1971, *1973*
  and hydroelectric power 6:*755*
Richter scale 4:486; 12:1530
ridges, ocean *see* ocean ridges
rills 5:561
rime 13:1579
Ring Nebula 1:*121*; 9:1090, *1091*
"ring of fire" 15:1861
rivers and lakes 2:192; 12:**1465–1470**
  creation of landforms and landscapes
    7:824–825; 12:1467–1468
  erosion by rivers 5:561–562;
    12:1465–1466, 1467–1468
  lakes 2:192; 6:700; 12:1467, 1468–*1469*
  river deltas 7:*824*; 12:*1467*
  stages of rivers 12:1465–1467
roches moutonnées 6:699
rock 12:**1483–1488**
  ages 6:683–684, 690
  igneous 6:689; 8:1012; 12:1483–1484,
    1488
  index (zone) fossils in 6:684, *685*, 690
  magnetism 7:893
  metamorphic 8:1013; 12:*1486*
  quarrying 8:*1019*–1020
  radioactive dating 6:684, 690, 691
  rock cycle 12:1486–*1487*
  samples 6:692
  sedimentary 6:689; 7:820, 825;
    8:1012–1013; 12:*1484*–1486
  strata 6:*690*; 12:1485
  structures and landscape 12:1487–1488
  weathering 5:559; 16:*1984–1988*
rock arches 7:824
rock flour 6:699–700
ROSAT (satellite) 1:125; 9:1136
ruby 8:1013; 15:1854
rutile 15:1829
RXTE (satellite) 9:1136

S
Sahara Desert 4:*414*, 417; 7:821
St. Helens, Mount 9:*1138*–1139
salt domes 9:*1145*
salt pans 4:*394*
Salyut space stations 13:1621, 1622–1623
San Andreas Fault 4:484, 486; 11:*1295*;
  12:*1530*
sand 16:1984
  glass manufacture from 6:701
sandstone 6:*689*; 8:1013, 1019; 12:*1484*,
  1485
San Francisco, earthquakes 4:484, *485*
sapphire 8:1013
satellites 12:**1517–1522**; 13:1621
  astronomical 9:1135, 1136; 12:1522;
    14:1713
  communications *see* communications
    satellites

satellites (*continued*)
first artificial **12:**1518
images of Earth from **6:***681*; **12:***1522*
launched **12:**1519
life times **12:**1519–1520
navigation **6:**705–706, *708*;
**9:**1086–1087; **12:***1522*
orbits **10:**1162–1163; **12:**1517–1518,
*1519*
satellite television **2:**237, 252–*253*;
**3:**352; **14:**1775
solar power (SPS) **13:**1602
spy **12:**1522
subsystems **12:**1520–1521
telemetry links to **12:**1446
used in mapmaking **8:***904*
use in archaeology **1:**96, 97
weather **3:**354–355; **8:***980*, 981;
**10:**1163; **12:**1522
*see also* space laboratories
Saturn **1:***122*; **12:**1523–1526; **13:**1604
Huygens and **6:**749
missions to **12:***1524, 1525, 1526*;
**13:***1628*, 1629, 1629–1630
moons **12:***1526*; **13:***1606, 1625*
rings **8:***927*; **12:**1524–1526
Schwarzschild radius **2:**199
seabed (ocean floor) **9:***1139*, 1140
mineral wealth **8:**1021; **9:***1144*
polymetallic nodules **8:**1021
seafloor (ocean) spreading **7:**893; **11:**1295
sea levels, rising **6:**712; **11:**1317
seamounts **9:**1140
seas **9:**1137–1138
seasons **4:***476, 477*, 478
sea stacks and sea arches **7:**825
sea walls **5:**564
seawater **16:**1966
desalination **16:***1972*
Sedna **1:**125
seiches **12:**1468
seismology **4:**486; **6:***692*, 693–694, *695*;
**12:**1530–1533
seismic surveying **5:**581; **6:***695–696*;
**9:***1146*; **12:**1532
seismic waves **12:**1531–1532
seismographs **10:**1213; **12:**1532–*1533*
*see also* earthquakes
septic tanks **13:**1549
seracs **6:**698
sewage treatment **13:**1546–1549
shales **12:**1485
shockwaves, earthquake **4:**486
shooting stars (meteors) **1:**116, *117*,
118
shrublands **2:**191
Shuttle Radar Topography Mission
(SRTM) **8:***904*
silicates **8:**1011

sills **9:**1138
siltstone **12:**1485
Silurian period **6:**686
singularities **2:***199*
sink holes **7:**825
Sirius **15:**1878, 1879, *1880*
*Skylab* space station **13:***1622*
slate **8:**1019
sleet **3:**345; **12:**1419; **13:**1578
smog **3:**339; **11:***1315*
SN 1987A (supernova) **9:**1110
snow and frost **13:**1578–1579
frost **13:**1579
hailstones **13:**1579
snow **3:**345; **12:**1419; **13:**1578, *1579*;
**16:***1990*
soil **13:**1593–1596
and climate **13:**1594–1596
core samples **13:***1593*
electrical resistance **1:**97
erosion **5:**560–561, *563*; **13:***1595*
fertility **13:**1594
horizons **13:**1593–*1594*
Solar and Heliospheric Observatory
(SOHO) **14:**1713
solar system **13:**1603–1606
origin **13:**1603–1605
other solar systems **13:**1606
planets revolve around the Sun
**3:***373*; **13:***1605*
*see also* asteroids, comets and meteors;
planets; Sun; and *names of individual
planets*
solar wind **11:**1285; **13:**1605–1606;
**14:**1715
solstices **4:**478; **14:**1712
Southern Ocean **9:**1137
spacecraft
navigation **9:**1088; **13:**1545
telemetry links to **12:**1446
*see also* space probes
SPACEHAB laboratory **13:***1623, 1634*
Spacelab **13:**1623–*1624*
space laboratories **12:**1520;
**13:**1621–1624
International Space Station **10:***1163*;
**13:***1621*, 1624, *1637*
*Mir* **13:***1622*, 1624, 1634–*1635*
Salyut space stations **13:**1621,
1622–1623
*Skylab* **13:***1622*
SPACEHAB **13:***1623, 1634*
Spacelab **13:**1623–*1624*
space shuttles and **13:**1624,
1634–*1635*
space probes **1:**125; **13:**1625–1630
powered **13:**1625; **14:***1787*
telemetry links to **12:**1446
*see also names of individual planets*

space shuttles **11:**1336; **12:***1489*, 1491;
**13:**1631–1636
and satellites **12:**1519, *1520*
tiles on **3:**308, *309*; **13:***1557, 1636*
space stations *see* space laboratories
space suits **13:**1637–1639
Space Transportation Systems (STSs)
*see* space shuttles
sperrylite **11:**1297
sphalerite **16:**2037, *2038*
Spitzer Space Telescope **14:**1766
springs (water), hot **16:**1970
*Sputnik 1* (satellite) **12:**1518
stacks **7:**824
sea **5:**563
stalactites and stalagmites **3:***297*; **16:***1969,
1985*, 1986
stars **1:**121; **14:**1670–1677
and black holes **2:**198, 199; **12:***1438*;
**14:**1676
and navigation **9:**1083–1084, 1088
binary **1:***122*; **2:**199; **6:**744; **9:**1109;
**14:**1676–1677
brightness **1:***122*; **15:**1878
closest to Earth **14:**1672; **15:**1878
clusters **14:**1677
constellations **1:***120*, 121; **14:**1670–1671
created in nebulas **9:**1089–1090;
**14:***1673*
distances from Earth **1:**122; **14:**1672,
1674
evolution of lives **1:**121–122;
**9:**1089–1091, 1107–1110; **14:***1673*,
1675–1676; **15:***1882*
fate **14:**1673
formation **9:**1089–1090; **13:**1603;
**14:***1673*, 1675
life time **14:**1672
locating **14:**1671
magnitude (brightness) **9:**1110;
**14:**1672–1674
main sequence **14:**1674
mass **14:**1672, 1674
moving **14:**1671–1672, *1674*
multiple **14:**1677
neutron stars **1:**121–122; **9:**1091,
1108–1109; **14:**1675–1676
new **1:**123
nuclear fusion in **1:**121; **9:**1117
oldest **15:**1880
pulsars **1:**122; **14:**1676, 1677; **15:**1824
radiation from **1:**121
spectral classes **14:**1674
speed of travel **14:**1674
temperature **14:**1672, 1674
traveling toward/away from Earth **4:**457
variable (Cepheids) **14:**1676; **15:**1880
*see also* galaxies; novas and supernovas;
Sun

stratigraphic sections 6:*690*
stratigraphy 6:691
stratopause 2:*133*, 134
stratosphere 2:*133*, 134; 11:*1398*; 15:*1801*
subduction 9:1063; 11:1295
subduction zones, volcanoes at 16:1941
Suez Canal 3:*273*, 276; 14:*1746–1747*
Sun 6:*652*; 14:1672, **1711–1716**
  and eclipses 4:*487–488*; 14:*1715*
  and tides 15:1807, 1808, *1809*
  atmosphere 14:*1715–1716*
  distance 14:*1711*
  elements in 14:*1716*
  heat from the 6:*738*
  magnitude (brightness) 14:*1673*
  mass 14:*1711*, 1715
  motion 14:*1712–1713*
  nuclear fusion in 1:121; 5:613; 6:*652*;
    14:*1714*, 1716
  observing the 14:*1712*, 1713
  prominences and flares 13:*1603*;
    14:*1714*, 1715
  radiative and convective zones 14:*1713*
  solar radiation 14:*1712*; 15:*1874–1875*
  solar spectrum 14:*1716*
  sunlight 7:*843*; 14:*1711*
  sunspots 14:1714
  surface 14:*1676*, 1713–1715
  temperature 14:*1713*, 1715
sunspots 14:1714
supergiants 14:1673, 1674, 1675
supernovas *see* novas and supernovas
Surtsey 16:1941
synclines 6:692; 12:1488

**T**
taiga 2:189, *190*
Tarantula Nebula 9:1089
temperature, air 16:1989
temperature inversions 11:1315; 16:1991
terraces, river 12:1468
terracing 5:561
Tertiary period 6:688
Thames Flood Barrier 4:*406*, 407;
  12:*1470*
Thera (Santorini), volcanic explosion
  16:1939
thermopause 2:*133*
thermosphere (ionosphere) 2:*133*, 134;
  7:795; 8:1002–1003; 11:*1398*
thunderstorms 15:1801–1802; 16:*1989*
  lightning 4:*504*; 7:**856–857**;
    15:1801–*1802*
  thunder 7:856
Tibetan Plateau 11:1295
tidal flooding 12:*1470*
tides 9:1043, 1138; 15:1804, **1807–1810**
  high and low 15:1807, *1808*
  spring and neap 15:1808, *1809*

till 6:700
timber industry 15:**1811–1814**
Titania (moon) 15:1886, 1888
topaz 8:*1009*
topography 7:821
tornadoes 15:**1836–1837**; 16:*1994*
  *see also* cyclones (hurricanes; typhoons)
Trapezium 9:1089–1090
trenches, ocean 4:484; 9:*1140*; 11:1294
  Mariana Trench 9:1141
Triassic period 6:687
Triton (moon) 9:*1095*
tropopause 2:*133*; 16:2007
troposphere 2:132–*133*; 3:345; 11:*1398*
tsunamis 15:1808, **1859–1861**
tundra 2:189–190; 13:1595
twisters *see* tornadoes
typhoons *see* cyclones (hurricanes;
  typhoons)

**U**
Umbriel (moon) 15:1888
Union Carbide disaster 11:*1308*
universe 15:**1877–1882**
  age 15:1879, 1880
  background (fireball) radiation
    15:*1879*, 1880–1881
  big bang and 1:123; 2:198; 5:*538*;
    12:1438; 15:*1877*, *1879*
  death of 15:1881–1882
  early understanding of 1:120;
    3:372–373; 15:1877–1878
  expanding 1:123; 4:457; 15:1879–1880
  inflation 15:1881
  measuring distances in 15:1880
  missing mass in 15:1882
  open or closed 15:1881
  oscillating 15:1881
  scale of 15:1878–1879
  steady-state theory 15:1881
  *see also* black holes; nebulas; novas and
    supernovas; solar system; stars; Sun
uraninite 15:*1883*
Uranus 13:1605; 15:**1885–1888**
  discovery 6:*744*; 15:1885
  effect of Neptune on 9:1092–1093
  magnetic field 15:1888
  moons 15:1886, 1888
  rings 15:*1887–1888*
  tilting axis 15:1887

**V**
V838 Monocerotis 9:*1107*
valleys
  hanging 6:699
  rift 7:824; 12:1488
  U-shaped 6:699; 7:*821*, 824
  V-shaped 6:699; 7:824
Van Allen belts 11:1285

Venus 13:1604; 15:**1904–1907**
  atmosphere 15:1904–1907
  atmospheric temperature 14:1777
  missions to 1:125; 13:1627; 15:*1905*
  phases of 15:1904
  rotation 15:1905
  surface 11:*1396*; 13:*1605*; 15:*1904*, *1906*,
    *1907*
*Venus 7* (space probe) 13:1626
Very Large Telescope (VLT) 1:124
Very Large Telescope Interferometer
  (VLTI) 9:*1135*
Very Long Baseline Array (VLBA) 9:1135
Vesuvius, Mount 16:1941
*Viking 1* (space probe) 13:1626, 1628
*Viking 2* (space probe) 13:1628
volcanic bombs 16:1938
volcanoes 6:691; 7:822–823; 11:*1294*;
  **16:1938–1941**
  active 16:*1938–1939*
  causing tsunamis 15:1860
  cinder cones 16:*1939*
  composite 16:*1939*
  eruptions 16:1939–1940
  extinct 16:1938
  fissure 16:*1939*
  intermediate 16:1940–1941
  quiet 16:1939, 1940
  shield 16:*1939*, 1940
  why volcanoes occur 16:1941
Voyager space probes 6:*656*; 13:1626,
  *1627*, 1629–1630
  data about Uranus and its moons
    15:*1885*, 1886, 1887–*1888*
  to Neptune 9:*1094–1095*; 13:*1628*, 1630
  to Saturn and its moons 12:*1524*, *1525*,
    *1526*; 13:*1628*, 1629
Vulcan, search for 8:955
vulcanology 6:692

**W**
wadis (arroyos) 4:414
warfarin 10:1224
waste 11:1312
  disposal 11:1319
  factory 11:1314
  radioactive (nuclear) 5:551;
    9:1116–*1117*; 11:1318
  toxic 11:1318–1319
water cycle 4:492; 12:1418;
  **16:1967–1970**
waterfalls 16:*1967*
waterspouts 15:1837
water supply 16:**1971–1974**
water table 16:1970
wave-cut platforms 7:825
waves, ocean 9:*1137*; 16:*1975*, 1976
  and coastal erosion 5:562, 563
  providing energy 5:552

waves (*continued*)
  tidal *see* tsunamis
  wave power **16:1979–1982**
weather **16:**1989–1990
  global warming and **6:**711, 712
  *see also* climate; clouds; weather
    systems
weather forecasting **8:**981, *982*
  chaos theory and **3:**312–313
  *see also* meteorology
weathering **5:***559*–561; **12:**1487;
  **16:1983–1988**
  biological **16:***1988*
  chemical **16:***1984*–1987
  mechanical **16:***1987*–1988
  rates **16:**1988
  *see also* erosion
weather stations **8:**980, *983*
weather systems **16:1989–1994**
  air masses **16:**1990, 1991
  anticyclones **16:**1993–1994
  cyclones (depressions) **12:**1419, 1470;
    **16:**1992–1993
  destructive *see* cyclones (hurricanes;
    typhoons)
  fronts **12:**1419; **16:**1990–1991,
    1992–1993
  *see also* meteorology
weeds, control **10:***1224*, 1226–1227
westerlies **16:**2008
wetlands **2:***192*
white dwarfs **1:**121; **9:**1091, 1109;
  **14:**1673, 1675, 1716
white holes **2:**199
wind **16:**1990, **2007–2010**
  anabatic winds **16:**2009
  Beaufort scale **16:**2009, 2010
  chinook winds **16:***2009*, 2010
  jet streams **16:**1991, 2010
  katabatic winds **16:***2009*
  monsoon winds **16:**2008–2009
  patterns **3:**337
  skyscrapers built to withstand
    **13:**1571
  trade winds **16:**2007–2008
  weathering by **5:**559; **16:**1987
  wind power **5:**552; **11:***1339*, 1341;
    **15:***1866*; **16:**2011–2014
wind shear **16:**2010
wood tin **15:***1826*
World Meteorological Organization
  **8:**983
World Ocean Circulation Experiment
  **8:**985
wormholes **2:**199
wulfenite **8:***1009*

**Y**
years **4:**475

# LIFE SCIENCES AND MEDICINE

**A**
abaca (Manila hemp) **5:**597
abscesses, dental **4:**411
acetaminophen **11:**1308
acetylcholine **2:**213
acinar glands **5:**575
actin **11:**1368–1369
adaptations **4:**490–491; **5:**569
adenine **9:**1039
adenoids **7:**884
adrenal glands **5:**547–548
AIDS (acquired immune deficiency
    syndrome) **1:31–32; 4:**441
  virus (HIV) **1:**31–*32*; **4:**441; **15:***1917*
alanine **10:***1165*
albumin **11:**1369
algae **10:**1274–1275
  blooms **9:**1142; **11:***1313*
  blue-green *see* cyanobacteria
  brown **11:**1371
  photosynthesis **10:**1253
  planktonic **9:**1142
  seaweeds **9:**1141
  zooxanthellae **3:***339*; **9:**1141
alleles **6:**679
allergens **1:**55, *56*
allergies **1:55–56**
alternation of generations **10:**1275–1276
alveoli **12:***1461*, 1462
Alzheimer's disease **9:**1101
*Amanita* **6:***648*
amino acids **1:**15, **68–71; 2:**179; **4:**454;
    **5:**557; **11:**1367–1368
  essential **1:***68*, 70–71; **11:**1367
  *see also* proteins
amniocentesis **11:**1344
amniotic sac **11:**1343
amoebas **10:***1171*; **11:***1370*, 1372
amphibians **1:**82
  metamorphosis **8:**979
anabolism **5:**557; **8:**957
androstenal **10:**1229
androsterone **10:**1229
anemia **9:**1130
  sickle-cell **3:**331; **4:**443, *455*
anesthetics **1:76–78; 6:***660*; **8:**938,
    943; **14:**1726–1727
  dental **1:**77–78; **4:**410–411
angiogenin **11:**1369
angioplasty, balloon **8:**943
animal kingdom **1:79–82**
  mountain animals **9:**1065–*1066*
  remote animal tracking **12:***1447*;
    **16:**2045
  *see also* zoology

ankylosaurs **4:**435
anorexia **9:**1132
anthrax **4:***443*; **10:**1211
antibiotics **1:91–93; 4:**464, *465*; **5:***617*;
    **8:**988
  bacteriostatic and bacteriocidal **1:**92
  discovery **1:**91, *92*; **2:***154*
  fermentation and **1:**93; **5:**591
  in agriculture **1:**92
  in wheat seeds **6:***676*
  narrow- and broad-spectrum **1:**92
  resistance to **1:**93
  side effects **1:**93
  *see also* penicillin
antibodies **6:**764, 765; **7:**884
  allergies and **1:**55
  monoclonal **6:***676*
  vaccination and **15:**1889, 1890
antidepressants **11:**1376
antidiuretic hormone (ADH) **5:**547
antigens **15:**1891
antiseptics **1:94–95; 7:**866–*867*
ants, and pheromones **10:**1228
anxiety **11:**1373
*Apatosaurus* **4:**435
apomixis **3:**341
aquaculture **1:**24
archaebacteria **8:**989
*Archaeopteryx* **4:***437*
archosaurs **4:**433–434
*Argentinosaurus* **4:**434
armadillos **3:**340
arms
  artificial **11:**1364
  bones **13:**1564
aromatherapy **10:**1229
arteries **3:***326*, *328*
  pulmonary artery **12:***1460*
arthritis **4:**443; **6:**764; **13:**1563
arthropods **1:**82
ascorbic acid *see* vitamins, vitamin C
asepsis **7:**867
aspirin **2:**213
asthma **1:**56; **9:**1071
astrocytes **2:***215*
atherosclerosis **5:***588*
athlete's foot **4:**441
ATP (adenosine triphosphate) **8:**957,
    958; **10:**1231
*Australopithecus* **13:**1563
autoimmune diseases **6:**764
Avogadro's number **3:**316
axolotls **8:***976*
axons (nerve fibers) **9:***1098*, 1099–*1100*

**B**
babies
  bone development **13:**1564
  need for touch **15:**1839

sleeping 13:*1572*
statistics and 14:1682, *1683*
backbone 13:*1562*, 1564
bacteria **2:152–155**; **8:**987–988
aerobic and anaerobic **10:**1210
and disease **2:**153–154; **4:**439–440, *443*
antibiotic-resistant **1:**93
genetic engineering and **6:**673–674, 676
Gram-positive and Gram-negative **1:**92
nitrogen-fixing **7:**779; **9:**1106
reproduction **2:***155*
use **2:**152–153; **6:**673–674, 676
*see also* antiseptics
balance **4:**472
barley, genetically engineered **2:***211*
basal metabolic rate (BMR) **8:***957*, 958
basophils **6:***733*
bats
in caves **3:***298*
pipistrelle **2:***181*
bees **8:***978*
pheromones **10:***1228*
behaviorism **11:**1378
bends, the **4:**450–451; **10:**1179
beriberi **16:**1931
bile **4:**426; **5:**574
bilharzia (schistosomiasis) **10:**1196
bilirubin **5:**574
binary fission **2:**155
biodiversity **2:180–183**
bioinformatics **9:**1039
biology **2:184–187**
*see also* botany; zoology
biorhythms **2:194–196**
birds **1:**82
cave **3:***298*
evolution from dinosaurs **1:**82; **4:**437
Black Death **4:***440*
bladder **5:***571*
blind people **15:***1838*–1839
blood **12:***1460*
plasma **7:**881
red blood cells **11:***1368*; **12:***1461*, 1463
blood pressure **6:***734*
monitors **8:**939–*940*
blue-green algae *see* cyanobacteria
body parts, artificial **8:**944
bollworms **3:***381*
bones
broken **13:**1564
marrow **7:***883*; **13:**1563
skeletal systems and **13:***1561, 1562, 1563*–1564
transplants **4:**413
botany **2:210–213**
*see also* plant kingdom
botulism **1:***91*; **2:***154*
*Brachiosaurus* **4:**432, 434
Braille **15:***1838*, 1839

brain **2:214–220**
electroencephalographs (EEGs) and
brain waves **8:**941; **13:***1572–1573, 1574*
scans **10:***1263*; **11:***1405*
virtual reality map of **15:***1913*
breathing **12:***1463–1464*
breeding, livestock **1:**25–26
bronchi **12:**1462
cilia **6:***763*
bronchioles **12:**1462
BSE (bovine spongiform encephalopathy) **4:**439
budding, by yeasts **16:**2036
bulimia **9:**1132
bulimia nervosa **11:**1375
burns, treatment of **13:**1567
butter **5:**621
butterflies **8:***977*

**C**

cacti **4:***416*, 417; **10:***1274*
caffeine **13:***1575*
calciferol *see* vitamins, vitamin D
camels **4:***414*, 417
camouflage **1:***80*
*Campylobacter* **8:***989*
cancer **3:**304–305; **4:**442; **5:***577*
breast **14:**1788
diet and **9:**1132
genes causing **9:**1039
lung **12:**1464
lymphomas **7:***884*
skin **14:***1712*; **15:**1875
treatment using anticancer drugs **7:**779; **10:***1166*, 1167; **11:**1298
treatment using radiotherapy **8:**943; **11:***1404–1405*; **16:**1933, 2034
vaccines for **15:**1892
*see also* leukemia; tumors
candidiasis **16:**2036
capillaries **3:**328
carbohydrates **3:279–282**; **9:**1129
metabolism **8:**956–957
caries, dental **4:**411
carnivores **5:**624
cartilage **13:**1561, 1563
catabolism **5:**557; **8:***956*–957
cataracts **5:**584
caterpillars **8:**977–978
cauterization **14:**1730
cell membrane **3:**301
receptors on **3:**303–304
cells **2:**179; **3:300–305**
animal **1:***79*
communication **3:**303–304
division **3:**303; **6:***678*; **9:**1039
organelles **3:***301–302*
plant **3:***282, 302*
cellulose **10:**1275

cell wall **3:***302*
central nervous system (CNS) **2:**214–215
centrioles **3:***301*, 303
cereals, dietary **9:**1129
cerebrospinal fluid **2:**215
cerebrum **2:**218–219, 220
cervix **12:**1450, 1452
chameleons **1:***80*
cheese **2:***153*; **5:***590*, 621–622
chemosynthesis **9:**1143
chicken pox **4:***439*
chickens
battery **1:***27*
parasites of **10:**1193
childbirth, pain relief during **1:**78
chimpanzees **16:***2044*
classification **3:**334
chitin **13:**1561–1562
*Chlamydomonas* **2:**213
chlorophyll **2:**178; **10:**1253, 1254, *1255*, 1274
chloroplasts **3:***302*; **8:**989; **10:**1254
cholesterol **5:**588–589; **9:**1130
chorionic villi sampling **11:**1343–1344
choroid **5:**583
chromosomes **3:**303; **4:***453*; **6:**677–678, 680
sex **6:**678
*see also* genes
chronic fatigue syndrome (CFS) **11:**1375, 1376
chrysalids **8:***977*, 978–979
chyle **7:**884
chyme **4:**424, *425*
cilates **11:**1372
circadian rhythms **2:**194; **11:***1380*; **13:**1574
circulatory systems **3:326–331**
CJD (Creutzfeldt-Jakob disease) **2:**220; **4:**439; **9:**1100–*1101*
cladistics **3:**334–335
classes **3:**333
classification **3:332–335**
Aristotle and **1:**111; **3:**332
Linnaeus and **2:**185; **3:**332, *333*; **7:**860–861
clavicle **13:**1564
clocks, biological (body clock) **2:**194; **13:**1574
cloning **3:340–343**; **6:**675
*Clostridium* spp. **1:***91*; **2:***154*
clotting, blood **6:***733*
cocaine **4:**411, 464
coccyx **13:**1564
cochlea **4:**471–472
codons **1:**70; **6:**680
coenzymes **5:**558
colds **6:**765; **15:**1916
vaccines for **15:**1892

collagen **11:***1369*
color blindness **4:**402
complement proteins **6:**762
*Compsognathus* **4:**434
coniferous plants (conifers) **10:**1277
connective tissues **11:***1369*
contact lenses **5:**585
contraception **11:***1326*
copepods **9:**1142
coral and coral reefs **9:***1141*–1142;
   **10:**1276
  global warming and **3:***339*; **6:**712
corn, genetically engineered **2:**210
cornea **5:**582
corticosteroids **5:**547
cowpox **7:**804, 805; **15:**1889–1890
cows
  immune to *Staphylococcus aureus* **6:**675
  milking **1:***28*
crabs, shell **13:**1561
cramp **12:***1459*
creation science **5:**567
crocodiles **1:**82; **4:***434*
crowns, dental **4:**412
cryosurgery **4:**393
cyanobacteria (blue-green algae) **2:**132;
  **8:**989; **10:**1253
cyanocobalmin **16:**1932
cycads **10:**1277
cystic fibrosis **5:**577; **6:**679
cytoplasm **3:***301*
cytosine **9:**1038

**D**

death, forensic science and **5:**632
decomposers **5:**624
decompression sickness (the bends)
  **4:**450–451; **10:**1179
deer, musk **10:**1228, 1229
dentistry **4:**410–413
  drills **4:***458*–459
  ultraviolet light used in **15:**1875, 1876
  X-rays **16:**2033
dentures **4:**412–413
deoxyribonucleic acid *see* DNA
depression (mental illness) **11:**1373, 1376
dermis, of the skin **13:***1566*, 1567
diabetes **2:**179; **5:**547; **6:**764; **8:***959*;
  **9:**1132
dialysis, kidney **5:***573*; **8:***944*
diaphragm **12:**1464
diatoms **5:**632; **11:***1372*
diet, balanced **8:***958*
digestion **2:**178
digestive system **4:**424–427
  enzymes **5:**558
dinosaurs **4:**432–437
  extinction **1:**118; **2:**183; **6:***687*–688
  fossils **2:***186*; **6:**686

*Diplodocus* **4:***435*
diseases **4:438–443**
  autoimmune **6:**764
  bacterial **2:**153–154; **4:**439–440, *443*
  carried in water **13:**1547
  genetic **6:***680*
  lymphatic system and **7:***883*–884
  parasitic **10:***1193*, 1194–1197
  viral **4:**440–441
disinfectants **1:**94
dizziness **4:**472
DNA (deoxyribonucleic acid) **3:**302–303,
  333–334; **4:452–455**; **6:**680
  and protein synthesis **1:**70; **4:**454–455;
    **6:**680; **9:**1038, 1039
  and the genetic code **4:**452–453,
    454–455; **8:**987; **9:**1038
  cloning **3:**341–342
  discovery of **8:**986–987
  fingerprinting (genetic
    fingerprinting) **2:***187*; **4:**455;
    **5:***534, 535, 633*; **7:***878*; **16:**2044
  "junk" **6:**680
  mutations **4:***455*
  plasmid **1:**29; **3:**341–342, *343*; **6:**674
  recombinant **6:***674*
  sequencing **9:***1039*
  structure **4:**390–391, *453*, 454; **8:**987;
    **9:***1038*–1039
  viral **4:**440–441; **15:**1914–1915
dogs, breeds of **3:***332*
Dolly the sheep **3:**340, *342*
dopamine **9:**1101
Down's syndrome **6:***680*; **11:***1344*
drinks, isotonic **13:**1661
drug industry **4:462–465**; **8:**943
  drug design and development **4:**463;
    **15:**1913
  drug testing **4:**463–464; **15:**1912
  *see also* anesthetics; antibiotics; drugs
drugs **4:**462–463; **8:**942–943
  anticancer **7:**779; **10:***1166*, 1167; **11:**1298
  antiparasite **10:**1196–*1197*
  inorganic molecules as **7:**779
  metabolism **5:**574
  placebo effect **4:**465
  poisonous **11:**1307
  side effects **4:**463
  used for mental disorders **11:***1376*
  *see also* anesthetics; antibiotics;
    drug industry

**E**

eardrums **4:**471; **13:**1617
ears and hearing **4:470–472**; **13:**1613;
  **15:**1870
  hearing damaged by noise **13:***1616*
Earth Summit (1992) **2:***183*
earthworms, skeleton **13:**1562

eating disorders **9:**1132
ecdysis **8:**978
ECGs *see* electrocardiograms and
  electrocardiographs
edema **7:**882
eelworms **10:**1225
eggs, in the diet **9:**1130
ejaculation **12:**1451–1452
electrocardiograms and electrocardiographs (ECGs) **3:***330*; **8:**940
electroconvulsive therapy (ECT) **11:**1374
elephantiasis **10:**1194
embryos
  development **3:**305
  storage **4:***392*
emphysema **12:**1464
endangered species, conservation of
  **3:**343
endocrine system **5:546–548**
endoplasmic reticulum **3:***301, 302*
endorphins **2:***219*
enteroviruses **15:**1916
enzymes **3:**296, 302; **5:557–558**;
  **11:**1366, 1369
  digestive **4:**425–426; **5:**558
  metalloenzymes **7:**779
eosinophils **6:***733*
epidermis, of the skin **13:**1565, *1566*, 1567
epididymis **12:**1450, *1451*
epidurals **1:**77, 78
Epigenome Project **6:**680
epinephrine **5:**547–548
Epstein-Barr virus **15:**1892
*Escherichia coli* (*E. coli*) **2:***152*; **8:**988
esophagus **4:**424
estrogen **5:**548; **11:**1343
ethics, medical **8:**945
*Euglena* **3:***335*
eukaryotes **3:**335; **11:**1371
eustachian tubes **4:**471
evolution **1:**81; **2:**186–187; **4:**409;
  **5:565–570**; **6:**685
excretory system **5:571–574**
exercise, anaerobic **12:***1459*
exocrine system **5:575–577**
exoskeletons **13:**1561–1562
extinction **2:**183; **6:***687*–688
  mass **2:**182
  of the dinosaurs **1:**118; **4:**437
eyes and vision **5:582–585**
  color vision **5:**582; **7:***848*

**F**

fallopian tubes **12:**1450, 1452
families (classification) **3:**333
farsightedness *see* hyperopia
fats **5:588–589**; **8:**959
  absorption in the intestines **7:**884
  dietary **5:***588–589*; **8:***958*; **9:**1130–1131

food technology and **5**:619–620
saturated and unsaturated **5**:588;
**9**:*1130–1131*
feet, prosthetic **11**:*1363*
fermentation **5**:*590–591*; **11**:*1372*;
**16**:2035, *2036*
and antibiotics **1**:*93*; **5**:591
and bread making **2**:227; **5**:590; **11**:*1372*
Pasteur and **10**:1210; **16**:2035
fertilization **3**:*305*; **12**:1449, *1452*
fetus
development **11**:1344–1345
ultrasound and **11**:*1344*; **13**:*1615*, 1616
fiber, dietary **9**:1128
fibrin and fibrinogen **6**:*733*
fillings, dental **4**:*411–412*
fimbriae **2**:*155*
finches, Galápagos (Darwin's finches)
**2**:182; **4**:409; **5**:*569*
fingerprinting **5**:630–631; **13**:*1565*
genetic *see* DNA, fingerprinting
fireflies **7**:*880*
fish **1**:*79*, 82
evolution **1**:82; **6**:686
farming **1**:24
fossilized **5**:*565*
flagellates **11**:*1372*
Flavr-savr tomatoes **6**:675
flies
black **10**:1195–1196
fruit **3**:305; **10**:1223
flowers, nectar production **2**:195
flukes **4**:441
blood **10**:*1194*
fly agaric **6**:*648*
food *see* nutrition
Food and Drug Administration (FDA)
**4**:462, 465
foraminiferans **11**:*1372*
foxes, fennec **4**:*417*
fractures **13**:1564
frogs **8**:*979*
desert **4**:417
frostbite **4**:439
fruits **10**:*1276*
in the diet **9**:1129; **16**:*1930*
preservation **10**:1172
processing **5**:618
fungi kingdom **6**:648–649; **8**:*988*–989;
**10**:1197
and disease **1**:92; **4**:441
classification **10**:1276
parasitic fungi **10**:*1196*, 1197
*see also* penicillin

## G

gametes **12**:1449
gametophytes **10**:1276, 1277
geese, snow **1**:*81*

gene flow **2**:181, 182
genera **3**:333
genes **4**:452–453; **6**:*678–679*, 680
alleles **6**:679
decoding **4**:453–454
dominant and recessive **6**:*679*
effect or "penetrance" **6**:679–680
Hox **3**:305
"jumping" **6**:680
mapping *see* Human Genome Project
mutations **6**:679
gene therapy **9**:1039
genetic drift **2**:182
genetic engineering **3**:342; **6**:**673–676**;
**9**:1039
and corn **2**:210
and wheat **2**:210, *213*; **6**:*676*
engineered bacteria **6**:*673–674*, 676
farm animals **1**:28–29
monoclonal antibodies **6**:676
plants **1**:29–*30*; **2**:210, *211*, 212, *213*;
**3**:*341*; **6**:*676*
to make vaccines **6**:676
*see also* cloning
genetic fingerprinting *see* DNA,
fingerprinting
genetic modification (GM) *see* genetic
engineering
genetics **6**:**677–680**
evolution and **5**:570
Mendel and **8**:946–*947*
*see also* chromosomes; DNA; genes;
genetic engineering
genome **6**:680; **9**:1039
Human Genome Project **6**:*680*; **9**:1039
germicides **1**:94
germ theory of disease **8**:*986*
gibberellic acid **2**:213
gigantism **5**:548
gingkoes **10**:1277
glands
endocrine **5**:*546*–548
exocrine **5**:575–577
glaucoma **5**:584
glial cells **2**:*215*, 216
globulin **11**:1369
glomeruli **5**:571, *572*
glucose, catabolism **8**:956–957
gluteus maximus **9**:1068
glycogen **5**:589
glycolysis **8**:957
GM (genetic modification) *see*
genetic engineering
goats, mountain **9**:*1066*
goiter **5**:548
Golgi apparatus **3**:*301*, 302
gonads, hormones **5**:548
goosebumps **13**:1567
gorillas **1**:*82*

granulocytes **3**:329
Great Irish Famine **6**:649
greenflies, pest control **10**:1223–1224
growth hormone **5**:548
guanine **9**:1038
guard cells **10**:*1253*, 1255
guinea worms **10**:1195
gum disease **4**:413

## H

habitats **2**:188
hairs **13**:*1566*, 1567
hands, artificial **11**:*1364*
haustoria **10**:1197, 1275
hay fever **1**:*55*
hearing *see* ears and hearing
heart and blood **6**:**731–734**
blood **3**:328–329; **6**:*733*–734
blood cells **1**:79; **3**:*300*, 329; **4**:*455*;
**6**:*733*, 762; **7**:*883*, 884
blood clotting **6**:*733*
blood diseases **3**:331
blood groups **3**:330; **6**:734
blood pigments **1**:79
blood plasma **7**:881
blood pressure **6**:*734*; **8**:*939–940*
blood transfusions **3**:330; **6**:734
defibrillation of the heart **8**:*941*
heart **3**:*327*, 328; **6**:*731–732*
heart diseases **3**:330–331; **4**:*442*, 443;
**9**:1132
heart transplants **3**:331; **14**:1730
monitoring the heart **3**:*330*; **8**:940–941
optimum heart rate during exercise
**13**:1659–1660
pacemaker **6**:731–732
heart attacks **3**:330, 331
heart-lung machines **3**:331
hemocyanin **1**:79
hemoglobin **1**:79; **3**:329; **6**:*733*; **9**:1129;
**11**:*1368*, 1369
synthetic **6**:734
hemophilia **4**:443; **6**:679
AIDS and **1**:31–32
hemostats **14**:1728
hemp **5**:596, 597
hepatitis, virus **15**:1916
herbivores **5**:624
herbs **10**:*1277*
heredity, Mendel's experiments **5**:570;
**6**:677; **8**:*946–947*
heroin **2**:*212*
hibernation **2**:*195*, 196
in caves **3**:298
hip replacements **11**:*1363*; **15**:*1828*
histamines **1**:55–56
HIV *see* human immunodeficiency
virus
Hodgkin's disease **7**:881

hominids **13**:1563
*Homo floresienses* **13**:*1563*
honeybees, pheromones **10**:*1228*
hookworms **10**:*1194*
hormones **2**:179; **3**:303; **11**:1369
　as pheromones **10**:1229
　drugs resembling **4**:464
　plant **2**:213
horticulture **1**:28
Hox genes **3**:305
human chorionic gonadotropin (hCG)
　　**11**:1343, 1344
Human Genome Project **6**:*680*; **9**:1039
human growth hormone (HGH) **8**:988
human immunodeficiency virus (HIV)
　　**1**:*31–32*; **4**:441
humans
　cloning **3**:343
　preserved in peat **1**:*100–101*
hybrids **2**:181
*Hylonomus*, fossils **6**:*684*
hyperopia **5**:583, 585
hypersensitization **1**:56
hypertension **6**:*734*
hyphae **6**:648; **10**:1197
hypothalamus **2**:218; **5**:546, 577

I

*Iguanodon* **4**:433
immune system **6**:762–765
　acquired immunity **6**:763
　allergens and **1**:56
　and parasites **10**:1196
　cell-mediated immunity **15**:1890, 1891
　immune response of someone with
　　HIV **1**:*32*
　natural immunity **6**:762, *763*
immunization **6**:*765*
indigestion **4**:425
influenza **4**:441
　vaccines for **15**:*1890*, 1892
　viruses **6**:765; **15**:*1890*, 1915, 1916
inheritance, genetic **6**:*677*
insects
　pheromones **10**:*1228*, 1229
　social **10**:1228
insomnia **13**:1575
insulin **2**:179; **5**:546, *548*; **6**:764; **9**:1132;
　　**11**:1368, 1369
　genetically engineered **6**:673–674; **8**:988
intensive care units (ICUs) **8**:942
intercourse, sexual **12**:1451–1452
interstitial fluid **7**:881, 882
intestines **4**:425, 426–427; **5**:574
　villi **4**:*426*; **7**:*882*
invertebrates **1**:81–82
ion channels **3**:*304*
iris **5**:582
IVP (intravenous pyelography) **5**:*571*

J

Japanese encephalitis (JE) virus **15**:*1891*
jaundice **5**:574
joints, artificial **11**:*1363*, 1365; **15**:*1828*

K

Karvonen formula **13**:1659–1660
keratin **11**:1369; **16**:2023
kidneys **5**:*571–573*
　dialysis **5**:*573*
　transplants **5**:574; **14**:*1731*
kingdoms **3**:333, 335
knees **13**:*1564*
　prosthetic **11**:1363
　surgery **13**:*1661*
Krausse end bulbs **15**:1838, *1839*
Krebs cycle **8**:957

L

lactic acid, in muscles **9**:1070–1071;
　　**12**:*1459*
*Lactobacillus* **8**:988
larvae **8**:977–978
larynx **16**:1934
learning **2**:220
　cognitive **11**:*1377*
leaves **10**:*1252, 1253–1254*
leishmaniasis **11**:1371
lenses, eye **4**:482, *483*
leucine **1**:71
leukemia **4**:399
lichens **10**:1276
lie-detector tests **5**:577
life
　extraterrestrial **1**:69
　origins of **5**:565–567; **8**:989
ligaments **13**:1563, *1564*
lignin **10**:1188
lignocaine **1**:78
limbs, artificial **11**:*1362–1364*
lipase **10**:*1164*; **11**:1369
liver **5**:574, 589
lungs **5**:574; **12**:*1460, 1461*–1462
　cilia **6**:*763*
　disorders **12**:*1462*, 1464
　transplants **14**:1731
lymphatic system **7**:881–884
　lymph **7**:*881, 882*, 883
　lymph nodes **1**:*31*; **6**:764; **7**:*882*,
　　883–884
lymphocytes **3**:329; **6**:*733*, 763, *764*;
　　**7**:*883*, 884
　B-cells **6**:764, 765
　T-cells **1**:*32*; **6**:*762*, 764–765
lymphomas **7**:*884*
lysine **1**:71
lysosomes **3**:*301*
lysostaphin **6**:*675*
lysozyme **5**:*616–617*

M

macromolecules **9**:1038
macrophages **6**:762; **7**:883
mad cow disease (BSE) **4**:439
malaria **4**:*441–442*; **10**:1194–1195, 1196;
　　**11**:1371
　antimalarial drugs **10**:*1197*
malnutrition **9**:1127, *1131*; **11**:*1327*
mammals **1**:82; **3**:*334*
　the rise of **6**:688
mammary glands **5**:577
Manila hemp **5**:597
manure **5**:*592*, 593, 595
marmots **9**:1066
marsupials **1**:82
meats
　preservation **5**:*622*
　processing **5**:*619*
meiosis **3**:303; **6**:*678*
Meissner corpuscles **15**:1838
melanin **13**:1567
melatonin **5**:547
memory **2**:220
meningitis **9**:1101
menstruation **12**:1452
mental illness **4**:443
metabolism **2**:179; **5**:557; **8**:956–959
　disorders **8**:*959*
　metabolic rate **8**:957–958; **9**:1127, *1132*
metalloenzymes **7**:779
metamorphosis **8**:976–979
methionine **1**:71
mice **10**:*1227*
microbiology **8**:986–989
　discovery of microorganisms **8**:998
　Pasteur's understanding of
　　microorganisms **10**:1210, 1211
　*see also* bacteria; fungi kingdom; protist
　　kingdom; viruses, biological
microsurgery **5**:584; **14**:1730
microvilli **14**:1751
migration **16**:2044
　salmon **2**:*196*
milk and milking **5**:*621*
Minamata disease **11**:1314
minerals, dietary **9**:1127–1128
mistletoe **10**:1197
mites **4**:441
　red **10**:1224
mitochondria **3**:*300, 301, 302*;
　　**8**:989; **12**:1459
mitosis **3**:303
mohair **5**:597
mole **3**:316
molecular biology **9**:**1038–1039**
moles, on the skin **13**:*1567*
mollusks **1**:81
monocytes **6**:*733*
monotremes **1**:82

mosquitoes
  and disease 4:*441*–442; 10:*1193*, 1194–1195, 1197
  studying 16:*2045*
moths
  pest control 10:*1229*
  pheromones 10:*1228*
multiple sclerosis (MS) 9:1101
muscular system 9:**1067–1072**
  cardiac muscle 9:1069, *1072*
  muscle performance 9:1070–1071
  muscle proteins 11:1368–1369
  skeletal (voluntary; striated) muscles 9:*1067, 1068, 1069*–1070
  smooth muscles 9:1068–1069, 1071–1072
mutations 6:679
  and evolution 5:*570*
  causing 1:29–30
  DNA 4:*455*
  somatic 6:764
mycelium 6:648
mycoprotein 5:619
mycorrhizae 6:649
myelin 2:216; 9:*1100*
myofibrils 9:*1068*, 1070
myoglobin 1:79
myopia 5:583, 584, 585
myosin 11:1368–1369
myxomatosis 10:1224

**N**
narcolepsy 13:1575
natural killer cells 6:762
natural selection 2:181, 186; 4:409; 5:568, 569, 570
nearsightedness *see* myopia
nematodes 10:1193, 1197
neoteny 8:*976*
nephrons 5:571
nervous system 9:**1096–1101**
  and taste 14:1751
  autonomic (ANS) 9:*1096*, 1099
  central nervous system (CNS) 9:*1096*, 1097–1099
  cranial nerves 9:1099
  disorders 9:1100–*1101*
  how nerves work 9:1099–1100
  motor nerves 3:*303*; 9:1099
  nerve cells *see* neurons
  nerve pathways 2:219–220
  nerves and touch 15:1838
  peripheral (PNS) 9:*1096, 1098*, 1099
  sensory nerves 9:1099
  somatic (voluntary) 9:*1096*, 1099
  speed of impulses 9:1099
neurons (nerve cells) 9:*1096, 1098*, 1099, *1100*
  brain 2:*215*, 216

neurotransmitters 3:303; 9:1100
neutrophils 6:*733*
nitrogenases 7:779
nucleic acids *see* DNA; RNA
nucleotides 4:*391*
nucleus, cell 3:*301, 302*–303
nutrition 9:**1127–1132**
  balanced diet 8:*958*; 9:1127, 1131–1132
  carbohydrates and 9:1129
  cereals 9:1129
  convenience foods 9:1128
  dairy products 9:1130
  diets and dieting 9:1132
  eating disorders and 9:1132
  fats and 5:*588–589*; 8:958; 9:1130–1131
  fiber 9:1128
  fruit and vegetables 9:1129; 16:*1930*
  how food is used in the body 8:958–959
  malnutrition 9:1127, *1131*; 11:*1327*
  meat and fish 9:1129–1130
  minerals and 9:1127–1128
  proteins and 1:70–71; 8:958; 9:1129; 11:*1366*, 1367–1368
  sports 13:1661
  sugars 9:1130, 1131
  water 9:1128
  *see also* metabolism; vitamins
nymphs 8:979

**O**
obesity 9:1127, 1128, 1132
obsessive-compulsive disorder (OCD) 11:1376
obstetricians 11:1343, *1344*
olfactory bulb 13:1576, 1577
onchocerciasis *see* river blindness
operating rooms 14:*1727*
orders 3:333
orgasm 12:1451–1452
Ornithischia 4:435–436
ornithopods 4:436
otters, sea 5:625
ova (eggs) 12:1449, 1452
ovaries 5:*546*; 12:1449–1450
  hormones 5:548
ovulation 12:1450
oxytocin 11:1345

**P**
pacemaker(s)
  artificial 6:732
  natural 6:731–732
pachycephalosaurs 4:436
Pacinian corpuscles 15:1838
pain 15:1839
pancreas
  as an endocrine gland 5:*546*
  as an exocrine gland 5:575

panspermia 5:566
parasitoids 10:1193
parasitology 10:**1193–1197**
  antiparasitic drugs 10:1196–*1197*
  ectoparasites and endoparasites 10:1193
  life cycles of parasites 10:1193–1194
  parasite defences 10:1196
  parasitic diseases 10:*1193*, 1194–1197
  pest-control parasites 10:1197
  plant and fungal parasites 10:*1196*, 1197, 1275
parathyroid glands 5:*546*, 547
Parkinson's disease 2:*218*; 9:1101
pasteurization 5:621; 8:986; 10:1211
patch clamping 3:*304*, 305
pea plants, Mendel's experiments 8:*946*–947
pellagra 16:1931
pelvis 13:*1563*
penicillin 5:591, *617*
  discovery 1:91, *92*; 2:*154*; 5:617; 8:*942*
  side effects 1:93
*Penicillium* spp.
  and antibiotics 1:91, 93; 2:*154*; 5:*617*
  and cheese 2:*153*
penis 12:1450, 1451, *1452*
pepsin 4:426; 5:558; 11:1369
peristalsis 4:424, *425*; 9:1071
peroxisomes 3:*301*
pests, cotton 3:*381*
phagocytes 6:762
phenylalanine 1:*68*, 71
pheromones 10:**1228–1229**; 11:*1343*
phloem 10:1277
photosynthesis 2:*178*; 10:**1252–1255**, 1274–1275
  dark reaction 10:1255
  light reaction 10:1254
  oxygen from 10:*1176*, 1177, 1253, 1255
phyla 3:333
phylloquinone *see* vitamins, vitamin K
physiology 10:**1262–1263**
physiotherapists 13:*1659*
pineal gland 5:547
pituitary gland 5:*546*–547, 548
placebos 4:465
placenta 5:*547*; 11:1343, *1345, 1346*
plague, bubonic 4:440
plankton 9:1142; 16:2045
plant kingdom 10:**1274–1277**
  alternation of generations 10:1275–1276
  asexual reproduction 3:340–341
  basic features 10:1274–1275
  binomial classification 7:861
  biorhythms 2:195
  breeding 1:29
  cells 3:*282, 302*

plant kingdom (*continued*)
  communication **2:**212
  desert **4:***416,* 417
  diversity **10:**1276
  fibers from **5:**597
  food chains and **5:**624
  food production *see* photosynthesis
  genetically engineered plants **1:**29–*30;*
    **2:**210, *211,* 212, *213;* **3:***341;* **6:***676*
  hormones **2:**213
  nonvascular plants **10:***1275,* 1276
  parasitic plants **10:**1197, 1275
  roots causing weathering **16:***1988*
  saprophytic plants **10:**1275
  seed- and nonseed plants **10:**1277
  vascular plants **10:**1276–1277
  water uptake **10:***1254*
  *see also* botany
plaque, dental **4:**411, 413
plasma (in blood) **7:**881
plasmids, DNA **1:**29; **3:**341–342, *343;*
  **6:**674
*Plasmodium* **4:**441–442; **11:***1371*
plastids **3:**302
platelets **3:**329; **6:**733
poisons **11:1306–1309**
  toxic wastes **11:**1318–1319
polio
  vaccine (Sabin vaccine) **15:**1890–1891
  virus **15:**1916
polygenes **6:**678
poppies, opium **2:***212*
post-traumatic stress disorder (PTSD)
  **11:**1375
potatoes, glowing **2:**212
pregnancy and birth **11:1343–1346;**
  **12:**1452
  birthing process **11:**1345–*1346*
  fetal heart-rate monitoring **8:**940–941
  the placenta **5:***547;* **11:**1343, *1345, 1346*
  *see also* reproductive system
premedication **1:**77, 78
prick test **1:**56
prions, and CJD **9:**1100–*1101*
progesterone **5:**548; **11:**1343, 1344
prokaryotes **8:**987; **11:**1370
prolactin **5:**547
prostaglandins **2:**213; **11:**1345
prostate gland **5:**577
  cancer **5:***577*
prosthetics **11:1362–1365**
  hip replacements **11:***1363;* **15:***1828*
proteins **1:**68–69; **3:**302; **11:1366–1369**
  complement **6:**762
  dietary **1:**70–71; **8:**958; **9:**1129;
    **11:**1367–1368
  enzymes as **5:**557
  formed from amino acids **1:**69–*70;* **8:**959
  genetically engineered **6:**673–674

iron-sulfur **7:**779
  structural **11:**1366
  structure of **11:***1367*
  synthesis **1:**70; **2:**179; **4:**454–455; **6:**680
  transport **11:**1366
  *see also* amino acids
protist kingdom **11:1370–1372**
  and diseases **4:**441–442; **11:***1371*
protozoans **11:**1370
Prozac **11:***1376*
psychiatry **11:1373–1376**
psychoanalysis **11:**1374
psychology **11:1377–1380**
  cognitive **11:**1378–1379
  Gestalt **11:**1378
  sports **13:**1661
psychotherapy **11:**1373, *1374*
pterosaurs **4:**436
puffer fish **11:**1309
pulse rate **2:**194
pupae **8:**978–979
pupil **5:**582
Purkinje cells **2:***215*
putrefaction **5:**591
pyridoxine **16:**1932
pyruvic acid **8:**957

# Q

Quorn **5:**619

# R

rabbits, myxomatosis **10:**1224
rabies **9:**1101; **10:***1211;* **15:**1916
raccoons **5:**625
radiation therapy *see* radiotherapy
radiolarians **11:**1372
radiology, interventional **8:**943
radiotherapy **6:***658;* **7:**801; **8:**943;
  **11:1404–1405;** **16:***1933,* 2024
radius and ulna **13:**1564
*Rafflesia* **10:**1197, 1275
rashes, skin **1:***56*
RDAs (recommended daily allowances)
  **9:**1131–1132
red tides **9:**1142
reflexes **2:**220; **9:***1097*–1099
relaxin **11:**1344
reproduction
  asexual **1:**81; **3:**340–341; **12:**1452
  sexual **1:**81; **12:**1449
reproductive system **12:1449–1452**
  female **12:**1449–*1450*
  male **12:***1450–1451*
  *see also* pregnancy and birth
reptiles **1:**82
respiration **10:***1177,* 1178; **12:**1459–1461
  aerobic **9:**1070
  anaerobic **9:**1070
  cellular **8:**956–957

respiratory system **12:1459–1464**
restriction fragment length
  polymorphisms (RFLPs) **1:**29
retina **5:***582*
retinol *see* vitamins, vitamin A
Rhesus factor **6:**734
rhodopsin **2:**213; **3:**304
riboflavin **16:**1932
ribonucleic acid *see* RNA
ribosomes **3:***301, 302;* **4:**454; **9:**1082
rickets **2:**179; **15:**1876; **16:***1933*
river blindness (onchocerciasis) **4:**442;
  **10:**1194, 1195–1196
RNA (ribonucleic acid) **3:**303
  and protein synthesis **4:**454–455;
    **9:**1039
  viral **15:**1914, 1915
rodents, teeth **4:**411
root canal therapy **4:**412
rubella **11:**1343
rubisco **10:**1255
Ruffini corpuscles **15:**1838, *1839*

# S

*Saccharomyces cerevisiae* **16:**2035
salivary glands **5:**575–576
salmon **2:***196*
salvarsan **5:**616; **8:**942
saprophytes **6:**649
Saurischia **4:**434–435
sauropods **4:***435*
scabies **4:**441
scapula **13:**1564
schistosomiasis (bilharzia) **10:**1196
schizophrenia **11:***1375*
sclera **5:**582
scurvy **2:**179; **16:**1931
sea anemones **10:**1276
sea urchins **5:**625
seaweeds **9:**1141
sebaceous glands **5:**575, 576; **9:**1072;
  **13:***1566*
seeds **10:**1277
*Seismosaurus* **4:**434
selection, natural *see* natural selection
semen **12:**1451, *1452*
semicircular canals **4:**471
senses
  biorhythms and **2:**194–195
  *see also* ears and hearing; smell; taste;
    touch; vision
serotonin **1:**71; **11:**1376
sheep
  breeding **1:**25–26
  mountain **9:**1066
  shearing **16:**2024
shrews **5:***624*
"sick building syndrome" **2:**248
sickle-cell anemia **3:**331; **4:**443, *455*

silkworms 10:1211
sinoatrial node 6:731–732
sisal 5:597
skeletal system 13:1561–1564
skin 13:1565–1567
  and touch 15:1838, 1839
  burn treatment 13:1567
  color 13:1567
  excretion through 5:574
  hairs 13:1566, 1567
  natural immunity and 6:762, 763
  rashes 1:56
skulls 13:1562
  fossil 13:1563
sleep and dreams 11:1380; 13:1572–1575
  dreams 13:1574–1575
  stages of sleep 13:1572–1574
sleeping pills 13:1575
sleeping sickness 4:442; 10:1194; 11:1371
slime molds 11:1372
smallpox 6:676; 15:1914, 1916
  vaccination 7:804–805; 10:1211;
    15:1889–1890, 1891–1892
smell 13:1576–1577
  see also pheromones
smoking, tobacco 3:331; 11:1309
  effect on the lungs 12:1462
snakes 1:82
  venom 11:1306, 1307
species 3:333
  cryptic 2:181
  definition 2:181
  endangered see endangered species,
    conservation of
  formation 2:181–182
  number on Earth 2:181
spectacles 5:584–585
speech 13:1617, 1650–1651; 16:1934
  speech problems 16:1937
  speech therapists 16:1936
  synthesized 16:1934, 1935, 1937
sperm 3:305; 12:1449, 1450, 1451, 1452
sphygmomanometers 6:734
spinal cord 9:1097–1099
spine 13:1562, 1564
spontaneous generation 5:565
spores, fungal 6:648
sporophytes 10:1275, 1276
sports science 13:1659–1661
stammering 16:1937
Staphylococcus aureus, division 2:155
stegosaurs 4:435
stem cells 3:343; 8:945
sterilization (microbial) 7:866–867;
    15:1875, 1876
stomach 4:424–426, 427
stomata 10:1253, 1254–1255
streptomycin 1:91
strokes 3:330, 331; 4:443; 16:1937

stuttering 16:1937
subphyla 3:333
subspecies 2:181; 3:333
sugar, processing 5:620
surgery 8:943–944; 13:1580; 14:1726–1731
  and stitches 14:1728
  antiseptic 1:94; 7:866–867; 14:1727
  aseptic 14:1727
  cryosurgery 4:393
  holography and 7:829
  laser 5:584; 7:828, 829; 8:945; 14:1729
  microsurgery 5:584; 14:1730
  minimal access (MAS; keyhole) 8:938;
    13:1661; 14:1728, 1730
  operating rooms 14:1727
  orthopedic 14:1731
  surgeons 14:1728–1729
  surgical instruments 14:1727–1728
  telesurgery 12:1480
  using robotics 12:1480; 14:1729, 1731
  see also anesthetics; transplants
sweat 5:575, 576, 577; 13:1567
sweat glands 5:576; 9:1072
symbiosis 10:1193, 1276
  mycorrhizae and 6:649
  see also parasitology
synapses 9:1100
synesthesia 13:1577
syphilis, treatment 5:616

T
tapeworms 4:441; 10:1196, 1197
tartar 4:413
taste 14:1750–1751
  and smell 13:1576
tears 5:576, 583
teeth
  artificial 4:412–413
  decay 4:411–412, 413; 15:1891
  structure 4:411
temperature, body 13:1565
  biorhythms and 2:194, 195
  control 13:1567
tendons 9:1069; 13:1563
testes 12:1450, 1451
  hormones 5:548
testosterone, drugs similar to 10:1166
tetracycline 1:92
tetrodotoxin 11:1309
textured vegetable protein (TVP)
    5:619
thalamus 2:218
therapods 4:434–435
thiamine 16:1932
threonine 1:71
thrombin 6:733
thymine 9:1039
thymus 6:765
thyroglobulin 11:1369

thyroid gland 2:195; 5:546, 547
thyrotropin 5:548
tibia and fibula 13:1564
tocopherol see vitamins, vitamin E
tomatoes, genetically engineered
    2:210; 6:675
tongue, taste buds 14:1750–1751
tonsils 7:884
touch 15:1838–1839
  plants' sense of 2:210–212
trachea 12:1461–1462
transgenic organisms 1:29; 6:675–676
transpiration 16:1969
transplants 8:943–944; 14:1730–1731
  bone 4:413
  heart 3:331; 14:1730
  kidney 5:574; 14:1731
  lung 14:1731
tree rings, to date objects 1:99–100
trees
  felling 15:1812
  hardwood 15:1811, 1812
  softwood 15:1811–1812
Triceratops 4:436
trilobites 6:685
Troodon 4:435
trophic levels 5:625
truffles 6:649
tryptophan 1:71
tumors
  detected using thermography
    14:1788
  see also cancer
twins, identical 3:340; 6:677
Tyrannosaurus rex 4:434
tyrosine 1:71

U
ureters 5:571
urethra 12:1450–1451
uterus 11:1344–1345, 1346

V
vaccinations 15:1889–1892, 1917
  bioengineered vaccines 6:676
  Jenner and 7:805; 15:1889–1890
  Pasteur and 10:1211
  smallpox 7:804–805; 10:1211;
    15:1889–1890, 1891–1892
vacuoles 3:302
vagina 12:1450
valine 1:71
vas deferens 12:1450
vegetables
  in the diet 9:1129
  processing 5:618
vegetarians 9:1130
veins 3:326–327, 328
  pulmonary vein 12:1460

velociraptors **4**:434–*435*
vertebrae **13**:*1562*, 1564
vertebrates **1**:80, 82
villi **4**:*426*; **7**:*882*
viruses, biological **8**:989; **15**:**1914–1917**
  and disease **4**:440–441; **6**:765
  classification **3**:*335*
  discovery **8**:986
  DNA **4**:440–441; **15**:*1914–1915*
  grown in the laboratory **15**:*1917*
  influenza **6**:765; **15**:*1890*, 1915, 1916
  multiplication of **15**:*1915–1916*
  rabies **10**:*1211*
  spread **15**:*1916*
  structure and shapes **15**:*1915*
  types **15**:*1915*
  *see also* AIDS
vision
  color **5**:582; **7**:*848*
  ion channels in **3**:304
  persistence of **14**:*1773*
vitamins **9**:1127, 1129; **16**:**1930–1933**
  vitamin A (retinol) **9**:1129, 1130;
    **16**:1930, 1931, 1932, 1933
  vitamin B **9**:1129, 1130; **16**:1930–1931,
    1932, 2036
  vitamin C (ascorbic acid) **1**:*14*; **9**:1127,
    1129; **16**:*1931*, 1932, 1933
  vitamin D (calciferol) **14**:*1712*; **15**:1876;
    **16**:1931, 1932, *1933*
  vitamin E (tocopherol) **16**:1931, 1932
  vitamin K (phylloquinone) **9**:1129;
    **16**:1932
VO2 max **13**:*1660–1661*
vomiting **9**:1071

**W**

wasps **2**:212; **8**:*1001*
  as parasitoids **10**:1193
  gall **10**:1194
West Nile virus **10**:1197
wetas **9**:1066
whales, humpback **9**:*1142*
wheat, genetically engineered **2**:210,
  *213*
wheat take-all **6**:*676*
wounds, treatment **1**:95

**X**

xylem **10**:*1254*, 1277

**Y**

yeasts **5**:590; **8**:988–989; **11**:1372;
  **16**:**2035–2036**
  and beer making **5**:*591*
  and bread making **2**:227, 228; **5**:590
  and wine making **5**:590; **16**:*2036*
yellow fever **10**:*1193*; **16**:*2045*
*Yersinia pestis* **4**:440

**Z**

zoo **16**:**2040–2043**
zoology **16**:**2044–2045**
  *see also* animal kingdom; evolution;
    parasitology; zoo
zooplankton **16**:2045
zooxanthellae **3**:*339*; **9**:1141
zygote **12**:1452

## MATHEMATICS

**A**

abacuses **3**:*263*, 358; **9**:*1123*
algebra **1**:**52–54**; **8**:*921*, 924
arithmetic **8**:922
  mental **8**:923
averages **14**:1679

**B**

binary number system **3**:362; **9**:1123,
  *1126*; **13**:*1587*
biostatistics **14**:1678–1679

**C**

calculus **3**:**265–266**; **8**:**924–925**;
  **10**:1259
censuses **14**:1678, 1683
chemometrics **14**:1679

**D**

decimal number system **9**:1123–1124
decimal points **9**:1126
demography **14**:1679
derivatives **3**:265
distances, measurement **8**:*928–929*

**E**

*Elements, The* (Euclid) **8**:*920*, 921
equations, algebraic **1**:*52*, 53–54;
  **8**:924

**F**

frequency curves **14**:1679–1680
functions **8**:925

**G**

geometry **8**:923
  analytical (Cartesian) **8**:921, *922*,
    925
  and the ancient Greeks **8**:920–921
  differential **3**:266
  fractal **3**:*313*

**H**

histograms **14**:1680

**L**

logarithms (logs) **3**:263; **8**:921

**M**

mathematics **8**:**920–925**
  algebra **1**:**52–54**; **8**:*921*, 924
  Archimedes and **1**:102–103
  arithmetic **8**:922, 923
  calculus **3**:**265–266**; **8**:**924–925**; **10**:1259
  historical developments **8**:*920–922*
  logarithms (logs) **3**:263; **8**:921
  Pythagoras and **11**:1387–1388
mean **14**:1679
measurement **8**:**928–931**
median **14**:1679
mode **14**:1679
modeling, population **3**:266

**N**

numbers, SI (*Système International*)
  prefixes **8**:930, 931
number systems **9**:**1123–1126**
  bases **9**:1125–1126
  binary **3**:362; **9**:1123, *1126*; **13**:*1587*
  decimal **9**:1123–1124
  decimal points **9**:1126
  fractions **9**:1126
  of ancient civilizations **9**:1124–*1125*
  places of digits **9**:1125

**P**

Pascal's triangle **14**:*1683*
pie charts **14**:1680
probability **14**:1680–1681

**S**

SI (*Système International*) units **8**:931;
  **11**:*1335*
statistics **14**:**1678–1683**

**T**

tally system **9**:1124
triangulation **8**:*928–929*

## PHYSICS AND CHEMISTRY

**A**

abrasives **1**:**12–13**
  diamond **1**:13; **4**:419
absolute zero **4**:393; **6**:664; **14**:1777
acceleration **9**:1050
  gravity and **8**:917
acceleration of free fall **6**:718
accelerometers **6**:719–720
accumulators **2**:170
acetate **5**:599
acetic acid **1**:14
acids and alkalis **1**:**14–16**
  acids **1**:*14–15*; **12**:1513
  alkali metals **1**:15–16
  alkalis **1**:15; **12**:1513

indicators 1:*15, 16*
   reactions of 12:1514
   the pH scale 1:16
acoustics 10:1260
   resonance 12:1458
acrylic 5:599; 14:1784
adhesives 1:17–18
advanced gas-cooled reactors (AGRs)
   9:1114
aerodynamics 1:19–22
aerogel 13:1557, 1609
agarose 5:535
Agent Orange 11:*1307*
airfoils 1:19; 15:1903
alchemists 3:*320*–321; 4:444, 445
alcohol
   an antiseptic 1:95
   from fermentation 5:590, *591*
aliphatic compounds 10:1166
alkalis *see* acids and alkalis
alkanes 9:1144
alkenes 9:1144; 10:1166
allotropes, of sulfur 14:1709
alloys 1:57–60; 8:*962*, 963–964, 967, 968
   platinum group 11:1298–1299
   solder 7:838; 15:1825
   tested 13:1648
   *see also* brass; bronze; pewter
Alnico 7:889; 15:1854
alpha particles 7:795, 800; 11:1402;
   15:1883
alumina 1:12–13; 3:310
aluminum 1:64–67; 8:967
   alloys 1:58, 64
   extraction from ore 1:*64*, 65–66
   mining 1:*64*, 65
   ores 1:*64*–65; 8:*963*
   recycling 1:*67*; 12:1427
amalgams 1:59; 8:951; 16:2038
ammeters 4:499–500
ammonia
   and refrigeration 12:1433–1434
   chemical bonds 15:*1897*
   dissolves in water 12:1513
   manufacture 3:296; 9:1105
ammonium chloride 9:1105
   mixed with water 12:1514
ammonium hydroxide 9:1105
ammonium nitrate 5:593; 9:1105
ammonium phosphate 5:593
ammonium sulfate 5:593
amperes (amps) 4:499, *508*
Ampère's law 4:508
amplitude 12:1457; 15:1870; 16:1975
angle of incidence 10:1156–1157, 1158
angle of reflection 10:1157
angstroms 13:1647
anions 7:794, 795
annealing 8:968; 15:1831

anode 5:520–521
antihydrogen atoms 10:*1208*
antimatter, detection 11:*1392*
antimony 7:838; 8:963
antineutrons 10:1207
antiparticles 10:1207
aqua regia 11:1297
arenes 9:1144
argon 7:*774*, 775
arsenic 8:963
arylide 10:*1182*
ascorbic acid 1:*14*
astatine 5:541
atomic beam magnetic resonance
   15:1822
atomic mass 2:137
   relative (RAM) 3:315, 316
atomic number 2:136; 5:540; 7:800;
   10:1217, 1218
atomic piles 9:1112
atomic theory, Dalton and 4:403
atomic weight 2:137; 10:1215
atoms and molecules 2:136–139; 10:1206
   atomic structure 2:138–*139*, 205; 5:540;
      9:1119; 10:1214

**B**
Bakelite 11:*1286*
barium 8:963
barium oxide 10:1179
barium sulfate 16:2033
barium titanate 10:1264, *1265*; 15:1871
bases, chemical 1:15, 16
basic oxygen process (BOC) 7:*798*, 799
bearings, molecular 10:*1167*
benzene 10:1166
beryllium 8:963; 10:1216
beta particles 7:800; 11:1402–1403
bimetallic strips
   in thermometers 15:1798
   in thermostats 15:1799–1800
biochemistry 2:178–179
bioluminescence 7:880
biophysics 10:1258–1259
bisphenols 1:95
bits (binary digits) 9:1126
blackbodies 11:1389
blast furnaces 7:798
blueshift 4:457; 14:1674
boiling points 4:392; 14:1776; 15:1900
boiling water reactors (BWRs) 11:1339
bonds, chemical *see* chemical bonds
borazon (cubic boron nitride) 4:397;
   9:1106
boron nitride 9:1106
   cubic (borazon) 4:397; 9:1106
bosons 5:629; 10:1207, 1209
Boyle's law 6:*663*–664
brass 1:58, 60; 2:225–226; 3:374; 8:963

Bravais unit cells 4:395
bromine 10:*1216*
bronze 1:57, 60; 2:240; 3:374; 8:963;
   15:1825, 1826, 1831
   molds made of 3:292–293
   tarnished 10:*1173*
Brownian motion 4:495
bubble chambers 10:1201, *1203–1204*,
   *1206*
buckminsterfullerene (buckyball) 3:*284*,
   285; 10:1257
bulk modulus 4:498
burning *see* combustion

**C**
calcium 8:963
   dietary 9:1128, 1130
   in fertilizers 5:594
calcium carbonate 3:284; 13:1562
   reaction with hydrochloric acid
      3:315, 316, 318
calculators 3:263–264; 8:*923*
   of Charles Babbage 2:150; 3:359
calendars
   Coligny Calendar 9:*1125*
   Gregorian 9:1124; 15:1815
   Julian 15:1815
caloric 6:735
camera obscura 10:1237
candelas 7:848
capacitors (condensers) 3:277–278; 4:506
capillary action 14:1725
carbon 3:283–286, 316; 10:1164–1165
   isotopes 1:99; 3:287–288; 7:800, 801;
      10:1217; 11:1403
   *see also* carbon dating; diamond;
      graphite
carbonation 16:1986
carbon black 3:286
carbon dating 1:99, *100*; 3:287–288;
   11:*1401*, 1403
carbon dioxide 3:283, 286
   as a greenhouse gas 3:339; 6:*710*–711;
      11:1317
   exhaled from the lungs 5:574; 6:731
   in fire extinguishers 5:*604*
   in blood 6:731
   solid (dry ice) 6:662; 13:*1610*;
      14:*1695*–1696
carbon fibers 3:289–291, *311*; 11:1363;
   13:*1654*
carbonic acid 16:1986
carbon monoxide 3:*286*; 11:1307
carboplatin 7:779
carborundum (silicon carbide) 3:310;
   4:397
casting 3:292–294; 8:969, 971; 15:1831
   brass 2:225–226
   ceramics 3:311

casting (*continued*)
  die **3:**294; **16:**2039
  sand **3:**294
catalysts **3:**295–296, 318, 323
  enzymes as **10:**1167
  platinum metals as **11:**1297–1298
cathode **5:**520
cathode rays **5:**526
cations **7:**794, 795
caustic potash (potassium hydroxide)
  **1:**15; **6:**645
caustic soda *see* sodium hydroxide
cavitation **11:**1360
celluloid **11:**1286
cellulose **3:***282*; **10:**1184; **11:***1320*
cellulose acetate **11:**1286
cellulose nitrate **11:**1286
cement **3:**296
ceramics, industrial **3:**308–311;
  **11:**1329–1330
  superconducting **14:**1720
CERN (European Organization for
  Nuclear Research) **2:***136, 205*;
  **10:***1198, 1201*
  and time dilation **12:**1437
  Large Hadron Collider **10:**1200
  particle detector **10:***1205*
cesium **1:**15–16; **8:**962–963; **15:***1817*
chain reaction **5:**615; **9:**1111, 1113–1114,
  1120
chaos theory **3:**312–313; **10:**1257
Charles's law **6:**664
chemical bonds
  covalent **15:***1896, 1897*
  ionic (electrovalent) **7:**794; **15:***1896*, 1897
  metallic **8:**961–962
chemical reactions **3:**314–319
  and electron shells **10:**1219
  chemical synthesis **3:***319*
  direction **3:**318–319
  exothermic **3:***316, 318*
  rate **3:**317–318
  *see also* catalysts; chemistry
chemiluminescence **7:**880
chemistry **3:**320–323
  biochemistry **2:**178–179
  inorganic **3:**322; **7:**778–779
  organic **3:**283, 322; **10:**1164–1167
  periodic table **3:**322; **5:**541; **8:**949;
  **10:**1214–1219
  physical **3:**322; **10:**1256–1257
  *see also* chemical reactions
Chernobyl disaster **9:***1116*
Chile saltpeter (sodium nitrate) **9:**1105
chlorine
  as an antiseptic **1:**95
  ions **7:**794
  production **5:**521
  reaction with sodium **10:**1219; **13:**1585

chromatography **3:**324–325; **5:**631
chromium **8:**967, 968–969; **15:***1854*
chromium chloride **12:***1513*
chronometers **15:***1816, 1820*–1821
circuit breakers *see* fuses and
  circuit breakers
cisplatin **7:**779
citric acid **1:***14*
clathrates **7:**774
clepsydras **15:***1816, 1819*
clocks *see* timekeeping devices
cloud chambers **10:**1203
cobalt chloride **12:***1513*
cochineal **10:**1180
coke **2:**200
cold fusion **6:**654
color **7:***848*; **8:**926
combustion **5:***541*; **10:**1175, 1177
compasses **3:**356–357; **9:**1083, *1084*
composites **11:**1291
compounds **2:**138; **3:**323
  chemical energy **3:**316
  ionic **7:**794
Compton effect **11:**1390–1391
concentration, effect on chemical
  reactions **3:**317–318
condensation **3:**344; **4:**444; **7:**863; **13:**1578
condensers, electrical *see* capacitors
condensers, steam **15:**1827–1828
conduction (heat) **6:**738
conductors **7:**781; **12:**1453, 1455
  lightning **7:***857*
  metals as **8:**962
  superconductors **14:**1719–1720
  *see also* semiconductors
convection **6:***737*, 738
Cooper pairs **14:**1718
coordination theory **15:**1853
copolymers **11:**1320
copper **3:**294, 374–376
  alloys **1:**57
  blister **8:***966*
  corrosion **3:**377
  early use of **3:**374; **15:**1830–1831
  mining **3:***375*; **8:**1018
  refining **3:**376; **5:***521*; **8:***966*, 967–968;
  **15:**1828
  resistivity **7:**780
  smelting **1:**59; **8:**966
  *see also* brass; bronze
copper oxide **3:**375; **10:***1173*
copper sulfate **3:***376*; **10:***1217*; **12:***1513*;
  **15:**1854
copper sulfides **3:**375, 376
Coriolis effect **15:**1810; **16:**1992,
  1993, 2007
corrosion **3:**377–378
  prevention **3:**378; **5:**536; **8:**974
  *see also* electroplating

cracking **9:**1149
  catalytic **3:***295*; **9:**1149
critical mass **5:***613*, 614; **9:**1120
critical point **15:**1900
cryogenics **4:**392–393; **14:**1717
cryopreservation **4:***392*
crystallography **6:**692
  X-ray **4:**394, 395–396; **16:**2034
crystals **4:**394–397; **8:**1010
  ionic **7:**794
  liquid *see* liquid crystals
  photonic **10:**1161
  piezoelectric **10:***1264–1265*; **13:**1557;
  **15:**1817, 1822, 1871
  structure **4:**394–395
  symmetry **4:**395
  synthetic **4:**394, 396–397
curium **4:**398
currents (electrical) *see* electrical
  currents
cyanide process **13:**1559
cycloalkanes **9:**1144
cyclohexane **10:**1166
cyclopropane **3:***285*
cyclotrons **10:**1199, *1200*; **14:**1719
Czochralski technique **4:**397

**D**

Dacron **11:**1287, 1288
damping **12:**1457
deceleration **5:**626
decibels **4:***472*; **13:**1616
deflagration **5:**579
density **1:**102
  relative *see* specific gravity
depth of field **10:**1238
*De Re Metallica* (Agricola) **8:***967*, 1015
desalination **4:**445; **10:***1172*; **16:***1972*
detergents *see* soaps and detergents
deuterium **5:**552; **6:**652, *653, 654*, 760
  and nuclear fusion **9:**1117, 1118, 1122
diamond **3:***284–285*; **4:**394, **418–419**;
  **5:***540*; **8:**1011, 1013
  an abrasive **1:**13; **4:**419
  cutting **4:**419
  industrial uses **1:**13; **4:**419
  set in platinum **11:***1299*
  synthetic **4:**396–397, 418
dielectric **3:**277, 278
diesel oil **9:**1149
diffraction
  light **7:**846, *847*; **10:***1158*, 1159; **16:***1978*
  sound **13:**1615
dipoles **1:**90; **7:**890, *892*; **10:**1264
disaccharides **3:***281*
displacement **13:***1643*
distillation **4:444–445**
  fractional **4:**445; **9:**1104, *1148*; **10:**1179
  of air **9:**1104; **10:**1179

of crude oil **9:**_1148_–1149
vacuum **9:**_1148_
Doppler effect **4:456–457**; **9:**1087;
   **13:**1615–1616
and expansion of the universe **4:**457;
   **15:**1879–1880
drag **1:**_19_, 41; **9:**_1051_
dry ice **6:**662; **13:**_1610_; **14:**_1695_–1696
dyes and dyeing **4:466–469**; **14:**_1781_
   fading **15:**1876
   photographic **10:**1244
   wool **16:**2025, _2026_
   _see also_ paints
dynamics **10:**1260
dynamite **5:**579–580, _579_; **8:**1015–1016

## E
eddy currents **13:**1608
elasticity **4:497–498**; **14:**1668
elastic limit **4:**497
electrical currents **2:**169–170;
   **4:**506–_507_, _508_
   alternating (AC) **6:**671, 672; **11:**1341
   direct (DC) **6:**671–672; **11:**1341
   lightning **7:**857
   _see also_ induction
electrical measurement **4:499–501**
electric-arc furnaces **7:**_799_
electric circuits **4:502–503**, _507_
   batteries and **2:**170; **4:**502
   capacitors **3:**_278_
   fuses and circuit breakers **6:650–651**
   relays **12:1439–1440**
   resistors **4:**503; **12:1455–1456**
   series and parallel **4:**502–_503_
electricity **4:504–509**
   and magnetism _see_ electromagnetism
   batteries and **2:**169–172; **4:**502
   cables **7:**_780_; **11:**_1342_; **14:**1719
   capacitors and **3:**277–278
   fuel cells and **6:**644–645
   generation **11:**1337–1338
   meters **4:**_500_, 501
   pylons **11:**_1342_
   static **4:**505–506; **10:**1232
   stored using superconductors **14:**1719
   supply **11:**1341–1342; **14:**1719
   thermoelectricity **14:1786–1787**
   _see also_ electrical currents; electrical
      measurement; electric circuits
electrodes
   in batteries **2:**170, 171
   in fuel cells **6:**644, 645
electrodynamic suspension **7:**859
electroluminescence **7:**_879_–880
electrolysis **4:**507; **5:520–521**; **7:**795
   aluminum obtained by **1:**65–66
   copper obtained by **3:**376; **5:**_521_;
      **15:**1828

electroplating **5:536–537**; **8:**973, 974;
   **13:**1560; **15:**1828
   silver obtained by **13:**1559
   sodium obtained by **13:**1586
electrolytes **5:**520; **7:**795
electromagnetic force **10:**1209
electromagnetic radiation **4:**509
   spectrum **7:**_843_–844; **13:**1644–1645
electromagnetic suspension **7:**859
electromagnetism **4:507–508**; **5:522–525**,
   629; **7:**891–892; **10:**1261
   Ampère and **1:**73; **4:507–508**
   and maglev trains **7:**_875_; **9:**1041; **14:**_1718_
   electromagnetic induction _see_ induction
   electromagnets for lifting **5:**522, 525
   electromagnets in generators **6:**_672_
   electromagnets in motors **5:**517, 518,
      _519_; **7:**_859_
   Faraday and **4:**508; **5:**523, 524–525,
      _587_; **7:**772
   Maxwell's equations **4:**508–509
   superconducting electromagnets
      **14:**1719
electromotive force (emf) **5:**525; **16:**1943
electron avalanches **6:**670
electronics **5:526–529**
electrons **2:**136
   and electrical charge **4:**504
   and electron microscopes **5:**530
   antiparticles of **10:**1207
   as beta particles **11:**1402–1403
   Cooper pairs **14:**1718
   discovery **5:**539; **10:**1206
   energy levels and luminescence **7:**879
   energy levels and radiation **13:**1646
   orbitals **10:**1219; **15:**1852
   shells (orbits) around the atomic
      nucleus **5:**540, 541; **7:**794;
      **10:**1218–1219; **15:**1852, 1896–1897
   valence **15:**1896–1897
   wave nature **11:**_1389_, 1392
electrophoresis **5:534–535**
electroplated nickel silver (EPNS) **13:**1560
electroplating **5:536–537**; **8:**973, 974;
   **13:**1560; **15:**1828
electropolishing **8:**973
electrostatics
   electrostatic induction **4:**_505_
   electrostatic machines **4:**505, 506
elements, chemical **2:**136; **3:**322;
   **5:538–541**
   Dalton's chart of **4:**_403_
   discovery **3:**_321_; **5:**540
   stars and the creation of **1:**123
   _see also_ periodic table
emulsions, nuclear **10:**1202
energy **5:549–552**
   electrical **5:**_552_
   geothermal **5:**552

heat **6:**736
kinetic **5:**549, _550, 551, 552_; **10:**_1258_;
   **12:**1493
latent **5:**549, _550_
lost in food chains **5:**625
mass-energy equation **5:**551, 614; **6:**653;
   **8:**919, 924; **9:**1113; **12:**1438; **14:**1716
nuclear **5:**550–552, 613
potential **5:**_549_, 550; **12:**1493
renewable resources **15:**1803
transfer **5:**627
water **5:**552
enzymes **10:**1167
equivalence, principle of **12:**1438
equivalent weight **5:**521
ethane **3:**_285_
ether (chemical compound) **4:**410
ether (hypothetical medium) **12:**1435
ethylene oxide **13:**1583
evaporation **2:**138; **3:**344; **7:**863; **15:**1900
explosive forming **5:**581
explosives **5:578–581**
   _see also_ fireworks and flares

## F
fabric conditioners **13:**1583
feedstock, chemical **9:**1149
femtoseconds **10:**1257
Fermilab **10:**1200
ferromagnets **7:**889
fertilizers **5:592–595**; **7:**779; **9:**1105, _1106_
   and the agricultural revolution **1:**25
   and water pollution **1:**30; **4:**492; **5:**_595_;
      **11:**_1313_–1314
   from sewage **13:**1546, _1548_, 1549
fiberglass, Teflon-coated **2:**247
firedamp **8:**1016–1017
fireworks and flares **5:607–608**; **13:**_1586_
fission, nuclear **5:**551, **613–615**; **9:**1111,
   1112–1113; **11:**1339
   and nuclear weapons **9:**1119–_1121_
flares **5:**_608_
flex, electric **7:**_780_
flight
   airplanes **1:**40–42
   history of **1:**_36_–40
   hypersonic **14:**1722
   Leonardo da Vinci and **7:**_840_
   subsonic **14:**1722
   supersonic _see_ supersonic flight
   transonic **14:**1722
flotation separation **8:**967, _968_; **11:**_1297_
flow
   laminar **16:**1928, 1929
   turbulent **16:**1928
flowmeters, venturi **15:**_1903_
fluids
   pressure in **11:**1347; **15:**1902, 1903
   _see also_ gases; liquids

fluorescence 7:879; 10:1159; 15:*1874*, 1875
  and solar energy 13:1598–1599
foam
  polyurethane 11:1289
  structural 11:1291
focal point 7:*846*
foot-pound system 5:550
force, measuring 11:1335
forces 5:626–629
  contact 5:*627*
  fundamental 5:629; 10:1206, 1209
  shear 4:498
forensic science 5:630–633; 13:1648
  *see also* electrophoresis
forging 8:*970*, 971
  tools 15:1831
Formica 11:1287, 1289
fractal geometry 3:*313*
fractional distillation 4:445; 9:1104,
  *1148*; 10:1179
fractions 9:1126
francium 1:15
Fraunhofer lines 13:*1648*
frequency 15:1870; 16:1975–1976
  natural 12:1457
friction 2:173; 5:636–637; 12:1454
  and electrical charge 4:504, 505
  overcoming 7:876
  viscosity and 12:1454; 16:1928
fructose 3:*280*
fuel rods, nuclear 10:*1219*
fulcrums 7:*842*
fullerenes 3:285; 10:*1257*
fuses and circuit breakers 6:650–651
fusion, nuclear 5:551–552; 6:652–654
  cold fusion 6:654
  in hydrogen bombs 5:551; 9:1117, 1122
  in nuclear reactors 6:654; 9:1117–*1118*
  in stars and the Sun 1:121; 5:613; 6:652;
    14:*1714*, 1716
  plasmas and 11:1285

## G

gallium 8:949; 10:1218
gallium arsenide 13:1540, 1543
galvanizing 3:378; 16:2039
galvanometers 1:*73*; 4:499–500
gamma rays 5:615; 6:657–658; 7:795,
  800; 13:1644
  and radiotherapy 11:1404
  from space 1:125; 9:1136
gases 2:138; 6:659–662
  inert *see* inert gases
  ionization 7:795
  kinetic theory of 8:926–927
  natural *see* natural gas
  pressurized 6:*659*, 660, 661; 11:*1348*
  viscosity 12:1454
gas laws 6:663–664

gasoline
  lead in 7:838
  octane numbers 9:1149
  production 9:1149
Geissler tubes 7:*794*
germanium 8:949, 963; 10:1218;
  13:1540; 15:1848
G-force 3:307; 5:627
glass 6:701–704; 13:*1556*; 15:1825
  fibers 11:*1298*
  laminated 1:18; 2:147
  recycling 12:1427–*1428*, *1429*
  stained 6:703–*704*
  types 6:702–703
  waste 12:1426
glass ceramics 3:310–311
glass-reinforced plastic (GRP) 11:1291
  for boatbuilding 13:*1553*–1554
  for trucks 15:1858
glucose 3:279–281
glue 1:*17*, 18
gluons 5:629; 10:1209
glycerin 13:1581
gold 6:713–715; 15:*1851*
  alloys 1:59
  bacterial concentration of 2:153
  casting 3:*292*
  extraction and refining 6:713–714
  gold rushes 6:*713*
  mining 6:713, *715*; 8:1019, 1020
  specific gravity 8:1010
  therapeutic value 7:779
  turning inexpensive metals into 10:1198
graphite 3:*284*, 285; 4:394, 418; 5:*540*, 604
  in pencils 7:838
gravimeters 6:694; 9:1146
gravitons 5:629; 10:1209
gravity 5:*628*, 629; 6:716–718; 10:1260;
  16:1997
  and acceleration 8:917
  and black holes 2:198; 12:*1438*
  and G-force 5:627
  center of 6:717
  Einstein's theory *see* relativity,
    general theory of
  fundamental force 10:1209
  inverse square law 6:718
  measuring 6:694
  pendulums and 10:1212
  potential energy and 5:550
gum arabic 1:18
guncotton 5:580
gutta-percha 12:*1498*

## H

Haber-Bosch process 9:1105
hadrons 2:*136*; 10:1208
half life 7:801; 11:1402
  of carbon-14 3:287–288; 11:1403

Hall-Héroult process 1:65–*66*
halogens 10:*1218*
heat 6:735–738
  insulators 6:738; 7:781; 11:1290
  *see also* temperature
heat treatment processes 15:1831
helium
  and nuclear fusion 1:121; 6:652, *653*;
    14:1716
  atomic structure 2:*137*
  discovery 7:775
  in balloons 2:164
  lights 7:774
  liquid 4:393; 14:1719
  uses 2:164; 7:*774*, 775
henrys 7:*773*
Hooke's law 4:497, 498
horsepower 11:1336
hourglasses 15:*1815*, 1816, 1819
hydrocarbons 10:1165
hydrochloric acid 1:14; 12:1513
  in the stomach 4:425, 426
  reaction with calcium carbonate
    3:315, 316, 318
  reaction with sodium chloride 12:1514
  reaction with zinc 3:*318*; 12:*1514*
hydrocracking 9:1149
hydrogen 6:662, 760–761
  as a fuel 6:662, 760–761
  and nuclear fusion 1:121; 5:551–552;
    6:652, *653*; 9:1117–1118, 1122; 14:1716
  and pH 1:16
  atoms 3:317; 5:540; 6:760; 10:*1208*
  hydrogen-powered fuel cells
    6:644–645, 760
  isotopes 6:760; 7:800; 9:1122
  liquid 10:1203
  plasma 9:1117–*1118*
  traced by radio telescopes 14:1763–1764
hydrogen fluoride, chemical bonds
  15:*1897*
hydrogen peroxide, an antiseptic 1:95
hydrolysis 13:1581
hyperons 10:1208–1209

## I

illuminance 7:848
ilmenite 10:*1181*
indicators, chemical 1:*15*, 16
indium antimonide 13:1540
inductance 15:1846
induction (electromagnetic induction)
  4:508; 5:524–525, 587; 6:671–672,
  756; 7:772–773, 892
  induction coils 7:*773*
inert gases (noble gases) 3:323; 6:662;
  7:774–775
inertia 5:627–628; 9:1049, 1050
  mass and 8:917

infrared radiation **7:**776–777, 844;
  **13:**1644
  and photography **12:**1448
  detection using thermal imaging **7:**777;
    **10:***1161*; **14:**1788
  observed from space **9:**1136
  uses **6:**722; **7:***776–777*; **9:**1029; **10:**1221;
    **12:***1442*, 1443; **14:**1789
inorganic chemistry **3:**322; **7:**778–779
insulators **7:**780–781
  electrical **7:***780–781*; **11:**1290; **12:**1453,
    1455; **15:**1847
  thermal **6:**738; **7:**781; **11:**1290
interference **16:**1977–1978, *1978*
  and wave nature of electrons **11:**1392
  and wave nature of matter **11:**1392
  light **7:**846; **10:**1159
  sound **13:***1614*, 1615
invar **10:**1213
inverse square law **6:**718
iodine **10:***1218*
  as an antiseptic **1:**95
  deficiency **5:**548
  sublimation **14:***1696*
ionization chambers **10:**1202
ions and ionization **7:**794–795
  complex ions **15:**1853–1854
  identifying substances using ions
    **13:**1649
  ion exchange **7:**795
  ionization **7:**795
  ions **1:**14; **5:**520; **7:***794–795*
iridium **8:**943, 963, 967; **11:**1296, 1297;
    **13:**1609
iron and steel **7:**796–799; **15:**1831
  alloy steels **8:**964
  building with **2:**245–246; **8:***961*; **13:**1569
  carbon steel **7:**797
  cast iron **1:**58; **7:**797, 798
  corrosion (rusting) **3:***377*, 378; **7:**797;
    **10:***1174*, 1175; **16:**1984, 1985
  iron **1:**60; **7:***796–797*; **8:***964*
  iron extraction **2:**200–203; **7:**797; **8:**967
  iron in blood **9:**1129–1130
  iron isotopes **7:**800
  iron ores **8:**964, 1013
  nickel-chrome steel **14:**1743
  pig iron **7:**798
  recycling **12:**1427
  sheet steel **8:***972*, 973
  stainless steel **1:**58; **7:**797; **8:**968–969
  steel **1:**58, *59*, 60; **2:***203*; **6:**737; **7:**796;
    **8:**963–964
  steel combustion **5:***541*
  steelmaking **7:**797–798, *799*; **10:**1178
  tempered steel **6:**736
  wrought iron **7:***797*, 798
iron carbonyl **15:**1854
iron chlorides **12:***1513*; **15:**1853

iron oxide, hydrated **10:***1174*, 1175
isomers, of monosaccharides **3:**281
isoprene **12:***1498*
isopropanol **1:**95
isotopes **2:**137; **7:**800–801; **10:**1217
  and radiometric dating of rocks **6:**684
  carbon **1:**99; **3:**287–288; **7:**800, 801;
    **10:**1217; **11:**1403
  hydrogen **6:**760; **7:**800; **9:**1122
  mass spectroscopy and **13:**1649
  radioisotopes **7:***800–801*; **11:**1403
  separation **7:**801
  uranium **5:**614, 615; **7:**801; **9:**1114,
    1119–1120; **15:**1884

**J**
JET (Joint European Torus) **6:***654*
Josephson effect **14:**1720
joules **5:**550
Joule-Thomson effect **7:***816*
junction boxes **6:**651

**K**
kaons **10:**1208
Kea, Mount, telescope on **1:***123*, 124
kelvins **7:**816
Kelvin temperature scale **4:**393; **6:**664;
    **7:**816; **14:**1777
kieselguhr **5:**580
kilograms, standard **8:***930*
kilowatts **11:**1335
kinematics **10:**1260
kinetic theory **7:**862–863
kinetoscopes **9:**1052
klystrons **10:***1199*
knots (speed) **9:**1084
krypton **7:***774*, 775

**L**
lactic acid **1:**14
Large Hadron Collider **10:**1200
latex rubber **3:***378*; **12:***1497*, 1498–1499
laughing gas (nitrous oxide) **1:**77, 78;
    **4:**410; **6:***660*
lead **7:**836–838
  alloys **1:**59, 60; **7:**838
  extraction and refining **7:**836–837; **8:**968
  in paint **7:**838; **10:**1180
  in pigments **10:**1181
  ore **7:***836*
  poisoning **7:***837*–838
  shot **7:**838
  smelting **1:**60
  uses **7:**836
lead azide **9:**1105–1106
lenses **7:**846; **10:**1158–1159; **12:**1431
  camera **10:**1238–1240, *1241*
  concave and convex **10:***1157*, 1158;
    **12:**1431

contact **5:**585
convergent and divergent **10:**1239
fisheye **10:**1240
focal length **10:**1238–1239, 1240, 1250
Fresnel **7:**851
microscope **8:**999–1000; **10:***1157*
on camcorders **3:**267
spherical and chromatic aberration
    **10:**1159
telephoto **10:**1239, 1250
telescopic **10:***1241*
wide-angle **10:**1239, 1250
zoom **10:**1239–1240, 1250
leptons **10:**1207–1208
levers **7:**841–842
lift force **1:**19, 40, *41*; **15:**1903
ligands **15:**1854
light **7:**843–848; **13:**1645
  and color **7:***848*; **8:**926
  and fiber optics **5:***600–602*
  and shadows **10:**1156
  blueshifted **4:**457; **14:**1674
  coherent and incoherent **7:**826, *827*
  curves toward a massive body **6:**718;
    **12:***1437*
  diffraction **7:**846, *847*; **10:***1158*, 1159;
    **16:**1978
  fluorescence **7:**879; **10:**1159; **15:***1874*
  interference **7:**846; **10:**1159
  measuring **7:**847–848
  particle nature **7:**846–847;
    **11:**1389–1390, *1390*, 1391
  phosphorescence **7:**879; **10:**1159
  polarization **10:**1159; **11:1310–1311**
  prisms and **6:***749*; **7:***844*, 845; **9:**1103;
    **10:***1156*; **13:**1645
  redshifted **4:**457; **14:**1674
  speed of **5:**628; **9:**1048; **10:**1158;
    **12:**1436, 1437–1438
  wave nature **6:***749*; **7:**846, *847*; **8:**927;
    **10:**1159; **16:***1977*, 1978
  wave-particle duality **11:**1391;
    **16:**1976–1977
  *see also* optics; reflection and refraction
lime **5:**594
liquid crystals **3:**264; **7:**864–865
  liquid crystal displays (LCDs) **7:**865;
    **10:***1160*; **14:***1772*
liquids **2:**138; **7:***862–863*
  and pressure **11:**1348
  specific gravity measured **13:**1643
  *see also* distillation
lithium **1:**15; **8:**962–963, 967
  reaction with water **10:***1175*
lithium deuteride **9:**1122
lithium fluoride **15:***1896*, 1897
litmus paper **1:**16
load **11:**1335
lodestones **3:**356; **7:**889

lubricants **7**:876–877
  oils and greases **7**:863, *876–877*; **16**:1929
lumens **7**:848
luminance **7**:848
luminescence **7**:878–880
  fluorescence **7**:879; **10**:1159;
    **13**:1598–1599; **15**:*1874*, 1875
luminous flux **7**:*847*, 848
luminous intensity **7**:847, 848
lux **7**:848

# M

Mach numbers **1**:45; **14**:1721, 1722, *1723*
magnesium **3**:*315*; **8**:963; **9**:1130
magnesium hydroxide **1**:14
magnetic flux density **5**:523
magnetism **7**:889–893
  and electricity *see* electromagnetism
  magnetic resistance **12**:1453–1454
  measuring **1**:98; **6**:*694*; **7**:*892*–893
  paramagnetism **15**:1854
magnetite **3**:296
magnetometers **1**:98; **6**:*694*; **7**:*892*; **9**:1146
  fluxgate **7**:893
  proton **7**:893
  spinner **7**:893
Magnox reactors **9**:1114
maltose **3**:281
Mandelbrot set **3**:*313*
manganese, in seabed nodules **8**:1021
manganese dioxide **3**:295
Manhattan Project **9**:1112, 1121
marble **3**:284
mass and weight **8**:917–919
  gravity and **6**:717
  space-time curved by mass **12**:*1436*, 1438
  weightlessness **6**:*717*; **8**:918–*919*;
    **12**:*1435*; **16**:1997–1998
mass-energy equation **5**:551, 614; **6**:653;
    **8**:919, 924; **9**:1113; **12**:1438; **14**:1716
matches **10**:*1230*
matter
  states of **4**:392; **6**:659; **7**:862
  wave nature **11**:1391, 1392
  *see also* atomic theory, Dalton and
mauveine **4**:*466*
mechanics **5**:626; **10**:1259–1260
melting **2**:138; **14**:1776
Mendelevium **10**:1218
mercury, metal **8**:950–*951*, 967
  alloys **1**:59
  as a superconductor **14**:1719
  glowing ions of **7**:*794*
  in barometers **2**:167–168; **8**:951
  in thermometers **8**:951; **15**:1797
  poisoning **11**:1314
Mersenne Twister **8**:*924*
mesons **2**:139; **10**:1206, 1207, 1208
metalloids **13**:1540, 1556

metallurgy **8**:966–969
  powder (sintering) **8**:*969*
metals **8**:960–965
  alkali metals **1**:15–16; **8**:962–963; **10**:1216
  alkaline earth metals **8**:963
  discovery **8**:965
  extraction from ores **8**:967–968
  metalloids **8**:963
  mixtures *see* alloys
  ores **8**:*963*, 964–965, *1016*
  properties **8**:960–*961*, 968
  reaction with acids **12**:1514
  recycling **12**:1427
  structure **8**:961–962
  transition metals **8**:963; **10**:*1217*, 1219;
    **12**:*1513*
  *see also* metallurgy; metalworking
metalworking **8**:970–975
  *see also* casting; electroplating
meters, standard **8**:930–931
methane **3**:*285*; **6**:662
  as a greenhouse gas **3**:339; **6**:710, 711,
    *712*; **11**:1317
  bonding of atoms in **15**:*1896, 1897*
  discovery **16**:1943
  from bacteria **8**:987
  in coal mines **3**:346; **8**:1016–1017
methanol, toxicity **11**:1308
methyl isocyanate **11**:1308
methyl orange **1**:*15*
micelles, soap **13**:*1581*
micrometers **8**:996–997
microwave radiation **8**:1002–1003; **13**:1644
  and communications satellites
    **3**:353–354; **14**:1757
  and radar **8**:1003
  and television transmission **8**:1003
  communications using **8**:907,
    *1002*–1003; **14**:1757
  microwave ovens **8**:*1003*
  solar energy and **13**:1602
  to carry telephone signals **1**:*90*
mirages **10**:1157; **12**:1431
mirrors **7**:*845*; **10**:1156, 1157;
    **12**:*1430*–1431
  concave **10**:1157; **12**:1430–1431
  convex **10**:1157; **12**:1430
  parabolic **13**:*1597, 1599*
  solar energy using **5**:550; **13**:*1597,
    1599–1600*
  virtual images **10**:1157
modeling, weather **3**:312–313
molecular weight **2**:137
molecules **2**:137
  valency and **15**:1896
monomers **11**:1320, 1321–1322
monosaccharides **3**:279–281
MOPVE technology **7**:778
mordanting **4**:466

motion **9**:1048–1051
  circular **5**:626
  close to the speed of light **5**:628; **9**:1051
  Galileo's studies of **6**:655; **9**:*1049*–1050
  linear **9**:1048
  Newton's laws of **5**:627–628; **7**:806;
    **9**:1050–1051, 1103; **12**:1489
  rotational **9**:1048
  simple harmonic **9**:1049
  translational **9**:1048
muons **12**:1437

# N

naphthalene **14**:1785
natural gas **5**:550; **6**:*662*; **9**:1148
  exploration for **6**:695–696
  pipelines **10**:1266–1267
neon **7**:775
  lights **6**:662; **7**:*774*, 775
neptunium **5**:541
neutrinos **6**:717; **10**:1201, *1203*, 1205,
    1207; **15**:1882
neutrons **2**:136, 139; **5**:540; **10**:1206, 1214
  and isotopes **7**:800
  and nuclear fission **5**:*614*, 615
  antiparticles of **10**:1207
newtons **5**:629; **11**:1335, 1347
Newton's rings **7**:*846*
nickel **15**:*1853*
  and the magnetostrictive effect **15**:1872
nickel nitrate **12**:*1513*
nickel silver **2**:226
nitric acid **12**:1513
  production **4**:445; **9**:1105; **11**:1298
nitrocellulose **5**:580
nitrogen **6**:662; **9**:1104–1106
  and "the bends" **10**:1178–1179
  compounds of **9**:1105–1106
  cycle **9**:1106
  fertilizers **5**:592–593; **9**:1105, *1106*
  liquid **4**:*393*; **6**:662; **9**:*1104*; **11**:*1349*;
    **14**:1719
  production of **9**:1104
  uses **9**:1104
nitroglycerine **5**:579, 580
nitrous oxide **9**:1105
  an anesthetic **1**:77, 78; **4**:410; **6**:*660*
  as a greenhouse gas **3**:339
noble gases *see* inert gases
nucleons **10**:1208
nucleus, atomic **5**:614; **10**:1206, 1214
  and radioactive decay **11**:1402–1403
  binding force in **10**:1209
  bombarded in particle accelerators
    **10**:1198
  electron shells (orbits) around **5**:540,
    541; **7**:794; **10**:1218–1219; **15**:1852,
    1896–1897
nylon **5**:598, *599*; **11**:1288, 1321; **14**:1784

**O**

octane numbers **9:**1149
"octaves, law of" **10:**1216
oil
  as a lubricant **7:**876–877; **16:**1929
  grading of motor oil **7:**876
  in paint binder **10:**1181–1182
  linseed **10:**1181
  recycling **12:**1428–1429
  viscosity **7:**863; **16:**1929
oligosaccharides **3:**281
opaque substances **10:**1156
open-hearth process **7:**799
optics **10:1156–1159**, 1260
  geometric **10:**1159, 1260
  physical **10:**1159, 1260
  quantum **10:**1159
  the eye and vision **5:**583
  see also light; reflection and refraction
optoelectronics **10:1160–1161**
orbitals, electron **10:**1219; **15:**1852
organic chemistry **3:**283, 322;
  **10:1164–1167**
osmium **8:**967; **11:**1296; **13:**1609
osmosis **10:1170–1172**
  osmotic pressure **10:**1171
  reverse **10:**1171–1172
oxidation and reduction **10:1173–1175**
oxidation number **10:**1174
oxygen **10:1176–1179**
  abundance **10:**1176
  atoms **10:**1176
  breathing **10:**1178, 1179
  cycle **10:**1178
  discovery **3:**321; **7:**835; **10:**1177
  from photosynthesis **10:**1176, 1177,
    1253, 1255
  liquid **4:**393; **10:**1176, 1178
  production **10:**1179
  reactivity **10:**1176
  uses **6:**661–662; **10:**1178–1179
  see also ozone
ozone **10:**1179
  ground-level **3:**339

**P**

paints **10:1180–1183**
  artists' **10:**1180, 1181, 1182–1183
  lead **7:**838; **10:**1180
  luminous **7:**879
  manufacture **10:**1183
  see also dyes and dyeing
palladium **11:**1296
paramagnetism **15:**1854
Parkesine **11:**1286
partial pressures, law of **4:**403
particle physics **10:1206–1209**
  antiparticles **10:**1207
  cosmic rays and **10:**1207

families of particles **10:**1207–1209
particle detectors **10:1202–1205**
particles for the fundamental forces
  **5:**629; **10:**1206, 1209
string theory **10:**1209
pascals **11:**1347; **15:**1893
patio process **13:**1559
Peltier effect **14:**1786, 1787
pendulums **6:**749; **10:1212–1213**;
  **15:**1816
pentaerythritol tetranitrate (PETN)
  **5:**580, 581
penumbra **10:**1156
periodic table **3:**322; **5:**541; **8:**949;
  **10:1214–1219**
petroleum plants **3:**295
pewter **1:**59, 60; **7:**838; **15:**1825
pH **1:**16
phenol **7:**866
phenols, as antiseptics **1:**95
phlogiston **3:**321; **7:**834–835
phosphates **10:**1231
phosphorescence **7:**879; **10:**1159
phosphorus **10:1230–1231**
  in fertilizers **5:**593–594
photochemical reactions **13:**1598
photoelectric effect **10:**1159; **11:**1390
photoluminescence **7:**879, 880
photometry **7:**847–848
photons **5:**629; **6:**717; **7:**847; **10:**1159,
    1207, 1209; **11:**1390, 1391;
    **16:**1976–1977
  and lasers **7:**827, 828
  gamma-ray **6:**657
  X-ray **16:**2031
physical chemistry **3:**322; **10:1256–1257**
physics **10:1258–1261**
  astrophysics **1:**123–124; **10:**1258
  biophysics **10:**1258–1259
  classical (Newtonian) **10:**1259–1261
  geophysics **6:**692, 693–696; **10:**1258
  particle **10:**1206–1209
piezoelectricity **4:**398; **10:1264–1265**;
  **15:**1822
  ceramics **3:**310
pigments **10:**1180–1181, 1182, 1183
pions **10:**1208
pitch (sound) **13:**1613–1614
pitch (substance), viscosity **16:**1929
Planck's constant **10:**1273; **11:**1389
plasma physics **6:**654; **11:1284–1285**;
  **13:**1609
  hydrogen **9:**1117–1118
plastic deformation **4:**497
plastics **11:1286–1291**
  carbon fibers mixed with **3:**291
  forming processes using **11:**1289, 1290
  glass-reinforced (GRPs) **11:**1291;
    **13:**1553–1554; **15:**1858

insulating **7:**780; **11:**1290
pipes **10:**1267, 1271
polymerization **11:**1287
recycling **11:**1291; **12:**1428
silicone **7:**781
thermoplastics **10:**1271; **11:**1289
thermosetting **11:**1289
waste **12:**1426
see also names of various plastics
plating see electroplating
platinum **11:**1296, 1297, 1298–1299
platinum group metals **11:1296–1299**;
  **15:**1851
plutonium **5:**541, 551
  and thermoelectric generators **14:**1787
  isotope **7:**801
  nuclear devices using **9:**1120–1121;
    **15:**1884
polarization **10:**1159; **11:1310–1311**
polonium **4:**398, 399; **11:**1401, 1402
polyacrylonitrile (PAN) **3:**290, 291
polycarbonate **11:**1290
polyester **5:**599; **11:**1288–1289; **14:**1784
  PVC-coated **2:**247–248
polyetheretherketone (PEEK) **11:**1291
polyethylene (polythene) **10:**1166;
  **11:**1287, 1289, 1320, 1321, 1323
  pipes **10:**1271
polyethylene terephthalate (PET)
  **11:**1288
polymerization **11:1320–1323**
  addition **11:**1320
  and synthetic fibers **5:**598–599; **11:**1321
  bulk **11:**1322–1323
  condensation **11:**1320
  direct **11:**1320
  emulsion **11:**1323
  of plastics **11:**1287
  suspension **11:**1323
polymers **10:**1165–1166
polypropylene **11:**1288, 1322
polysaccharides **3:**279, 281–282
polystyrene **11:**1287–1288, 1320
polytetrafluoroethylene (PTFE; Teflon)
  **7:**780; **11:**1288, 1290; **12:**1495
polythene see polyethylene
polyurethane **11:**1289
polyvinyl chloride (PVC) **11:**1288, 1289,
  1320
  pipes **10:**1271
positrons **10:**1207; **11:**1403
potassium **1:**16; **8:**962–963
  in fertilizers **5:**594
potassium aluminum sulfate **12:**1514
potassium bicarbonate **5:**604
potassium ferricyanide **12:**1514
potassium hydroxide (caustic potash)
  **1:**15; **6:**645
potassium nitrate **9:**1105; **12:**1514

potentiometers **4**:500–501
  sliding-wire **4**:501
power **11:1334–1336**
  electrical **11**:1335, *1336*
precession **6**:730
precipitation, chemical, and sewage
    treatment **13**:1546–1547
pressure **11:1347–1349**
  absolute **11**:1349
  atmospheric **6**:660; **11**:1347–1348
  differential **11**:1349
  gauge **11**:1349
  osmotic **10**:1171
  static and dynamic **15**:1902
pressurized water reactors (PWRs)
    **9**:*1114*; **11**:1339
prisms **6**:*749*; **7**:844, 845; **9**:1103; **13**:1645
  raindrops as **10**:*1156*; **12**:1420
protons **2**:136; **5**:540; **10**:1206, 1214
  and antiprotons **10**:*1209*
  and electrical charge **4**:504
  collisions **2**:*136*
PTFE *see* polytetrafluoroethylene
PVC *see* polyvinyl chloride
pyrolysis **3**:290

## Q

quanta **2**:205; **7**:846–847; **10**:*1273*;
    **11**:*1390*; **13**:1645–1646
quantum entanglement **10**:1273
quantum theory **7**:846–847; **9**:1051;
    **10**:1273; **11:1389–1392**
  Compton effect **11**:1390–1391
  Einstein and the photoelectric effect
    **11**:1389–1390
  Planck and **2**:205; **10**:1272–1273;
    **11**:1389; **13**:1645–1646
  quantum mechanics **11**:1391–1392
  uncertainty principle **11**:1392
  wave nature of electrons **11**:*1389*, 1392
  wave nature of matter **11**:1391, 1392
  wave-particle duality of light **11**:1391
quarks **10**:1208–1209

## R

radar **11:1393–1396**
  airfield-control **1**:50
  antennas **11**:1394, *1395*
  displays **11**:1395
  Doppler **11**:1396
  ground-penetrating **1**:98; **6**:695;
    **11**:1396
  microwaves and **8**:1003
  tracking **11**:1395
  two-way **11**:1396
  use in archaeology **1**:97, 98
  use in astronomy **9**:1135; **11**:*1396*
  use in navigation systems **9**:1086
  use in weather-detection **8**:982

radiation **7**:795
  in nuclear power stations **11**:1339–1340
radiation (heat) **6**:*735, 738*
radio **11:1397–1400**
  amplitude modulation (AM) **1**:89, 90;
    **11**:*1398*, 1399–1400
  antennas and **1**:89, 90; **11**:1298–1299,
    1394, 1400
  astronomy **1**:124–*125*; **9**:1134–1135;
    **14**:1763–*1765*
  broadcasting **2**:*234*–235; **11**:1397–*1398*,
    1399
  carrier waves **11**:*1398*, 1399, 1400
  digital **11**:*1399*, 1400
  frequency modulation (FM) **1**:89, 90;
    **11**:*1398*, 1400
  Marconi and **8**:*906–907*; **11**:1397
  modulation **11**:*1398*, 1399
  ranges (bands) **8**:1002; **11**:1400
  speed of waves **11**:1394, 1399
  stations **1**:90
  tuning receivers **12**:1458
  use in aircraft-landing systems **1**:51
  use in MRI scans **8**:935
  use in navigation systems **9**:1085–1086
  use in remote control **12**:*1441*–1442,
    1446
  use in transmitting television
    **14**:1770–1771
  waves **1**:89–90; **11**:1399; **13**:1644
  *see also* radar
radioactivity **5**:541, 614; **11:1401–1403**;
    **15**:1883
  alpha decay **11**:1402
  and gamma rays **6**:657
  beta decay **11**:1402–1403
  carbon-14 isotope **3**:287–288
  dating rocks using **6**:684, 690, 691
  detection **6**:*669–670*; **10**:1205
  gamma ray emission **11**:1403
  natural **6**:670
  radioactive and nuclear waste **5**:551;
    **9**:1116–*1117*; **11**:1318
  work of Becquerel **3**:322; **4**:399;
    **10**:1261; **11**:1401
  work of Marie and Pierre Curie **4**:399;
    **11**:1401, *1402*
  work of Rutherford **12**:1502
  *see also* carbon dating
radiocarbon dating *see* carbon dating
radioisotopes **7**:800–*801*; **11**:1403
radium **4**:398, 399; **11**:1401, *1402*
radon **2**:248; **7**:775; **12**:1502
rainbows **10**:*1156*; **12:1420–1421**
rare gases *see* inert gases
rayon **5**:598; **14**:1784
RDX (cyclonite) **5**:580, *581*
redox reactions **2**:200; **10**:1174, 1175
redshift **4**:457; **14**:1674

reduction *see* oxidation and reduction
reflection and refraction **10**:*1260*;
    **12:1430–1431**
  double refraction **8**:1011
  of sound **13**:1614–1615
  reflection **7**:*845*; **10**:1156–1157;
    **12**:1430–1431; **13**:1614
  refraction **6**:*749*; **7**:*845*; **10**:1157–1158;
    **12**:1420, *1431*; **13**:1614–1615, 1645
  total internal reflection **5**:600; **10**:1158
refraction *see* reflection and refraction
refractive index **7**:845; **10**:1158
relative atomic mass (RAM) **3**:315, 316
relative density *see* specific gravity
relativity **12:1435–1438**
  general theory of **3**:266; **4**:496; **6**:718;
    **12**:1438
  special theory of **4**:495–496; **8**:955;
    **12**:1436–1438
reluctance **12**:1454; **15**:1847
resins
  epoxy **1**:18
  vinyl **1**:18
resistance **12:1453–1454**
  air **5**:637
  electrical **4**:503; **7**:780–781; **12**:*1453*,
    *1455*; **14**:1717–1718; **15**:1800
  friction and **12**:1454
  magnetic (reluctance) **12**:1453–1454
resistivity **7**:780–781
  meters **1**:97
resonance **12:1457–1458**
retrosynthetic analysis **10**:1166–1167
rhodium **5**:*536*; **11**:1296, 1297
rigidity modulus (shear modulus) **4**:498
Rochelle salt **15**:1871
rolling metal **8**:*972–973*
röntgenoluminescence **7**:880
rotameter flow gauges **15**:*1903*
rubber **4**:*498*; **12:1497–1500**
  latex **3**:*378*; **12**:*1497*, 1498–1499
  neoprene and nitrile **12**:1499
  polyurethane **12**:*1499*
  styrine-butadiene rubber (SBR) **12**:1499
  silicone **7**:781
  synthetic **1**:18; **12**:1499
rubber cement **1**:18
rubidium **1**:15–16; **8**:962–963
rust **3**:*377*; **7**:797; **10**:*1174*, 1175;
    **16**:1984, 1985
ruthenium **11**:1296–1297

## S

saffron yellow **10**:1180
salt (sodium chloride) **3**:323; **5**:539
  crystals **4**:*394*; **10**:1264, *1265*
  electrolysis of **5**:520, 521
  in solution **16**:1966
  production **12:1515–1516**

reaction with hydrochloric acid
12:1514
saltpeter (potassium nitrate) 9:1105
salts, chemical 12:1513–1514
  simple, double, and complex 12:1514
saponification 13:1581
scandium 8:949, 963
  electron structure 15:1852
Schrödinger equation 11:1392
Seebeck effect 14:1786–1787
selenium 8:963
semiconductors 5:528; 12:1453, 1455;
  13:1540–1543
  doped 13:1541; 15:1848
  in digital cameras 10:1246–1247
  in silicon chips 13:1543
  in thyristors 13:1543
  in transistors 13:1542–1543; 15:1848
  junctions 13:1541–1542
  lasers made from 13:1543
  LEDs 13:1543
  n-type and p-type 13:1541; 15:1848
  pure 13:1540–1541
Semtex 5:580, 581
shear forces 4:498
shear modulus (rigidity modulus) 4:498
shockwaves, from supersonic flight
  14:1722–1723
silica (silicon dioxide) 13:1556–1557
silicates 13:1556
silicon 8:963; 13:1556–1557
  as a semiconductor 13:1540–1541, 1556
silicon carbide (carborundum) 3:310;
  4:397; 16:2038
silicone plastics 7:781
silicone rubber 7:781
silicones 13:1557
silver 8:967; 13:1558–1560
  alloys 1:59; 13:1560
  ores 8:1013
  plate 13:1560
  sterling 13:1560
  tarnish 10:1175
silver bromide 10:1243, 1244; 13:1560
silver chloride 13:1560
silver nitrate 1:95; 10:1242; 13:1559
silver sulfide 13:1558, 1560
sintering 8:969
SI (Système International) units,
  prefixes 8:930, 931
smelting 1:59–60; 2:200; 8:966
Snell's law 10:1158
soaps and detergents 13:1580–1583
  and surface tension 13:1580; 14:1724
  hard water and 7:795
  soap flakes 13:1582
  soap manufacture 13:1580–1581
  soap powder 13:1582
  synthetic detergents 13:1582–1583

sodium 1:15; 8:962–963; 13:1584–1586
  ions 7:794; 13:1585
  liquid 13:1599
  making pure sodium 13:1586
  properties 13:1585–1586
  reactions, general 13:1584–1585
  reaction with air 13:1584
  reaction with chlorine 10:1219; 13:1585
  reaction with water 3:317
  sodium-vapor discharge lamps 7:855
  storage 13:1584
  tarnishing 13:1584
  uses 7:855; 13:1585, 1586
sodium acetate 12:1514
sodium bicarbonate 3:323; 4:425;
  12:1514
sodium carbonate 12:1514
sodium chloride see salt
sodium dioxide 13:1584
sodium hydroxide (caustic soda) 1:15;
  5:521; 10:1187; 12:1513
sodium monosulfite 10:1188
sodium nitrate 9:1105
sodium sulfate 10:1187
sodium thiosulfate 10:1244
solder 1:59; 7:838; 15:1825
solids 2:138; 13:1609–1610
  and pressure 11:1348
sonar 10:1265; 13:1611–1612
  torpedoes and 9:1032, 1033
sonic booms 1:20; 14:1722
sound 4:470, 472; 13:1613–1616;
  16:1976
  and sonar 13:1611
  and the Doppler effect 4:456–457;
  13:1615
  decibels 4:472; 13:1616
  noise 13:1616
  speed of 13:1611–1612, 1613;
  14:1721–1722
  ultrasound see ultrasonics
  waves 13:1614–1615
sound barrier 14:1721
space-time 15:1818
  curved by mass 12:1436, 1438
Spandex 14:1784
spark chambers 10:1204–1205
specific gravity (relative density) 1:102;
  13:1642–1643
speed 5:626
Stanford Linear Accelerator (SLAC)
  10:1201, 1207
starch 3:279, 281–282
statics 10:1260
steam 6:737
steel see iron and steel
stills 4:444–445
stopwatches 15:1822
strain 4:498

streamlines 9:1051
stress 4:498
  shear 4:498
strong nuclear force 5:629; 10:1209
strontium 8:963; 11:1403
subatomic particles 2:136, 139
  in particle accelerators 10:1198–1201
  muons 12:1437
  see also particle physics
sublimation 6:662; 13:1609; 14:1695–1696
sucrose 3:281
sugar 3:281, 282
sulfadiazine 13:1559
sulfur 14:1709–1710
sulfuric acid 1:14, 15
  molecules 2:138
sundials 15:1816, 1819
superconductivity 4:393; 7:778, 779;
  12:1453; 14:1717–1720
  superconductor types 14:1719–1720
superfinishing 8:974
supersonic flight 1:20, 45; 14:1721–1723
  scramjets 1:45
surface tension 7:863; 13:1580;
  14:1724–1725
surfactants 13:1580–1581
switchers, for fiber-optic systems 4:397
symbols, chemical 3:314, 315, 323
syncho-cyclotrons 10:1199
synchrotrons 4:395–396; 10:1200–1201;
  14:1719
Système International (SI) number
  prefixes 8:930, 931

T
talc 5:604
technetium 5:540; 7:779
Teflon see polytetrafluoroethylene
tellurium 10:1216–1217
temperature 6:736; 14:1776–1777
  absolute zero 4:393; 6:664; 14:1777
  affecting chemical reactions 3:318
  and the triple point 14:1777
  centigrade (Celsius) scale 14:1777;
  15:1796
  changes caused by 6:736–737
  extremes 8:931; 14:1776, 1777
  Fahrenheit scale 14:1766, 1776; 15:1796
  Kelvin scale 4:393; 6:664; 7:816; 14:1777
  Réamur scale 14:1777
tempering 15:1831
Terylene 11:1288
Tesla coil 14:1778–1779
thermionic emission 5:532
thermoelectricity 14:1786–1787
thermoplastics 10:1271; 11:1289
Thomson effect 14:1787
thorium 4:399
thrust 1:41

time **15**:1815–1818
  measures of **8**:931; **9**:1124
  sidereal and solar **15**:1816
  theory of relativity and **12**:1437; **15**:1818
  time zones **15**:1817–1818
  *see also* calendars; timekeeping devices
timekeeping devices **15**:1816–1817, **1819–1824**
  atomic clocks **6**:706; **8**:931; **15**:*1817*, 1822–1823, *1824*
  chronometers **15**:*1816*, *1820*–1821
  clepsydras (water clocks) **15**:1816, 1819
  digital watches **7**:865; **15**:1822
  electrical clocks and watches **15**:*1821*, 1822
  event timers **15**:*1823*, 1824
  hourglasses **15**:*1815*, 1816, 1819
  mechanical clocks and watches **15**:*1819*–1822
  pendulum clocks **10**:*1212*, 1213; **15**:1816, 1820
  quartz clocks and watches **10**:*1264*; **15**:1817, 1822
  stopwatches **15**:*1822*
  sundials (shadow clocks) **15**:1816, 1819
  time switches **15**:1823–1824
tin **15**:**1825–1826**
  alloys **15**:1825
  block **15**:1826
tin chloride **15**:1826
tin oxides **15**:1826
tinplate **15**:1825
titanium **15**:**1827–1829**
  alloys **11**:1363; **15**:1827
  production **15**:*1829*
  uses **15**:*1827*–1828
titanium dioxide **10**:1180, *1181*; **15**:1829
titanium oxide **15**:1827
titanium tetrachloride **15**:1829
TNT (trinitrotoluene) **5**:580; **9**:1106
tokamaks **6**:654; **9**:1117–*1118*
  Tokamak Fusion Test Reactor **11**:1285
torques **5**:626; **6**:729
Torricellian vacuum **2**:167
torrs **15**:1893
transcendental numbers **9**:1126
transition elements **15**:**1851–1854**
translucent substances **10**:1156
transmutation **5**:541
transparent substances **10**:1156
transuranic elements **5**:541; **10**:1218
"triads, law of" **10**:1215
triple point of water **14**:1777
tritium **5**:552; **6**:652, *653*, 760
  and nuclear fusion **9**:1117, 1118, 1122
tungsten **15**:*1852*
tuning forks **13**:*1613*
turbulence, air **1**:22

**U**
ultrasonics **15**:**1870–1873**
  for drilling **15**:*1873*
  for welding **15**:*1873*; **16**:2002
  medical uses **8**:*937*; **11**:*1344*; **13**:*1615*, 1616; **15**:*1871*, 1873
  to clean materials **15**:1873
  to test materials **15**:*1872*, 1873
  ultrasound **8**:937; **13**:1616; **15**:*1870*–1871
  undersea **15**:1873
ultraviolet **7**:844; **13**:1644; **15**:**1874–1876**
  and fluorescence **15**:1875
  observatories and **9**:1136
  uses **15**:*1875–1876*
umbra **10**:1156
uncertainty principle **11**:1392
unified field theory **4**:496
uranium **5**:540; **11**:1401; **12**:*1502*; **15**:**1883–1884**
  and nuclear fission **5**:551, 613, *614–615*; **9**:1113, 1114, 1119–1120; **11**:1339; **15**:1884
  and the atomic bomb **5**:614; **9**:1120, 1121
  enriched **9**:1121; **15**:1884
  fuel rods **10**:*1219*
  half life **5**:615; **7**:801
  isotopes **5**:614, 615; **7**:801; **9**:1114, 1119–1120; **15**:1884
  ores and mining **15**:1883
  prospecting for **6**:670
  refining **15**:1884
uranium hydroxide **15**:*1883*
uranium oxide **15**:*1883*, 1884

**V**
vacuum **15**:**1893–1895**
  heat in a **6**:738
  vacuum coating **15**:1894–1895
vacuum drying, salt **12**:1516
valence **5**:541; **10**:1216, 1219; **15**:**1896–1897**
vanadium **8**:963
Van de Graaf generators **4**:*506*
vapor **15**:*1900*–1901
vaporization **4**:444
vapor pressure **15**:**1900–1901**
velocity **5**:626
  terminal **6**:718; **16**:1929
  vector nature **9**:*1050*
venturi effect **15**:**1902–1903**
verdigris **3**:377
vibratory systems **12**:1457
viscosity **7**:*863*; **12**:1454; **16**:**1928–1929**
  coefficient of **16**:1929
voltage **4**:502
  ratios **15**:1847–1848
  SI (*Système International*) number prefixes **8**:930

voltmeters **4**:*499*, 500
volts **16**:1942, 1943
von Patera process **13**:1559
vulcanization **12**:1497, *1498*, 1499

**W**
watches *see* timekeeping devices
water **16**:**1965–1966**
  boiling point **4**:393; **6**:737
  chemical bonds **15**:*1897*
  electrolysis of **5**:520
  freezing point **4**:393; **16**:1965
  freshwater from seawater **4**:445; **10**:1171, *1172*
  hard **7**:795; **16**:1966, 1973
  molecules **2**:138; **16**:1965–1966
  properties **16**:1965
  required by the body **9**:1128; **16**:*1965*, 1967
  softening **7**:795; **16**:1973
  solubility **16**:1965–1966
  states of **4**:392
  testing **7**:*837*
  treatment plants **16**:*1971*
  triple point **14**:1777
  vapor **15**:*1900*; **16**:1967, 1968
watts **5**:550; **11**:1335; **12**:1455
wave motion **16**:**1975–1978**
  amplitude **15**:1870; **16**:1975
  period **16**:1975
  transverse and longitudinal **16**:*1976*
  velocity **16**:1976
  wave frequency **15**:1870; **16**:1975–1976
  wavelength **15**:1870; **16**:1975
  *see also* diffraction; interference
weakly interacting massive particles (WIMPS) **15**:1882
weak nuclear force **5**:629; **10**:1208, 1209
weight *see* mass and weight
weightlessness **6**:*717*; **8**:918–*919*; **12**:*1435*; **16**:**1997–1998**
wet oil **9**:1148
wetting agents **14**:1725
wind tunnels **1**:21–22; **16**:*2010*
wings **1**:19, 22, 40, *41*
  supersonic **14**:1723
woad **10**:1180
work, measuring **11**:1335
W particles **10**:1208, *1209*

**X**
xenon **7**:*774*, 775
X-rays **13**:1644; **16**:**2031–2034**
  and radiation therapy **8**:943
  computerized axial tomography (CAT; CT) scans **8**:*934*, *939*; **16**:2033–*2034*
  dangers of **16**:2034
  dental **16**:2033
  discovery **8**:932; **16**:2031

images of Egyptian mummies **15:**1913
industrial uses **16:**2034
in medicine **8:***932–934,* 939; **14:**1729;
   **16:***2031,* 2032–*2033*
making X-ray pictures **16:**2032
observed from space **9:**1136
production **16:***2031–2032*
radiotherapy and **11:**1404; **16:**2034
security X-ray machines **1:***49*
X-ray crystallography **4:**394, 395–396;
   **16:**2034
X-ray diffraction **4:***454;* **10:**1256

## Y
Young's modulus **4:**498

## Z
zinc **16:2037–2039**
   alloys *see* brass
   reaction with hydrochloric acid **3:***318;*
      **12:***1514*
zinc chloride **12:***1514*
zinc oxide **16:**2037, 2038, *2039*
zinc sulfide **16:**2037, 2039
zirconium boride **3:**310
Z particles **10:***1204,* 1208, 1209

# TECHNOLOGY

## A
A4 Pacifics (locomotives) **7:**872–873
Aardman Animations **1:***86,* 87
ABMs (antiballistic-missile missiles)
   **9:**1032
Abrams tanks **14:***1743,* 1744, *1745*
accelerator mass spectrometer (AMS)
   **1:**99
accelerators *see* particle accelerators
Adobe Photoshop Album **10:***1250*
ADSL (Asymmetric Digital Subscriber
   Line ADSL)**14:**1758
advance warning equipment (AWARE)
   **15:**1843
adzes **15:**1830
Aibo (robot) **12:***1479*
ailerons **1:***41*
AIM-120 Slammer missiles **9:**1031
air bags, used for water power **16:***1982*
airborne early warning (AEW) systems
   **11:**1396
air-conditioning **1:34–35**
   *see also* refrigeration
aircraft carriers **16:**1958, *1960,* 1961
air-cushion vehicles (ACVs)
   *see* hovercraft
air-delivered seismic instrument devices
   (ADSIDs) **12:**1447–1448
air-gun arrays **6:***695*

airplanes **1:36–45**
   aerodynamics **1:**19–*20,* 22
   aeronautical engineers and **5:***555,* 556
   afterburners **7:**809
   anatomy **1:**42–43
   autopilots **1:***42;* **9:**1086; **13:***1544,* 1545
   brakes **2:***224*
   cockpit **1:***40*
   Doppler devices **4:***457;* **11:**1396
   emergency oxygen in **10:**1179
   examined using X-rays **16:**2034
   flight recorders **1:***41*
   gyrocompasses **6:**730
   hydraulic equipment **6:**753
   jet **7:***787,* 807, *808,* 809, 810; **15:***1869;*
      **16:**1953–1954
   jet airliners **1:**39–40, 41–42, 43
   landing **1:**50–51
   landing gear **1:***66*
   navigation systems in **9:**1085–*1086*
   pilotless **1:**45; **12:***1443*
   principles of flight **1:**40–42
   radar devices in **11:**1396
   speed calculated **11:**1396; **15:***1902,* 1903
   speed record **16:**1955
   stealth aircraft **1:**44; **16:***1958*
   subsonic flight **1:**19
   supersonic **1:***20;* **7:**809
   tilt-rotor **16:**1961
   tires **12:**1500
   torpedoes dropped from **9:**1032, 1033
   types **1:***43–45*
   VR helmets used in **15:**1912
   V/STOL aircraft **7:***808;* **16:1944–1947,**
      1958, 1960
   weightlessness and the "Vomit Comet"
      **16:**1998
   *see also* airports; helicopters;
      parachutes; warplanes
airports **1:46–51**
airships **2:**163
   *Hindenburg* **6:***761*
air-traffic control **1:**49–*50;* **11:***1393,*
   1394, 1396
Akashi Kaikyo Bridge **2:**232
alarms, smoke **5:***606*
all-terrain vehicles (ATVs) **1:**75
alternative fuel vehicles **1:61–63; 14:**1694
   biofuels **1:**62
   electric **1:***61,* 62–63
   fuel cells and **1:***63;* **6:**645
   hybrid vehicles **1:**61
   solar-powered **1:**62; **13:***1600, 1601*
alternators **6:**671; **11:**1337
*Alvin* (submersible) **14:**1708
ammunition
   cartridge **6:**724, 725, 727
   *see also* bullets
amphibious vehicles **1:74–75**

Amphicar **1:**75
amplifiers **10:**1234
amplitude modulation (AM) **1:**89, 90;
   **11:***1398,* 1399–1400
analytical engines **2:***151;* **3:**359; **13:**1588,
   *1589*
angiography **8:**935
angledozers **4:**480
animation **1:83–88**
   computer **1:***83,* 84, *87–88;* **3:***370, 371*
antennas **1:89–90**
   cable network **2:***253*
   dish **1:***89,* 90
   platinum and **11:**1298–1299
Apple computers **3:***360,* 361
   Mac OS **3:**365
   PowerBooks **3:**361, *362*
   Safari **3:**361
aqualungs **4:**448
aqueducts **2:***231*
archaeology **1:96–101**
   remote sensors used in **12:**1448
Archimedes screws **1:**103; **8:**910;
   **11:**1383–1384
architecture **1:104–109**
   ancient Greek **1:**105
   ancient Roman **1:**106
   Asian **1:***107,* 108–109
   baroque **1:**107
   Chinese **1:***105,* 108; **2:**241–242
   Gothic **1:***106;* **2:**241
   "green" **2:**248
   in the Americas **1:***104,* 107
   Islamic **1:**106
   Japanese **1:**108; **2:***242*
   Mesopotamian **2:**241
   modern **1:***109*
   neoclassical **1:**107
   Renaissance **1:**107
   rococo **1:**107
   *see also* building techniques; pyramids;
      skyscrapers
Arpanet **7:**788
*Artemis* satellite **3:***353*
artificial intelligence (AI) **1:**88, **112–115;**
   **3:**367
   *see also* robotics
artillery **6:**728
ASIMO (robot) **12:***1477*
asphalt cutters **7:***802,* 803
assault ships **16:**1961
astrolabes **9:**1083–1084
Asymmetric Digital Subscriber Line
   (ADSL) **14:**1758
Atlas missiles **9:**1029
ATMs (automated teller machines)
   **13:***1592*
ATVs (all-terrain vehicles) **1:**75
automatons **1:**112; **12:***1477*

automobiles **2:**140–149
  aerodynamics **1:***19, 20*
  alternative-fuel *see* alternative fuel
    vehicles
  axles **14:**1737
  batteries **2:**171, *172*
  brakes **2:**141, 144–145, 146, 221–*222*,
    223; **6:**753
  catalytic converters **3:***296*; **11:**1316
  computer systems **2:**148
  cooling system **2:**145
  engine **2:**142–*143*; **7:***773, 782–784,* 787
  fuel gauges **15:**1844
  headlights **15:***1895*
  history **2:**140–142
  ignition system **2:**145
  motor oils for **7:**876
  navigation systems in **2:***145*; **6:***708*;
    **9:***1087–1088*; **15:**1843
  onboard television **14:***1775*
  painting **10:**1183
  production **5:***554*; **12:**1482
  race cars **2:**147–*149*
  safety **2:**145–147
  spark plugs **3:***309*; **11:**1299
  starter motors **13:***1607–1608*
  steam cars **14:**1687
  steering **2:***144,* 145
  suspension **2:**144; **14:***1736–1737*
  tires **14:**1736
  traffic-avoidance systems **15:**1843
  transmission (gear system) **2:**144
  wheels **16:***2004*
  windshields **1:**18; **3:***310*
autopilots **1:**42; **9:**1086; **13:***1544,* 1545
AV-8 (aircraft) **16:***1945,* 1946
AWARE (advance warning equipment)
    **15:**1843
axes **15:**1830
axles **14:**1737

**B**

B-2 (aircraft) **16:***1956*
B-52 (aircraft) **16:***1953*
Baby, The (computer) **13:**1589–1590
backstaffs **9:**1084
balances and weighing machines
    **2:156–159**; **8:***917,* 929
ballistics **2:160–161**
balloons **2:162–164**
bar codes and scanners **2:165–166**;
    **7:**828, 829
bassoons **9:**1077
"batching pigs" **10:**1267
bathyscaphes **14:***1704–*1706
bathyspheres **14:***1703–*1704
batteries **2:**169–172; **4:**502
  camcorder **3:**272
  digital-camera **10:**1249

invention **2:***170*; **16:***1942, 1943*
  lithium-ion (Li-ion) **3:**272
  rechargeable **2:**172
  *see also* fuel cells
battleships **16:**1958
bearings **2:173–174**
Bell X-1 (aircraft) **14:**1723
bicycles **2:175–177**
  development **2:**175–176
  streamlined **1:***22*
binoculars **10:**1158
biochips **4:**455
bioengineering **5:**555
  bioengineered vaccines **6:**676
biosensors **8:**941
bits (binary digits) **3:**362
  and digital camcorders **3:**271
bits, drill **4:**459, 460; **15:**1831
black boxes **1:**41
blacktop roads **12:**1474, *1475*
blast furnaces **2:200–203**
block and tackle pulleys **11:***1381–*1382
Bluetooth **7:***793*; **9:***1037*; **10:**1221
boats
  boatbuilding **13:***1551–*1554
  carvel construction **13:**1552–1553
  clinker construction **13:**1552
  hydrofoil **6:758–759**
  steam-powered **8:**909–910
bombers (aircraft) **16:***1952–1953,* 1955
bombs and shells **2:206–209**; **5:***613*
  atomic bombs **2:**209; **5:**614;
    **9:**1112–1113, 1114, *1120–*1121
  hydrogen bombs **2:**209; **5:**551; **9:**1117,
    1122
  shells **2:**206–207; **5:**581; **14:**1743
  smart bombs **2:**209; **6:***721*
box scrapers **12:**1474
brake systems **2:221–224**; **5:**637
  airplane **2:***224*
  automobile **2:**141, 144–145, 146,
    221–*222*, 223; **6:**753
  bicycle **2:**177
  high-performance disks **3:***311*
  mountain railroads **3:**261
  regenerative **12:**1425
  rheostatic **12:**1425
  train **2:**222–223, 224; **12:**1425
  truck **2:**222, 224; **15:***1856*
bread making **2:227–229**; **5:**590
breathing apparatus **12:**1463
bricks and brickmaking **2:**240, *243–*244
bridges **2:230–233**
  resonance and **12:***1457,* 1458
broadband **7:**791
broadcasting **2:234–239**
  radio **2:***234–*235; **11:***1397–1398,* 1399
  television **2:***235–239*; **8:**1003;
    **14:**1770–1771

buildings, world's tallest **13:**1570
building techniques **2:240–249**
  bridges **2:**232–233
  building materials **2:**242–246
  dams **4:**404
  equipment *see* cranes; earthmovers;
    winches and windlasses
  "green" architecture **2:**248
  modern **2:***246–*248
  skyscrapers **13:**1569–1571
  *see also* architecture
bulk carriers **13:**1555
bulldozers **4:**480, *481*
bullets **1:***21*; **2:***160–*161
bull-roarers **9:**1073
buses **14:***1693–1694*
bytes **3:**362; **9:**1126; **13:**1589

**C**

cables
  coaxial **2:***251*
  electric flex **7:***780*
  high-voltage **11:***1342*; **14:**1719
  undersea and transatlantic **7:**816;
    **10:**1160; **14:***1754,* 1757
  wire-rope **16:***2017–*2018
cable television **2:**236–237, **250–253**
cable travel **3:260–262**
  cable cars **3:***261–262*; **14:**1691, *1693*
caissons **2:**232; **7:**850
calendar stacks **10:***1188,* 1189
calendering **14:**1785
camcorder **3:267–272**
cameras **10:**1237
  box **10:**1236–1237
  compact **10:**1238, *1242*
  depth of field **10:**1238
  diaphragm in **10:**1237–1238
  digital **10:***1240, 1246–*1251
  digital video **9:**1054–1055
  films **10:**1236, *1243,* 1244–1245
  flash **10:**1241, 1245
  focal length of lenses **10:**1238–1239,
    1240, 1250
  focusing **10:**1238
  in cell phones **10:***1240*
  lenses **10:**1238–1240, *1241*
  movie **9:**1053–*1055*
  reflex **10:**1238, *1239*
  rostrum **1:**85
  Schmidt **10:**1244
  shutters **10:**1236, 1237, *1238*
  speed cameras **15:***1842*
  television **14:**1769–1770
  thermal-imaging **7:**777
canning **5:**622–623
cannons **6:***723*
  hand **6:**723
capstans, power-driven **16:**2006

carburetors 7:784
carpets and rugs 14:*1784, 1785*
cars *see* automobiles
cartridge ammunition 6:724, 725
  shotgun 6:727
cassette tapes 7:885–886
*Castora Sei* (lay-barge) 10:1269, 1270
catalytic converters 3:*296*; 11:1316
*Catch-Me-Who-Can* (locomotive)
  14:*1687*
cathode-ray tubes 5:*532–533*; 14:*1770*
CAT scans *see* computerized axial
  tomography
CCTV (closed-circuit television)
  14:*1770*
CDs (compact discs) 4:429, *430–431*;
  7:*830–833*
  CD-players 7:*830*
cellular phones (cell phones; mobile
  phones) 5:*529*; 7:*793*; 8:*990*;
  9:*1034*–1037; 12:*1522*; 14:*1753*,
  *1758–1759*
  3G 15:1909
  cameras in 10:*1240*
cement 2:*244*–245
central heating systems
  thermostats 15:*1799*, 1800
  timers 15:1824
central processing units (CPUs)
  3:362; 9:1126
centrifuges 3:**306–307**
chair lifts 3:261, *262*
Channel Tunnel 6:707–708; 15:*1862*,
  *1864*, 1865
charge-coupled devices (CCDs)
  3:*267*–268; 9:1054, 1134; 11:*1351*
  and spectrographs 13:1648
  in digital cameras 10:1246–1247, 1249
  in image scanners 12:1528, 1529
  in television cameras 14:1769–1770
  in the Hubble Space Telescope 14:1767
*Charlotte Dundas* (steamboat) 8:909–910
Chicago L rapid transit system 12:*1424*
Chinese, ancient
  fireworks 5:607
  forges 2:201
  papermaking 10:1184–1185
  porcelain 11:1330–1331
  printing 11:1352
  rafts and boats 13:1551
chips *see* silicon chips
circuit boards 5:*527*; 15:*1850*
  *see also* printed circuits
clarinets 9:1077
clavichords 9:1078
*Clermont* (steamship) 8:910
closed-circuit television *see* CCTV
CN Tower, Toronto 13:1570
coal, turned into oil 2:152–153

coal mining 3:**346–349**; 8:*1015*,
  1016–1017, *1018*, 1021
Cockerell's raft 16:*1982*
Code Red computer virus 16:1926
cog railroads 3:**350–351**
cog wheels *see* gears
color separation overlay (CSO) 14:*1773*
Colossus (computer) 3:359
combine harvesters 1:*25*, 26
Comet (airliner) 1:39
commutators 5:*517*–518
compressors, and jackhammers 7:802, 803
computer-aided design (CAD) 3:371;
  5:554
computer-generated imagery (CGI)
  9:*1056*
computer graphics 3:**368–371**
computerized axial tomography (CAT;
  CT) scans 8:*934, 939*; 16:*2033–2034*
computers 3:**358–367**; 5:527, 529; 8:*925*
  and printing 11:*1358, 1359*
  as musical synthesizers 9:1080
  Babbage's analytical engines 2:*151*;
    3:359; 13:1588, *1589*
  binary numbers 9:*1126*; 13:*1587*
  bugs 13:1590, 1592
  CD and DVD recording drives 7:*831*
  CPU 3:362, 368
  disks 7:887–888; 13:1588
  DNA 4:455
  electronic 3:359–360
  embedded 3:364
  expert systems 1:114
  games 3:*370*, 371
  graphical user interface (GUI) 3:*365*;
    7:*819*; 13:*1591*
  handheld 3:364
  image scanners and 12:*1528*
  in animation 1:*83, 84, 87–88*; 3:370, *371*
  in medicine 8:944–945
  Josephson memory 14:1720
  laptop 3:*362*, 364; 7:865
  light-operated 10:1161
  magnetic tape as storage devices
    13:1588
  main components 3:362–363
  mainframe 3:364
  mechanical 3:358–359
  memory 13:1587
  monitors 7:865
  mouse 7:*819*
  networks 3:364–365
  neural networks 1:114–115; 3:367;
    12:1478
  palmtop 8:*995*
  personal digital assistants (PDAs)
    **10:1220–1221**
  personal (PCs) 3:360–361, 363–364;
    5:*526*; 13:1587, 1589

quantum 3:367
robots controlled by 12:1479, 1480,
  *1482*
speech synthesis 16:*1934*, 1935, *1937*
supercold 14:1720
supercomputers 3:*363*, 364; 14:*1720*
  used in mapmaking 8:*905*
viruses 3:366; 16:**1924–1927**
*see also* artificial intelligence; Internet;
  software; virtual reality
Concorde (airplane) 1:*20, 43, 45, 47*;
  14:*1722*, 1723
concrete
  pipes 10:*1268*, 1271
  roads 12:1474–1475
containers and container ships
  13:*1555*
convertiplanes 16:*1944*
coolidge tubes 16:*2031*
Copperhead shells 2:207, *208*
cotton 3:**379–381**; 5:596, *597*; 14:1780,
  *1782*
cotton gins 1:26; 3:*380*–381; 5:596
cranes 4:**388–389**
crash barriers 12:1476
cross-staffs 9:1084
cruisers 16:1958, *1961*
CT scans *see* computerized axial
  tomography
cullet 6:702
cut-and-cover construction 12:1424
cybernetics 12:1479

**D**

Dalles Dam 6:*757*
Daniell cells 2:171, 172
data synchronization 10:1221
da Vinci robots 14:1731
Decca navigation 5:611; 9:1085–1086
decompression chambers 4:*450*, 451
defibrillators 8:*941*
demolition 2:248–*249*
depth charges 2:208–209
depth sounding 15:1873
derricks 4:460–461
destroyers, guided-missile 16:1960
detonators 5:580–581
diesel engines 4:**420–423**; 7:783,
  786–787
  common-rail 4:421
  fuel-injection system 6:646–647
  in ships 8:*909*
diffusion pumps, vapor 15:1893–*1894*
digital audio software 4:**428–431**
digital compact cassettes (DCCs) 7:888
Digital Scene Matching Area Correlator
  (DSMAC) 6:720
digital signal processors (DSPs) 9:1036
Digital Subscriber Line (DSL) 14:1758

digital technology 5:528
  and animation 1:86
  and cell phones 9:1035
  and telephones 14:1758
  camcorders 3:270–272
  digital audio software 4:428–431
  digital audio tapes (DATs) 7:888
  digital cameras 10:1240, 1246–1251
  digital projector technology 9:1059
  digital radio 11:1399, 1400
  digital television 2:238; 5:528–529
  digital video 9:1053, 1054–1055
  laser discs 7:832
  photocopiers using 10:1233
digital versatile (video) discs (DVDs)
  7:830–833; 14:1774, 1775
diodes 5:527, 533; 13:1541
  light-emitting (LEDs) 3:264; 7:855;
  13:1543
discharge lamps 7:795, 854, 855, 879
disks
  computer 7:887–888
  magneto-optical (MODs) 7:888
distance measuring equipment (DME)
  9:1086
diving 4:446–451
  atmospheric 4:451
  deep-sea 4:449–451; 10:1178–1179
  saturation 4:451
  scuba 4:446, 447, 448–449
diving bells 4:446, 449, 450–451; 14:1698
Dolby Digital 9:1058
Dolby Stereo 9:1058
Doppler radar 11:1396
drawknives 15:1833
dredgers 4:481–482
drilling rigs 4:460–461; 6:662;
  9:1146, 1147
drills 1:13; 4:458–459; 15:1832
  bow 15:1830
  drill bits 4:459, 460; 15:1831
  drill presses 15:1835; 16:2022
  gears 6:668
  hammer 8:1016
  pneumatic 4:472
  steam-driven 8:1016
  tips 8:969
  ultrasonic 15:1873
  see also jackhammers
drones 1:45
drums 9:1073, 1077, 1078
dry spinning 5:599
dump trucks (dumpers) 4:481
Duplex Universal Karriers, Wheeled
  (DUKWs) 1:74, 75
DVD camcorders 3:271
DVD recorders 7:832; 14:1775
DVDs (digital versatile (video) discs)
  7:830–833; 14:1774, 1775

E
earthmovers 4:479–482; 12:1474
echo sounders 5:610; 13:1611, 1612
EEGs see electroencephalographs and
  electroencephalograms
Egyptians, ancient
  agriculture 1:23
  calendar 15:1815
  idea of the universe 15:1877
  locks (security) 7:868–869
  metal extraction 8:967
  mortar 2:244
  papyrus 10:1184
  pyramids 1:105; 2:240, 241; 8:1019;
  13:1568; 14:1733
  quarrying 8:1019
  rafts and boats 13:1551, 1552
  surveying 14:1733
  timekeeping 15:1819
electric motors 5:516–519
  DC 5:517–518
  induction 5:518–519
  linear 7:858–859; 12:1496
  rotary 7:858, 859
  synchronous 5:519
  to power vehicles 1:61, 62–63
electroencephalographs and
  electroencephalograms, (EEGs) 8:941;
  13:1572–1573, 1574; 16:1936
electronic countermeasures (ECMs)
  9:1032; 16:1955–1956
Electronic Numerical Integrator
  Calculator (ENIAC) 3:359, 360;
  13:1589
electron microscopes 5:530–531; 8:987,
  1000–1001
  scanning (SEMs) 5:531; 8:999,
  1000–1001; 9:1100
  transmission (TEMs) 5:530; 8:999,
  1001
electron tubes 5:532–533; 8:990; 15:1848
elevators and escalators 5:542–545;
  13:1569
  effect of falling elevators on weight
  8:918–919
e-mail 7:788, 791, 791
  viruses 16:1926
  see also Internet
endoscopes 5:602; 8:936, 938
engineering 5:553–556
engines
  automobile 2:142–143
  diesel see diesel engines
  four-stroke 7:782–783, 785; 9:1061
  fuel-injection 6:646–647
  gasoline 7:783–786
  heat engines 6:738
  internal combustion see internal
  combustion engines
  jet see jet engines
  marine-propulsion 8:909–911
  Newcomen's 8:1016; 14:1684, 1685
  steam see steam engines
  Stirling (air) 14:1689–1690
  Trevithick's 14:1686–1687
  two-stroke 7:785–786; 8:912; 9:1061
  Wankel (rotary) 7:787; 8:912;
  14:1685–1686; 16:1948–1949
  Watt's 14:1685–1686
  see also rockets; turbines
ENIAC see Electronic Numerical
  Integrator Calculator
ENIGMA code 3:359
escalators 5:543–545
evaporators, flash-chamber 16:1972
excavators 4:479–480
  for tunneling 15:1863–1864
expert systems 1:114
explosive reactive armor (ERA) 14:1744
extrusion process 11:1289, 1290
Eyematic 1:87

F
F-22 Raptor (aircraft) 16:1956
F-35 Joint Strike Fighter 16:1946–1947
fantails 13:1544; 16:2014
"Fat Man" atomic bomb 9:1120
faucets, valves in 15:1898
feedback control 13:1545; 15:1800
felt 14:1785
fetal heart-rate monitors 8:940–941
fiber 5:596–599
  forensic science and 5:631
  synthetic 5:597–598; 14:1784
  see also textiles
fiber optics 5:600–602; 10:1160
  and cable television 2:237, 253
  switchers 4:397
  telephones and 5:602; 14:1755, 1757
fiberscopes 5:602
files (tools) 15:1833
firefighting 5:603–606
fishing industry 5:609–612
flash, camera 10:1241, 1245
flashlights 4:502
flash memory 10:1248
flax (linen) 5:596, 597
flight simulation 15:1911–1912
flintlocks 6:724
Flintstones, The 1:85
float-glass process 6:702, 703
floppy disks, computer 7:887–888
fluoroscopes 16:2033
flutes 9:1073, 1075, 1076
"fly-by-light" systems 1:42
"fly-by-wire" systems 1:42
Flyer (aircraft) 1:37
flying shuttles 14:1782

focal length **10:**1238–1239, 1240, 1250
Fokker **1:**18
food technology **5:618–623**
  additives **4:***469;* **5:**623
  *see also* bread making; refrigeration
Ford, Model T **2:***141*–142
forklift trucks **5:634–635**
Formula One racing **2:**147–148
foundations **2:**246
Fourdrinier machines **10:**1185, 1189
freeze-drying **5:**623; **12:**1434; **14:**1695;
  **15:**1895
freezing **14:***1776*
  food **5:**622; **12:**1434
frequency modulation (FM) **1:**89, 90;
  **11:***1398,* 1400
frigates **16:**1959–1960
fuel cells **1:**63; **6:644–645,** 760
  *see also* batteries
fuel gauges, automobile **15:**1844
fuel injection **6:646–647**
funiculars **3:***260*–261
fuses, bomb **2:**207–208

**G**
GADFLY missiles **9:**1030
gas-discharge lamps *see* discharge lamps
gas mantles, incandescent **7:**853
gas turbines **5:**518; **6:665–666; 7:**787,
  807; **15:***1869*
  in power stations **11:**1338
gears **6:667–668**
  automobile **2:**144
  bicycle **2:***176*–177
  worm **6:**668; **7:***876*
Geiger-Müller detectors (Geiger counters)
  **6:**658, **669–670; 10:**1205; **15:**1876
generators **5:***518,* 519; **6:671–672**
  in hydroelectric power plants **6:**756
geodimeters **14:**1733
gimbals **6:***730*
Glen Canyon Dam **6:***754*
gliders **16:***2008*
Global Positioning System (GPS) **1:**42;
  **5:***610,* 611; **6:705–708**
  and bomb guidance **6:***721*
  satellites **9:**1087–1088
  used by mapmakers **8:***902,* 903
  used in aircraft **16:**1956
  used in farming **1:**30
  used in navigation **9:**1087–*1088*
  used in vehicles **15:**1843
*GM Sunraycer* **13:**1600, *1601*
Golden Gate Bridge **2:***233*
Google (search engine) **7:**790, *791*
governors **13:**1544–*1545*
GPS *see* Global Positioning System
GRAIL missiles **9:**1030
gramophones **13:**1618

Grand Coulee Dam **6:**756
Grande Dixence Dam **4:**405
Grand Prix races **2:**148
graphical user interface (GUI) **3:***365;*
  **7:**819; **13:***1591*
graphics, computer **3:368–371**
gravity meters **13:***1642*
gravure **11:**1358–1359
*Great Western* (steamship) **8:**910
Greeks, ancient
  algebra **1:**52–53
  and the elements **5:**538
  architecture **1:**105
  building techniques **2:**240
  geometry **8:***920*–921
  idea of the universe **15:**1877
  mortar **2:**244
  underwater craft **14:**1697
grinding machines **15:**1835
grinding wheels **1:**13
ground stations, satellite **3:**353, *354*
GSM (global system for mobile
  communications) **9:**1036
Guggenheim Museum **2:***246*
guidance systems **6:719–722**
  inertial **6:**719, *720;* **9:**1029, 1086
  remote **6:**721–*722*
  wire **9:**1029, 1033
gunpowder (black powder) **5:**578–579,
  607
guns **6:723–728**
  recoilless **6:**728
  *see also* bullets; cartridge ammunition
gyrocompasses **6:**730; **13:**1545
gyroscopes **6:729–730**
  in guidance systems **6:**720
  rate gyroscopes **6:**720
gyrostabilizers **6:**730

**H**
hacksaws **15:**1832
hammers **15:**1832
hand stars **5:**608
hard disks, computer **7:**887–888
harpsichords **9:**1078–1079
harquebuses **6:**724
Harrier aircraft **16:**1945, 1946, *1954,* 1958
headlights **15:***1895*
headphones **13:***1640*
heart-lung machines **6:***731*
heart rate monitors **13:**1660
heat engines **6:**738
HEAT (high-explosive antitank) shells
  **14:**1743
helicopters **6:739–742**
heliostats **13:**1599, *1600*
Hellfire missiles **9:**1031
HESH (high-explosive squash heads)
  **14:**1743

*Hindenburg* (airship) **6:***761*
Hiroshima **2:**209; **5:**614
*Holland,* USS **14:**1697
hollanders **10:**1188
holography and holograms **7:**828–*829;*
  **10:***1159;* **13:**1612
hones **15:**1835
Hoover Dam **4:***406,* 508
horns, English **9:**1077
horse collars **1:**24
HOT missiles **9:**1029
hovercraft (air-cushion vehicles) **1:**75;
  **6:745–747; 16:**1961
hovertrains **9:**1041
howitzers **6:***728*
hulls
  oil-tanker **14:**1747–1748
  submarine **14:**1699–1700
hydrapulpers **10:**1188
hydraulics **6:750–753**
  and forklift trucks **5:**635
  and prostheses **11:**1365
  and robotics **12:**1479
  brakes **2:**221–*222*
  shock absorbers **14:**1736, *1737*
  springs **14:**1669
Hydrocar **1:**75
hydroelectric power **4:**407; **5:**552;
  **6:754–757; 11:**1335, 1337, 1340–1341
  tidal power **6:**757; **9:**1143;
  **15:1803–1806,** 1810
  turbines **6:**755–756; **15:**1803, 1867–1868
hydrofoils **6:758–759**
hydrometers **13:**1643
hydrophones, Captor's **8:**1007
hyperfiltration **10:**1172
HyperText Transfer Protocol (HTTP)
  **7:**789

**I**
IBM *see* International Business Machines
ICBMs (intercontinental ballistic
  missiles) **9:**1028–*1029*
imaging, medical *see* medical imaging
induction motors **5:**518–*519*
Industrial Revolution **8:**975
  and architecture **1:**109
  and mining **8:**1015–1016
inertial guidance systems **6:**719, *720;*
  **9:**1029, 1086
ingots **3:***292,* 293–*294*
instrument landing system (ILS) **1:**51
instruments, musical *see* musical
  instruments
integrated circuits
  thick film resistors as **12:**1456
  *see also* silicon chips
Integrated Service Digital Network
  (ISDN) **14:**1758

Intelsat **3:**353, *355*
intercoolers **15:**1858
internal combustion engines **4:**420–421;
    **7:782–787**
  starter motor **13:***1608*
  valves **15:**1899
  *see also* diesel engines; gas turbines;
    jet engines
International Business Machines (IBM)
    **3:**359
Internet **3:***358*; **7:788–793**
  optoelectronic technology and
    **10:**1160
  wireless **7:***792–793*; **14:***1757*
  *see also* e-mail
Internet Service Providers (ISPs) **7:**788,
    789; **10:**1221
interstate highway **12:***1472*
IRBMs (intermediate range ballistic
    missiles) **9:**1030
irrigation **1:**27; **16:***1974*
ISDN (Integrated Service Digital
    Network) **14:**1758
isostatic pressing **3:**311

**J**
jackhammers **7:802–803**
*Jahre Viking* (ship) **14:**1747
Javelin missiles **9:**1030
jeeps, amphibious **1:**74
jenny, spinning **14:**1782; **16:**2025–2026
jet engines **1:**39; **6:**666; **7:***787*, **806–810**;
    **15:**1869
  pulse-jets **7:**810
  ramjets **7:**810
  scramjets **1:**45; **7:**810
  turbofan **1:***37*; **7:***806*, *808–809*
  turbojet **7:**807–808
  turboprop **7:**808
Jim suits **4:***451*
Joint Direct Attack Munitions (JDAM)
    bombs **6:***721*
jointers **16:**2021
Joint European Torus (JET) **6:***654*;
    **11:***1284*, 1285
JPEG files **10:**1248–*1249*
jumbo jets **1:***38*, 40, 46–47

**K**
keels **13:**1552–1553, 1554
keyboard instruments **9:**1074,
    1078–1079
keyboards and typewriters **7:817–819**;
    **16:**2030
kilns **11:**1332–1333
Kismet (robot) **1:***115*
knitting **14:**1781, 1785
knives **15:**1832
kraft process **10:**1185, 1187–1188

**L**
lamps
  arc **7:**853–854
  fluorescent **15:**1875
  gas-discharge **7:**795, 854, *855*, 879
  mercury vapor **7:**855
  oil **7:***852*, 853
  sodium vapor **13:***1585*
  sun **15:**1875
landing craft **16:**1961
Landing Vehicles, Tracked (LVTs) **1:**74
laser discs **7:830–833**
lasers **7:826–829**; **10:***1158*; **13:***1543*
  and bar codes **2:**165, 166
  and fiber optics **5:**602; **14:***1756–1757*
  laser drills **4:**459
  used for cutting cloth **14:***1783*
  used in dentistry **4:**413
  used in distance-measuring **8:***928*
  used in holography **7:**828–829;
    **10:***1159*
  used in making laser discs **7:***833*
  used in missile guidance **6:**722;
    **9:**1031
  used in nuclear fusion **9:**1118
  used in physical chemistry
    **10:**1256–1257
  used in playing laser discs **7:***830*,
    831–832
  used in range finding **6:**722; **14:**1734
  used in surgery **5:**584; **7:**828, *829*;
    **8:**945; **14:**1729
  used in welding **16:**2001–2002
  used to vaporize carbon **10:**1257
lathes **15:***1833–1834*; **16:***2019*
lay-barges **10:***1269–1270*
LCDs *see* liquid crystal displays
Lear jets **1:***43*
LEDs *see* light-emitting diodes
life-support machines (ventilators)
    **8:**942, *945*
lightbulbs **7:**775, *853*, 854
  Edison and **4:***493*, 494; **7:**854
  energy-efficient **7:**855
light-emitting diodes (LEDs) **3:**264;
    **7:**855; **13:***1543*
lighthouses **7:849–851**
lighting **7:852–855**
  fluorescent **7:**854, 855, 879–880
  neon **6:**662; **7:***774*, 775
  street **7:**855; **12:***1476*
  *see also* lightbulbs
light meters **10:***1242*
lightships **7:***851*
linear electric motors **7:858–859**;
    **12:**1496
linear variable differential transformers
    (LVDTs) **15:**1845
Linotype **11:***1356*

liquid crystal displays (LCDs) **7:**865;
    **10:***1160*
  LCD projectors **9:**1059
  LCD television screens **14:***1772*, 1774
lithography **11:**1356–1358
"Little Boy" atomic bomb **5:**614
local-area networks (LANs) **2:**253;
    **3:**364–365
locks (security) **7:868–869**; **12:***1504*–1505
locomotives **7:870–875**
  diesel **7:***872*, 873
  diesel-electric **7:***873*, 874–875; **12:**1413
  electric **7:***874–875*
  steam **7:***870–873*, 874; **14:***1686*, 1687,
    1688
  *see also* trains
longlining **5:***611*, 612
looms **14:***1780*, 1781
  operated using punched cards
    **13:**1587–1588
  power **14:***1783*
Loran **9:**1085–1086
*Lord of the Rings* trilogy (movies) **1:**87,
    *88*
lost-wax process **3:**293
loudspeakers *see* speakers
Lüger **6:**727

**M**
machine guns **6:***725–726*
  on tanks **14:**1745
machine tools **15:**1833–1835
McMath-Pierce telescope **14:***1712*, 1713
maglev trains **7:***858*, 859, 875; **9:**1041;
    **10:***1261*; **14:***1718*
magnetic resonance imaging (MRI) scans
    and scanners **2:***216*; **8:**934–935, 939
magnetic storage **7:885–888**
  camcorder tapes **3:**269
magnetrons **8:***1003*; **11:***1394*
mains, water **16:**1971
*Mallard* (locomotive) **7:**872–873
manipulators, hydraulic **6:**753
manometers **8:**951
marine propulsion **8:908–912**
  *see also* hydrofoils; sailing
masers **7:**826–827
mass production **2:***142*; **14:***1783*
mass spectroscopy **13:**1648–1649
  mass spectrometers **1:***100*; **6:**691; **11:***1401*
matchlocks **6:***724*
medical imaging **8:932–937**
  angiography **8:**935
  computerized axial tomography (CAT;
    CT) scans **8:***934*, 939; **16:**2033–*2034*
  endoscopy **5:***602*; **8:**936, *938*
  magnetic resonance imaging (MRI)
    scans and scanners **2:***216*;
    **8:**934–935, 939

positron emission tomography (PET)
  scans 2:*216*; 7:*801*; 8:935–937, 939;
  11:*1375*
thermography 14:1788, *1789*
ultrasound 8:*937*; 11:*1344*; 13:*1615*,
  1616; 15:*1871*, 1873
X-ray images 8:*932*–934, 939; 14:1729;
  16:*2031*, 2032–*2033*
medical sensors 8:941
medical technology 8:**938–945**
  computers 8:944–945
  imaging *see* medical imaging
  medical ethics 8:945
  monitoring equipment 8:939–942
  nanomedicine 9:1082
  treatment 8:942–944
  virtual reality systems 15:1912–*1913*
memory cards, camcorder 3:272
metal detectors 1:98; 8:962, *965*
  airport 1:49
metronomes 10:*1213*
Métro, Paris 12:1423
microchips *see* silicon chips
microelectronics 8:**990–995**
  *see also* printed circuits; silicon chips
microlights 1:43
microphones 10:1265; 13:1618–*1619*
microprocessors 5:*526*; 8:*991*; 12:1479
microscopes 8:987, **998–1001**
  atomic force (AFMs) 8:1001; 9:1081
  electron *see* electron microscopes
  optical light 2:*185*; 5:530–531; 8:*999*,
    1000, 1001; 10:*1157*
  scanning acoustic 8:1001
  scanning electron (SEMs) 5:531; 8:*999*,
    *1000–1001*; 9:*1100*
  scanning probe 8:1001
  scanning tunneling (STMs) 8:987, 1001
  specimens and slides 8:1001
  underwater 8:1001
microwave landing system (MLS) 1:51
milling machines 15:*1834*–1835
mills
  tide 15:1810
  *see also* windmills and wind pumps
mine, explosive 8:**1004–1007**; 16:1962
minesweepers 8:1007; 16:1962
minibrowsers 9:1037
minidiscs 7:832
mining and quarrying 8:**1014–1021**
  aluminum 1:*64*, 65
  coal 3:*346–349*; 8:*1015*, 1016–1017,
    *1018*, 1021
  copper 3:*375*; 8:1018
  diamonds 4:418, *419*
  explosives used in 5:581; 8:1015–1016,
    1017–1018, *1020*, 1021
  gold 6:713, *715*; 8:1019, 1020
  history 8:1014–1016

iron 7:*796*
lead 7:*836*, *837*
quarrying 8:1014, 1019–1020
safety 8:1016–1017
salt 12:1515–1516
sulfur 14:1710
surface mining 8:*1016*, 1017–1019
underground mining 8:*1018*, 1020–1021
underwater mining 8:*1018*, 1021
*Minority Report* (movie) 15:1911
Minuteman missiles 9:*1029*
missiles and torpedoes 9:**1028–1033**
  air-to-air and air-to-ground missiles
    9:1030–1031
  antiaircraft missiles 9:*1030*
  antiballistic-missile missiles
    (ABMs) 9:1032
  antimissile weapons 9:1032
  cruise missiles 6:*719*; 9:*1028*,
    *1031*–1032
  intercontinental ballistic missiles
    (ICBMs) 9:1028–*1029*
  intermediate range ballistic missiles
    (IRBMs) 9:1030
  missiles 6:*719*, 721–*722*; 9:1028;
    16:1955–1956, 1959
  sea-launched missiles 9:1031
  submarine-launched ballistic missiles
    (SLBMs) 9:1029; 14:1701–*1702*
  torpedoes 9:1028, *1032–1033*; 14:*1701*
mobile communication 9:**1034–1037**
  and the Internet 7:792–793; 9:*1037*
  cell phones 5:*529*; 7:793; 8:990;
    9:*1034*–1037
  future 7:793
  personal digital assistants 10:1221
  videophones 9:1037
mobile phones *see* cellular phones
mobile telephone switching offices
  (MTSOs) 9:1034, 1035
molding
  ceramics 3:311
  plastics 11:*1289*, 1290
molds, for casting 3:292–293
monorails 9:**1040–1041**
Moore's law 3:366–367
Morse code 14:1753
mortars 2:206
mortisers 16:2021–2022
Mosaic (web browser) 7:790
motion-capture technology 1:87; 9:1056
motion pictures 9:**1052–1059**
  film 9:1053
  history 9:1052–1053
  movie cameras 9:1053–*1055*
  projectors 9:1053, *1058–1059*
  sound track 9:*1057*–1058
  special effects 9:1055–1057
  *see also* animation

motorcycles 9:**1060–1062**
motor racing 2:147–149
motors
  electric *see* electric motors
  outboard 8:*911*–912
mouse, computer 7:*819*
movies *see* motion pictures
Moving Pictures Experts Group (MPEG)
  4:429
MP3s 4:428, *429–431*
MRI *see* magnetic resonance imaging
mule, spinning 14:1782; 16:2026
multiple independently targetable
  reentry vehicles (MIRVs) 9:1029
Multiple Mirror Telescope (MMT)
  14:1761
multiplexing 12:1446
multirole combat aircraft (MRCA)
  16:1955
musical instrumental digital interface
  (MIDI) 9:1080
musical instruments 9:**1073–1080**
  brass 2:*226*; 9:*1076*, 1077; 12:1458
  keyboard 9:1074, 1078–1079
  percussion 9:*1077*–1078
  science of music 9:1074
  stringed 9:1074–1075; 11:1388; 12:*1458*
  synthesizers 9:1079–*1080*
  wind (woodwind) 9:1073, 1074,
    *1075*–1077; 12:1458
Music Teller stations 4:*431*
muskets 6:724
MYCIN 1:114

N
nanotechnology (nanoengineering)
  5:554; 8:994–995; 9:**1081–1082**
  nanorobots 8:995; 9:*1081*; 12:1482
  nanotubes 8:1001; 10:*1257*
Natachata (computer program) 1:113
*Nautilus* (submarine) 14:1697
navigation 9:**1083–1088**
  aircraft 9:1085–*1086*, *1087*–1088
  automobile 2:*145*; 6:*708*; 9:*1087*–*1088*;
    15:1843
  gyrocompasses and 6:730
  measuring longitude 9:1084–1085;
    15:*1816*
  navigation satellites 6:705–706, *708*;
    9:1086–1087; 12:1522
  ship 9:*1083*–1088
  spacecraft 9:1088
  submarine 14:1702
  using astrolabes 9:1083–1084
  using cross-staffs and sextants
    9:1084, *1085*
  using GPS 9:1087–*1088*
  using quadrants 9:1084
  using radar 9:1086

navigation (*continued*)
  using radio aids **9:**1085–1086
  *see also* guidance systems
needles, manufacture **16:**2017, *2018*
nets, for fishing **5:**611, 612
networks, computer (LANs and WANs)
  **3:**364–365
neural networks **1:**114–115; **3:**367; **12:**1478
neutron activation analysis **11:**1403
newspapers, printing **11:***1355*
Nipkow discs **14:***1769*
Notre Dame cathedral **1:***106*
NTSC system **14:**1770, 1771
nuclear magnetic resonance (NMR)
  **7:***893*; **10:***1256*
nuclear reactors **9:**1111–1118
  and transuranic elements **10:**1218
  chain reaction **5:**615; **9:**1111,
    1113–1114; **15:**1884
  design **9:**1114
  electromagnetic pumps and **11:**1386
  fast breeder **15:***1884*
  history of nuclear power **9:**1111–1112
  nuclear fission **9:**1111, 1112–1113;
    **15:**1884
  nuclear fusion **6:**654; **9:**1117–*1118*
  nuclear power plants **5:***615*; **9:***1111*,
    1112, *1113*, *1114*, *1115*; **11:**1318, *1337*,
    1338, *1341*
  safety **9:**1115–*1116*
  types **9:**1114–*1115*; **11:**1339
  waste **9:**1116–*1117*
nuclear weapons **2:***209*; **9:**1119–1122;
  **10:**1260
  atomic bombs **2:**209; **5:**614;
    **9:**1112–1113, 1114, *1120*–1121
  hydrogen bombs **2:**209; **5:**551;
    **9:**1117, 1122

**O**

oboes **9:**1077
oil rigs *see* drilling rigs
oil tankers *see* tankers
oil wells, drilling **4:**460–461
olfactometers **16:***2045*
Omega system **9:**1085–1086
Omnirange **9:**1085–1086
ophthalmoscopes **5:**584
optical character recognition (OCR)
  **12:**1527
oscillating water columns (OWCs)
  **16:***1980*, 1981
oscilloscopes **5:**533; **10:**1168–1169;
  **15:***1848*; **16:***1977*

**P**

P-51 Mustang (aircraft) **16:***1952*
packet switching **14:***1758*
pagodas **2:***242*

Panamax vessels **14:***1747*
pantographs **12:***1425*
paper and papermaking **10:**1184–**1189**
  recycling paper **12:**1426–1427
papyrus **10:***1184*
parachutes **10:**1190–**1192**
parchment **10:**1185
Parthenon **1:**105
particle accelerators **2:**139; **5:***629*;
  **10:**1198–**1201**
  and transuranic elements **10:**1218
  circular **10:***1198*, 1199
  cyclotrons **10:**1199, *1200*; **14:**1719
  insulators **7:***781*
  linear **10:***1198–1199*
  Stanford Linear Accelerator (SLAC)
    **10:***1201*, *1207*
  superconducting **14:**1719
  syncho-cyclotrons **10:**1199
  synchrotrons **4:***395–396*; **10:***1200*–1201;
    **14:**1719
particle detectors **10:**1202–**1205**
  bubble chambers **10:**1201, *1203–1204*,
    *1206*
  cloud chambers **10:**1203
  spark chambers **10:**1204–1205
PDAs *see* personal digital assistants
Peacekeeper missiles **9:**1029
pens, ink **16:***2028–2030*
penstocks **6:**755
personal-area networks (PANs) **9:**1037
personal digital assistants (PDAs)
  **10:**1220–**1221**
PET *see* positron emission tomography
Petronas Towers, Malaysia **2:***247*;
  **13:***1569*
phonographs **4:***494*; **13:**1617–*1618*
photoconductive cells **10:**1235
photocopiers **10:**1232–**1233**
photodiodes (photoemissive cells)
  **10:**1234, *1235*
photoelectric cells **10:**1234–**1235**
photoemissive cells **10:**1234, *1235*
photoengraving **8:**905
photogrammetry **8:**903
photography **10:**1236–**1245**
  aerial **1:**96; **8:***903*; **14:***1735*
  digital **10:**1246–**1251**
  early **10:**1236
  films **10:**1236, *1243*, 1244–1245
  high-speed **10:**1245
  infrared **12:**1448; **14:**1789
  light meters **10:***1242*
  printing techniques **10:**1245, *1251*
  processing films **10:**1242–1245
  Schlieren **10:***1245*
  silver salts and **10:**1243, 1244;
    **13:**1560
  space **8:**904

used in mapmaking **8:***904*, 905
  *see also* cameras
photomultipliers **7:***848*; **12:***1529*
photonics **10:***1160*
phototubes (photoemissive cells)
  **10:**1234, *1235*
phototypesetting **11:**1359
photovoltaic cells **10:**1235
photovoltaic effect **10:**1235
pianos **9:***1078*, 1079
  player **13:***1588*
pickling **5:**622
pinions **6:**667
pipelines **10:**1266–**1271**
  clay pipes **10:**1270–1271
  concrete pipes **10:***1268*, 1271
  history **10:**1266
  laying **10:**1267–1270
  oil and gas **10:***1266–1267*
  pipe manufacture **10:**1270
  plastic pipes **10:***1267*, *1271*
  pumping stations **10:**1267
pistols, automatic **6:**727
pitot tubes **15:***1902*, 1903
pixels **3:**369; **7:**865
  digital camera **10:**1246, *1247–1248*
planers **16:**2021
planes **15:**1832–1833
planing machines **15:**1834
plan position indicators (PPIs)
  **11:**1394, 1395
plasma vapor deposition (PVD)
  **11:***1285*
plastic forming, ceramics **3:**311
*Plongeur* (submarine) **14:**1698
plows **1:***23*, *24*; **11:**1300–**1301**
plywood boats **13:**1553
pneumatic drills **4:***472*
pneumatic tools **7:**802
polymerase chain reaction (PCR)
  **3:**342
porcelain **11:**1330–*1332*, *1333*
positron emission tomography (PET)
  scans **2:***216*; **7:***801*; **8:**935–937, 939;
  **11:***1375*
pottery **11:**1328–**1333**
  dating **1:**100
power generation and distribution
  **4:***500*, 509; **6:**738; **11:**1337–**1342**
  combined cycle power stations
    **11:**1338–1339
  fossil-fuel power stations **11:**1338
  hydroelectric power plants **6:***754*,
    *755*–757; **11:**1337
  nuclear power plants **5:***615*; **9:***1111*,
    1112, *1113*, *1114*, *1115*; **11:***1337*,
    1338, *1341*
  power lines **4:***509*
  solar power stations **13:***1597*

steam condensers **15:**1827–1828
wave power **16:1979–1982**
wind power **5:**552; **11:***1339*, 1341; **15:***1866*; **16:**2011–2014
*see also* tidal power
power shovels **4:**479
power tools **15:***1832*, 1833
pressure gauges **11:**1348–*1349*
printed circuits **11:1350–1351**
  printed circuit boards (PCBs) **8:**990, *991*, *994*
  *see also* silicon chips
printing **11:1352–1359**
  computers and **11:***1358*, *1359*
  dye-sublimation **10:***1251*; **14:**1696
  early presses **11:***1354*
  gravure **11:**1358–1359
  Gutenberg and **11:**1353
  Linotype **11:***1356*
  lithography **11:**1356–1358
  Monotype **11:**1356
  moveable type **11:**1353
  photographs **10:**1245, *1251*
  phototypesetting **11:**1359
  stereotyping **11:***1355*–1356
  typesetting **11:**1354–1355
  woodblock **11:***1352*–*1353*
projectors, motion-picture **9:**1053, *1058*–*1059*
propellers **1:**41; **8:***910–911*; **11:1360–1361**
  aircraft **1:**41; **11:***1361*
  ships' **8:***910–911*; **11:**1360–1361
propulsors, electrical **8:***910*
pulleys **11:1381–1382**
pulse-jets **7:**810
pumps **11:1383–1386**
  centrifugal **11:***1385*–1386
  electromagnetic **11:**1386
  jet **11:**1386
  peristaltic **11:**1385
  positive displacement **11:***1383*, 1384–*1385*
  reciprocating **11:**1385
  rotary **11:**1384, *1385*; **15:**1893
  screw **8:**910; **11:**1383–1384
  steam **8:**1016
  vapor diffusion pumps **15:**1893–*1894*
  wind pumps **16:***2013*, 2014
purse seining **5:**611
pyramids
  Egyptian **1:**105; **2:***240*, 241; **8:**1019; **13:**1568; **14:**1733
  Mayan **1:***104*
  ziggurats **1:**105; **13:**1568

**Q**

quadrants **9:**1084
quarrying **8:**1014, 1019–1020

**R**

racing
  motorcycles **9:**1062
  motor racing **2:**147–149
  race car tires **12:**1500
rack-and-pinion system **3:***350*, *351*
rackets
  squash and badminton **13:**1655
  tennis **13:**1652, *1654*
radio data systems (RDSs) **15:**1843
radiology **8:**932–937
radiosondes **15:**1845
rafts, used for water power **16:***1982*
railroad systems **12:1412–1417**
  cable railroads **3:***260*–*261*
  car brakes **2:**222, 223
  cog railroads
  elevated **12:***1422*
  light **12:***1422–1423*
  marshaling yards **12:**1416–*1417*
  monorails **9:1040–1041**
  signaling and traffic control **12:**1414–*1416*
  transcontinental **12:**1413, *1414*
rallying **2:**149
ramjets **7:**809
ramp metering, for traffic control **15:**1842
rams, hydraulic **11:**1386
random-access memory (RAM) **3:**264, 362, 363
rapid transit systems **12:1422–1425**
  light railways **12:**1422–1423
  monorails **9:1040–1041**
  subway systems **12:**1423–*1424*, *1425*
  trains used in **12:**1425
  trams **14:***1692*, 1694
  trolleybuses **12:**1422; **14:***1691*, 1692
  *see also* streetcars and buses
RDSs (radio data systems) **15:**1843
read-only memory (ROM) **3:**264, 362
rechargeable batteries **2:**172
records, vinyl **13:**1618, *1619*
refrigeration **5:***622*; **6:**661; **12:1432–1434**
  *see also* air-conditioning
relays **12:1439–1440**
remote control **12:1441–1446**, *1481*
  Remotely Operated Vehicles **14:***1706*
remote handling **12:**1443–1444
remote sensors **12:1447–1448**
  animal-tracking **12:***1447*; **16:**2045
  geological **12:**1448
  in archaeology **12:**1448
  military **12:**1447–1448
resistors **4:**503; **12:1455–1456**
respirators **12:***1464*
revolvers **6:***726*–727
rheostats **4:**501

rifles **6:**724
  assault **6:**726
  cartridge **6:**725
roads and road construction **12:1471–1476**; **15:**1840
  *see also* traffic control
road trains **15:**1857
Robodoc **14:**1731
robotics **1:**112–113, *114*, *115*; **12:1477–1482**; **14:***1708*
  and virtual reality systems **15:**1912
  for surgery **12:***1480*; **14:***1729*, 1731
  metalworkers **8:**974, 975
  nanobots (nanorobots) **8:**995; **9:***1081*; **12:**1482
  remote-controlled robots **12:***1444*
  *see also* artificial intelligence
*Rocket* (locomotive) **7:***870*, 871
rockets **2:**160; **7:**806; **12:1489–1492**
  hybrid **12:***1490*
  propellants **10:**1179; **12:***1490*, 1491–*1492*
roller coasters **12:1493–1496**
Romans, ancient
  agriculture **1:**24
  architecture **1:**106
  brickmaking **2:**243
  bridges **2:**230, *231*
  buildings **2:**240–241
  calendar **15:**1815
  firefighting **5:**606
  locks (security) **7:**869
  mortar **2:**244
  numerals **9:**1124, *1125*
  pipes **10:**1266
  roads **12:**1471
rotoscoping **9:**1056–1057
rumble strips **10:***1268*, 1271

**S**

safes and vaults **12:1503–1506**
  *see also* locks
sailing **8:**908; **12:1507–1512**
Salford transverse oscillators **15:***1804*
Salter's duck **16:***1981*, 1982
sandblasting **1:**12, *13*
sanders **1:***12*; **16:***2021*, 2022
*saqiyas* **11:**1383
sawmills **15:***1813*
saws **15:***1831*, 1832
  band saws and jigsaws **16:**2021
  circular (table) **16:**2019–*2020*, 2021
  radial **16:**2020
saxophones **9:***1076*, 1077
scales *see* balances and weighing machines
scanners, image **12:1527–1529**
  *see also* photocopiers
SCOOT (split-cycle-and-off-set-optimizing technique) **15:**1841–1842

scramjets **1:**45; **7:**810
scrapers, motor **4:**481
screwdrivers **15:***1830*
scuba diving **4:***446, 447,* 448–449
Scud missiles **9:**1030
Sea Fighter **16:***1962*
seaplanes **1:***44*
search engines, Internet **7:**790, *791,* 792
seat belts, car **2:**146–147
seed drills **1:**26
Seikan Tunnel **15:**1865
seining, purse **5:**611
Semantic Web **7:**793
sensors
  medical **8:**941
  remote *see* remote sensors
  robotic **12:**1480–1481
separators **3:**307
servomechanisms **13:1544–1545;**
  **15:**1800
servomotors **13:**1545
sextants **9:**1084, *1085*
*shadufs* **11:**1383
shapers **15:**1834; **16:**2021
shells *see* bombs and shells
ships and shipbuilding **13:1550–1555**
  autopilots **13:**1545
  boatbuilding **13:***1551–1554*
  bulk carriers **13:***1555*
  container ships **13:***1555*
  cruise ships **13:***1550*
  drill ships **9:**1147
  dry cargo vessels **13:**1555
  gyrocompasses **6:**730
  gyrostabilizers **6:**730
  lay-barges **10:***1269–1270*
  propulsion *see* marine propulsion
  ship navigation **9:***1083*–1088
  sonar **13:**1611–*1612*
  speedboats **13:***1554*
  stability **13:**1550–1551
  steamships **8:***908*
  tankers **13:**1555; **14:1746–1749**
  warships **16:1957–1962**
  *see also* hovercraft; hydrofoils; sailing
shock absorbers **14:**1736, *1737*
shotguns **6:**727
shrapnel **2:**206
*Shrek* (movie) **1:***83*
Sidewinder missiles **9:**1031
silencers **6:**727
silicon chips (integrated circuits;
  microchips) **3:**359, *360,* 362; **5:***526,*
  *527;* **8:***990,* 991–994; **11:**1350–1351;
  **13:**1557
  future uses of **8:**995
  identity implants **8:**995
  in calculators **3:**264
  in televisions **14:**1774

production of **7:**778; **8:**991–992;
  **13:***1540, 1556*
  switches in **14:***1739*
  transistors in **8:**991
silk **5:***596,* 597; **14:**1780, 1781, 1782
SIM (subscriber identification module)
  cards **9:**1036
skyscrapers **1:**109; **2:**246–*247;* **6:**708;
  **13:1568–1571**
  *see also* building techniques
Skysweeper guns **9:**1030
slides (transparencies) **10:***1244,* 1245
smart technology **8:**990
  bombs **2:**209; **6:***721*
  shells **2:**207
smoke alarms (detectors) **5:***606;* **15:***1850*
smokejacks **6:**665
smoking, food **5:**622
software **3:**365; **13:1587–1592**
  antivirus **16:***1926*–1927
  bugs **13:**1590, 1592
  computer programs **3:**361, 362;
    **13:**1588, *1589*–1591
  graphical user interface (GUI) **3:***365;*
    **7:**819; **13:***1591*
  software engineering **13:**1591–1592
  voice-recognition **16:***1935*
  word-processing programs **16:**1935,
    2030
solar energy **13:1597–1602**
  solar panels **5:***552;* **13:**1597–*1598*
  solar ponds **13:**1601–1602
  solar-powered vehicles **1:***62;* **13:**1600,
    *1601*
  solar power generators **14:***1786*
  solar power satellites (SPSs) **13:**1602
  solar water heaters **13:**1597–1598, 1601
  using mirrors **5:**550; **13:***1597,*
    *1599–1600*
  using solar (photoelectric) cells **5:**550;
    **10:***1234,* 1235; **13:***1602,* 1625
solenoids **5:***523;* **7:***891*–892;
  **13:1607–1608**
Sopwith F1 Camel **16:***1951*
sound recording **13:1617–1620**
  digital **13:**1620
  Edison's phonograph **4:***494;*
    **13:**1617–*1618*
  microphones **10:**1265; **13:**1618–*1619*
  records **13:**1618
  using tape **13:**1620
  *see also* CDs (compact discs); speakers
spark plugs **3:***309;* **11:**1299
Sparrow missiles **9:**1031
speakers (loudspeakers) **5:***525;* **13:***1614,*
  1619, **1640–1641;** **15:***1845*
  moving-coil **13:***1641*
  ribbon **13:**1641
spectrograms, speech **16:**1934–1935

spectroscopy **10:**1256; **13:1644–1649**
  absorption and emission spectra
    **13:**1646
  and compounds **13:**1646–1647
  and light emitted by stars **13:***1648;*
    **14:**1674
  mass spectroscopy **13:**1648
  spectrographs **13:**1645, 1647–1648
  spectrometers **13:***1645, 1646,* 1647
  spectrophotometers **13:**1647, 1648
  spectroscopes **7:**844; **13:***1647;* **14:***1674,*
    1716
  ultraviolet **15:**1876
  *see also* nuclear magnetic resonance
speedboats **13:***1554*
speed cameras **15:***1842*
speed increasers **6:**667
speed reducers **6:**667
sphygmomanometers **8:**939–*940*
spillways **6:***757*
spinning **14:**1781, 1782, 1784; **16:**2023,
  *2025*
  spinning jenny **14:**1782; **16:**2025–2026
  spinning mule **14:**1782; **16:**2026
spirit levels **14:***1733*
split-cycle-and-off-set-optimizing
  technique (SCOOT) **15:**1841–1842
spoilers **1:**41–42
spokeshaves **15:**1833
sports equipment **13:1652–1658**
  athletics **13:***1656*–1657
  badminton **13:**1655
  baseball **13:***1657*–1658
  football **13:***1658*
  golf **13:**1655–1656
  ice hockey **13:**1658
  squash **13:**1655
  tennis **13:**1652, *1654*–1655
spread-spectrum frequency hopping
  **9:**1037
springs **14:1668–1669,** 1736
  air **14:**1669, 1736–1737
  coil **14:**1736, *1737*
  extension **14:**1668
  leaf **14:**1668–*1669,* 1736
  torsion-bar **14:***1737*
sprinklers, water **1:**59
SQUIDS *see* superconducting quantum
  interference devices
SR-N1 (hovercraft) **6:***746,* 747
Starstreak missiles **9:**1029
stealth technology
  aircraft **1:**44; **16:***1958*
  ships **16:**1962
steam engines **1:**26; **2:**140; **7:**870;
  **8:**909–910; **14:1684–1688**
  boilers **14:**1686, 1688
  compound **14:**1687–1688
  double-acting **14:**1686, *1687*

governors 13:1544–*1545*
single-acting 14:*1686*
steam locomotives 7:*870*–873, 874; 14:*1686*, 1687, 1688
*see also* turbines, steam
stereotyping 11:*1355*–1356
stethoscopes 8:939, *940*
Stinger missiles 9:*1030*
Stirling engines 14:**1689–1690**
stock-car racing 2:149
STOL aircraft 1:44
*see also* V/STOL aircraft
streetcars and buses 14:**1691–1694**
buses 14:*1693*–1694
cable cars 3:*261*; 14:*1691*, *1693*
streetcars 12:*1422*; 14:*1691*–*1692*, 1694
trams 14:*1692*, 1694
trolleybuses 12:1422; 14:*1691*, 1692
streetlights 7:855; 12:*1476*; 15:1824
submachine guns 6:726
submarines 14:**1697–1702**
breathing underwater 14:1699
diving and surfacing 14:1698, *1699*
earliest 14:*1697*
engines 14:1698
navigation 14:1702
nuclear-powered 14:1698, 1702
propulsion 8:910
steering 13:1545; 14:*1699*, *1700*
the hull 14:1699–1700
weapons 9:*1032*–*1033*; 14:1700–*1702*
submersibles 14:**1703–1708**
bathyscaphes 14:*1704*–1706
bathyspheres 14:*1703*–1704
diving bells 4:449, 450–451
propulsion 14:1708
uses 14:1706–*1708*
*see also* submarines
Subroc missiles 9:1031
subscriber identification module cards
*see* SIM cards 9:1036
substations, electricity 11:*1340*, 1342; 15:*1846*
subway systems 12:*1423*–*1424*
trains 12:*1425*
supercharging 4:422–423
supercomputers 3:*363*, 364
superconducting quantum interference devices (SQUIDS) 14:1719
surface mounting 11:*1350*
surveying 14:**1732–1735**
and mapmaking 8:*901*, 903
geodetic 14:1732
plane 14:1732
seismic 5:581; 6:695–696; 9:*1146*; 12:1532
using triangulation 14:1732–1733
using trilateration 14:1732

suspension 14:**1736–1737**
automobile 2:144; 14:*1736*–*1737*
bicycle 2:177
hydropneumatic 14:1742
swamp buggies 1:75
switches 14:**1738–1739**
mercury 15:1799–1800
solenoids and 13:1608
time 15:1823–1824
Sydney Harbor Bridge 2:233

**T**
tablet PCs 3:*363*
tachymetry 14:1735
Tacoma Narrows Bridge 2:*232*; 12:*1457*
tailraces 6:755
tankers 13:1555; 14:**1746–1749**
hydraulic valves 6:753
tanks 14:**1740–1745**
amphibious 1:74–75
anti-tank mines and 8:1005, 1006, 1007
bridge-laying 14:1745
underwater 1:75
tape recorders 13:1620
tapered channels (TAPCHANs) 16:1981
tapes, magnetic-storage 7:*885*–*887*, 888
Tarbela Dam 4:405
telecommunications 14:**1752–1759**
fiber-optic 5:602; 10:1160; 14:*1755*, 1756–1757
*see also* telegraphy; telephones; videophones
telegraphy 14:**1752–1753**
Edison and 4:493
Marconi and 8:*906*–907
telemetry 12:1444–*1446*, 1520
telephones
Bakelite 11:*1286*
cables 14:*1754*, 1756–1757
development 5:526–527; 14:*1752*, 1753–1754
Edison and 4:494
fiber-optic systems 5:602; 14:*1755*, 1756–1757
making connections 14:1754–1756
microwave signals 1:*90*
multiplexed signals 14:1758
receivers 14:1754–1755
transmitters 14:1754
video 14:*1774*
*see also* cellular phones
telescopes 14:*1672*, 1760–1767
aperture synthesis 14:1765
gamma-ray 1:125
Hubble Space Telescope (HST) 1:124; 5:*538*; 9:*1136*; 11:*1304*; 13:*1602*; 14:*1766*–1767
infrared 7:777
Keplerian 14:1760

large space telescopes 1:124
of Galileo 6:655–656; 14:1760
of Herschel (William) 6:743
of Huygens 6:749
of Newton 9:*1103*; 14:1760–1761
radio 1:124–*125*; 9:1135; 14:*1762*–*1765*; 15:*1878*
reflecting 14:1760–1762, *1763*
refracting 14:1760, 1762, *1763*
Schmidt camera 10:1244
solar 14:*1712*, 1713
space 13:*1644*; 14:1766–1767
transits 14:1734
television 14:**1768–1775**
and color separation overlay (CSO) 14:*1773*
antennas 1:90; 11:1311
broadcasting 2:*235*–*239*; 8:1003; 14:1770–1771
cable 2:236–237, **250–253**; 14:1770
cameras 14:1769–1770
cathode-ray tubes in 5:532–533; 14:*1770*
closed-circuit (CCTV) 14:1770
color 14:1769, *1770*, 1771–1772
digital 2:238; 5:528–529; 14:1775
flat-screen 7:865
in vehicles 14:*1775*
LCD screens 14:*1772*, 1774
master antenna (MATV) 2:250–251
microchip technology and 14:1774
plasma screen 14:*1768*, 1774–1775
receiving 14:1771–1773
remote controls 7:793
satellite 2:237, 252–253; 3:352; 14:1775
screens 7:*879*; 14:*1768*, *1772*, 1774–1775
signals 11:1311
stations 1:90
Tesla coils 14:*1779*
video recording 14:1774
tellurometers 14:1733
terrain contour matching (TERCOM) system 6:720
Teton Dam, Idaho 4:405–406
tetrahertz scanners 10:1161
textiles 14:**1780–1785**
dyes 4:466–469; 14:*1781*
finishing treatments 14:1785
"intelligent" fabrics 14:1784
uses in industry 14:1783
*see also* cotton; fiber; silk; wool
thaumotropes 9:*1053*
theodolites 8:*901*; 14:1733, *1734*, 1735
thermal imaging 7:777; 10:*1161*
thermocouples 11:1299; 14:1787; 15:1798
thermography 7:*776*; 8:933; 14:**1788–1789**; 15:1798

thermomechanical generators 14:1690
thermometers 15:1796–1798
  bimetallic strip 15:1798
  bulb 8:980; 15:1796, 1797
  digital 15:1797
  electrical 15:1798
  liquid crystals used in 7:864
  liquid-in-glass 15:1796
  maximum-minimum 15:1797–1798
  mercury 8:951; 15:1797
  strip 15:1798
  tympanic (infrared) 15:1798
  see also thermocouples
thermoresistors (thermistors) 15:1798
thermos flasks (vacuum flasks) 15:1895
thermostats 12:1432, 1440;
  15:1799–1800
Thor missiles 9:1029
Three Gorges Dam 4:407
Thrust SSC (jet-powered car) 2:147
thyristors 13:1543; 14:1738–1739
tidal power 5:552; 6:757; 9:1143;
  15:1803–1806, 1810
TIFF files 10:1248, 1249
tiles, ceramic 3:308, 309, 311
tiltmeters 16:1941
tires 12:1497, 1500; 14:1736
  bicycle 2:176
  racing car 2:148
Titanic (ship) 14:1708
Titan missiles 9:1029
toilets 13:1549
Tomahawk missiles 9:1028, 1031–1032
Tom Thumb (locomotive) 12:1412
tools and tool manufacture
  15:1830–1835
  see also woodworking
torches, oxyacetylene 10:1178
torpedoes 9:1028, 1032–1033; 14:1701
touch-screen technology 10:1220, 1221
towers 13:1571
tracked air-cushion vehicles 9:1041
traffic control 12:1476; 15:1840–1843
  speed limits 12:1476
trains
  automatic 12:1425
  brakes 2:222–223, 224; 12:1425
  bullet 7:874, 875
  electric 12:1425
  maglev 7:858, 859, 875; 9:1041;
    10:1261; 14:1718
  rapid-transport-system 12:1425
  see also locomotives
trams 14:1692, 1694
transducers 10:1265; 13:1640;
  15:1844–1845
  capacitative 15:1845
  displacement 15:1844
  electrostrictive 15:1872

inductive 15:1845
  magnetostrictive 15:1871–1872
  micromechanical friction 15:1844
  piezoelectric 15:1871
  potentiometric 15:1844–1845
  strain-gauge 2:158; 15:1845
  ultrasound 8:937; 15:1871–1872
  see also microphones; speakers
transformers 6:672, 756–757;
  7:772, 773; 11:1337–1338, 1340,
  1342; 15:1846–1847
  flyback 14:1779
  the first 7:772
transistors 5:527–528, 533; 8:990, 994;
  14:1768; 15:1848–1850
  field effect (FETs) 13:1543; 15:1850
  in microchips 8:991
  insulated-gate field effect (IGFETs)
    15:1850
  invention 3:360; 5:527; 13:1542;
    14:1768; 15:1849
  junction (bipolar) 13:1542;
    15:1849–1850
  junction-gate field effect (JFETs)
    13:1542, 1543; 15:1850
  light-emitting 10:1161
  semiconductors 15:1848–1849
transits 14:1734
Transrapid system 7:859
TRANSYT system 15:1841
travelators 5:545
trawling, stern 5:612
Trident missiles 9:1029; 14:1702
Trieste (submersible) 14:1706
triodes 5:527, 533; 11:1398
Trojan horses 3:366
Trojans (computer viruses) 16:1925
trolleybuses 12:1422; 14:1691, 1692
trombones 9:1077
trucks 15:1855–1858
  brakes 2:222, 224; 15:1856
  forklift 5:634–635
trumpets 9:1077
Tube, London 12:1423, 1424
tunneling 12:1424; 15:1862–1865
turbines 15:1866–1869
  gas see gas turbines
  hydraulic 5:518; 6:755–756
  impulse 6:755–756; 15:1867
  reactor 6:756
  steam 5:518; 6:738; 8:910; 14:1688;
    15:1867, 1868–1869
  Straflo 15:1805, 1806
  water 6:755–756; 15:1803, 1805, 1806,
    1866–1868
  wind 5:518; 11:1339; 15:1866; 16:2014
Turbinia (ship) 8:910
turbochargers 4:422–423; 15:1857–1858
Turing test 1:113

turntables, record 13:1620
tweeters 13:1641
typesetting 11:1354–1355
typewriters see keyboards and
  typewriters

U
UHT process 5:621
ultracentrifuges 3:307
ultrafiltration 10:1172
ultralights 1:43
unattended ground sensors (UGSs)
  12:1448
Universal Product Code (UPC) 2:165
Universal Resource Locators (URLs)
  7:790

V
V-1 missiles 9:1028, 1031
V-2 rockets 12:1491
V22 Osprey (aircraft) 16:1961
vacuum cleaners 15:1893, 1895
vacuum (thermos) flasks 15:1895
vacuum tubes (thermionic valves)
  5:526, 527, 533
  diodes 5:527, 533
  triodes 5:527, 533; 11:1398
valves 15:1898–1899
  artificial heart-valves 15:1899
  balance 15:1898
  check 15:1899
  demand 4:448, 449
  gate 15:1898, 1899
  globe 15:1899
  hydraulic 6:753
  internal combustion engine 15:1899
  lift 15:1898
  needle 15:1899
  slide 15:1899
  steam 15:1899
  stop 15:1898–1899
  thermionic see vacuum tubes
vaults 12:1504, 1506
vellum 10:1185
ventilators 8:942, 945
Verrazano Narrows Bridge 2:233
very high frequency omnidirectional
  radio (VOR) 9:1086
Very Large Array (VLA) 1:89; 14:1764,
  1765
very large-scale integration (VLSI)
  8:991
very long baseline interferometry
  (VLBI) 14:1765
videophones 9:1037; 15:1908–1909
video recording 14:1774
  videocassette recorders (VCRs) 7:887
  videocassettes 7:887
  videotape recorders (VTRs) 7:887

violins 9:*1074*, 1075; 12:*1458*
virtual reality (VR) 3:*367*; 15:**1910–1913**
viruses, computer 3:366; 16:**1924–1927**
viscometers 16:1928–1929
voice analysis 16:**1934–1937**
voltaic pile 2:169–*170*; 16:*1943*
"Vomit Comet" 16:1998
V/STOL aircraft 7:*808*; 16:**1944–1947**, 1958, 1960
VTOL aircraft 1:44–45

## W

Wankel engines (rotary engines) 7:787; 8:912; 14:1685–1686; 16:**1948–1949**
WAP *see* wireless application protocol
warplanes 16:**1951–1956**
  against ships 16:1957–1958
warships 16:**1957–1962**
  nuclear-powered 16:*1960*, 1961
washboards, on boats 13:1551
washing machines 16:**1963–1964**
water frames 14:1782; 16:2026
waterjets 8:911, *912*
water wheels 15:1866; 16:*2003*
watt-hour meters 4:501
wave power 16:**1979–1982**
weaving 14:1780–1781, 1782; 16:2026
webcams 7:789
weighing machines *see* balances and weighing machines
welding 16:**1999–2002**
  arc 11:1285; 16:1999–*2000*
  electron-beam 16:2001
  explosion 16:2002
  friction 16:2002
  gas 16:1999
  laser 16:2001–*2002*
  plasma 16:*2000*–2001
  resistance 16:2002
  using ultrasonics 15:1873; 16:2002
wheel-locks 6:724
wheels 16:**2003–2004**
  bicycle 2:176
wide-area networks (WANs) 3:364–365
winches and windlasses 16:**2005–2006**
windlasses 16:2005, *2006*
windmills and wind pumps 16:**2011–2014**
  windmills 13:1544; 15:1866; 16:*2011*–2014
  wind pumps 16:*2013*, 2014
  wind turbines 5:518; 11:*1339*; 15:*1866*; 16:*2014*
windows, stained-glass 6:703–704
wingsails 12:1512
wire and cable 16:**2015–2018**
wire guidance systems 9:1029, 1033
wireless application protocol (WAP) 9:1036

wood
  building with 2:*242*–243
  paper made from wood pulp 10:1185, *1186–1187*
woodworking 16:**2019–2022**
woofers 13:1641
wool 5:596–597; 14:1780; 16:**2023–2026**
  *see also* spinning
Woolworth Building 13:1569
World Product Code (WPC) 2:166
World Wide Web 7:*789*–790
worms (computer viruses) 16:1925
  Code Red 16:1926
writing tools 16:**2027–2030**
  ink pens 16:*2028–2030*
  keyboards and typewriters 7:**817–819**; 16:2030
  word processors 16:1935, 2030

## X

X-29 (aircraft) 16:1953, 1956
xerography 10:1232

## Y

yachts 12:*1508*, 1511

## Z

Zeya Dam 4:405
ziggurats 1:105; 13:1568
zoetropes 1:84; 9:1052

## PEOPLE

## A

Abbe, Ernst 8:999
Adams, John Couch 9:1092–*1093*
Ader, Clément 1:37
Agassiz, Louis 6:690
Agricola (Georg Bauer) 8:*967*, 1015
Airy, George 9:1093
Alcock, John 1:39
Aldrin, Edwin "Buzz" 9:1042, *1043*
Alvarez, Walter 6:*687*
Amati, Andrea 9:1075
Ampère, André-Marie 1:**72–73**; 4:507–*508*
Anaximander the Elder 5:538, 567
Andreessen, Marc 7:790
Angström, Anders Jonas 13:1647
Appolonius of Perga 8:921
Arago, François 4:508
Archimedes 1:**102–103**; 3:265; 6:751; 7:841; 8:910; 11:1383; 13:*1643*
Argand, Aimé 7:853
Aristotle 1:**110–111**, 114, 120; 3:320; 10:1259
  and classification 1:111; 3:332
  and motion 9:1049

and the elements 5:538
diving bell 4:446
Arkwright, Richard 14:1782; 16:2026
Armstrong, Edwin H. 11:1398
Armstrong, Neil A. 9:1042, *1043*
Arrhenius, Svante 5:566
Asimov, Isaac 12:1478
Atanasoff, John Vincent 3:360
Avogadro, Amadeo 10:1215

## B

Baade, Walter 9:1107
Babbage, Charles 2:**150–151**; 3:359; 13:1588
Bacon, Francis 6:644
Bacon, Roger 5:578
Baekeland, Leo Hendrik 11:1286
Baeyer, Adolf von 11:1286
Baird, John Logie 2:*235*; 14:1768, 1771
Bakewell, Robert 1:25–26
Barber, John 6:665
Bardeen, John 3:360; 5:527; 13:1542; 14:1768; 15:1849
Barker, Robert 15:1866
Barlow, Edward 15:1820
Barnard, Christiaan 14:1730
Barron, Robert 7:869
Bartlett, Neil 7:774
Barton, Otis 14:1703
Basov, Nikolai 7:827
Bauer, Georg *see* Agricola
Becquerel, Antoine-Henri 3:322; 4:399; 10:1261; 11:1401
Beebe, Charles William 14:1703
Beijerinck, Martinus 8:986
Bell, Alexander Graham 5:526–527; 8:965; 14:*1752*, 1753–1754
Bell-Burnell, Jocelyn 14:1677
Benz, Karl 2:141; 7:783
Berger, Hans 8:941
Berliner, Emile 13:1618
Berners-Lee, Timothy 7:*789*, 793
Bernoulli, Daniel 15:1902
Bernoulli, Jakob and Johann 8:922
Bertin, Jean 9:1041
Berzelius, Jöns Jakob 3:314, 315; 11:1296–1297
Bessemer, Henry 7:799
Biró, László and Georg 16:2029
Bjerknes, Vilhelm 8:981
Blériot, Louis 1:37
Bohr, Niels 2:139, **204–205**; 3:322; 5:540
Bolsover, Thomas 13:1580
Boltzmann, Ludwig 8:927
Bolyai, János 8:922
Bondi, Hermann 15:1881
Booth, Hubert Cecil 15:1895
Borchardt, Hugo 6:727
Bosch, Robert 6:646, *647*

Bourne, William **14**:1697
Boyle, Robert **5**:538–539; **6**:*663*
Braithwaite, John **5**:606
Bramah, Joseph **6**:751
Branly, Edouard-Eugéne **11**:1397
Brattain, Walter **3**:360; **5**:527; **13**:1542; **14**:1768; **15**:1849
Braun, Anton **7**:783
Braun, Karl **8**:907
Bray, John **1**:84
Breazeal, Cynthia **1**:*115*
Breguet, Louis-Charles **6**:742
Brentano, Franz **11**:1378
Briggs, Robert **3**:342
Brin, Sergey **7**:*791*
Broglie, Louis-Victor-Pierre-Raymond de **11**:1391
Brongniart, Alexandre **11**:1332
Brunel, Isambard Kingdom **14**:1752
Brunel, Marc Isambard **12**:1424; **15**:1862
Bunsen, Robert **13**:1645
Burdin, Claude **15**:1867
Bushnell, David **14**:*1697*

**C**

Calley, John **14**:1684
Cannizzaro, Stanislao **8**:948–949; **10**:1215
Carlisle, Anthony **4**:507
Carlson, Chester F. **10**:1232
Carothers, W. H. **5**:598; **11**:1321
Cartwright, Edmund **14**:1783
Cascariolo, Vincenzo **7**:878
Caxton, William **11**:1353
Cayley, George **1**:36
Celsius, Anders **15**:1796
Chabaneau, François **11**:1296
Chadwick, James **2**:139; **5**:540
Chain, Ernst **1**:91; **5**:617
Challis, James **9**:1093
Chancourtois, Alexandre-Émile Béguyer de **10**:1215–1216
Chandrasekhar, Subrahmanyan **2**:197–198
Chapman, Colin **2**:148
Chargaff, Erwin **9**:1038–1039
Charles, Jacques-Alexandre-César **2**:163; **6**:664
Christy, James **11**:1305
Cierva, Juan de la **6**:742
Claude, Georges **7**:854
Clausius, Rudolf **8**:926–927
Clement, William **15**:1820
Cockerell, Christopher **6**:*746*
Cohl, Émile **1**:84
Cohn, Ferdinand **8**:986
Coke, Thomas **1**:25
Collins, Michael **9**:*1043*
Colmar, Charles Thomas de **3**:263

Colt, Samuel **6**:*726*, 727
Compton, Arthur Holly **11**:*1390*
Congreve, William **12**:1490
Connolly, J. **11**:1373
Cookworthy, William **11**:1331
Coolidge, William David **16**:2031
Cooper, Peter **7**:871; **12**:1412
Copernicus, Nicolaus **1**:120; **3**:372–373; **14**:1711; **15**:1877
Coriolis, Gustave de **16**:2007
Correns, Carl Erich **6**:677; **8**:947
Cousteau, Jacques **4**:*447*, 448
Craigie, Andrew **4**:462
Crick, Francis, and James Watson **4**:390–391, 454; **8**:987
Cristofori, Bartolomeo di Francesco **9**:1079
Crompton, Samuel **14**:1782; **16**:2026
Ctesibius of Alexandria **9**:1074
Cugnot, Nicolas **2**:140; **7**:870
Curie, Marie and Pierre **3**:322; **4**:398–399; **11**:1401, *1402*
Curtiss, Glenn **1**:38
Czochralski, Jan **4**:397

**D**

Daguerre, Louis-Jacques-Mandé **10**:1243
Dahl, Carl **10**:1185
Daimler, Gottlieb **2**:141; **7**:*783*; **9**:1060
Dalton, James **4**:402–403; **10**:1261
Dalton, John **3**:321
Darby, Abraham **2**:202, 231
Darwin, Charles **2**:186; **3**:332; **4**:408–409; **5**:*568–569*; **6**:685
  inspired by Linnaeus **7**:860
Davenport, Thomas **5**:516
Davis, John **9**:1084
Davis, William Morris **6**:690; **7**:821–822; **12**:1467–1468
Davy, Humphry **3**:*321*; **4**:507; **5**:540, 586; **7**:853; **8**:965
  and aluminum **1**:67
  and photography **10**:1242
  and sodium **13**:1586
  safety lamp **8**:1016–1017
Deere, John **1**:26; **11**:1301
De Forest, Lee **5**:527; **11**:1398
Democritus (Demokritos) **5**:539; **10**:1206, 1261
Descartes, René **8**:921, *922*; **11**:1377; **12**:1421
Dewar, James **15**:1895
Dick, Philip K. **1**:112–113
Diesel, Rudolph **4**:*421*; **7**:783
Diophantus of Alexandria **1**:53
Dirac, Paul **11**:*1392*
Disney, Walt **1**:84, 85; **9**:1058
Döbereiner, Johann **10**:1215
Dobzhansky, Theodoosius **5**:570

Domagk, Gerhard **8**:943
Doppler, Christian Johann **4**:456; **9**:1087; **13**:1615
Drake, Edwin L. **9**:1145
Drebbel, Cornelius van **14**:1697, 1698; **15**:1799
Duesbury, William **11**:1331
Dunlop, John Boyd **2**:175; **14**:1736
du Pont, Eleuthère Irénée **7**:*834*
Duryea, Charles and Frank **2**:141
Dvorak, August **7**:818–819

**E**

Eastman, George **10**:1243
Eckert, John Presper **3**:360
Edison, Thomas **4**:493–494
  and the telephone **4**:494
  electric lamps (lightbulbs) **3**:289; **4**:*493*; **7**:854
  kinetoscope **9**:1052
  phonograph **4**:*494*; **13**:1617–*1618*
  power plant **4**:509; **11**:1337
Ehrlich, Paul **8**:942
Einstein, Albert **2**:197; **4**:495–496; **10**:1259; **12**:*1436*
  and calculus **3**:266
  and light **7**:826–827; **11**:1389–1390
  and motion close to the speed of light **5**:628; **9**:1051
  and nuclear fission **9**:1112, 1121
  and the photoelectric effect **11**:1390
  and time **15**:1818
  general theory of relativity **3**:266; **4**:496; **6**:718; **12**:1438
  mass-energy equation **5**:551, 614; **6**:653; **8**:919, 924; **12**:1438
  special theory of relativity **4**:495–496; **8**:955; **12**:1436–1438
Einthoven, Willem **8**:940
Emphedocles **5**:538
Engelbart, Douglas **7**:819
Eratosthenes **8**:929
Ericsson, John **5**:606
Euclid **8**:*920*
Eudoxus of Cnidus **8**:921
Euler, Leonhard **8**:922
Evinrude, Ole **8**:911

Faraday, Michael **5**:586–587
  and electromagnetism **4**:508; **5**:523, 524–525, *587*; **7**:772
  and the first transformer **7**:*772*, 773
  laws of electrolysis **5**:521, 587
Farenheit, Daniel Gabriel **8**:951; **15**:1796
Farnsworth, Philo **14**:1769
Feng, Milton **10**:1161
Ferdinand II, Grand Duke **15**:1796
Fermi, Enrico **9**:1112
Feynman, Richard **9**:1081, *1082*

Fibonacci, Leonardo **8:**921
Fischer, Emil **3:***280*
Fisher, R. A. **5:**570
Fitch, John **8:**909
Fitzroy, Robert **8:**981
Flamsteed, John **8:**996
Fleischer, Max **1:**84
Fleming, Alexander **1:***92*; **2:***154*;
    **5:***616–617*; **8:***942*
Fleming, John Ambrose
   diode **5:**527
    left-hand rule **5:***524*
    right-hand rule **5:***524*, 525
Flettner, Anton **6:**742
Florey, Howard **1:**91; **5:**617
Focke, Heinrich **6:**742
Focke, Wilhelm Olbers **8:**947
Fokker, Anthony **1:**38–39
Ford, Henry **2:***141*; **12:**1472
Fortin, Jean, barometer **2:**167–168
Fossett, Steve **2:***164*
Fourneyron, Benoit **15:**1867
Francis, James **6:**756
Franklin, Benjamin **4:**506; **7:**857
Franklin, Rosalind **4:**391, 454
Frasch, Hermann **14:**1710
Fraunhofer, Joseph von **13:**1645, *1648*
Fresnel, Augustin **7:**851
Freud, Sigmund **11:***1373*, 1374
Frye, Thomas **11:**1331
Fuller, Buckminster **10:**1257
Fulton, Robert **8:**910; **14:**1697
Fust, Johann **11:**1353

**G**

Galen **3:**326; **4:***462*
Galileo Galilei **6:**655–656
   and gravity **6:**716; **8:**917
   and pendulums **15:**1816
   and the Copernican theory **1:**120;
    **6:***655*, 656, **15:**1879
   and the planets **6:***656*; **7:**813
   telescopes **6:**655–656; **10:**1260;
    **14:**1760
Galle, Johann Gottfried **9:**1093
Galvani, Luigi **2:**169; **4:**506–507
Garnerin, André-Jacques **10:**1190
Garros, Roland **16:**1952
Gascoigne, William **8:**996
Gates, William **3:***360*; **13:**1591
Gauss, Carl **8:**922
Gay-Lussac, Joseph-Louis **6:***664*
Geiger, Hans Wilhelm **6:**669
Gilbert, William **4:**505; **7:**891
Glaser, Donald A. **10:**1203
Glidden, Carlos **7:**817
Goddard, Robert H. **12:**1490
Godfrey, Thomas **9:**1084
Gold, Thomas **15:**1881

Gould, Gordon **7:**826
Graham, Thomas **10:***1170*
Greathead, James Henry **15:**1862
Green, Andy **2:**147
Gresley, Nigel **7:**874
Grew, Nehemiah **8:**998
Guarneri, Andrea **9:**1075
Guericke, Otto von **4:**505
Guettard, Jean-Etienne **7:**834
Gurdon, John **3:**342
Gutenberg, Johannes **10:**1185; **11:**1353
Guth, Alan **15:**1881

**H**

Hadley, John **9:**1084
Hahn, Otto **9:**1111–1112
Haigh, John George **1:**15
Haldane, J. B. S. **5:**570
Hale, William **12:**1490
Hall, Asaph **8:**914
Hall, Charles Martin **1:**67
Halley, Edmund **1:**119
Hamilton, William **8:**911
Hanna, William, and Joseph Barbera
   **1:***85*
Hargreaves, James **14:**1782
Harrison, John **9:**1085; **15:***1816*, *1820*,
   1821
Harvey, William **3:**326–328; **8:**938;
   **10:**1263
Hauksbee, Francis **4:**505
Hawking, Stephen **2:**199; **16:***1934*
Heisenberg, Werner Karl **11:**1392
Helmholtz, Hermann von **5:**584
Henry, Joseph **7:**772, *773*
Henslow, John **4:**408
Heracleides **8:**952
Hero of Alexandria **1:**112; **7:**870;
   **10:**1263
Héroult, Paul **1:**67
Herschel, Caroline **6:**743, 744
Herschel, John **2:**150; **15:**1878
Herschel, William **6:**743–744; **15:**1878,
   1885, 1886
Hertz, Heinrich Rudolf **2:**234; **4:**509;
   **5:**527; **11:**1397
Hickman, Henry Hill **1:**76–77
Hipparchus **14:**1670
Hippocrates **8:**938; **14:***1726*
Holland, John P. **14:**1697
Hollerith, Hermann **3:**359
Holonyak, Nick **10:**1161
Homer **14:**1709
Hooke, Robert
   and elasticity **4:**497
   and Jupiter **7:***812*
   microscopy **3:**300; **8:**986, 998
   quarrel with Newton **9:**1103
Horner, William George **1:**84

Hounsfield, Godfrey **8:***939*
Hoyle, Fred **15:**1881
Hubble, Edwin Powell **1:**123; **15:**1878
Humboldt, Alexander von **6:**664
Hutton, James **6:**689
Huygens, Christiaan **6:748–749**
   and light **6:***749*; **7:**846, *847*
   clock **6:***748*; **9:**1085; **10:**1213; **15:**1820
   experiment with engines **7:**782
   telescope **6:**749
Hyatt, John Wesley **11:**1286

**I**

Imhotep **5:**553

**J**

Jacquard, Joseph-Marie **13:**1587–1588
James, William **11:**1378
Jansky, Karl **14:**1763
Janssen, Zacharias **8:**998
Jenkins, C. F. **14:**1768
Jenner, Edward **7:804–805**; **8:**938;
   **15:**1889–1890
Jenny, William **13:**1569
Jobs, Steve **3:***360*
Joliot-Curie, Irène and Frédéric **4:**399
Josephson, Brian **14:**1720
Joule, James **7:***816*; **11:***1335*

**K**

Kasparov, Gary **1:***112*, 114
Kay, John **14:**1782, 1783
Kekulé von Stradonitz, Friedrich
   **10:**1166
Kellogg, Edward W. **13:**1640
Kelvin, Lord (William Thomson) **4:**393;
   **6:**664; **7:**815–816; **14:**1777, 1787
Kepler, Johannes **1:**120
Khorana, Har **8:**987; **9:**1038
Khwarizmi, Muhammad ibn Musa al-
   **1:**53, 54; **8:**921; **9:***1124*
Kilburn, Tom **13:**1589
King, Augusta Ada (Countess of
   Lovelace) **2:**151; **3:**364; **13:**1588, *1589*
King, Tom **3:**342
Kingsford Smith, C. E. **1:**39
Kirchoff, Gustav **13:**1645
Klaproth, Martin Heinrich **15:**1883
Klaus, Karl Karlovich **11:**1297
Klietsch, Karl **11:**1358
Koch, Robert **8:**986
Kolff, Willem **8:**944
König, Friedrich **11:**1354

**L**

Lagrange, Joseph **8:**922
Lamarck, Jean-Baptiste-Pierre-Antoine
   de **5:**568

Land, Edwin Herbert **11**:1310–1311
Langley, Samuel **1**:37
Laplace, Pierre-Simon de **2**:197; **7**:835
Lartigue, Charles **9**:1040
Lassell, William **9**:1095
Latimer-Needham, C. H. **6**:746
Lauste, Eugene **9**:1057
Lavassor, Émile **2**:141
Lavoisier, Antoine-Laurent **3**:321; **5**:539;
    **7**:834–835; **10**:1177, 1214; **14**:1709
Lecoq de Boisbaudran, Paul-Emile
    **10**:1217–1218
Leeuwenhoek, Anthony (Anton; Antoni)
    van **3**:300; **8**:986, 998; **11**:1370
Leibniz, Gottfried **3**:265, 358–359; **6**:749;
    **8**:922; **10**:1259
Lemaître, Georges-Henri **15**:1879
Lenoir, Jean Joseph Etienne **7**:782
Lenormand, Louis-Sébastien **10**:1190
Leonardo da Vinci **7**:839–840; **10**:1190;
    **14**:1697
    flying-machine design **1**:36
    helicopter design **6**:*741*
    tank design **6**:*741*
    the lathe **16**:2019
Leverrier, Urbain **9**:1093
Libby, Willard **3**:*287*
Lilienthal, Otto **1**:37
Lim, Drahoslav **5**:585
Lindbergh, Charles **1**:39
Linnaeus, Carolus **2**:185; **3**:332, *333*;
    **7**:860–861
Lippershey, Hans **14**:*1760*
Lister, J. J. **8**:999
Lister, Joseph **1**:94; **7**:866–867; **8**:938;
    **14**:1727
Lobachevsky, Nikolay **8**:922
Lodge, Oliver **2**:234; **11**:1397; **13**:1640
Lord, Peter **1**:86–87
Lorenz, Hendrik **2**:139
Lorin, René **7**:806
Lovelace, Countess of (Augusta Ada
    King) **2**:151; **3**:364; **13**:1588, *1589*
Lovell, Bernard **14**:1764–1765
Lowell, Percival **8**:915
Lumière, Auguste and Louis **9**:1052
Lyell, Charles **4**:408; **5**:568; **6**:689

## M

McAdam, John Loudon **12**:*1472*
McCay, Winsor **1**:84
McCormick, Cyrus Hall **1**:26
Macmillan, Kirkpatrick **2**:175
Malpighi, Marcello **8**:998
Malthus, Thomas **5**:568
Mantell, Gideon **4**:432–433
Marconi, Guglielmo **2**:234, 235;
    **8**:906–907; **11**:1397
Mariotte, Edme **6**:*663*

Martin, Pierre-Emile **7**:799
Mauchly, John **3**:360
Maxim, Hiram Stevens **1**:37; **6**:725–726
Maxwell, James Clerk **4**:508–509; **7**:816;
    **8**:926–927; **10**:1261
Mayer, Adolf **8**:986
Mayr, Ernst **5**:570
Meitner, Lise **9**:1111–1112
    mendelevium **8**:949
Mendeleyev, Dmitry (Dmitri Mendeleev)
    **3**:322; **5**:541; **8**:948–949; **10**:*1214*,
    1216–1218
    and transition elements **15**:1851
Mendel, Gregor **2**:186–187; **5**:570; **6**:677,
    *678*; **8**:946–947
Meucci, Antonio **14**:1753
Michell, John **2**:197
Michelson, Albert **12**:1435
Miescher, Johann Friedrich **8**:986
Miles, G. W. **11**:1286
Miller, Stanley **1**:*71*; **5**:566
Minkowski, Rudolph **9**:1107
Minton, Thomas **11**:1332
Möbius, August **8**:922
Mohs, Friedrich **8**:1010
Montgolfier brothers **2**:162–*163*
Moore, Daniel McFarlane **7**:854
Moore, Gordon **3**:366
Moore, Henry **1**:*57*
Morley, Edward **12**:1435
Morse, Samuel **8**:981; **14**:1752–1753
Morton, William T. G. **4**:410
Mudge, Thomas **15**:1822
Mueller, Erwin **8**:1001
Müller, Walther **6**:669

## N

Napier, John **8**:921
Nasmyth, James **7**:872
Neilson, James **2**:202
Newcomen, Thomas **8**:1016; **14**:1684,
    *1685*
Newlands, John **10**:1216
Newton, Isaac **9**:1102–1103; **10**:1260
    and calculus **3**:265, *266*; **8**:922, 924;
    **10**:1259
    and gravity **1**:120; **6**:716; **9**:1102–1103;
    **15**:1808
    and light **7**:846; **9**:1103; **13**:1645
    and telescopes **9**:*1103*; **14**:1760–1761
    and viscosity **16**:*1929*
    laws of motion **5**:627–628; **7**:806;
    **9**:1050–1051, 1103; **12**:1489
Nicholson, Vanessa-Mae **9**:*1074*
Nicholson, William **4**:507
Nicol, William **11**:1311
Niépce, Joseph-Nicéphore **10**:1236,
    1242–1243
Nipkow, Paul **14**:1768

Nirenberg, Marshall **8**:987; **9**:1038
Noble, Alfred **5**:579, 580
Nollet, Jean-Antoine **10**:1170

## O

O'Brien, Willis **1**:86
Ohain, Hans von **7**:807
Omar Khayyam **1**:53
Onnes, Heike Kamerlingh **14**:1718
Oparin, Aleksandr Ivanovich **5**:566
Orsted, Hans Christian **1**:67, 72; **4**:507;
    **5**:522, 587
Osann, Gottfried **11**:1296–1297
Otis, Elisha **5**:543, 544; **13**:1569
Otto, Nikolaus **2**:141; **7**:783
Owen, Richard **4**:*433*

## P

Page, Lawrence **7**:*791*
Panhard, René **2**:141
Papin, Denis **7**:782; **8**:909; **14**:1684
Paracelsus **8**:942
Paré, Ambroise **11**:1362
Parkes, Alexander **11**:1286
Park, Nick **1**:86–87
Parsons, Charles Algernon **6**:*665*
Parsons, William **14**:1761
Pascal, Blaise **3**:263, 358; **6**:749, 750
Pasteur, Louis **10**:1210–1211
    and fermentation **10**:1210; **16**:2035
    and pasteurization **10**:1211
    and the silkworm industry **10**:1211
    disproves spontaneous generation
    **5**:565–566
    germ theory of disease **7**:866; **8**:938,
    *986*; **10**:1211
Peltier, Jean **14**:1787
Pelton, Lester Allen **6**:756
Penzias, Arno **15**:*1879*, 1880
Peress, Joseph **4**:451
Perkin, William **4**:*466*
Pfleumer, Fritz **7**:885
Picard, Jean **4**:505
Piccard, Auguste **14**:1706
Pilkington, Alastair **6**:703
Pine, Courtney **9**:*1076*
Pinel, Philippe **11**:1373
Planché, Andrew **11**:1331
Planck, Max **2**:205; **10**:1159, **1272–1273**;
    **11**:1389; **13**:1645–1646
Plato **1**:110, 111
Poincaré, Jules **8**:922
Popov, Alexsandr **11**:1397
Poulsen, Valdemar **7**:885
Powell, John Wesley **6**:690
Priestley, Joseph **3**:321; **10**:1177
Prochorov, A. M. **7**:827
Ptolemy **15**:1877
Pythagoras **8**:921; **11**:1387–1388**

## R

Rabi, Isidor **15**:1822
Ramsay, William **7**:*775*
Ransome, Robert **11**:1301
Rayleigh, Lord **7**:775; **10**:1260
Reber, Grote **14**:1763
Redi, Francesco **5**:565
Reinitzer, Friedrich **7**:865
Reno, Jesse W. **5**:543
Reynaud, Émile **1**:84
Rhind, Alexander Henry **8**:920
Rice, Chester W. **13**:1640
Richter, C. F. **4**:486
Riemann, Georg Bernhard **8**:923
Riva-Rocci, Scipione **8**:940
Robert, M. N. **2**:163
Robert, Nicholas-Louis **10**:1185
Röntgen, Wilhelm **8**:932, 939; **16**:2031
Rudbeck, Olof, the Younger **7**:860
Rutherford, Ernest **2**:*138*, 205; **3**:322;
    **6**:657; **12**:1501–1502
  and atomic structure **2**:*139*; **5**:539–540;
    **10**:1206

## S

Sainte-Claire Deville, Henri **1**:65
Salter, Stephen **16**:1982
Savery, Thomas **8**:1016; **14**:1684
Sax, Antoine-Joseph (Adolph) **9**:1077
Schawlow, Arthur **7**:827
Scheele, Carl Wilhelm **9**:1104
Schmidt, Bernard **10**:1244
Schöffer, Peter **11**:1353
Schönbein, Christian Friedrich
    **11**:1286
Schott, Otto **8**:999–1000
Schrödinger, Erwin **11**:*1391*, 1392
Schulze, Johann Heinrich **10**:1242
Schwarzschild, Karl **2**:*197*
Seaborg, Glenn Theodore **5**:540
Seebeck, Thomas J. **14**:1786
Seeberger, Charles D. **5**:543
Senefelder, Aloys **11**:1357
Seysenegg, Erich von **8**:947
Shockley, William **3**:360; **5**:527;
    **13**:1542; **14**:1768; **15**:1849
Shortt, William **15**:1822
Sickdhar, Radhanath **9**:1064
Sidgier, Henry **16**:1963–1964
Siebe, Augustus **4**:446
Siemens, William **7**:799
Sikorsky, Igor **6**:*742*
Simpson, James Young **1**:77
Smith, William **6**:689–*690*
Snell, Willebrord **10**:1158
Soddy, Frederick **12**:1502
Sörensen, Sören **1**:16
Soulé, Samuel **7**:817
Spemann, Hans **3**:341

Spode, Josiah **11**:1332
Stanhope, Charles **11**:1354
Stanley, Francis Edgar **14**:1687
Stanley, Freelan Oscar **14**:1687
Staudinger, Hermann **11**:1287
Stephenson, George **7**:871; **8**:1016
Stephenson, Robert **7**:*870*, 871;
    **14**:*1686*
Stevens, John **7**:871; **12**:1412
Stirling, Robert **14**:1689
Stradivari, Antonio **9**:1075
Strassman, Fritz **9**:1111–1112
Stringfellow, John **1**:37
Strowger, Almon **14**:1755
Struve, Wilhelm von **8**:997
Sulston, John **6**:*680*
Swammerdam, Jan **8**:998
Swan, Joseph **5**:598; **7**:854
Swinton, A. A. Campbell **14**:1768
Symington, William **8**:909
Szilard, Leo **9**:1112

## T

Tait, Peter Guthrie **7**:816
Talbot, William Henry Fox **10**:1243
Taylor, F. B. **11**:1292
Telford, Thomas **12**:1472
Tennant, Smithson **11**:1296
Tesla, Nikola **14**:1778
Thales of Miletus **5**:538; **8**:921
Theophrastus **2**:185
Thomson, J. J. **2**:139, 204–205; **5**:539;
    **10**:1206; **12**:1501
Thomson, Robert William **12**:1500
Tighman, Benjamin **10**:1185
Tombaugh, Clyde **11**:*1302*
Torricelli, Evangelista **2**:*167*; **11**:1348
Towneley, Richard **8**:996
Townes, Charles H. **7**:826, 827
Townshend, Charles **1**:25
Trésaguet, Pierre-Marie-Jérôme
    **12**:1471–1472
Trevithick, Richard **7**:870; **8**:1016;
    **14**:1686–1687
Truman, Harry S. **2**:*234*
Tschermak von Seysenegg, Erich
    **6**:677
Tsiolkovsky, Konstantin Eduardovich
    **12**:1490
Tsvet, Mikhail **3**:324
Tull, Jethro **1**:26
Turing, Alan **1**:113; **3**:359
Turri, Peregrino **7**:817
Tusi, Nasir ad-Din at- **8**:921

## U

Ulloa, Antonio de **11**:1296
Urey, Harold **1**:*71*; **5**:566
Ussher, James **4**:473; **6**:689

## V

Venturi, Giovanni **15**:1902
Vesalius, Andreas **2**:185; **8**:938
Vidie, Lucien **2**:168
Villard, Paul **6**:657; **11**:1403
Volta, Alessandro **2**:169–*170*; **4**:506;
    **10**:1260; **14**:1752; **16**:*1942–1943*
von Braun, Wernher **12**:1490–1491
Vries, Hugo de **6**:677; **8**:947

## W

Walcott, Charles **6**:685
Wallace, Alfred Russel **2**:186; **4**:409; **5**:569
Walters, W. Grey **1**:113
Wankel, Felix **7**:787; **16**:*1948*
Waterman, Lewis E. **16**:2028
Watson, James *see* Crick, Francis, and
    James Watson
Watson, John Broadus **11**:1378
Watson-Watt, Robert **11**:1393–1394
Watt, James **8**:1016; **11**:1336; **13**:1544;
    **14**:1685–1686
Weaver, Warren **9**:1038
Wedgwood, Thomas **10**:1242
Wegener, Alfred **6**:690; **11**:1292–1293;
    **15**:1853; **16**:*1995–1996*
Wells, Horace **4**:410
Welsbach, Carl Auer, Count of **7**:853
Wenner-Gren, Axel L. **9**:1040
Wertheimer, Max **11**:1378
Wheatstone, Charles **14**:1752, 1753
Wheeler, John **2**:198
Whitehead, Robert **9**:1032
Whitelaw, James **15**:1866
Whitney, Eli **1**:26; **3**:*380*–381; **5**:596
Whittle, Frank **1**:39; **7**:806–*807*
Wichterle, Otto **5**:585
Wilkins, Maurice **4**:391, *454*
Wilkinson, John **2**:202
Wilmut, Ian **3**:342
Wilson, Edward O. **2**:181
Wilson, Robert **15**:*1879*, 1880
Wöhler, Friedrich **1**:67; **10**:1164
Wollaston, William **11**:1296
Woskressensky, Alexander **8**:948
Wright, Orville and Wilbur **1**:*36*, 37
Wright, Sewall **5**:570
Wundt, Wilhelm **11**:*1378*

## Y

Yablonovitch, Eli **10**:1161
Yale, Linus **7**:*868*, 869
Yeager, Chuck **1**:45
Young, Thomas **16**:1978

## Z

Zeiss, Carl **8**:999
Zwicky, Fritz **9**:1107, *1109*
Zworykin, Vladimir **14**:1768

# General index

Numbers in **bold** refer to volume; page numbers in **bold** refer to main articles; page numbers in *italics* refer to illustrations.

**A**

A4 Pacifics (locomotives) **7:**872–873
*aa* (lava) **16:**1940
Aardman Animations **1:**86, 87
abaca (Manila hemp) **5:**597
abacuses **3:***263,* 358; **9:***1123*
Abbe, Ernst **8:**999
ABMs (antiballistic-missile missiles) **9:**1032
Abrams tanks **14:***1743,* 1744, *1745*
abrasives **1:12–13**
  diamond **1:**13; **4:**419
abscesses, dental **4:**411
absolute zero **4:**393; **6:**664; **14:**1777
acceleration **9:**1050
  gravity and **8:**917
acceleration of free fall **6:**718
accelerator mass spectrometer
    (AMS) **1:**99
accelerators *see* particle accelerators
accelerometers **6:**719–720
accretion disks **13:**1604
accumulators **2:**170
acetaminophen **11:**1308
acetate **5:**599
acetic acid **1:**14
acetylcholine **2:**213
acid rain **2:***135;* **3:**339; **4:**490; **5:***564;*
    **10:**1178; **11:***1316, 1318*
acids and alkalis **1:14–16**
  acids **1:***14–15;* **12:**1513
  alkali metals **1:**15–16
  alkalis **1:**15; **12:**1513
  indicators **1:***15, 16*
  reactions of **12:**1514
  the pH scale **1:**16
acinar glands **5:**575
acoustics **10:**1260
  resonance **12:**1458
acquired immune deficiency syndrome
    *see* AIDS
acrylic **5:**599; **14:**1784
actin **11:**1368–1369
ACVs (air-cushion vehicles)
    *see* hovercraft

Adams, John Couch **9:**1092–*1093*
adaptations **4:**490–491; **5:**569
adenine **9:**1039
adenoids **7:**884
Ader, Clément **1:**37
adhesives **1:17–18**
Adobe Photoshop Album **10:***1250*
adrenal glands **5:**547–548
ADSIDs (air-delivered seismic
    instrument devices) **12:**1447–1448
ADSL (Asymmetric Digital Subscriber
    Line) **14:**1758
advanced gas-cooled reactors (AGRs)
    **9:**1114
advance warning equipment (AWARE)
    **15:**1843
adzes **15:**1830
aerodynamics **1:19–22**
aerogel **13:**1557, 1609
agar **8:***987*
agarose **5:**535
Agassiz, Louis **6:**690
Agent Orange **11:***1307*
agriculture **1:23–30**
  antibiotics in **1:**92
  breeding livestock **1:**25–26, 28
  breeding plants **1:**29
  crop rotation **1:**25; **10:**1222
  genetically engineered plants **1:**29–30
  history **1:***23–26*
  intensive farming **1:**27–28
  irrigation **1:**27
  machinery **1:***25,* 26, 30
  organic farming **1:**26
  plows **1:***23, 24;* **11:1300–1301**
  slash and burn **4:***489*
  water and **16:**1974
  *see also* crops; pest control
Aibo (robot) **12:***1479*
AIDS (acquired immune deficiency
    syndrome) **1:31–32;** **4:**441
  virus (HIV) **1:***31–32;* **4:**441; **15:***1917*
ailerons **1:**41
AIM-120 Slammer missiles **9:**1031

air **1:33**
  air pressure **1:***33;* **16:**1989–1990, *1991,*
    1992–1993
  fractional distillation **9:**1104; **10:**1179
  freezing constituents of **13:**1610
  liquid **4:**393; **9:**1104
  *see also* atmosphere
air bags, used for water power **16:***1982*
airborne early warning (AEW) systems
    **11:**1396
air-conditioning **1:34–35**
  *see also* refrigeration
aircraft carriers **16:***1958, 1960,* 1961
air-cushion vehicles *see* hovercraft
air-delivered seismic instrument
    devices (ADSIDs) **12:**1447–1448
airfoils **1:**19; **15:**1903
air-gun arrays **6:***695*
air masses **16:**1990, 1991
airplanes **1:36–45**
  aerodynamics **1:***19–20,* 22
  aeronautical engineers and **5:***555,* 556
  afterburners **7:**809
  anatomy **1:42–43**
  autopilots **1:**42; **9:**1086; **13:***1544,* 1545
  brakes **2:***224*
  cockpit **1:***40*
  Doppler devices **4:***457;* **11:**1396
  emergency oxygen in **10:**1179
  examined using X-rays **16:**2034
  flight recorders **1:***41*
  gyrocompasses **6:**730
  hydraulic equipment **6:**753
  jet **7:***787,* 807, *808,* 809, 810; **15:**1869;
    **16:**1953–1954
  jet airliners **1:**39–40, 41–42, 43
  landing **1:**50–51
  landing gear **1:**66
  navigation systems in **9:**1085–*1086*
  pilotless **1:***45;* **12:***1443*
  principles of flight **1:**40–42
  radar devices in **11:**1396
  speed calculated **11:**1396; **15:***1902,*
    1903
  speed record **16:**1955

stealth aircraft **1:**44; **16:***1958*
subsonic flight **1:**19
supersonic **1:***20*; **7:**809
tilt-rotor **16:**1961
tires **12:**1500
torpedoes dropped from **9:**1032, 1033
types **1:***43–45*
VR helmets used in **15:**1912
V/STOL aircraft **7:***808*; **16:1944–1947**, 1958, 1960
weightlessness and the "Vomit Comet" **16:**1998
*see also* airports; helicopters; parachutes; warplanes
airports **1:46–51**
airships **2:**163
  *Hindenburg* **6:***761*
air-traffic control **1:**49–*50*; **11:***1393*, 1394, 1396
Airy, George **9:**1093
Akashi Kaikyo Bridge **2:**232
alanine **10:***1165*
alarms, smoke **5:***606*
albumin **11:**1369
alchemists **3:***320*–321; **4:**444, 445
Alcock, John **1:**39
alcohol
  as an antiseptic **1:**95
  from fermentation **5:**590, *591*
Aldrin, Edwin "Buzz" **9:**1042, *1043*
algae **10:**1274–1275
  blooms **9:**1142; **11:***1313*
  blue-green *see* cyanobacteria
  brown **11:**1371
  photosynthesis **10:**1253
  planktonic **9:**1142
  seaweeds **9:**1141
  zooxanthellae **3:***339*; **9:**1141
algebra **1:52–54**; **8:***921*, 924
aliphatic compounds **10:**1166
alkalis *see* acids and alkalis
alkanes **9:**1144
alkenes **9:**1144; **10:**1166
alleles **6:**679
allergens **1:**55, *56*
allergies **1:55–56**
allotropes, of sulfur **14:**1709
alloys **1:57–60**; **8:***962*, 963–964, 967, 968
  platinum group **11:**1298–1299
  solder **7:**838; **15:**1825

tested **13:**1648
  *see also* brass; bronze; pewter
all-terrain vehicles (ATVs) **1:**75
alluvial deposits, gold **6:**713
alluvium **13:**1596
Alnico **7:**889; **15:**1854
Alpha Centauri **14:**1677
alpha particles **7:**795, 800; **11:**1402; 15:1883
Alps **6:***688*
alternation of generations **10:**1275–1276
alternative fuel vehicles **1:61–63**; **14:**1694
  biofuels **1:**62
  electric **1:***61*, 62–63
  fuel cells and **1:***63*; **6:**645
  hybrid vehicles **1:**61
  solar-powered **1:***62*; **13:**1600, *1601*
alternators **6:**671; **11:**1337
altitude
  and mountain habitats **9:**1065
  climate and **3:**336–337
alumina **1:**12–13; **3:**310
aluminum **1:64–67**; **8:**967
  alloys **1:**58, 64
  extraction from ore **1:***64*, 65–66
  mining **1:***64*, 65
  ores **1:***64*–65; **8:***963*
  recycling **1:***67*; **12:**1427
aluminum oxide *see* alumina
Alvarez, Walter **6:***687*
alveoli **12:***1461*, 1462
*Alvin* (submersible) **14:**1708
Alzheimer's disease **9:**1101
amalgams **1:**59; **8:**951; **16:**2038
*Amanita* **6:***648*
Amati, Andrea **9:**1075
amino acids **1:**15, **68–71**; **2:**179; **4:**454; **5:**557; **11:**1367–1368
  essential **1:***68*, 70–71; **11:**1367
  *see also* proteins
ammeters **4:**499–500
ammonia
  and refrigeration **12:**1433–1434
  chemical bonds **15:***1897*
  dissolves in water **12:**1513
  manufacture **3:**296; **9:**1105
ammonium chloride **9:**1105
  mixed with water **12:**1514
ammonium hydroxide **9:**1105
ammonium nitrate **5:**593; **9:**1105

ammonium phosphate **5:**593
ammonium sulfate **5:**593
ammunition
  cartridge **6:**724, 725, 727
  *see also* bullets
amniocentesis **11:**1344
amniotic sac **11:**1343
amoebas **10:***1171*; **11:***1370*, 1372
Ampère, André-Marie **1:72–73**; **4:**507–*508*
amperes (amps) **4:**499, *508*
Ampère's law **4:**508
amphibians **1:**82
  metamorphosis **8:**979
amphibious vehicles **1:74–75**
Amphicar **1:**75
amplifiers **10:**1234
amplitude **12:**1457; **15:**1870; **16:**1975
amplitude modulation (AM) **1:**89, 90; **11:***1398*, 1399–1400
anabolism **5:**557; **8:**957
analytical engines **2:***151*; **3:**359; **13:**1588, *1589*
Anaximander the Elder **5:**538, 567
Andreessen, Marc **7:**790
androstenal **10:**1229
androsterone **10:**1229
anemia **9:**1130
  sickle-cell **3:**331; **4:**443, 455
anemometers **8:**980
anesthetics **1:76–78**; **6:***660*; **8:**938, 943; **14:**1726–1727
  dental **1:***77*–78; **4:**410–411
angiogenin **11:**1369
angiography **8:**935
angioplasty, balloon **8:**943
angledozers **4:**480
angle of incidence **10:**1156–1157, 1158
angle of reflection **10:**1157
anglesite **7:**836
Ångström, Anders Jonas **13:**1647
angstroms **13:**1647
animal kingdom **1:79–82**
  mountain animals **9:**1065–*1066*
  remote animal-tracking **12:***1447*; **16:**2045
  *see also* zoology
animation **1:83–88**
  computer **1:***83*, 84, *87–88*; **3:**370, *371*
anions **7:**794, 795
ankylosaurs **4:**435
annealing **8:**968; **15:**1831

anode **5:**520–521

anorexia **9:**1132

Antarctica

  a polar desert **4:**415

  hole in ozone layer **2:***135*

  ice shelves **6:***697*

antennas **1:89–90**

  cable network **2:***253*

  dish **1:***89*, 90

  platinum and **11:**1298–1299

anthrax **4:***443*; **10:**1211

antibiotics **1:91–93**; **4:**464, *465*; **5:***617*; **8:**988

  bacteriostatic and bacteriocidal **1:**92

  discovery **1:**91, *92*; **2:***154*

  fermentation and **1:***93*; **5:**591

  in agriculture **1:**92

  in wheat seeds **6:***676*

  narrow- and broad-spectrum **1:**92

  resistance to **1:**93

  side effects **1:**93

  *see also* penicillin

antibodies **6:**764, 765; **7:**884

  allergies and **1:**55

  monoclonal **6:**676

  vaccination and **15:**1889, 1890

anticlines **6:**692; **12:**1488

  oil reservoirs **9:***1145*

anticyclones (highs) **16:**1993–1994

antidepressants **11:**1376

antidiuretic hormone (ADH) **5:**547

antigens **15:**1891

antihydrogen atoms **10:***1208*

antimatter, detection **11:***1392*

antimony **7:**838; **8:**963

antineutrons **10:**1207

antiparticles **10:**1207

antiseptics **1:94–95**; **7:**866–*867*

ants, and pheromones **10:**1228

anxiety **11:**1373

*Apatosaurus* **4:**435

aphids, pest control **10:**1224, *1226*

Apollo space missions **9:**1042, *1043*, 1045

apomixis **3:**341

Apple computers **3:***360*, 361

  Mac OS **3:**365

  PowerBooks **3:**361, *362*

  Safari **3:**361

apples, dried **10:**1172

Appolonius of Perga **8:**921

aquaculture **1:**24

aqualungs **4:**448

aqua regia **11:**1297

aqueducts **2:***231*

aquifers **16:**1970

Arago, François **4:**508

Aral Sea, pollution **11:**1314–1315

archaebacteria **8:**989

archaeology **1:96–101**

  remote sensors used in **12:**1448

*Archaeopteryx* **4:***437*

arches

  rock **6:***689*

  sea **5:**563

Archimedes **1:102–103**; **3:**265; **6:**751; **7:**841; **8:**910; **11:**1383; **13:***1643*

Archimedes screws **1:**103; **8:**910; **11:**1383–1384

architecture **1:104–109**

  ancient Greek **1:**105

  ancient Roman **1:**106

  Asian **1:***107*, 108–109

  baroque **1:**107

  Chinese **1:***105*, 108; **2:**241–242

  Gothic **1:***106*; **2:***241*

  "green" **2:**248

  in the Americas **1:***104*, 107

  Islamic **1:**106

  Japanese **1:**108; **2:***242*

  Mesopotamian **2:**241

  modern **1:***109*

  neoclassical **1:**107

  Renaissance **1:**107

  rococo **1:**107

  *see also* building techniques; pyramids; skyscrapers

archosaurs **4:**433–434

Arctic, global warming and **6:**711–712

Arecibo, radio telescope **9:**1135; **14:**1765

arenes **9:**1144

Argand, Aimé **7:**853

argentine **13:**1558

*Argentinosaurus* **4:**434

argon **7:***774*, 775

Ariel (moon) **15:***1886*, 1888

Aristotle **1:110–111**, 114, 120; **3:**320; **10:**1259

  and classification **1:**111; **3:**332

  and motion **9:**1049

  and the elements **5:**538

  diving bell **4:**446

arithmetic **8:**922

  mental **8:**923

Arkwright, Richard **14:**1782; **16:**2026

armadillos **3:**340

armalcolite **9:**1043

arms

  artificial **11:**1364

  bones **13:**1564

Armstrong, Edwin H. **11:**1398

Armstrong, Neil A. **9:**1042, *1043*

aromatherapy **10:**1229

Arpanet **7:**788

Arrhenius, Svante **5:***566*

arroyos (wadis) **4:**414

arsenic **8:**963

*Artemis* satellite **3:***353*

arteries **3:**326, *328*

  pulmonary artery **12:***1460*

arthritis **4:**443; **6:**764; **13:**1563

arthropods **1:**82

artificial intelligence (AI) **1:**88, **112–115**; **3:**367

  *see also* robotics

artillery **6:**728

arylide **10:***1182*

ascorbic acid **1:***14*

  *see* vitamins, vitamin C

asepsis **7:**867

ash, volcanic **16:***1940*

ASIMO (robot) **12:***1477*

Asimov, Isaac **12:**1478

asphalt cutters **7:***802*, 803

aspirin **2:**213

assault ships **16:**1961

astatine **5:**541

asteroids, comets, and meteors **1:116–119**

  asteroids **1:**116, 117–118; **6:**687–688; **13:**1603

  comets **1:**116, *117*, 119; **13:**1606; **14:**1696

  meteorites **1:**116, *118*, 119; **4:**437; **9:**1139

  meteoroids **1:**116, 118

  meteors (shooting stars) **1:**116–118

  space probes sent to **13:**1630

asthenosphere **11:**1294

asthma **1:**56; **9:**1071

astrocytes **2:***215*

astrolabes **9:**1083–1084

astronauts, and weightlessness **8:**918, *919*; **12:***1435*; **16:***1997*, *1998*

astronomy **1:120–125**

  Copernicus **1:**120; **3:**372–373; **14:**1711

development of **1:**120
Galileo and **6:**655–656
Herschel (William) and **6:***743–744*; **15:**1885
radar astronomy **9:**1135; **11:***1396*
radio astronomy **1:**124–*125*; **9:**1134–1135; **14:***1763–1765*
*see also* black holes; planets; solar system; stars; universe
astrophysics **1:**123–124; **10:**1258
Asymmetric Digital Subscriber Line (ADSL) **14:**1758
Atacama Desert **4:**416
Atanasoff, John Vincent **3:**360
atherosclerosis **5:***588*
athlete's foot **4:**441
Atlantic Ocean **9:**1137
*Atlantis* (space shuttle) **13:**1624, 1634–*1635*, *1636*
Atlas missiles **9:**1029
atmosphere **2:132–135; 4:**473
and radio **11:***1398*
gases in the **1:**33; **6:**661; **9:**1104
in the past **2:**132; **6:**710
water vapor in **15:**1901
*see also* air
ATMs (automated teller machines) **13:***1592*
atomic beam magnetic resonance **15:**1822
atomic mass **2:**137
relative (RAM) **3:**315, 316
atomic number **2:**136; **5:**540; **7:**800; **10:**1217, 1218
atomic piles **9:**1112
atomic theory, Dalton and **4:**403
atomic weight **2:**137; **10:**1215
atoms and molecules **2:136–139; 10:**1206
atomic structure **2:**138–*139*, 205; **5:**540; **9:**1119; **10:**1214
ATP (adenosine triphosphate) **8:**957, 958; **10:**1231
attrition **12:**1465
ATVs (all-terrain vehicles) **1:**75
auroras **3:**313; **7:***795*; **11:**1284–1285
*Australopithecus* **13:**1563
autogiros **6:**742
autoimmune diseases **6:**764
automated teller machines (ATMs) **13:***1592*
automatons **1:**112; **12:**1477

automobiles **2:140–149**
aerodynamics **1:***19, 20*
alternative-fuel *see* alternative fuel vehicles
axles **14:**1737
batteries **2:**171, *172*
brakes **2:**141, 144–145, 146, 221–*222*, 223; **6:**753
catalytic converters **3:***296*; **11:**1316
computer systems **2:**148
cooling system **2:**145
engine **2:**142–*143*; **7:***773, 782*, 783, *784*, 787
fuel gauges **15:**1844
headlights **15:***1895*
history **2:**140–142
ignition system **2:**145
motor oils for **7:**876
navigation systems in **2:***145*; **6:***708*; **9:**1087–*1088*; **15:**1843
onboard television **14:***1775*
painting **10:**1183
production **5:***554*; **12:**1482
race cars **2:**147–*149*
safety **2:**145–147
spark plugs **3:***309*; **11:**1299
starter motors **13:**1607–*1608*
steam cars **14:**1687
steering **2:***144*, 145
suspension **2:**144; **14:**1736–*1737*
tires **14:**1736
traffic-avoidance systems **15:**1843
transmission (gear system) **2:**144
wheels **16:***2004*
windshields **1:**18; **3:***310*
autopilots **1:**42; **9:**1086; **13:***1544*, 1545
auxin herbicides **10:**1226
AV-8 (aircraft) **16:***1945*, 1946
averages **14:**1679
Avogadro, Amadeo **10:**1215
Avogadro's number **3:**316
AWARE (advance warning equipment) **15:**1843
axes **15:**1830
axles **14:**1737
axolotls **8:***976*
axons (nerve fibers) **9:***1098*, 1099–*1100*

**B**
B-2 (aircraft) **16:***1956*
B-52 (aircraft) **16:***1953*
Baade, Walter **9:**1107

Babbage, Charles **2:150–151**; **3:**359; **13:**1588
babies
bone development **13:**1564
need for touch **15:**1839
sleeping **13:***1572*
statistics and **14:**1682, *1683*
Baby, The (computer) **13:**1589–1590
Babylonians, and mathematics **8:**920; **9:**1124; **11:**1387–1388
backbone **13:***1562*, 1564
backstaffs **9:**1084
Bacon, Francis **6:**644
Bacon, Roger **5:**578
bacteria **2:152–155; 8:**987–988
aerobic and anaerobic **10:**1210
and disease **2:**153–154; **4:**439–440, *443*
antibiotic-resistant **1:**93
genetic engineering and **6:**673–*674*, 676
Gram-positive and Gram-negative **1:**92
nitrogen-fixing **7:**779; **9:**1106
reproduction **2:***155*
use **2:**152–153; **6:**673–*674*, 676
*see also* antiseptics
Baekeland, Leo Hendrik **11:**1286
Baeyer, Adolf von **11:**1286
Bailey's Beads **4:**488
Baird, John Logie **2:***235*; **14:**1768, 1771
Bakelite **11:***1286*
Bakewell, Robert **1:**25–26
balance **4:**472
balances and weighing machines **2:156–159; 8:***917, 929*
*see also* mass and weight
ballistics **2:160–161**
balloons **2:162–164**
balls, spinning **15:**1903
Barber, John **6:**665
bar codes and scanners **2:165–166**; **7:**828, 829
Bardeen, John **3:**360; **5:**527; **13:**1542; **14:**1768; **15:**1849
barium **8:**963
barium oxide **10:**1179
barium sulfate **16:**2033
barium titanate **10:**1264, *1265*; **15:**1871
Barker, Robert **15:**1866
barley, genetically engineered **2:***211*

Barlow, Edward **15**:1820
Barnard, Christiaan **14**:1730
barometers **1**:33; **2**:167–168; **8**:951, *981*
 aneroid **2**:168; **11**:1349
Barron, Robert **7**:869
Bartlett, Neil **7**:774
Barton, Otis **14**:1703
barycenter **10**:1163
basal metabolic rate (BMR) **8**:*957*, 958
basalt **8**:*1012*; **12**:1484
bases, chemical **1**:15, 16
basic oxygen process (BOC) **7**:*798*, 799
basins **7**:824
basophils **6**:*733*
Basov, Nikolai **7**:827
bassoons **9**:1077
"batching pigs" **10**:1267
bathyscaphes **14**:*1704–1706*
bathyspheres **14**:1703–1704
bats
 in caves **3**:*298*
 pipistrelle **2**:181
batteries **2**:169–172; **4**:502
 camcorder **3**:272
 digital-camera **10**:1249
 invention **2**:*170*; **16**:*1942, 1943*
 lithium-ion (Li-ion) **3**:272
 rechargeable **2**:172
 *see also* fuel cells
battleships **16**:1958
Bauer, Georg *see* Agricola
bauxite **1**:*64–65*; **8**:*963*, 965; **13**:1595
bays **9**:1138
beaches **5**:564
bearings **2**:173–174
 molecular **10**:*1167*
Beaufort scale **16**:2009, 2010
Becquerel, Antoine-Henri **3**:322; **4**:399;
 **10**:1261; **11**:1401
Beebe, Charles William **14**:1703
bees **8**:*978*
 pheromones **10**:*1228*
behaviorism **11**:1378
Beijerinck, Martinus **8**:986
Bell, Alexander Graham **5**:526–527;
 **8**:965; **14**:*1752*, 1753–1754
Bell-Burnell, Jocelyn **14**:1677
Bell X-1 (aircraft) **14**:1723
bends, the **4**:450–451; **10**:1179
benzene **10**:1166
Benz, Karl **2**:141; **7**:783
Berger, Hans **8**:941

*bergschrunds* **6**:699
beriberi **16**:1931
Berliner, Emile **13**:1618
Berners-Lee, Timothy **7**:*789*, 793
Bernoulli, Daniel **15**:1902
Bernoulli, Jakob and Johann **8**:922
Bertin, Jean **9**:1041
beryl **8**:*1009*
beryllium **8**:963; **10**:1216
Berzelius, Jöns Jakob **3**:314, 315;
 **11**:1296–1297
Bessemer, Henry **7**:799
beta particles **7**:800; **11**:1402–1403
Bhopal, and the Union Carbide
 disaster **11**:*1308*
bibles, Gutenberg **11**:1353
bicycles **2**:175–177
 development **2**:175–176
 streamlined **1**:*22*
big bang **1**:123; **2**:198; **5**:*538*; **12**:1438;
 **15**:*1877, 1879*
big crunch **15**:1881
bile **4**:426; **5**:574
bilharzia (schistosomiasis) **10**:1196
bilirubin **5**:574
bimetallic strips
 in thermometers **15**:1798
 in thermostats **15**:1799–1800
binary fission **2**:155
binary number system **3**:362; **9**:1123,
 *1126*; **13**:*1587*
binoculars **10**:1158
biochemistry **2**:178–179
biochips **4**:455
biodiversity **2**:180–183
bioengineering **5**:555
 bioengineered vaccines **6**:676
 *see also* prosthetics
biogeography **6**:682
bioinformatics **9**:1039
biology **2**:184–187
 *see also* botany; zoology
bioluminescence **7**:880
biomes and habitats **2**:188–193
 biomes **2**:188–*193*; **4**:490
 cave life **3**:298–299
 mountain habitats **9**:*1065*
 *see also* food webs
biophysics **10**:1258–1259
biorhythms **2**:194–196
biosensors **8**:941
biostatistics **14**:1678–1679

birds **1**:82
 cave **3**:298
 evolution from dinosaurs **1**:82; **4**:437
Biró, László and Georg **16**:2029
bisphenols **1**:95
bits (binary digits) **3**:362; **9**:1126
 and digital camcorders **3**:271
bits, drill **4**:459, 460; **15**:1831
Bjerknes, Vilhelm **8**:981
blackbodies **11**:1389
black boxes **1**:41
Black Death **4**:*440*
black holes **1**:122, 124; **2**:197–199;
 **6**:718; **9**:1109; **12**:*1438*; **14**:1676;
 **15**:*1881*
black smokers **9**:*1143*
blacktop roads **12**:1474, *1475*
bladder **5**:*571*
blast furnaces **2**:200–203; **7**:798
Blériot, Louis **1**:37
blind people **15**:*1838*–1839
blizzards **13**:1579
block and tackle pulleys **11**:*1381*–1382
blood **12**:*1460*
 plasma **7**:881
 red blood cells **11**:*1368*; **12**:*1461*, 1463
blood pressure **6**:*734*
 monitors **8**:939–*940*
blowholes **5**:563
blue-green algae *see* cyanobacteria
blueshift **4**:457; **14**:1674
Bluetooth **7**:793; **9**:*1037*; **10**:1221
boardsailing **12**:*1506*
boat lifts **3**:275
boats
 boatbuilding **13**:*1551*–1554
 carvel construction **13**:1552–1553
 clinker construction **13**:1552
 hydrofoil **6**:758–759
 steam-powered **8**:909–910
body parts, artificial **8**:944
Bohr, Niels **2**:139, **204–205**; **3**:322;
 **5**:540
boiling points **4**:392; **14**:1776; **15**:1900
boiling water reactors (BWRs)
 **11**:1339
bollworms **3**:*381*
Bolsover, Thomas **13**:1580
bolsters **15**:1832
Boltzmann, Ludwig **8**:927
Bolyai, János **8**:922
bombers (aircraft) **16**:1952–*1953*, 1955

bombs and shells **2:206–209**; **5:***613*
  atomic bombs **2:**209; **5:**614;
    **9:**1112–1113, 1114, *1120*–1121
  hydrogen bombs **2:**209; **5:**551; **9:**1117,
    1122
  shells **2:**206–207; **5:**581; **14:**1743
  *see also* explosives
Bondi, Hermann **15:**1881
bonds, chemical *see* chemical bonds
boneblack **3:**286
bonemeal **5:**593–594
bones
  broken **13:**1564
  marrow **7:***883*; **13:**1563
  skeletal systems and **13:***1561, 1562,*
    *1563*–1564
  transplants **4:**413
Booth, Hubert Cecil **15:**1895
borazon (cubic boron nitride) **4:**397;
  **9:**1106
Borchardt, Hugo **6:**727
boreholes **6:**693
bores, river **15:**1810
boron nitride **9:**1106
  cubic (borazon) **4:**397; **9:**1106
Bosch, Robert **6:**646, *647*
bosons **5:**629; **10:**1207, 1209
botany **2:210–213**
  *see also* plant kingdom
botulism **1:***91*; **2:***154*
boulder clay **6:**700
bounce **12:**1439
Bourne, William **14:**1697
bovine spongiform encephalopathy
  (BSE) **4:**439
box scrapers **12:**1474
Boyle, Robert **5:**538–539; **6:***663*
Boyle's law **6:***663*–664
*Brachiosaurus* **4:**432, 434
Braille **15:***1838*, 1839
brain **2:214–220**
  electroencephalographs (EEGs)
    and brain waves **8:**941;
    **13:***1572*–*1573, 1574*
  scans **10:***1263*; **11:***1405*
  virtual reality map of **15:***1913*
Braithwaite, John **5:**606
brake systems **2:221–224**; **5:**637
  airplane **2:***224*
  automobile **2:**141, 144–145, 146,
    221–*222*, 223; **6:**753

bicycle **2:**177
  high-performance disks **3:***311*
  mountain railroads **3:**261
  regenerative **12:**1425
  rheostatic **12:**1425
  train **2:**222–223, 224; **12:**1425
  truck **2:**222, 224; **15:***1856*
Bramah, Joseph **6:**751
Branly, Edouard-Eugéne **11:**1397
brass **1:**58, 60; **2:225–226**; **3:**374; **8:**963
Brattain, Walter **3:**360; **5:**527; **13:**1542;
  **14:**1768; **15:**1849
Braun, Anton **7:**783
Braun, Karl **8:**907
Bravais unit cells **4:**395
Bray, John **1:**84
bread making **2:227–229**; **5:**590
breathing **12:**1463–*1464*
breathing apparatus **12:**1463
Breazeal, Cynthia **1:***115*
breeding, livestock **1:**25–26
Breguet, Louis-Charles **6:**742
Brentano, Franz **11:**1378
bricks and brickmaking **2:**240,
  *243*–244
bridges **2:230–233**
  resonance and **12:***1457*, 1458
Briggs, Robert **3:**342
Brin, Sergey **7:***791*
broadband **7:**791
broadcasting **2:234–239**
  radio **2:***234*–235; **11:***1397*–*1398*, 1399
  television **2:***235*–239; **8:**1003;
    **14:**1770–1771
Broglie, Louis-Victor-Pierre-Raymond
  de **11:**1391
bromine **10:**1216
bronchi **12:**1462
  and cilia **6:***763*
bronchioles **12:**1462
Brongniart, Alexandre **11:**1332
bronze **1:***57*, 60; **2:**240; **3:**374; **8:**963;
  **15:**1825, 1826, 1831
  molds made of **3:**292–293
  tarnished **10:**1173
Brownian motion **4:**495
Brunel, Isambard Kingdom **14:**1752
Brunel, Marc Isambard **12:**1424; **15:**1862
BSE (bovine spongiform
  encephalopathy) **4:**439
bubble chambers **10:**1201, *1203*–*1204*,
  *1206*

buckminsterfullerene (buckyball)
  **3:***284*, 285; **10:**1257
budding, by yeasts **16:**2036
buildings, world's tallest **13:**1570
building techniques **2:240–249**
  bridges **2:**232–233
  building materials **2:**242–246
  dams **4:**404
  equipment *see* cranes; earthmovers;
    winches and windlasses
  "green" architecture **2:**248
  modern **2:***246*–248
  skyscrapers **13:**1569–1571
  *see also* architecture
bulimia **9:**1132
  bulimia nervosa **11:**1375
bulk carriers **13:**1555
bulk modulus **4:**498
bulldozers **4:**480, *481*
bullets **1:***21*; **2:***160*–161
bull-roarers **9:**1073
Bunsen, Robert **13:**1645
Burdin, Claude **15:**1867
Burgess Shale **6:**685, 686
burning *see* combustion
burns, treatment of **13:**1567
buses **14:**1693–*1694*
Bushnell, David **14:***1697*
butter **5:**621
butterflies **8:***977*
buttes **7:**824
bytes **3:**362; **9:**1126; **13:**1589

## C

cables
  coaxial **2:***251*
  electric flex **7:***780*
  high-voltage **11:***1342*; **14:**1719
  undersea and transatlantic **7:**816;
    **10:**1160; **14:***1754*, 1757
  wire-rope **16:***2017*–2018
cable television **2:**236–237, **250–253**
cable travel **3:260–262**
  cable cars **3:***261*–262; **14:**1691, *1693*
cacti **4:***416*, 417; **10:***1274*
caffeine **13:***1575*
caissons **2:**232; **7:**850
calciferol *see* vitamins, vitamin D
calcite **12:**1488
calcium **8:**963
  dietary **9:**1128, 1130
  in fertilizers **5:**594

calcium carbonate **3:**284; **13:**1562
  reaction with hydrochloric acid
    **3:**315, 316, 318
calculators **3:**263–264; **8:***923*
  of Charles Babbage **2:**150; **3:**359
calculus **3:**265–266; **8:**924–925;
  **10:**1259
calendars
  Coligny Calendar **9:***1125*
  Gregorian **9:**1124; **15:**1815
  Julian **15:**1815
calendar stacks **10:***1188*, 1189
calendering **14:**1785
Calley, John **14:**1684
caloric **6:***735*
Cambrian period **6:**686
  Cambrian explosion **1:**81
camcorder **3:**267–272
camels **4:***414*, 417
camera obscura **10:**1237
cameras **10:***1237*
  box **10:**1236–1237
  compact **10:**1238, *1242*
  depth of field **10:**1238
  diaphragm in **10:**1237–1238
  digital **10:***1240*, *1246–1251*
  digital video **9:**1054–1055
  films **10:**1236, *1243*, 1244–1245
  flash **10:**1241, 1245
  focal length of lenses **10:**1238–1239,
    *1240*, 1250
  focusing **10:**1238
  in cell phones **10:***1240*
  lenses **10:**1238–1240, *1241*
  movie **9:**1053–*1055*
  reflex **10:**1238, *1239*
  rostrum **1:**85
  Schmidt **10:**1244
  shutters **10:**1236, 1237, *1238*
  speed cameras **15:***1842*
  television **14:**1769–1770
  thermal-imaging **7:**777
camouflage **1:***80*
*Campylobacter* **8:***989*
canals **3:**273–276
cancer **3:**304–305; **4:**442; **5:***577*
  breast **14:**1788
  diet and **9:**1132
  genes causing **9:**1039
  lung **12:**1464
  lymphomas **7:***884*
  skin **14:***1712*; **15:**1875

treatment using anticancer drugs
    **7:**779; **10:***1166*, 1167; **11:**1298
  treatment using radiotherapy **8:**943;
    **11:***1404–1405*; **16:**1933, 2034
  vaccines for **15:**1892
  *see also* leukemia; tumors
candelas **7:**848
candidiasis **16:**2036
candles **7:**852–853
canning **5:**622–623
Cannizzaro, Stanislao **8:**948–949;
  **10:**1215
cannons **6:***723*
  hand **6:**723
canyons **7:**824
capacitors (condensers) **3:**277–278;
  **4:**506
capillaries **3:**328
capillary action **14:**1725
cap rock **9:**1145
capstans, power-driven **16:**2006
carbohydrates **3:**279–282; **9:**1129
  metabolism **8:**956–957
carbon **3:**283–286, 316; **10:**1164–1165
  cycle **4:**492
  isotopes **1:**99; **3:**287–288; **7:**800, 801;
    **10:**1217; **11:**1403
  *see also* carbon dating; diamond;
    graphite
carbonates, mineral **8:**1012
carbonation **16:**1986
carbon black **3:**286
carbon dating **1:**99, *100*; **3:**287–288;
  **11:***1401*, 1403
carbon dioxide **3:**283, 286
  as a greenhouse gas **3:**339; **6:***710*–711;
    **11:**1317
  exhaled from the lungs **5:**574; **6:**731
  in fire extinguishers **5:***604*
  in blood **6:**731
  solid (dry ice) **6:**662; **13:***1610*;
    **14:***1695*–1696
carbon fibers **3:**289–291, *311*; **11:**1363;
  **13:***1654*
carbonic acid **16:**1986
Carboniferous period **6:**686
carbon monoxide **3:***286*
  toxicity **11:**1307
carboplatin **7:**779
carborundum (silicon carbide) **3:**310;
  **4:**397
carburetors **7:**784

caries, dental **4:**411
Carlisle, Anthony **4:**507
Carlson, Chester F. **10:**1232
carnivores **5:**624
Carothers, W. H. **5:**598; **11:**1321
carpets and rugs **14:***1784*, *1785*
cars *see* automobiles
cartilage **13:**1561, 1563
cartridge ammunition **6:**724, 725
  shotgun **6:**727
Cartwright, Edmund **14:**1783
Cascariolo, Vincenzo **7:**878
cassette tapes **7:**885–886
*Cassini* (space probe) **13:***1625*, 1626,
  1630; **14:***1787*
Cassiopeia A (supernova remnant)
  **15:***1882*
cassiterite **15:***1826*
casting **3:**292–294; **8:**969, *971*; **15:**1831
  brass **2:**225–226
  ceramics **3:**311
  die **3:**294; **16:**2039
  sand **3:**294
Castor **14:**1677
*Castora Sei* (lay-barge) **10:**1269, 1270
catabolism **5:**557; **8:***956*–957
catalysts **3:**295–296, 318, 323
  enzymes as **10:**1167
  platinum metals as **11:**1297–1298
catalytic converters **3:***296*; **11:**1316
cataracts **5:**584
*Catch-Me-Who-Can* (locomotive)
  **14:**1687
caterpillars **8:**977–978
cathode **5:**520
cathode rays **5:**526
cathode-ray tubes **5:**532–533; **14:***1770*
cations **7:**794, 795
CAT scans *see* computerized axial
  tomography
caustic potash (potassium hydroxide)
  **1:**15; **6:**645
cauterization **14:**1730
caves **3:**297–299
cavitation **11:**1360
Caxton, William **11:**1353
Cayley, George **1:**36
CCTV (closed-circuit television)
  **14:**1770
CDs (compact discs) **4:**429, 430–431;
  **7:**830–833
  CD-players **7:***830*

celestial sphere **14**:1670, *1671*
cell membrane **3**:301
  receptors on **3**:303–304
cell phones *see* cellular phones
cells **2**:179; **3**:**300–305**
  animal **1**:79
  communication **3**:303–304
  division **3**:303; **6**:*678*; **9**:1039
  organelles **3**:*301–302*
  plant **3**:*282, 302*
cellular phones (cell phones; mobile
    phones) **5**:*529*; **7**:793; **8**:990;
    **9**:*1034*–1037; **12**:1522; **14**:*1753,*
    1758–*1759*
  3G **15**:1909
  cameras in **10**:*1240*
celluloid **11**:1286
cellulose **3**:*282*; **10**:1184, 1275; **11**:*1320*
cellulose acetate **11**:1286
cellulose nitrate **11**:1286
cell wall **3**:*302*
Celsius, Anders **15**:1796
cement **2**:*244–245*; **3**:296
Cenozoic era **6**:688
censuses **14**:1678, 1683
central heating systems
  thermostats **15**:*1799*, 1800
  timers **15**:1824
central nervous system (CNS)
    **2**:214–215
central processing units (CPUs) **3**:362;
    **9**:1126
centrifuges **3**:**306–307**
centrioles **3**:*301*, 303
cephalosporins **1**:91
Cepheids (variable stars) **14**:1676;
    **15**:1880
ceramics, industrial **3**:**308–311**;
    **11**:1329–1330
  superconducting **14**:1720
cereals, dietary **9**:1129
cerebrospinal fluid **2**:215
cerebrum **2**:218–219, 220
Ceres (asteroid) **1**:117
CERN (European Organization for
    Nuclear Research) **2**:*136, 205*;
    **10**:*1198, 1201*
  and time dilation **12**:1437
  Large Hadron Collider **10**:1200
  particle detector **10**:*1205*
cerussite **7**:836
cervix **12**:1450, 1452

cesium **1**:15–16; **8**:962–963; **15**:*1817*
cesspools **13**:1549
CFCs *see* chlorofluorocarbons
CGRO (Compton Gamma Ray
    Observatory) **9**:1136
Chabaneau, François **11**:1296
Chadwick, James **2**:139; **5**:540
Chain, Ernst **1**:91; **5**:617
chain reaction **5**:615; **9**:1111,
    1113–1114, 1120
chair lifts **3**:261, *262*
chalcedony **8**:1010; **15**:1830
chalk **12**:*1485*
*Challenger* (space shuttle) **13**:1631,
    1632
Challis, James **9**:1093
chameleons **1**:*80*
Chancourtois, Alexandre-Émile
    Béguyer de **10**:1215–1216
Chandra (satellite) **9**:1136
Chandrasekhar, Subrahmanyan
    **2**:197–198
Channel Tunnel **6**:707–708; **15**:*1862,
    1864*, 1865
chaos theory **3**:**312–313**; **10**:1257
Chapman, Colin **2**:148
charcoal **3**:*283*, 285–286
Chargaff, Erwin **9**:1038–1039
charge-coupled devices (CCDs)
    **3**:*267–268*; **9**:1054, 1134; **11**:*1351*
  and spectrographs **13**:1648
  in digital cameras **10**:1246–1247,
    1249
  in image scanners **12**:1528, 1529
  in television cameras **14**:1769–1770
  in the Hubble Space Telescope
    **14**:1767
Charles, Jacques-Alexandre-César
    **2**:163; **6**:664
Charles's law **6**:664
*Charlotte Dundas* (steamboat)
    **8**:909–910
Charon (moon) **11**:*1305*
cheese **2**:*153*; **5**:*590*, 621–622
chemical bonds
  covalent **15**:*1896, 1897*
  ionic (electrovalent) **7**:794; **15**:*1896,*
    1897
  metallic **8**:961–962
chemical reactions **3**:**314–319**
  and electron shells **10**:1219
  chemical synthesis **3**:*319*

direction **3**:318–319
  exothermic **3**:*316, 318*
  rate **3**:317–318
  *see also* catalysts; chemistry
chemiluminescence **7**:880
chemistry **3**:**320–323**
  biochemistry **2**:**178–179**
  inorganic **3**:322; **7**:**778–779**
  organic **3**:283, 322; **10**:**1164–1167**
  periodic table **3**:322; **5**:541; **8**:949;
    **10**:**1214–1219**
  physical **3**:322; **10**:**1256–1257**
  *see also* chemical reactions
chemometrics **14**:1679
chemosynthesis **9**:1143
Chernobyl disaster **9**:*1116*
chernozems **13**:1596
Chicago L rapid transit system **12**:*1424*
Chichen Itza **1**:*104*
chicken pox **4**:*439*
chickens
  battery **1**:*27*
  parasites of **10**:1193
Chicxulub impact crater **1**:118; **6**:*688*
childbirth, pain relief during **1**:78
Chile saltpeter (sodium nitrate) **9**:1105
chimpanzees **16**:*2044*
  classification **3**:334
China, architecture **1**:*105*, 108;
    **2**:241–242
china clay (kaolin) **11**:1329, *1330*
Chinese, ancient
  fireworks **5**:607
  forges **2**:201
  papermaking **10**:1184–1185
  porcelain **11**:1330–1331
  printing **11**:1352
  rafts and boats **13**:1551
chips *see* silicon chips
chitin **13**:1561–1562
*Chlamydomonas* **2**:213
chlorine
  as an antiseptic **1**:95
  ions **7**:794
  production **5**:521
  reaction with sodium **10**:1219;
    **13**:1585
chlorofluorocarbons (CFCs) **2**:135;
    **6**:711; **10**:1179; **12**:1434
chlorophyll **2**:178; **10**:1253, 1254, *1255*,
    1274
chloroplasts **3**:*302*; **8**:989; **10**:1254

cholesterol 5:*588*–589; 9:1130
chorionic villi sampling 11:1343–1344
Christy, James 11:1305
chromatography 3:*324–325*; 5:631
chromium 8:967, 968–969; 15:*1854*
chromium chloride 12:*1513*
chromosomes 3:303; 4:*453*;
   6:*677–678*, 680
  sex 6:678
  *see also* genes
chromosphere 14:1715
chronic fatigue syndrome (CFS)
   11:1375, 1376
chronometers 15:*1816*, *1820*–1821
chrysalids 8:*977*, 978–979
chyle 7:884
chyme 4:424, *425*
Cierva, Juan de la 6:742
cilates 11:1372
cinnabar 8:950, *951*
circadian rhythms 2:194; 11:*1380*;
   13:1574
circuit boards 5:*527*; 15:*1850*
  *see also* printed circuits
circuit breakers *see* fuses and
   circuit breakers
circulatory systems 3:*326–331*
cirques 6:699
cisplatin 7:779
citric acid 1:*14*
CJD (Creutzfeldt-Jakob disease) 4:439;
   9:1100–*1101*
cladistics 3:334–335
clarinets 9:1077
classes 3:333
classification 3:*332–335*
  Aristotle and 1:111; 3:332
  Linnaeus and 2:185; 3:332, *333*;
   7:860–861
clathrates 7:774
Claude, Georges 7:854
Clausius, Rudolf 8:926–927
clavichords 9:1078
clavicle 13:1564
Clement, William 15:1820
clepsydras 15:1816, 1819
*Clermont* (steamship) 8:910
cliffs 7:825
  chalk 12:*1485*
climate 3:*336–339*; 6:681
  change 3:338–339; 8:*984–985*;
   11:1316–1318

effect of ocean currents on 9:1139
effect on soils 13:1594–1596
*see also* global warming; weather
*Climate Orbiter* (space probe) 13:1592
climax communities 4:491
clocks *see* timekeeping devices
clocks, biological (body clock) 2:194;
   13:1574
cloning 3:*340–343*; 6:675
closed-circuit television (CCTV)
   14:1770
*Clostridium* spp. (bacteria) 1:*91*; 2:*154*
clotting, blood 6:*733*
cloud chambers 10:1203
clouds 2:*132*; 3:*344–345*; 12:1419;
   15:*1900*, 1901; 16:1967, 1990
  altocumulus 3:*344*, 345
  altostratus 3:345; 16:1993
  and cyclones (depressions) 4:400,
   401; 16:1993
  cirrocumulus 3:345
  cirrostratus 3:345; 16:1993
  cirrus 3:*344*, 345; 16:1993
  cumulonimbus (thunderstorm)
   3:*344*, 345; 7:856; 15:*1801*, 1802,
   1836, 1837
  cumulus 3:*344*
  mammatus 16:*1989*
  nimbostratus 3:345; 16:1993
  nimbus 3:345
  stratus 16:1993
CN Tower, Toronto 13:1570
coal 5:550; 12:1485
  formation 3:*347*
  turned into oil 2:152–153
coal mining 3:*346–349*; 8:*1015*,
   1016–1017, *1018*, 1021
Coalsack Nebula 9:1091
coasts
  coastal deserts 4:416–417
  erosion 5:*561*, *562–564*; 7:825
  landforms 7:825
cobalt chloride 12:*1513*
COBE (cosmic background explorer)
   satellite 9:1135; 15:1881
cocaine 4:411, 464
coccyx 13:1564
cochineal 10:1180
cochlea 4:471–472
Cockerell, Christopher 6:*746*
Cockerell's raft 16:*1982*
Code Red computer virus 16:1926

codons 1:70; 6:680
coenzymes 5:558
cog railroads 3:*350–351*
cog wheels *see* gears
Cohl, Émile 1:84
Cohn, Ferdinand 8:986
coir 5:597
coke 2:200
Coke, Thomas 1:25
cold fusion 6:654
colds 6:765; 15:1916
  vaccines for 15:1892
collagen 11:*1369*
Collins, Michael 9:*1043*
Colmar, Charles Thomas de 3:263
colonization 4:491
color 7:*848*; 8:926
Colorado River 12:*1465*, *1468*
color blindness 4:402
color separation overlay (CSO)
   14:*1773*
Colossus (computer) 3:359
Colt, Samuel 6:*726*, 727
*Columbia* (space shuttle) 13:*1631*, 1632
combine harvesters 1:*25*, 26
combustion 5:*541*; 10:1175, 1177
Comet (airliner) 1:39
comets *see* asteroids, comets, and
  meteors
communications satellites 3:*352–355*;
   9:*1035*, 1037; 10:1163; 12:1518,
   *1520*, 1521–1522; 14:*1756*
  and radio 11:*1398*
  and television 2:237, 252–253; 3:352
  and videophones 15:1908–1909
commutators 5:*517–518*
companion stars 14:1676–1677
compasses 3:*356–357*; 9:1083, *1084*
complement proteins 6:762
composites 11:1291
compounds 2:138; 3:323
  chemical energy 3:316
  ionic 7:794
compressors, and jackhammers 7:802,
   803
*Compsognathus* 4:434
Compton, Arthur Holly 11:*1390*
Compton effect 11:1390–1391
Compton Gamma Ray Observatory
   (CGRO) 9:1136; 14:1766
computer-aided design (CAD) 3:371;
   5:554

computer-generated imagery (CGI) **9:***1056*

computer graphics **3:368–371**

computerized axial tomography (CAT; CT) scans **8:***934, 939*; **16:***2033–2034*

computers **3:358–367**; **5:**527, 529; **8:***925*

  and printing **11:***1358, 1359*

  as musical synthesizers **9:**1080

  Babbage's analytical engines **2:***151*; **3:**359; **13:***1588, 1589*

  binary numbers **9:***1126*; **13:***1587*

  bugs **13:***1590*, 1592

  CD and DVD recording drives **7:***831*

  CPU **3:**362, 368

  disks **7:***887–888*; **13:***1588*

  DNA **4:**455

  electronic **3:**359–360

  embedded **3:**364

  expert systems **1:**114

  games **3:***370*, 371

  graphical user interface (GUI) **3:***365*; **7:**819; **13:***1591*

  handheld **3:**364

  image scanners and **12:***1528*

  in animation **1:***83*, 84, *87–88*; **3:**370, *371*

  in medicine **8:**944–945

  Josephson memory **14:**1720

  laptop **3:***362*, 364; **7:**865

  light-operated **10:**1161

  magnetic tape as storage devices **13:***1588*

  main components **3:**362–363

  mainframe **3:**364

  mechanical **3:**358–359

  memory **13:***1587*

  monitors **7:**865

  mouse **7:***819*

  networks **3:**364–365

  neural networks **1:**114–115; **3:**367; **12:**1478

  palmtop **8:***995*

  personal digital assistants (PDAs) **10:1220–1221**

  personal (PCs) **3:***360–361, 363*–364; **5:***526*; **13:**1587, 1589

  quantum **3:**367

  robots controlled by **12:**1479, 1480, *1482*

  speech synthesis **16:***1934*, 1935, *1937*

  supercold **14:**1720

  supercomputers **3:***363*, 364; **14:***1720*

  used in mapmaking **8:***905*

  viruses **3:**366; **16:1924–1927**

  *see also* artificial intelligence; Internet; software; virtual reality

concentration, effect on chemical reactions **3:**317–318

Concorde (airplane) **1:***20*, 43, 45, 47; **14:***1722*, 1723

concrete

  pipes **10:***1268*, 1271

  roads **12:**1474–1475

condensation **3:**344; **4:**444; **7:**863; **13:***1578*

condensers, electrical *see* capacitors

condensers, steam **15:**1827–1828

conduction (heat) **6:**738

conductors **7:**781; **12:**1453, 1455

  lightning **7:***857*

  metals as **8:**962

  superconductors **14:**1719–1720

  *see also* semiconductors

conglomerates **12:**1484

Congreve, William **12:**1490

coniferous plants (conifers) **10:**1277

connective tissues **11:***1369*

Connolly, J. **11:**1373

conservation **3:**343; **4:**492; **16:**2044–2045

constellations **1:***120*, 121; **14:**1670–1671

contact lenses **5:**585

containers and container ships **13:***1555*

continental drift **4:**474–475, 484; **6:**690–691, 694; **7:**893; **11:**1293–*1294*; **16:***1995*–1996

  *see also* plate tectonics

continental shelves **9:**1140

continental slopes **9:**1140

contours **8:**902

contraception **11:***1326*

convection **6:***737*, 738

convertiplanes **16:***1944*

conveyor belt, global **9:**1139

Cookworthy, William **11:**1331

Coolidge, William David **16:**2031

coolidge tubes **16:**2031

Cooper, Peter **7:**871; **12:**1412

cooperite **11:**1297

Cooper pairs **14:**1718

coordination theory **15:**1853

copepods **9:**1142

Copernicus, Nicolaus **1:**120; **3:**372–373; **14:**1711; **15:**1877

copolymers **11:**1320

copper **3:***294*, **374–376**

  alloys **1:**57

  blister **8:***966*

  corrosion **3:**377

  early use of **3:***374*; **15:**1830–1831

  mining **3:***375*; **8:**1018

  refining **3:**376; **5:***521*; **8:***966*, 967–968; **15:**1828

  resistivity **7:**780

  smelting **1:**59; **8:***966*

  *see also* brass; bronze

Copperhead shells **2:**207, *208*

copper oxide **3:**375; **10:***1173*

copper sulfate **3:***376*; **10:***1217*; **12:***1513*; **15:**1854

copper sulfides **3:**375, 376

coral and coral reefs **9:***1141*–1142; **10:**1276

  global warming and **3:***339*; **6:**712

core, study of Earth's **6:**693–694

Corinth Canal **3:***275*

Coriolis, Gustave de **16:**2007

  Coriolis effect **15:**1810; **16:***1992*, 1993, 2007

corn, genetically engineered **2:**210

cornea **5:**582

corona, solar **14:**1715–1716

Correns, Carl Erich **6:**677; **8:**947

corrosion **3:377–378**

  prevention **3:**378; **5:**536; **8:**974

  *see also* electroplating

corticosteroids **5:**547

corundum **8:**1013

cosmic background explorer (COBE) satellite **9:**1135; **15:**1881

cosmic rays **6:**670; **10:**1207

  detection **10:**1202

cotton **3:379–381**; **5:**596, *597*; **14:**1780, *1782*

cotton gins **1:**26; **3:***380*–381; **5:**596

Cousteau, Jacques **4:***447*, 448

cowpox **7:**804, 805; **15:1889–1890**

cows

  immune to *Staphylococcus aureus* **6:***675*

  milking **1:***28*

Crab Nebula **9:***1090*, 1091, 1110

crabs, shells of **13:***1561*

cracking **9:**1149
  catalytic **3:***295;* **9:**1149
Craigie, Andrew **4:**462
cramp **12:***1459*
cranes **4:388–389**
crash barriers **12:**1476
Crater Lake **12:***1469*
craters, impact **1:**118; **6:***688;* **7:**821
cream **5:**621
creation science **5:**567
Cretaceous period **6:**687
Creutzfeldt-Jakob disease (CJD) **2:***220;*
  **4:**439; **9:**1100–*1101*
Crick, Francis, and James Watson
  **4:390–391**, 454; **8:**987
Cristofori, Bartolomeo di Francesco
  **9:**1079
critical mass **5:***613,* 614; **9:**1120
critical point **15:**1900
crocodiles **1:**82; **4:***434*
Crompton, Samuel **14:**1782; **16:**2026
crops
  rotation **1:**25; **10:**1222
  *see also* agriculture; pest control
cross-staffs **9:**1084
crowns, dental **4:**412
crude oil *see* oil, crude
cruisers **16:**1958, *1961*
crust, Earth's **9:**1063; **11:**1294
  rock cycle and **12:***1487*
cryogenics **4:392–393**; **14:**1717
cryopreservation **4:***392*
cryosurgery **4:**393
crystallography **6:**692
  X-ray **4:**394, 395–396; **16:**2034
crystals **4:394–397**; **8:**1010
  growing **4:**396
  ionic **7:**794
  liquid *see* liquid crystals
  photonic **10:**1161
  piezoelectric **10:***1264–1265;* **13:**1557;
    **15:**1817, 1822, 1871
  structure **4:**394–*395*
  symmetry **4:**395
  synthetic **4:**394, 396–397
Ctesibius of Alexandria **9:**1074
CT scans *see* computerized axial
  tomography
Cugnot, Nicolas **2:**140; **7:**870
cullet **6:**702
Curie, Marie and Pierre **3:**322;
  **4:398–399**; **11:**1401, *1402*

curium **4:**398
currents (electrical) *see* electrical
  currents
currents (oceanic) **9:***1138–*1139
  and coastal erosion **5:**563–564
  effect on climate **9:**1139
  global warming and **6:**712; **9:**1139
Curtiss, Glenn **1:**38
cut-and-cover construction **12:**1424
cyanide process **13:**1559
cyanobacteria (blue-green algae) **2:**132;
  **8:**989; **10:**1253
cyanocobalmin **16:**1932
cybernetics **12:**1479
cyberterrorism **3:**366
cycads **10:**1277
cycloalkanes **9:**1144
cyclohexane **10:**1166
cyclones (depressions; lows)
  *see* depressions
cyclones (hurricanes; typhoons)
  **4:400–401**; **8:***980,* 985; **15:**1836;
  **16:***1992, 1993,* 1994, *2007*
  *see also* tornadoes
cyclopropane **3:***285*
cyclotrons **10:**1199, *1200;* **14:**1719
Cygnus X-1 **2:**199
cystic fibrosis **5:**577; **6:**679
cytoplasm **3:***301*
cytosine **9:**1038
Czochralski, Jan **4:**397
Czochralski technique **4:**397

**D**

2,4-D **10:**1225, 1226
Dacron **11:**1287, 1288
Daguerre, Louis-Jacques-Mandé
  **10:**1243
Dahl, Carl **10:**1185
Daimler, Gottlieb **2:**141; **7:***783;* **9:**1060
Dalles Dam **6:**757
Dalton, James **4:402–403**; **10:**1261
Dalton, John **3:**321
damping **12:**1457
dams **2:***193;* **4:404–407**; **5:***549;* **6:***754,*
  *757;* **12:***1470;* **16:***1973*
Daniell cells **2:**171, 172
Darby, Abraham **2:**202, 231
Darwin, Charles **2:**186; **3:**332;
  **4:408–409**; **5:***568–569;* **6:**685
  inspired by Linnaeus **7:**860
data synchronization **10:**1221

Davenport, Thomas **5:**516
da Vinci robots **14:**1731
Davis, William Morris **6:**690;
  **7:**821–822; **12:**1467–1468
Davy, Humphry **3:***321;* **4:**507; **5:**540,
  586; **7:**853; **8:**965
  and aluminum **1:**67
  and photography **10:**1242
  and sodium **13:**1586
  safety lamp **8:**1016–1017
days **4:**475, 477
  sidereal and solar **15:**1816
DDT (dichlorodiphenyl-
  trichloroethane) **4:**492; **10:**1223;
  **11:**1313
death, forensic science and **5:**632
Decca navigation **5:**611; **9:**1085–1086
deceleration **5:**626
decibels **4:***472;* **13:**1616
decimal number system **9:**1123–1124
decimal points **9:**1126
decomposers **5:**624
decompression chambers **4:***450,* 451
decompression sickness (the bends)
  **4:**450–451; **10:**1179
*Deep Space 1* (space probe) **13:**1626,
  1630
deer, musk **10:**1228, 1229
Deere, John **1:**26; **11:**1301
defibrillators **8:***941*
deflagration **5:**579
De Forest, Lee **5:**527; **11:**1398
deforestation **15:**1814
  and global warming **6:**711
Deimos (moon) **8:**913
deltas **7:***824;* **12:***1467*
Democritus (Demokritos) **5:**539;
  **10:**1206, 1261
demography **14:**1679
demolition **2:**248–*249*
density **1:**102
  relative *see* specific gravity
dentistry **4:410–413**
  drills **4:***458–459*
  ultraviolet light used in **15:**1875, 1876
  X-rays **16:**2033
dentures **4:**412–413
deoxyribonucleic acid *see* DNA
depression (mental disease)
  **11:**1373, 1376
depressions (cyclones; lows) **12:**1419,
  1470; **16:**1992–1993

depth charges 2:208–209
depth of field 10:1238
depth sounding 15:1873
*De Re Metallica* (Agricola) 8:*967*, 1015
derivatives 3:265
dermis, of the skin 13:*1566*, 1567
derricks 4:460–461
desalination 4:445; 10:*1172*; 16:*1972*
Descartes, René 8:921, *922*; 11:1377;
  12:1421
desertification 4:416
deserts 2:191; 4:414–417, *475*; 7:*822*;
  12:1419
  polar 12:1419
destroyers, guided-missile 16:1960
detergents *see* soaps and detergents
detonators 5:580–581
deuterium 5:552; 6:652, *653*, 654, 760
  and nuclear fusion 9:1117, 1118, 1122
Devonian period 6:686
dew 15:*1901*
Dewar, James 15:1895
dew point 3:344; 12:1418; 13:1578;
  15:1901
diabetes 2:179; 5:547; 6:764; 8:*959*;
  9:1132
dialysis, kidney 5:*573*; 8:*944*
diamond 3:*284*–285; 4:394, **418–419**;
  5:*540*; 8:1011, 1013
  an abrasive 1:13; 4:419
  cutting 4:419
  industrial uses 1:13; 4:419
  set in platinum 11:*1299*
  synthetic 4:396–397, 418
diamond-ring effect 4:*487*, 488
diaphragm 12:1464
diatoms 5:632; 11:*1372*
dichlorodiphenyltrichloroethane
  (DDT) 4:492; 10:1223; 11:1313
Dick, Philip K. 1:112–113
dielectric 3:277, 278
Diesel, Rudolph 4:*421*; 7:783
diesel engines 4:**420–423**; 7:783,
  786–787
  common-rail 4:421
  fuel-injection system 6:646–647
  in ships 8:*909*
diesel oil 9:1149
diet, balanced 8:*958*
diffraction
  light 7:846, *847*; 10:*1158*, 1159; 16:1978
  sound 13:1615

diffusion pumps, vapor 15:1893–*1894*
digestion 2:178
digestive system 4:**424–427**
  enzymes 5:558
digital audio software 4:**428–431**
digital compact cassettes (DCCs) 7:888
Digital Scene Matching Area
  Correlator (DSMAC) 6:720
digital signal processors (DSPs) 9:1036
Digital Subscriber Line (DSL) 14:1758
digital technology 5:528
  and animation 1:86
  and cell phones 9:1035
  and telephones 14:1758
  camcorders 3:270–272
  digital audio software 4:**428–431**
  digital audio tapes (DATs) 7:*888*
  digital cameras 10:*1240*, *1246*–1251
  digital projector technology 9:1059
  digital radio 11:*1399*, 1400
  digital television 2:238; 5:528–529
  digital video 9:1053, 1054–1055
  laser discs 7:832
  photocopiers using 10:1233
digital versatile (video) discs (DVDs)
  7:830–*833*; 14:1774, *1775*
dikes 9:1138
dimension stones 8:1019, 1020, *1021*
dinosaurs 4:**432–437**
  extinction of 1:118; 2:183;
    6:*687–688*
  fossils 2:*186*; 6:686
diodes 5:527, *533*; 13:*1541*
  light-emitting (LEDs) 3:264; 7:855;
    13:1543
Diophantus of Alexandria 1:53
dioxin 10:1225
*Diplodocus* 4:*435*
dipoles 1:90; 7:890, *892*; 10:1264
Dirac, Paul 11:*1392*
disaccharides 3:*281*
discharge lamps 7:795, 854, *855*, 879
*Discovery* (space shuttle) 13:*1634*
diseases 4:**438–443**
  autoimmune 6:764
  bacterial 2:153–154; 4:439–440, *443*
  carried in water 13:1547
  genetic 6:*680*
  lymphatic system and 7:*883*–884
  parasitic 10:*1193*, 1194–1197
  viral 4:440–441
disinfectants 1:94

disks
  computer 7:887–888
  magneto-optical (MODs) 7:*888*
Disney, Walt 1:*84*, 85; 9:1058
distance measuring equipment (DME)
  9:1086
distances, measurement 8:*928*–929
distillation 4:**444–445**
  fractional 4:445; 9:1104, *1148*;
    10:1179
  of air 9:1104; 10:1179
  of crude oil 9:*1148*–1149
  vacuum 9:*1148*
diving 4:**446–451**
  atmospheric 4:451
  deep-sea 4:449–451; 10:1178–1179
  saturation 4:451
  scuba 4:*446*, *447*, 448–449
diving bells 4:446, 449, 450–451;
  14:1698
dizziness 4:472
DNA (deoxyribonucleic acid)
  3:302–303, 333–334; 4:**452–455**;
  6:680
  and protein synthesis 1:70;
    4:454–455; 6:680; 9:1038, 1039
  and the genetic code 4:452–453,
    454–455; 8:987; 9:1038
  cloning 3:341–342
  discovery 8:986–987
  fingerprinting (genetic
    fingerprinting) 2:*187*; 4:455; 5:*534*,
    535, 633; 7:*878*; 16:2044
  "junk" 6:680
  mutations 4:*455*
  plasmid 1:29; 3:341–342, *343*; 6:674
  recombinant 6:*674*
  sequencing 9:*1039*
  structure 4:*390–391*, 453, 454; 8:987;
    9:*1038*–1039
  viral 4:440–441; 15:1914–1915
Döbereiner, Johann 10:1215
Dobzhansky, Theodosius 5:570
dogs, breeds of 3:*332*
Dolby Digital 9:1058
Dolby Stereo 9:1058
doldrums 16:2007
Dolly the sheep 3:340, *342*
Domagk, Gerhard 8:943
dopamine 9:1101
Doppler, Christian Johann 4:456;
  9:1087; 13:1615

Doppler effect **4:**456–457; **9:**1087; **13:**1615–1616
  and expansion of the universe **4:**457; **15:**1879–1880
Doppler radar **11:**1396
Down's syndrome **6:**680; **11:***1344*
drag **1:***19*, 41; **9:***1051*
Drake, Edwin L. **9:**1145
drawknives **15:**1833
Drebbel, Cornelius van **14:**1697, 1698; **15:**1799
dredgers **4:**481–*482*
drift (glaciofluvial deposits) **6:**700
drift, longshore **5:**564
drilling rigs **4:**460–461; **6:**662; **9:***1146, 1147*
drills **1:**13; **4:**458–459; **15:***1832*
  bow **15:**1830
  drill bits **4:**459, 460; **15:**1831
  drill presses **15:**1835; **16:**2022
  gears **6:**668
  hammer **8:**1016
  pneumatic **4:***472*
  steam-driven **8:**1016
  tips **8:**969
  ultrasonic **15:***1873*
  see also jackhammers
drinks, isotonic **13:**1661
drones **1:***45*
drought **3:***337*
drug industry **4:**462–465; **8:**943
  drug design and development **4:**463; **15:***1913*
  drug testing **4:**463–*464*; **15:***1912*
  see also anesthetics; antibiotics; drugs
drugs **4:**462–463; **8:**942–943
  anticancer **7:**779; **10:***1166*, 1167; **11:**1298
  antiparasite **10:***1196–1197*
  inorganic molecules as **7:**779
  metabolism **5:**574
  placebo effect **4:**465
  poisonous **11:**1307
  side effects **4:**463
  used for mental disorders **11:***1376*
  see also anesthetics; antibiotics; drug industry
drumlins **6:**700; **7:**824
drums **9:**1073, *1077*, 1078
dry ice **6:**662; **13:***1610*; **14:***1695–1696*
dry spinning **5:**599
DSL (Digital Subscriber Line) **14:**1758

DSMAC (Digital Scene Matching Area Correlator) **6:**720
Duesbury, William **11:**1331
dugouts **13:**1551
DUKWs (Duplex Universal Karriers, Wheeled) **1:**74, *75*
dump trucks (dumpers) **4:**481
dunes **7:***822*, 825
  coastal **7:**825
Dunlop, John Boyd **2:**175; **14:**1736
Duplex Universal Karriers, Wheeled (DUKWs) **1:**74, *75*
du Pont, Eleuthère Irénée **7:***834*
Duralumin **1:**58
Duryea, Charles and Frank **2:**141
DVD camcorders **3:**271
DVD recorders **7:**832; **14:***1775*
DVDs (digital versatile discs) **7:**830–*833*; **14:**1774, *1775*
Dvorak, August **7:**818–819
dyes and dyeing **4:**466–469; **14:***1781*
  fading **15:**1876
  photographic **10:**1244
  wool **16:**2025, *2026*
  see also paints
dynamics **10:**1260
dynamite **5:**579–580, *579*; **8:**1015–1016

## E

eardrums **4:**471; **13:**1617
ears and hearing **4:**470–472; **13:**1613; **15:**1870
  hearing damaged by noise **13:***1616*
Earth **4:**473–478; **13:**1604
  age of **4:**473; **5:**566; **6:**689
  circumference **8:**902, 929
  history compressed into a year **6:**687
  layers **4:**473–474, *475*
  magnetic field **7:***890*, 891
  movements **4:**475–476
  solar heating **4:**476–477
  solar year **4:**477–*478*
  temperature **2:**133; **4:**474
  vegetation cover **7:***777*
  see also atmosphere; plate tectonics
earthmovers **4:**479–482; **12:**1474
earthquakes **4:**483–486
  causes **4:**483–484; **11:***1294*, 1295
  causing tsunamis **15:**1859–*1860*, *1861*
  epicenter **12:**1531
  focus **12:**1531
  prediction **4:**485; **12:**1533

  scales used to measure **4:**486; **12:**1530
  seismic waves (shockwaves) **4:**486; **6:**693–694; **12:**1531
  skyscrapers built to withstand **13:**1571
  see also seismology
Earth Summit (1992) **2:***183*
earthworms, skeleton **13:**1562
Easter Island **1:**99
Eastman, George **10:**1243
eating disorders **9:**1132
ecdysis **8:**978
ECGs see electrocardiograms and electrocardiographs
echo sounders **5:**610; **13:**1611, 1612
Eckert, John Presper **3:**360
eclipses **4:**487–488; **9:**1044–*1045*; **14:**1715
ECMs (electronic countermeasures) **9:**1032; **16:**1955–1956
ecology **4:**489–492
ecosystems **4:**489–490
  changing **4:**491
eddy currents **13:**1608
edema **7:**882
Edison, Thomas **4:**493–494
  and the telephone **4:**494
  electric lamps (lightbulbs) **3:**289; **4:***493*; **7:**854
  kinetoscope **9:**1052
  phonograph **4:***494*; **13:**1617–*1618*
  power plant **4:**509; **11:**1337
EEGs see electroencephalographs and electroencephalograms
eelworms **10:**1225
eggs, in the diet **9:**1130
Egyptians, ancient
  agriculture **1:***23*
  calendar **15:**1815
  idea of the universe **15:**1877
  locks (security) **7:**868–869
  metal extraction **8:**967
  mortar **2:**244
  papyrus **10:***1184*
  pyramids **1:**105; **2:***240*, 241; **8:**1019; **13:**1568; **14:**1733
  quarrying **8:**1019
  rafts and boats **13:**1551, 1552
  surveying **14:**1733
  timekeeping **15:**1819
Ehrlich, Paul **8:**942
Einstein (satellite) **9:**1136

El Niño Southern Oscillation (ENSO) **8**:985
e-mail **7**:788, 791, *791*
  viruses **16**:1926
  *see also* Internet
embryos
  development **3**:305
  storage **4**:*392*
emerald **8**:1013; **15**:*1854*
Emphedocles **5**:538
emphysema **12**:1464
emulsions, nuclear **10**:1202
endangered species, conservation **3**:343
end moraine **6**:700
endocrine system **5:546–548**
endoplasmic reticulum **3**:*301, 302*
endorphins **2**:*219*
endoscopes **5**:*602*; **8**:936, *938*
energy **5:549–552**
  electrical **5**:*552*
  geothermal **5**:552
  heat **6**:736
  kinetic **5**:549, *550, 551, 552*; **10**:*1258*;
    **12**:*1493*
  latent **5**:549, *550*
  lost in food chains **5**:625
  mass-energy equation **5**:551, 614;
    **6**:653; **8**:919, 924; **9**:1113; **12**:1438;
    **14**:1716
  nuclear **5**:550–552, 613
  potential **5**:*549*, 550; **12**:*1493*
  renewable resources **15**:1803
  solar *see* solar energy
  transfer **5**:627
  water **5**:552
Engelbart, Douglas **7**:819
engineering **5:553–556**
engines
  automobile **2**:142–*143*
  diesel *see* diesel engines
  four-stroke **7**:782–783, *785*; **9**:1061
  fuel-injection **6**:646–647
  gasoline **7**:783–786
  heat engines **6**:738
  internal combustion *see* internal
    combustion engines
  jet *see* jet engines
  marine-propulsion **8**:909–911
  Newcomen's **8**:1016; **14**:1684, *1685*
  steam *see* steam engines
  Stirling (air) **14:1689–1690**
  Trevithick's **14**:1686–1687

two-stroke **7**:785–*786*; **8**:912; **9**:1061
Wankel (rotary) **7**:787; **8**:912;
    **14**:1685–1686; **16:1948–1949**
Watt's **14**:1685–1686
  *see also* rockets; turbines
ENIAC calculating machine **3**:*359*, 360;
    **13**:1589
ENIGMA code **3**:359
enteroviruses **15**:1916
*Envisat* (satellite) **12**:*1521*
enzymes **3**:296, 302; **5:557–558**;
    **10**:1167; **11**:1366, 1369
  digestive **4**:425–426; **5**:558
  metalloenzymes **7**:779
eons, geological **6**:*683*
eosinophils **6**:*733*
epidermis, of the skin **13**:1565, *1566*,
    1567
epididymis **12**:1450, *1451*
epidurals **1**:77, 78
Epigenome Project **6**:680
epinephrine **5**:547–548
epochs, geological **6**:688
Epstein-Barr virus **15**:1892
equations, algebraic **1**:*52*, 53–54; **8**:924
equator **4**:476–477
equinoxes **4**:477, 478
equivalence, principle of **12**:1438
equivalent weight **5**:521
eras, geological **6**:*683*
Eratosthenes **8**:929
Ericsson, John **5**:606
erosion **5:559–564**; **7**:820, 824;
    **13**:*1595*; **16**:1983–1984
  average rate **16**:1987
  by rivers **5**:561–562; **12**:1465–1466,
    1467–1468
  cycles of **6**:690
  glacial **5**:564; **6**:699; **7**:*821*; **12**:1468
  soil **5**:560–561, *563*; **13**:*1595*
  *see also* weathering
erratics **6**:700
escalators **5**:543–*545*
*Escherichia coli* (E. coli) **2**:*152*; **8**:988
eskers **6**:700; **7**:824
esophagus **4**:424
estrogen **5**:548; **11**:1343
ethane **3**:*285*
ether (chemical compound) **4**:410
ether (hypothetical medium)
    **12**:1435
ethics, medical **8**:945

ethylene oxide **13**:1583
Etna, Mount **16**:1940
Euclid **8**:*920*
Eudoxus of Cnidus **8**:921
*Euglena* **3**:*335*
eukaryotes **3**:335; **11**:1371
Euler, Leonhard **8**:922
European Organization for Nuclear
    Research (CERN) **2**:*136, 205*;
    **10**:*1198, 1201*
eustachian tubes **4**:471
eutrophication **11**:1313–1314
evaporation **2**:138; **3**:344; **7**:863;
    **15**:1900
evaporators, flash-chamber **16**:*1972*
Everest, Mount **7**:821; **9**:*1063*
  height calculated **9**:1064
Everglades **2**:*192*
Evinrude, Ole **8**:911
evolution **1**:81; **2**:186–187; **4**:409;
    **5:565–570**; **6**:685
excavators **4**:*479–480*
  for tunneling **15**:1863–1864
excretory system **5:571–574**
exercise, anaerobic **12**:*1459*
exfoliation (weathering) **16**:1987
exocrine system **5:575–577**
Exosat **14**:1766
exoskeletons **13**:1561–1562
exosphere **2**:*133*, 135; **11**:*1398*
expert systems **1**:114
*Explorer 1* (satellite) **12**:1518
explosive forming **5**:581
explosive reactive armor (ERA)
    **14**:1744
explosives **5:578–581**
  *see also* bombs and shells; fireworks
    and flares
extinction **2**:183; **6**:*687–688*
  mass **2**:182
  of the dinosaurs **1**:118; **4**:437
extrusion process **11**:*1289*, 1290
Exxon *Valdez* oil spill **2**:152; **11**:1314;
    **14**:*1748*
Eyematic **1**:*87*
eyes and vision **5:582–585**
  color vision **5**:582; **7**:*848*

## F

F-22 Raptor (aircraft) **16**:1956
F-35 Joint Strike Fighter
    **16**:1946–1947

fabric conditioners **13**:1583
fallopian tubes **12**:1450, 1452
families (classification) **3**:333
fantails **13**:1544; **16**:2014
Faraday, Michael **5**:586–587
  and electromagnetism **4**:508; **5**:523,
    524–525, *587*; **7**:772
  and the first transformer **7**:*772*, 773
  laws of electrolysis **5**:521, 587
Fahrenheit, Daniel Gabriel **8**:951;
  **15**:1796
farming *see* agriculture
Farnsworth, Philo **14**:1769
farsightedness *see* hyperopia
"Fat Man" atomic bomb **9**:*1120*
fats **5**:588–589; **8**:959
  absorption in the intestines **7**:884
  dietary **5**:*588–589*; **8**:*958*;
    **9**:1130–1131
  food technology and **5**:619–620
  saturated and unsaturated **5**:588;
    **9**:1130–1131
faucets, valves in **15**:1898
faults **4**:*485*; **6**:692
  and earthquakes **4**:484
  and oil reservoirs **9**:*1145*
  and tsunamis **15**:1859–1860
  transform **11**:1295
feedback control **13**:1545; **15**:1800
feedstock, chemical **9**:1149
feet, prosthetic **11**:1363
felt **14**:1785
femtoseconds **10**:1257
Feng, Milton **10**:1161
Ferdinand II, Grand Duke **15**:1796
fermentation **5**:590–591; **11**:1372;
  **16**:2035, *2036*
  and antibiotics **1**:*93*; **5**:591
  and bread making **2**:227; **5**:590;
    **11**:1372
  Pasteur and **10**:1210; **16**:2035
Fermi, Enrico **9**:1112
Fermilab **10**:1200
ferromagnets **7**:889
fertilization **3**:*305*; **12**:1449, *1452*
fertilizers **5**:592–595; **7**:779; **9**:1105,
  *1106*
  and the agricultural revolution **1**:25
  and water pollution **1**:30; **4**:492;
    **5**:*595*; **11**:*1313*–1314
  from sewage **13**:1546, *1548*, 1549
fetal heart-rate monitors **8**:940–941

fetus
  development **11**:1344–1345
  ultrasound and **11**:*1344*; **13**:*1615*,
    1616
Feynman, Richard **9**:1081, *1082*
fiber **5**:596–599
  forensic science and **5**:631
  synthetic **5**:*597–598*; **14**:1784
  *see also* textiles
fiber, dietary **9**:1128
fiberglass, Teflon-coated **2**:247
fiber optics **5**:600–602; **10**:1160
  and cable television **2**:237, 253
  switchers **4**:397
  telephones and **5**:602; **14**:*1755*, 1757
fiberscopes **5**:602
Fibonacci, Leonardo **8**:921
fibrin and fibrinogen **6**:*733*
files (tools) **15**:1833
fillings, dental **4**:411–*412*
fimbriae **2**:*155*
finches, Galápagos (Darwin's finches)
  **2**:182; **4**:409; **5**:*569*
fingerprinting **5**:630–631; **13**:*1565*
  genetic *see* DNA, fingerprinting
firedamp **8**:1016–1017
firefighting **5**:603–606
fireflies **7**:880
fires, forest **15**:1812
fire-setting **8**:1015
fireworks and flares **5**:607–608;
  **13**:*1586*
Fischer, Emil **3**:*280*
fish **1**:*79*, 82
  evolution **1**:82; **6**:686
  farming **1**:24
  fossilized **5**:565
Fisher, R. A. **5**:570
fishing industry **5**:609–612
fission, nuclear **5**:551, **613**–615; **9**:1111,
  1112–1113; **11**:1339
  and nuclear weapons **9**:1119–*1121*
Fitch, John **8**:909
Fitzroy, Robert **8**:981
fjords **6**:699
flagellates **11**:1372
Flamsteed, John **8**:996
flares **5**:*608*
flash, camera **10**:1241, 1245
flashlights **4**:*502*
flash memory **10**:*1248*
Flavr-savr tomatoes **6**:675

flax (linen) **5**:596, 597
Fleischer, Max **1**:84
Fleming, Alexander **1**:92; **2**:154;
  **5**:616–617; **8**:*942*
Fleming, John Ambrose
  diode **5**:527
  left-hand rule **5**:*524*
  right-hand rule **5**:*524*, 525
Flettner, Anton **6**:742
flex, electric **7**:*780*
flies
  black **10**:1195–1196
  fruit **3**:305; **10**:1223
flight
  airplanes **1**:40–42
  history of **1**:*36*–40
  hypersonic **14**:1722
  Leonardo da Vinci and **7**:*840*
  subsonic **14**:1722
  supersonic *see* supersonic flight
  transonic **14**:1722
flight simulation **15**:1911–*1912*
flintlocks **6**:724
*Flintstones, The* **1**:*85*
float-glass process **6**:*702*, 703
flooding **8**:*984*; **12**:1469–1470
  flood barriers **4**:*406*, 407; **12**:*1470*
  tidal **12**:*1470*
floodplains **12**:1466
floppy disks, computer **7**:887–888
Florey, Howard **1**:91; **5**:617
flotation separation **8**:967, *968*;
  **11**:*1297*
flow
  laminar **16**:1928, 1929
  turbulent **16**:1928
flowers, nectar production **2**:195
flowmeters, venturi **15**:*1903*
fluids
  pressure in **11**:1347; **15**:1902, 1903
  *see also* gases; liquids
flukes **4**:441
  blood **10**:*1194*
fluorescence **7**:879; **10**:1159; **15**:*1874*,
  1875
  and solar energy **13**:1598–1599
fluorite **8**:1011
fluoroscopes **16**:2033
flutes **9**:1073, *1075*, 1076
fly agaric **6**:*648*
"fly-by-light" systems **1**:42
"fly-by-wire" systems **1**:42

*Flyer* (aircraft) **1**:37
flying shuttles **14**:1782
foam
  polyurethane **11**:1289
  structural **11**:1291
focal length **10**:*1238–1239*, 1240, 1250
focal point **7**:*846*
Focke, Heinrich **6**:742
Focke, Wilhelm Olbers **8**:947
Fokker **1**:18
Fokker, Anthony **1**:38–39
food *see* nutrition
Food and Drug Administration (FDA)
  **4**:462, 465
food chains **5**:624, *625*
  poisons and pesticides in **11**:1313,
  1314
food technology **5**:**618–623**
  additives **4**:*469*; **5**:623
  *see also* bread making; refrigeration
food webs **5**:**624–625**
foot-pound system **5**:550
foraminiferans **11**:1372
force, measuring **11**:1335
forces **5**:**626–629**
  contact **5**:*627*
  fundamental **5**:629; **10**:1206, 1209
  shear **4**:498
Ford, Henry **2**:*141*; **12**:1472
Ford, Model T **2**:*141*–142
forensic science **5**:**630–633**; **13**:1648
  *see also* electrophoresis
forests
  forestry **15**:1814
  helping forests regrow **15**:*1814*
  temperate **2**:190–191, 193
  tropical **2**:192
  *see also* rain forests
forging **8**:*970*, 971
  tools **15**:1831
forklift trucks **5**:**634–635**
Formica **11**:1287, 1289
Formula One racing **2**:147–148
Fortin, Jean, barometer **2**:167–168
Fossett, Steve **2**:*164*
fossil fuels **5**:550; **10**:1165
  and climate change **3**:339;
  **11**:1316–*1317*
  underwater **9**:1143
fossils **6**:685–687, 689–690, 692
  dinosaur **2**:*186*; **6**:*686*
  fish **5**:*565*

*Hylonomus* **6**:*684*
  index (zone) **6**:*684*, *685*, 690
  skulls **13**:1563
foundations **2**:246
Fourdrinier machines **10**:1185, 1189
Fourneyron, Benoit **15**:1867
foxes, fennec **4**:*417*
fractal geometry **3**:*313*
fractional distillation **4**:445; **9**:1104,
  *1148*; **10**:1179
fractions **9**:1126
fractures **13**:1564
Francis, James **6**:756
francium **1**:15
Franklin, Benjamin **4**:506; **7**:857
Franklin, Rosalind **4**:391, 454
Frasch, Hermann **14**:1710
Fraunhofer, Joseph von **13**:1645, *1648*
Fraunhofer lines **13**:*1648*
freeze-drying **5**:623; **12**:1434; **14**:1695;
  **15**:1895
freezing **14**:*1776*
  food **5**:622; **12**:1434
frequency **15**:1870; **16**:1975–1976
  natural **12**:1457
frequency curves **14**:1679–1680
frequency modulation (FM) **1**:89, 90;
  **11**:*1398*, 1400
Fresnel, Augustin **7**:851
Freud, Sigmund **11**:*1373*, 1374
friction **2**:173; **5**:**636–637**; **12**:1454
  and electrical charge **4**:504, 505
  overcoming **7**:876
  viscosity and **12**:1454; **16**:1928
frigates **16**:1959–1960
frogs **8**:*979*
  desert **4**:417
fronts, weather **12**:1419; **16**:1990–1991,
  1992–1993
frost **13**:1579
frostbite **4**:439
frost shattering **16**:1987
fructose **3**:*280*
fruits **10**:*1276*
  in the diet **9**:1129; **16**:*1930*
  preservation **10**:1172
  processing **5**:618
Frye, Thomas **11**:1331
fuel cells **1**:63; **6**:**644–645**, 760
  *see also* batteries
fuel gauges, automobile **15**:1844
fuel injection **6**:**646–647**

fuel rods, nuclear **10**:*1219*
fulcrums **7**:*842*
Fuller, Buckminster **10**:1257
fullerenes **3**:285; **10**:*1257*
Fulton, Robert **8**:910; **14**:1697
fumaroles **16**:1941
functions **8**:925
fungi kingdom **6**:648–649; **8**:*988*–989;
  **10**:1197
  and disease **1**:92; **4**:441
  classification **10**:1276
  parasitic fungi **10**:*1196*, 1197
  *see also* penicillin
funiculars **3**:*260*–261
fuses, bomb **2**:207–208
fuses and circuit breakers **6**:**650–651**
fusion, nuclear **5**:551–552; **6**:**652–654**
  cold fusion **6**:654
  in hydrogen bombs **5**:551; **9**:1117,
  1122
  in nuclear reactors **6**:654;
  **9**:1117–*1118*
  in stars and the Sun **1**:121; **5**:613;
  **6**:*652*; **14**:*1714*, 1716
  plasmas and **11**:1285
Fust, Johann **11**:1353

**G**
GADFLY missiles **9**:1030
Galápagos Islands **2**:182; **4**:409; **5**:568,
  *569*
galaxies **1**:122–123; **9**:*1135*; **14**:*1670*
  and black holes **2**:198
  clusters **14**:1677
  nearest **15**:1878
  receding **1**:123; **15**:1878
  *see also* Milky Way galaxy
Galen **3**:326; **4**:462
galena (lead sulfide) **7**:*836*; **8**:964,
  *1009*
Galileo (Global Positioning System)
  **6**:705, *707*
*Galileo* (space probe) **7**:814; **13**:1626,
  1630
Galileo Galilei **6**:**655–656**
  and gravity **6**:716; **8**:917
  and pendulums **15**:1816
  and the Copernican theory **1**:120;
  **6**:*655*, 656; **15**:1879
  and the planets **6**:656; **7**:813
  telescopes **6**:655–656; **10**:1260;
  **14**:1760

*Galileo Orbiter* (spacecraft) **9:**1046
Galle, Johann Gottfried **9:**1093
gallium **8:**949; **10:**1218
gallium arsenide **13:**1540, 1543
Galvani, Luigi **2:**169; **4:**506–507
galvanizing **3:**378; **16:**2039
galvanometers **1:***73*; **4:**499–500
gametes **12:**1449
gametophytes **10:**1276, 1277
gamma rays **5:**615; **6:***657–658*; **7:**795, 800; **13:**1644
  and radiotherapy **11:**1404
  from space **1:**125; **9:**1136
garbage **6:***712*
Garnerin, André-Jacques **10:**1190
garnet **8:***1009*, 1013
Garros, Roland **16:**1952
Gascoigne, William **8:**996
gas-discharge lamps *see* discharge lamps
gases **2:**138; **6:***659–662*
  inert *see* inert gases
  ionization **7:**795
  kinetic theory of **8:**926–927
  natural *see* natural gas
  pressurized **6:***659*, 660, 661; **11:***1348*
  viscosity **12:**1454
gas laws **6:663–664**
gas mantles, incandescent **7:**853
gas masks **6:***661*
gasoline
  lead in **7:**838
  octane numbers **9:**1149
  production **9:**1149
gas turbines **5:**518; **6:665–666**; **7:**787, 807; **15:***1869*
  in power stations **11:**1338
Gates, William **3:***360*; **13:**1591
Gauss, Carl **8:**922
Gay-Lussac, Joseph-Louis **6:***664*
gears **6:667–668**
  automobile **2:**144
  bicycle **2:***176–177*
  worm **6:**668; **7:***876*
geese, snow **1:***81*
Geiger, Hans Wilhelm **6:**669
Geiger-Müller detectors (Geiger counters) **6:**658, **669–670**; **10:**1205; **15:**1876
Geissler tubes **7:***794*
gemstones **8:**1013

gene flow **2:**181, 182
genera **3:**333
generators **5:***518*, 519; **6:671–672**
  in hydroelectric power plants **6:**756
genes **4:**452–453; **6:***678–679*, 680
  alleles **6:**679
  decoding **4:**453–454
  dominant and recessive **6:**679
  effect or "penetrance" **6:**679–680
  Hox **3:**305
  "jumping" **6:**680
  mapping *see* Human Genome Project
  mutations **6:**679
*Genesis* (space probe) **14:***1715*
gene therapy **9:**1039
genetic drift **2:**182
genetic engineering **3:**342; **6:673–676**; **9:**1039
  and corn **2:**210
  and wheat **2:**210, *213*; **6:***676*
  engineered bacteria **6:**673–*674*, 676
  farm animals **1:**28–29
  monoclonal antibodies **6:**676
  plants **1:**29–*30*; **2:**210, *211*, 212, *213*; **3:***341*; **6:***676*
  to make vaccines **6:**676
  *see also* cloning
genetic fingerprinting *see* DNA, fingerprinting
genetic modification (GM) *see* genetic engineering
genetics **6:677–680**
  evolution and **5:**570
  Mendel and **8:**946–*947*
  *see also* chromosomes; DNA; genes; genetic engineering
genome **6:**680; **9:**1039
  Human Genome Project **6:**680; **9:**1039
geodimeters **14:**1733
Geographical Information Systems (GISs) **6:**682
geography **6:681–682**
  biogeography **6:**682
  human **6:**681, *682*
  physical **6:**681
geologic timescale **6:683–688**
geology **6:689–692**
  geological remote sensors **12:**1448

geometry **8:**923
  analytical (Cartesian) **8:**921, *922*, 925
  and the ancient Greeks **8:**920–921
  differential **3:**266
  fractal **3:***313*
geomorphology **6:**691; **7:**820
  geomorphic cycle **7:**821–822
geophysics **6:**692, **693–696**; **10:**1258
germanium **8:**949, 963; **10:**1218; **13:**1540; **15:**1848
germicides **1:**94
germ theory of disease **8:***986*
geysers **16:***1970*
G-force **3:**307; **5:**627
gigantism **5:**548
Gilbert, William **4:**505; **7:**891
gimbals **6:***730*
gingkoes **10:**1277
*Giotto* (space probe) **13:***1626*, 1630
GISs *see* Geographical Information Systems
glaciation **6:697–700**; **16:***1966*, 1968–1969
  creation of landforms **7:***821*, 824
  glacial erosion **5:**564; **6:**699; **7:***821*; **12:**1468
glands
  endocrine **5:***546–548*
  exocrine **5:***575–577*
Glaser, Donald A. **10:**1203
glass **6:701–704**; **13:***1556*
  fibers **11:***1298*
  glassmaking **6:***701–702*; **15:***1825*
  laminated **1:**18; **2:**147
  recycling **12:**1427–*1428*, *1429*
  stained **6:**703–*704*
  types **6:**702–703
  waste **12:**1426
glass ceramics **3:**310–311
glass-reinforced plastic (GRP) **11:**1291
  for boatbuilding **13:***1553*–1554
  for trucks **15:**1858
glaucoma **5:**584
Glen Canyon Dam **6:***754*
glial cells **2:***215*, 216
Glidden, Carlos **7:**817
gliders **16:***2008*
global conveyor belt **9:**1139
Global Positioning System (GPS) **1:**42; **5:***610*, 611; **6:705–708**
  and bomb guidance **6:***721*
  satellites **9:**1087–1088

Global Positioning System (*continued*)
 used by mapmakers **8:***902*, 903
 used in aircraft **16:***1956*
 used in farming **1:**30
 used in navigation **9:***1087–1088*
 used in vehicles **15:***1843*
global warming **3:***339*; **6:709–712**;
 **11:***1317*–1318
globulin **11:**1369
glomeruli **5:***571, 572*
GLONASS **6:**705
glucose **3:**279–281
 catabolism **8:**956–957
glue **1:***17*, 18
gluons **5:**629; **10:**1209
gluteus maximus **9:**1068
glycerin **13:**1581
glycogen **5:**589
glycolysis **8:**957
GM (genetic modification) *see*
 genetic engineering
*GM Sunraycer* **13:**1600, *1601*
goats, mountain **9:***1066*
Gobi Desert **4:**416
Goddard, Robert H. **12:**1490
Godfrey, Thomas **9:**1084
goiter **5:**548
gold **6:713–715**; **15:***1851*
 alloys **1:**59
 bacterial concentration of **2:**153
 casting **3:***292*
 extraction and refining **6:**713–714
 gold rushes **6:***713*
 mining **6:**713, *715*; **8:**1019, 1020
 specific gravity **8:**1010
 therapeutic value **7:**779
 turning inexpensive metals into
 **10:**1198
Gold, Thomas **15:**1881
Golden Gate Bridge **2:***233*
Golgi apparatus **3:***301*, 302
gonads, hormones **5:**548
Google (search engine) **7:**790, *791*
goosebumps **13:**1567
gorges **7:**824, 825
gorillas **1:***82*
Gould, Gordon **7:**826
governors **13:**1544–*1545*
GPS *see* Global Positioning System
Graham, Thomas **10:***1170*
GRAIL missiles **9:**1030
gramophones **13:**1618

Grand Canyon **12:**1468
Grand Coulee Dam **6:**756
Grande Dixence Dam **4:**405
Grand Prix races **2:**148
Grand Teton National Park,
 Wyoming **4:***491*
granite **8:**1019; **12:**1483–1484
 energy from **6:**696
granulocytes **3:**329
graphical user interface (GUI) **3:**365;
 **7:**819; **13:***1591*
graphics, computer **3:368–371**
graphite **3:***284*, 285; **4:**394, 418; **5:***540*,
 604; **8:***1010*
 in pencils **7:**838
grasslands
 temperate **2:**191
 tropical **2:***191*
gravimeters **6:**694; **9:**1146
gravitons **5:**629; **10:**1209
gravity **5:***628*, 629; **6:716–718**;
 **10:**1260; **16:**1997
 and acceleration **8:**917
 and black holes **2:**198; **12:***1438*
 and G-force **5:**627
 center of **6:**717
 Einstein's theory *see* relativity,
 general theory of
 fundamental force **10:**1209
 inverse square law **6:**718
 measuring **6:**694
 pendulums and **10:**1212
 potential energy and **5:**550
gravity meters **13:***1642*
gravure **11:**1358–1359
grease, as a lubricant **7:***876*–877
Great Barrier Reef **7:***825*; **9:**1141–1142
Great Basin **6:**696
Greathead, James Henry **15:**1862
Great Irish Famine **6:**649
Great Lakes **12:**1468
*Great Western* (steamship) **8:**910
Greeks, ancient
 algebra **1:**52–53
 and the elements **5:**538
 architecture **1:**105
 building techniques **2:**240
 geometry **8:***920*–921
 idea of the universe **15:**1877
 mortar **2:**244
 underwater craft **14:**1697
Green, Andy **2:**147

greenflies, pest control **10:**1223–1224
greenhouse effect **6:**709–710
 greenhouse gases **2:**135; **3:**339; **6:**710,
 *712*; **8:**984; **11:**1317
green waves **15:**1841
Gresley, Nigel **7:**874
Grew, Nehemiah **8:**998
grinding machines **15:**1835
grinding wheels **1:**13
groins **5:***562*, 564
ground stations, satellite **3:**353, *354*
groundwater **16:***1969*, 1970, 1974
growth hormone **5:**548
GSM (global system for mobile
 communications) **9:**1036
guanine **9:**1038
guard cells **10:***1253*, 1255
Guarneri, Andrea **9:**1075
Guericke, Otto von **4:**505
Guettard, Jean-Etienne **7:**834
Guggenheim Museum **2:***246*
guidance systems **6:719–722**
 inertial **6:**719, *720*; **9:**1029, 1086
 remote **6:**721–*722*
 wire **9:**1029, 1033
gulfs **9:**1138
Gulf Stream **9:**1139
gullies **5:**561
gum arabic **1:**18
gum disease **4:**413
gummite **15:***1883*
guncotton **5:**580
gunpowder (black powder)
 **5:**578–579, 607
guns **6:723–728**
 recoilless **6:**728
 *see also* bullets; cartridge ammunition
Gurdon, John **3:**342
Gutenberg, Johannes **10:**1185; **11:**1353
Guth, Alan **15:**1881
gutta-percha **12:***1498*
gypsum **8:**1013; **16:**1985
gyrocompasses **6:**730; **13:**1545
gyroscopes **6:729–730**
 in guidance systems **6:**720
 rate gyroscopes **6:**720
gyrostabilizers **6:**730

**H**
Haber-Bosch process **9:**1105
habitats *see* biomes and habitats
hacksaws **15:**1832

Hadley, John **9:**1084
hadrons **2:***136*; **10:**1208
Hahn, Otto **9:**1111–1112
Haigh, John George **1:**15
hail **3:**345; **12:**1419
hailstones **7:**856; **13:**1579
hair dryers **10:***1235*
hairs **13:***1566*, 1567
Haldane, J. B. S. **5:**570
Hale, William **12:**1490
half life **7:**801; **11:**1402
   of carbon-14 **3:**287–288; **11:**1403
Hall, Asaph **8:**914
Hall, Charles Martin **1:**67
Halley, Comet **1:**119
Halley, Edmund **1:**119
Hall-Héroult process **1:**65–66
halogens **10:***1218*
halons **2:**135
Hamilton, William **8:**911
hammers **15:**1832
hands, artificial **11:***1364*
hand stars **5:**608
Hanna, William, and Joseph Barbera
   **1:***85*
hard disks, computer **7:**887–888
Hargreaves, James **14:**1782
harpsichords **9:**1078–1079
harquebuses **6:**724
Harrier aircraft **16:**1945, 1946,
   *1954*, 1958
Harrison, John **9:**1085; **15:***1816*,
   *1820*, 1821
Harvey, William **3:**326–328; **8:**938;
   **10:**1263
Hauksbee, Francis **4:**505
haustoria **10:**1197, 1275
Hawaiian Islands **9:**1063
Hawking, Stephen **2:**199; **16:***1934*
hay fever **1:***55*
headlights **15:***1895*
headphones **13:***1640*
hearing *see* ears and hearing
heart and blood **6:**731–734
   blood **3:**328–329; **6:***733*–734
   blood cells **1:**79; **3:***300*, *329*; **4:***455*;
      **6:***733*, 762; **7:***883*, 884
   blood clotting **6:***733*
   blood diseases **3:**331
   blood groups **3:**330; **6:**734
   blood pigments **1:**79
   blood plasma **7:**881

blood pressure **6:***734*; **8:**939–*940*
blood transfusions **3:**330; **6:**734
   defibrillation of the heart **8:***941*
   heart **3:***327*, 328; **6:***731*–*732*
   heart diseases **3:**330–331; **4:***442*, 443;
      **9:**1132
   heart transplants **3:**331; **14:**1730
   monitoring the heart **3:***330*;
      **8:**940–941
   optimum heart rate during exercise
      **13:**1659–1660
   pacemaker **6:**731–732
heart attacks **3:**330, 331
heart-lung machines **3:**331; **6:***731*
heart rate monitors **13:**1660
heat **6:**735–738
   insulators **6:**738; **7:**781; **11:**1290
   *see also* temperature;
      thermography
heat engines **6:**738
heaters, space heaters **6:***737*
HEAT (high-explosive antitank) shells
   **14:**1743
heat treatment processes **15:**1831
Heisenberg, Werner Karl **11:**1392
helicopters **6:**739–742
heliostats **13:**1599, *1600*
helium
   and nuclear fusion **1:**121; **6:**652,
      *653*; **14:**1716
   atomic structure **2:***137*
   discovery **7:**775
   in balloons **2:**164
   lights **7:***774*
   liquid **4:**393; **14:**1719
   uses **2:**164; **7:***774*, 775
Hellfire missiles **9:**1031
Helmholtz, Hermann von **5:**584
hematite **7:***796*, 797; **8:**967
hemocyanin **1:**79
hemoglobin **1:**79; **3:**329; **6:***733*;
   **9:**1129; **11:***1368*, 1369
   synthetic **6:**734
hemophilia **4:**443; **6:**679
   AIDS and **1:**31–32
hemostats **14:**1728
hemp **5:**596, 597
Henry, Joseph **7:**772, *773*
henrys **7:***773*
Henslow, John **4:**408
hepatitis, virus **15:**1916
Heracleides **8:**952

herbicides **10:**1226–1227
herbivores **5:**624
herbs **10:***1277*
heredity, Mendel's experiments **5:**570;
   **6:**677; **8:**946–947
heroin **2:***212*
Hero of Alexandria **1:**112; **7:**870;
   **10:**1263
Héroult, Paul **1:**67
Herschel, Caroline **6:**743, 744
Herschel, John **2:**150; **15:**1878
Herschel, William **6:**743–744; **15:**1878,
   1885, 1886
Hertz, Heinrich Rudolf **2:**234; **4:**509;
   **5:**527; **11:**1397
Hertzsprung-Russell diagrams
   **14:**1674–1675
HESH (high-explosive squash heads)
   **14:**1743
hibernation **2:***195*, 196
   in caves **3:**298
Hickman, Henry Hill **1:**76–77
hieroglyphics **16:**2027
highs *see* anticyclones
Himalayas, formation **9:***1063*,
   1064–1065; **11:**1295; **12:**1488
*Hindenburg* (airship) **6:***761*
Hipparchus **14:**1670
Hippocrates **8:**938; **14:***1726*
hip replacements **11:***1363*; **15:***1828*
Hiroshima **2:**209; **5:**614
histamines **1:**55–56
histograms **14:**1680
HIV (human immunodeficiency virus)
   **1:**31–*32*; **4:**441
Hodgkin's disease **7:**881
Holland, John P. **14:**1697
*Holland*, USS **14:**1697
hollanders **10:**1188
Hollerith, Hermann **3:**359
Holocene epoch **6:**688
holography and holograms **7:**828–*829*;
   **10:***1159*; **13:**1612
Holonyak, Nick **10:**1161
Homer **14:**1709
hominids **13:**1563
*Homo floresienses* **13:**1563
hones **15:**1835
honeybees, pheromones **10:***1228*
Hooke, Robert
   and elasticity **4:**497
   and Jupiter **7:***812*

Hooke, Robert (*continued*)
  microscopy 3:300; 8:986, 998
  quarrel with Newton 9:1103
Hooker Telescope 15:1878
Hooke's law 4:497, 498
hookworms 10:*1194*
Hoover Dam 4:*406, 508*
hormones 2:179; 3:303; 11:1369
  as pheromones 10:1229
  drugs resembling 4:464
  plant 2:213
horns, English 9:1077
horse collars 1:24
Horsehead Nebula 9:1090; 14:*1675*
horse latitudes 16:2007
horsepower 11:1336
horticulture 1:28
HOT missiles 9:1029
hot-rod racing 2:148
Hounsfield, Godfrey 8:*939*
hourglasses 15:*1815*, 1816, 1819
hovercraft (air-cushion vehicles) 1:75;
  6:745–747; 16:1961
howitzers 6:*728*
Hox genes 3:305
Hoyle, Fred 15:1881
Hubble, Edwin Powell 1:123; 15:1878
Hubble constant 15:1880
Hubble Space Telescope (HST) 1:124;
  5:*538*; 9:*1136*; 11:*1304*; 13:*1602*;
  14:*1766*–1767
hulls
  oil-tanker 14:1747–1748
  submarine 14:1699–1700
human chorionic gonadotropin (hCG)
  11:1343, 1344
Human Genome Project 6:*680*; 9:1039
human growth hormone (HGH) 8:988
human immunodeficiency virus (HIV)
  1:31–*32*; 4:441
humans
  cloning 3:343
  preserved in peat 1:100–101
Humboldt, Alexander von 6:664
humidity, relative 15:1901
hurricanes *see* cyclones
Hutton, James 6:689
*Huygens* (space probe) 12:1524, 1526;
  13:1630
Huygens, Christiaan 6:**748–749**
  and light 6:*749*; 7:846, *847*
  clock 6:*748*; 9:1085; 10:1213; 15:1820

experiment with engines 7:782
  telescope 6:749
Hyatt, John Wesley 11:1286
hybrids 2:181
hydrapulpers 10:1188
hydraulics 6:**750–753**
  and forklift trucks 5:635
  and prostheses 11:1365
  and robotics 12:1479
  brakes 2:221–*222*
  shock absorbers 14:1736, *1737*
  springs 14:1669
Hydrocar 1:75
hydrocarbons 10:1165
hydrochloric acid 1:14; 12:1513
  in the stomach 4:425, 426
  reaction with calcium carbonate
    3:315, 316, 318
  reaction with sodium chloride
    12:1514
  reaction with zinc 3:*318*; 12:*1514*
hydrocracking 9:1149
hydroelectric power 4:407; 5:552;
  6:**754–757**; 11:1335, 1337,
  1340–1341
  tidal power 6:757; 9:1143;
    15:**1803–1806**, 1810
  turbines 6:755–756; 15:1803,
    1867–1868
hydrofoils 6:**758–759**
hydrogen 6:662, **760–761**
  as a fuel 6:662, 760–761
  and nuclear fusion 1:121; 5:551–552;
    6:652, *653*; 9:1117–1118, 1122;
    14:1716
  and pH 1:16
  atoms 3:317; 5:540; 6:760; 10:*1208*
  hydrogen-powered fuel cells
    6:644–*645*, 760
  isotopes 6:760; 7:800; 9:1122
  liquid 10:1203
  plasma 9:1117–*1118*
  traced by radio telescopes
    14:1763–1764
hydrogen fluoride, chemical bonds
  15:*1897*
hydrogen peroxide, an antiseptic 1:95
hydrological cycle *see* water cycle
hydrolysis 13:1581
hydrometers 13:1643
hydrophones, Captor's 8:1007
hydrothermal vents 9:1143

hygrometers 1:35; 8:980; 15:1901
*Hylonomus*, fossils 6:*684*
hyperfiltration 10:1172
hyperons 10:1208–1209
hyperopia 5:583, 585
hypersensitization 1:56
hypertension 6:*734*
HyperText Transfer Protocol
  (HTTP) 7:789
hyphae 6:648; 10:1197
hypothalamus 2:218; 5:*546*, 577

I
IBM (International Business
  Machines) 3:359
ICBMs (intercontinental ballistic
  missiles) 9:1028–*1029*
ice
  global warming and polar ice
    6:711–712
  melting 6:*736*
ice ages 8:984–985
  mountain formation after 9:1065
  Pleistocene 6:697
icebergs 6:*697*; 16:1968
Iceland 9:1140
Iceland spar 8:1011
ice sheets 6:697, 698
ice shelves 6:*697*
ideograms 16:2027
idlers 6:668
*Iguanodon* 4:433
illuminance 7:848
ilmenite 10:*1181*; 15:1829
imaging, medical *see* medical
  imaging
Imhotep 5:553
immune system 6:**762–765**
  acquired immunity 6:763
  allergens and 1:56
  and parasites 10:1196
  cell-mediated immunity 15:1890,
    1891
  immune response of someone with
    HIV 1:*32*
  natural immunity 6:762, *763*
immunization 6:*765*
incineration, waste 11:1319
Indian Ocean 9:1137
indicators, chemical 1:*15, 16*
indigestion 4:425
indium antimonide 13:1540

inductance **15:**1846
induction (electromagnetic induction)
   **4:**508; **5:**524–525, 587; **6:**671–672,
   756; **7:**772–773, 892
   induction coils **7:***773*
induction motors **5:**518–*519*
Industrial Revolution **8:**975
   and architecture **1:**109
   and mining **8:**1015–1016
inert gases (noble gases) **3:**323; **6:**662;
   **7:**774–775
inertia **5:**627–628; **9:**1049, 1050
   mass and **8:**917
inertial guidance systems **6:**719, *720*;
   **9:**1029, 1086
influenza **4:**441
   vaccines for **15:***1890*, 1892
   viruses **6:**765; **15:***1890*, 1915, 1916
Infrared Astronomical Satellite (IRAS)
   **9:**1136; **14:**1766
infrared radiation **7:**776–777, 844;
   **13:**1644
   and photography **12:**1448
   detection using thermal imaging
   **7:**777; **10:***1161*; **14:**1788
   observed from space **9:**1136
   uses **6:**722; **7:***776–777*; **9:**1029;
   **10:**1221; **12:***1442*, 1443; **14:***1789*
   *see also* thermography
ingots **3:***292*, 293–*294*
inheritance, genetic **6:***677*
inorganic chemistry **3:**322; **7:**778–779
insecticides *see* pesticides and
   insecticides
insects
   pheromones **10:***1228*, 1229
   social **10:**1228
insomnia **13:**1575
instrument landing system (ILS) **1:**51
instruments, musical *see* musical
   instruments
insulators **7:**780–781
   electrical **7:***780–781*; **11:**1290;
   **12:**1453, 1455; **15:**1847
   thermal **6:**738; **7:**781; **11:**1290
insulin **2:**179; **5:**546, *548*; **6:**764;
   **9:**1132; **11:**1368, 1369
   genetically engineered **6:**673–674;
   **8:**988
integrated circuits
   thick film resistors as **12:**1456
   *see also* silicon chips

Integrated Service Digital Network
   (ISDN) **14:**1758
Intelsat **3:**353, *355*
*Intelsat VI* (satellite) **12:***1520*
*Intelsat IX* (satellite) **12:**1520
intensive care units (ICUs) **8:**942
intercoolers **15:**1858
intercourse, sexual **12:**1451–1452
interference **16:**1977–1978, *1978*
   and wave nature of electrons **11:**1392
   and wave nature of matter **11:**1392
   light **7:**846; **10:**1159
   sound **13:***1614*, 1615
interglacial periods **6:**697
internal combustion engines
   **4:**420–421; **7:**782–787
   starter motor **13:***1608*
   valves **15:**1899
   *see also* diesel engines; gas turbines;
   jet engines
International Business Machines
   (IBM) **3:**359
International Gamma-Ray
   Astrophysics Laboratory **10:***1259*
International Space Station **10:***1163*;
   **13:***1621*, 1624, *1637*
International Ultraviolet Explorer
   (IUE) **9:**1136; **14:**1766
Internet **3:***358*; **7:**788–793
   optoelectronic technology and
   **10:**1160
   wireless **7:***792–793*; **14:***1757*
   *see also* e-mail
Internet Service Providers (ISPs)
   **7:**788, 789; **10:**1221
interstate highway **12:***1472*
interstitial fluid **7:**881, 882
intestines **4:***425*, 426–*427*; **5:**574
   villi **4:***426*; **7:***882*
inverse square law **6:**718
invertebrates **1:**81–82
iodine **10:***1218*
   as an antiseptic **1:**95
   deficiency **5:**548
   sublimation **14:***1696*
ion channels **3:***304*
ionization chambers **10:**1202
ionosphere *see* thermosphere
ions and ionization **7:**794–795
   complex ions **15:**1853–1854
   identifying substances using ions
   **13:**1649

ion exchange **7:**795
ionization **7:**795
ions **1:**14; **5:**520; **7:***794–795*
IRBMs (intermediate range ballistic
   missiles) **9:**1030
iridium **8:**943, 963, 967; **11:**1296,
   1297; **13:**1609
iris **5:**582
iron and steel **7:**796–799; **15:**1831
   alloy steels **8:**964
   building with **2:**245–246; **8:***961*;
   **13:**1569
   carbon steel **7:**797
   cast iron **1:**58; **7:**797, 798
   corrosion (rusting) **3:***377*, 378; **7:**797;
   **10:***1174*, 1175; **16:**1984, 1985
   iron **1:**60; **7:***796–797*; **8:***964*
   iron extraction **2:**200–203; **7:**797;
   **8:**967
   iron in blood **9:**1129–1130
   iron isotopes **7:**800
   iron ores **8:**964, 1013
   nickel-chrome steel **14:**1743
   pig iron **7:**798
   recycling **12:**1427
   sheet steel **8:***972*, 973
   stainless steel **1:**58; **7:**797; **8:**968–969
   steel **1:**58, *59*, 60; **2:***203*; **6:***737*; **7:**796;
   **8:**963–964
   steel combustion **5:***541*
   steelmaking **7:**797–798, *799*; **10:**1178
   tempered steel **6:**736
   wrought iron **7:***797*, 798
iron carbonyl **15:**1854
iron chlorides **12:***1513*; **15:**1853
iron oxide, hydrated **10:***1174*, 1175
irrigation **1:**27; **16:***1974*
ISDN (Integrated Service Digital
   Network) **14:**1758
islands **7:**825
   barrier **7:**825
   formation **16:**1941
   speciation on **2:**182
isobars **16:**1992, 1993, 2010
isomers, of monosaccharides **3:**281
isoprene **12:***1498*
isopropanol **1:**95
isostasy **9:**1065
isostatic pressing **3:**311
isotopes **2:**137; **7:**800–801; **10:**1217
   and radiometric dating of rocks
   **6:**684

isotopes (*continued*)
  carbon **1:**99; **3:**287–288; **7:**800, 801;
    **10:**1217; **11:**1403
  hydrogen **6:**760; **7:**800; **9:**1122
  mass spectroscopy and **13:**1649
  radioisotopes **7:**800–*801*; **11:**1403
  separation **7:**801
  uranium **5:**614, 615; **7:**801; **9:**1114,
    1119–1120; **15:**1884
IVP (intravenous pyelography) **5:***571*

**J**

jackhammers **7:**802–*803*
Jacquard, Joseph-Marie **13:**1587–1588
*Jahre Viking* (ship) **14:**1747
James, William **11:**1378
James Webb Telescope **1:**124; **14:**1767
Jansky, Karl **14:**1763
Janssen, Zacharias **8:***998*
Japan, architecture **1:**108; **2:***242*
Japanese encephalitis (JE) virus
    **15:***1891*
jaundice **5:**574
Javelin missiles **9:**1030
JDAM (Joint Direct Attack Munitions)
    bombs **6:***721*
jeeps, amphibious **1:**74
Jenkins, C. F. **14:**1768
Jenner, Edward **7:**804–*805*; **8:**938;
    **15:**1889–1890
jenny, spinning **14:**1782; **16:**2025–2026
Jenny, William **13:**1569
JET (Joint European Torus) **6:***654*
jet engines **1:**39; **6:**666; **7:***787*, **806–810**;
    **15:**1869
  pulse-jets **7:**810
  ramjets **7:**810
  scramjets **1:**45; **7:**810
  turbofan **1:***37*; **7:***806, 808–809*
  turbojet **7:**807–808
  turboprop **7:**808
jet streams **16:**1991, 2010
Jim suits **4:***451*
Jobs, Steve **3:***360*
Joint Direct Attack Munitions (JDAM)
    bombs **6:***721*
jointers **16:**2021
Joint European Torus (JET) **6:***654*;
    **11:***1284*, 1285
joints, artificial **11:***1363*, 1365; **15:***1828*
Joliot-Curie, Irène and Frédéric **4:**399
Josephson, Brian **14:**1720

Josephson effect **14:**1720
Joule, James **7:***816*; **11:***1335*
joules **5:**550
Joule-Thomson effect **7:***816*
JPEG files **10:**1248–*1249*
jumbo jets **1:***38*, 40, 46–47
junction boxes **6:**651
Jupiter **7:**811–814; **10:***1162*; **13:**1604
  Great Red Spot **7:***812*
  missions to **13:**1629–1630
  moons **6:***656*; **7:***813*
Jurassic period **6:**687
Jutland, Battle of **16:**1957

**K**

kames **6:**700; **7:**824
kaolin (china clay) **11:**1329, *1330*
kaolinite **11:**1329
kaons **10:**1208
Karvonen formula **13:**1659–1660
Kasparov, Gary **1:***112*, 114
Kay, John **14:***1782*, 1783
Kea, Mount, telescope on **1:***123*, 124
Keck II Telescope **1:***123*, 124
keels **13:**1552–1553, 1554
Kekulé von Stradonitz, Friedrich
    **10:**1166
Kellogg, Edward W. **13:**1640
Kelvin, Lord (William Thomson)
    **4:**393; **6:**664; **7:**815–**816**;
    **14:**1777, 1787
kelvins **7:**816
Kelvin temperature scale **4:**393; **6:**664;
    **7:**816; **14:**1777
Kepler, Johannes **1:**120
keratin **11:**1369; **16:**2023
keyboard instruments **9:**1074,
    1078–1079
keyboards and typewriters **7:**817–**819**;
    **16:**2030
Khorana, Har **8:**987; **9:**1038
Khwarizmi, Muhammad ibn Musa al-
    **1:**53, 54; **8:**921; **9:***1124*
kidneys **5:**571–573
  dialysis **5:***573*
  transplants **5:**574; **14:***1731*
kieselguhr **5:**580
Kilauea **7:**821
Kilburn, Tom **13:**1589
kilns **11:**1332–1333
kilograms, standard **8:***930*
kilowatts **11:**1335

kimberlite **4:**418
kinematics **10:**1260
kinetic theory **7:**862–863
kinetoscopes **9:**1052
King, Augusta Ada (Countess
    of Lovelace) **2:**151; **3:**364;
    **13:**1588, *1589*
King, Tom **3:**342
kingdoms **3:**333, 335
Kingsford Smith, C. E. **1:**39
Kirchoff, Gustav **13:**1645
Kismet (robot) **1:***115*
Kitt Peak National Observatory
    (KPNO) **9:***1134*
Klaproth, Martin Heinrich **15:**1883
Klaus, Karl Karlovich **11:**1297
Klietsch, Karl **11:**1358
klystrons **10:***1199*
knees **13:***1564*
  prosthetic **11:**1363
  surgery **13:***1661*
knitting **14:**1781, 1785; **16:***2023*
knives **15:**1832
knots (speed) **9:**1084
Koch, Robert **8:**986
Koeppen, Wladimir **3:**338
Koeppen classification **3:**337–338
Kolff, Willem **8:**944
König, Friedrich **11:**1354
kraft process **10:**1185, 1187–1188
Krakatoa, volcanic eruption **15:**1860;
    **16:**1939
Krause end bulbs **15:**1838, *1839*
Krebs cycle **8:**957
krypton **7:***774*, 775
K-T boundary, extinctions at
    **6:**687–688
Kuiper belt **1:**119, 125; **13:**1606
Kyoto Protocol **6:**712

**L**

laccoliths **16:**1938
lactic acid **1:**14
  in muscles **9:**1070–1071; **12:***1459*
*Lactobacillus* **8:**988
Laerdal tunnel **15:**1864
Lagrange, Joseph **8:**922
lahars **16:**1939
lakes **2:**192; **6:**700; **12:**1468–1469
  oxbow **12:**1467, 1469
Lamarck, Jean-Baptiste-Pierre-Antoine
    de **5:**568

lampblack **3**:286

lamps
  arc **7**:853–854
  fluorescent **15**:1875
  gas-discharge **7**:795, 854, *855*, 879
  mercury vapor **7**:855
  oil **7**:*852*, 853
  sodium vapor **13**:*1585*
  sun **15**:1875

Land, Edwin Herbert **11**:1310–1311

landfills **11**:1319

landforms **7**:820–825
  biogenic **7**:825
  coastal and ocean **7**:825
  continental **7**:822–825
  streamlined **6**:699; **7**:824
  structural **7**:820

landing craft **16**:1961

Landing Vehicles, Tracked (LVTs) **1**:74

landslides, causing tsunamis **15**:1860

Langley, Samuel **1**:37

LANs (local area networks) **2**:253;
  **3**:364–365

lapilli **16**:1938

Laplace, Pierre-Simon de **2**:197; **7**:835

Large Hadron Collider **10**:1200

Large Magellanic Cloud, Tarantula
  Nebula **9**:1089

Lartigue, Charles **9**:1040

larvae **8**:*977–978*

larynx **16**:1934

laser discs **7**:830–833

lasers **7**:826–829; **10**:*1158*; **13**:*1543*
  and bar codes **2**:165, 166
  and fiber optics **5**:602; **14**:1756–1757
  laser drills **4**:459
  used for cutting cloth **14**:*1783*
  used in dentistry **4**:413
  used in distance-measuring **8**:*928*
  used in holography **7**:828–829;
    **10**:*1159*
  used in making laser discs **7**:*833*
  used in missile guidance **6**:722;
    **9**:1031
  used in nuclear fusion **9**:1118
  used in physical chemistry
    **10**:1256–1257
  used in playing laser discs **7**:*830*,
    831–832
  used in range finding **6**:722; **14**:1734
  used in surgery **5**:584; **7**:828, *829*;
    **8**:945; **14**:1729

used in welding **16**:2001–2002
used to vaporize carbon **10**:1257

Lassell, William **9**:1095

laterites **13**:1595

latex rubber **3**:*378*; **12**:*1497*,
  1498–1499

lathes **15**:*1833*–1834; **16**:*2019*

Latimer-Needham, C. H. **6**:746

latitude **8**:901–902
  climate and **3**:336
  measuring **9**:1084

latosols **13**:1595–*1596*

laughing gas (nitrous oxide) **1**:77, 78;
  **4**:410; **6**:*660*

Lauste, Eugene **9**:1057

lava **12**:*1483*, 1484; **16**:1938, *1940*
  pillow **16**:1941

lava caves **3**:297–298

Lavassor, Émile **2**:*141*

Lavoisier, Antoine-Laurent **3**:321;
  **5**:539; **7**:834–835; **10**:1177, 1214;
  **14**:1709

lay-barges **10**:*1269*–1270

LCDs *see* liquid crystal displays

leaching **13**:1594

lead **7**:836–838
  alloys **1**:59, 60; **7**:838
  extraction and refining **7**:836–837;
    **8**:968
  in paint **7**:838; **10**:1180
  in pigments **10**:1181
  ore **7**:*836*
  poisoning **7**:*837*–838
  shot **7**:838
  smelting **1**:60
  uses **7**:836

lead azide **9**:1105–1106

Lear jets **1**:*43*

learning **2**:220
  cognitive **11**:*1377*

leaves **10**:*1252*, 1253–*1254*
  dropping **10**:*1255*

Lecoq de Boisbaudran, Paul-Emile
  **10**:1217–1218

LEDs *see* light-emitting diodes

Leeuwenhoek, Antoni van **3**:300;
  **8**:986, 998; **11**:1370

legs, bones **13**:1564

Leibniz, Gottfried **3**:265, 358–359;
  **6**:749; **8**:922; **10**:1259

leishmaniasis **11**:1371

Lemaître, Georges-Henri **15**:1879

Lenoir, Jean Joseph Etienne **7**:782

Lenormand, Louis-Sébastien **10**:1190

lenses **7**:*846*; **10**:1158–1159; **12**:1431
  camera **10**:1238–1240, *1241*
  concave and convex **10**:*1157*, 1158;
    **12**:1431
  contact **5**:585
  convergent and divergent **10**:1239
  eye **4**:482, *483*
  fisheye **10**:1240
  focal length **10**:1238–1239, 1240,
    1250
  Fresnel **7**:851
  microscope **8**:999–1000; **10**:*1157*
  on camcorders **3**:267
  spherical and chromatic aberration
    **10**:1159
  telephoto **10**:1239, 1250
  telescopic **10**:*1241*
  wide-angle **10**:1239, 1250
  zoom **10**:1239–1240, 1250

Leonardo da Vinci **7**:839–840; **10**:1190;
  **14**:1697
  flying-machine design **1**:36
  helicopter design **6**:*741*
  tank design **6**:*741*
  the lathe **16**:*2019*

Leonid meteor shower **9**:1093

leptons **10**:1207–1208

leucine **1**:71

leukemia **4**:399

levees **12**:1466, 1470

Leverrier, Urbain **9**:1093

levers **7**:841–842

Libby, Willard **3**:*287*

lichens **10**:1276

life
  extraterrestrial **1**:69
  origins of **5**:565–567; **8**:989

life-support machines (ventilators)
  **8**:942, 945

lift force **1**:19, 40, *41*; **15**:1903

ligaments **13**:1563, *1564*

ligands **15**:1854

light **7**:843–848; **13**:1645
  and color **7**:*848*; **8**:926
  and fiber optics **5**:*600–602*
  and shadows **10**:1156
  blueshifted **4**:457; **14**:1674
  coherent and incoherent **7**:826, *827*
  curves toward a massive body **6**:718;
    **12**:*1437*

light (*continued*)
  diffraction 7:846, *847*; 10:*1158*, 1159; **16**:1978
  fluorescence 7:879; 10:1159; 15:*1874*
  interference 7:846; 10:1159
  measuring 7:847–848
  particle nature 7:846–847; **11**:1389–1390, *1390*, 1391
  phosphorescence 7:879; 10:1159
  polarization 10:1159; **11**:**1310–1311**
  prisms and 6:*749*; 7:*844*, 845; 9:1103; 10:*1156*; 13:1645
  redshifted 4:457; **14**:1674
  speed of 5:628; 9:1048; 10:*1158*; 12:1436, 1437–1438
  wave nature 6:*749*; 7:846, *847*; 8:927; 10:1159; 16:*1977*, 1978
  wave-particle duality 11:1391; **16**:1976–1977
  *see also* optics; reflection and refraction
lightbulbs 7:775, *853*, 854
  Edison and 4:*493*, 494; 7:854
  energy-efficient 7:855
light-emitting diodes (LEDs) 3:264; 7:855; 13:1543
lighthouses **7:849–851**
lighting **7:852–855**
  fluorescent 7:*854*, 855, 879–880
  neon 6:662; 7:*774*, 775
  street 7:855; 12:*1476*
  *see also* lightbulbs
light meters 10:*1242*
lightning 4:*504*; **7:856–857**; **15**:1801–*1802*
lightships 7:*851*
light-years 1:122; 14:1672
Lilienthal, Otto 1:37
limbs, artificial 11:*1362–1364*
Lim, Drahoslav 5:585
lime 5:594
limestone 7:821, 825; 8:*1019*; 12:1485
  caves 3:297; 7:825; 16:*1985*, 1986
  scenery 12:1488
limonite 8:964
Lindbergh, Charles 1:39
linear electric motors **7:858–859**; 12:1496
linear variable differential transformers (LVDTs) 15:1845
Linnaeus, Carolus 2:185; 3:332, *333*; **7:860–861**

Linotype 11:*1356*
lipase 10:*1164*; 11:1369
Lippershey, Hans 14:*1760*
liquid crystal displays (LCDs) 7:865; 10:*1160*; 14:*1772*
  LCD projectors 9:1059
  LCD television screens 14:*1772*, 1774
liquid crystals 3:264; **7:864–865**
liquids 2:138; **7:862–863**
  and pressure 11:*1348*
  specific gravity measured 13:1643
  *see also* distillation
Lister, J. J. 8:999
Lister, Joseph 1:94; **7:866–867**; 8:938; 14:1727
lithium 1:15; 8:962–963, 967
  reaction with water 10:*1175*
lithium deuteride 9:1122
lithium fluoride 15:*1896*, 1897
lithography 11:1356–1358
lithosphere 11:1294
litmus paper 1:*16*
"Little Boy" (atomic bomb) 5:614
liver 5:574, 589
load 11:1335
loaders 4:480
Lobachevsky, Nikolay 8:922
local area networks (LANs) 2:253; 3:364–365
locks (on canals) 3:*274*–275, *276*
locks (security) **7:868–869**; 12:*1504*–1505
locomotives **7:870–875**
  diesel 7:*872*, 873
  diesel-electric 7:*873*, 874–875; 12:1413
  electric 7:*874*–875
  steam 7:870–873, 874; 14:*1686*, 1687, 1688
  *see also* trains
locusts 10:*1225*
lodestones 3:356; 7:889
Lodge, Oliver 2:234; 11:1397; 13:1640
loess 12:1484–1485
logarithms (logs) 3:263; 8:921
logic 1:114
longitude 8:901, 902
  and time zones 15:1818
  measuring 9:1084–1085; 15:*1816*, 1821

longlining 5:*611*, 612
looms 14:*1780*, 1781
  operated using punched cards 13:1587–1588
  power 14:1783
Loran 9:1085–1086
Lord, Peter 1:*86*–87
*Lord of the Rings* trilogy (movies) 1:87, *88*
Lorenz, Hendrik 2:139
Lorin, René 7:806
lost-wax process 3:293
loudspeakers *see* speakers
Love Canal 11:1319
Lovelace, Countess of (Augusta Ada King) 2:151; 3:364; 13:1588, *1589*
Lovell, Bernard 14:1764–1765
Lowell, Percival 8:915
lows *see* depressions
lubricants **7:876–877**
  oils and greases 7:863, *876*–877; **16**:1929
Lüger 6:727
lumber yards 15:1814
lumens 7:848
Lumière, Auguste and Louis 9:1052
luminance 7:848
luminescence **7:878–880**
  fluorescence 7:879; 10:1159; 13:1598–1599; 15:*1874*, 1875
luminous flux 7:847, 848
luminous intensity 7:847, 848
*Lunar Orbiter 2* (space probe) 9:*1046*
*Lunar Prospector* (space probe) 9:1042
Luna space probes 9:1044; 13:1626
lungs 5:574; 12:*1460*, *1461*–1462
  cilia 6:*763*
  disorders 12:*1462*, 1464
  transplants 14:1731
lux 7:848
LVDTs (linear variable differential transformers) 15:1845
Lyell, Charles 4:408; 5:568; 6:689
lymphatic system **7:881–884**
  lymph 7:*881*, 882, 883
  lymph nodes 1:*31*; 6:*764*; 7:*882*, 883–884
lymphocytes 3:329; 6:*733*, 763, *764*; 7:*883*, 884
  B-cells 6:764, 765
  T-cells 1:*32*; 6:*762*, 764–765
lymphomas 7:*884*

lysine **1:**71
lysosomes **3:***301*
lysostaphin **6:***675*
lysozyme **5:***616*–617

# M

McAdam, John Loudon **12:***1472*
McCay, Winsor **1:**84
McCormick, Cyrus Hall **1:**26
McMath-Pierce telescope **14:***1712*,
   1713
machine guns **6:***725*–726
  on tanks **14:**1745
machine tools **15:**1833–1835
Mach numbers **1:**45; **14:***1721, 1722,*
   *1723*
Machu Picchu **1:**107–108
Macmillan, Kirkpatrick **2:**175
macromolecules **9:**1038
macrophages **6:**762; **7:**883
mad cow disease (BSE) **4:**439
*Magellan* (space probe) **1:**125; **13:**1558,
   *1605*; **15:**1905
maglev trains **7:***858*, 859, *875*; **9:**1041;
   **10:***1261*; **14:***1718*
magma **8:**1012; **16:**1938, 1939
magnesium **3:***315*; **8:**963; **9:**1130
magnesium hydroxide **1:**14
magnetic flux density **5:**523
magnetic resonance imaging (MRI)
   scans and scanners **2:***216*;
   **8:***934*–935, 939
magnetic storage **7:**885–888
  camcorder tapes **3:**269
magnetism **7:**889–893
  and electricity *see* electromagnetism
  magnetic resistance **12:**1453–1454
  measuring **1:**98; **6:**694; **7:***892*–893
  paramagnetism **15:**1854
  *see also* magnetic storage
magnetite **3:**296; **7:**797; **8:**964
magnetometers **1:**98; **6:***694*; **7:***892*;
   **9:**1146
  fluxgate **7:**893
  proton **7:**893
  spinner **7:**893
magnetrons **8:***1003*; **11:***1394*
Magnox reactors **9:**1114
malachite **8:***1011*
malaria **4:***441*–442; **10:***1194*–1195,
   1196; **11:***1371*
  antimalarial drugs **10:***1197*

*Mallard* (locomotive) **7:**872–873
malnutrition **9:**1127, *1131*; **11:***1327*
Malpighi, Marcello **8:**998
Malthus, Thomas **5:**568
maltose **3:**281
mammals **1:**82; **3:***334*
  the rise of **6:**688
mammary glands **5:**577
Mammoth Cave, Kentucky **3:**299
Mandelbrot set **3:***313*
manganese, in seabed nodules **8:**1021
manganese dioxide **3:**295
Manhattan Project **9:**1112, 1121
Manila hemp **5:**597
manipulators, hydraulic **6:**753
manometers **8:**951
Mantell, Gideon **4:**432–433
mantle, study of **6:**693–694
manure **5:***592*, 593, 595
mapmaking **8:**900–905
  distortions **8:**902–903
  from photographs **14:***1735*
  latitude and longitude **8:**901–902
  printing techniques **8:**905
  projections **8:**904–905
  scales **8:**901
  symbols **8:**902
marble **3:**284; **8:**1019; **12:***1486*
Marconi, Guglielmo **2:**234, 235;
   **8:**906–907; **11:**1397
Mariana Trench **9:**1141
marine propulsion **8:**908–912
  *see also* hydrofoils; sailing
Mariner space probes **13:**1626
  *Mariner 2* **13:**1626, 1627; **15:***1905*
  *Mariner 4* **13:**1626, 1628
  *Mariner 9* **13:**1628
  *Mariner 10* **8:***952*, 953, *955*; **13:**1626
Mariotte, Edme **6:***663*
marmots **9:**1066
Mars **1:***124*; **8:**913–916; **13:**1604
  life on **8:**915; **13:**1628–*1629*
  missions to **1:**125; **8:**915, *916*;
   **12:***1445*; **13:**1628–*1629, 1630*
  moons **8:**913, *914*
  poles **8:***913*, 914
  seismology **12:**1532
  surface **8:***913*, 914–*915*
  water on **8:**916
  weather **8:**913–914
Mars Exploration Rovers **13:***1629, 1630*
*Mars Express* (space probe) **13:**1629

Mars Global Surveyor, images from
   **8:***915*
*Mars Observer* (space probe) **13:**1628
*Mars Pathfinder* (space probe) **13:**1628
*Mars Rovers* (robotic vehicles) **13:**1626
marsupials **1:**82
Martin, Pierre-Emile **7:**799
masers **7:**826–827
mass and weight **8:**917–919
  gravity and **6:**717
  space-time curved by mass **12:***1436,*
   1438
  weightlessness **6:***717*; **8:***918*–919;
   **12:***1435*; **16:**1997–1998
  *see also* balances and weighing
   machines
mass-energy equation **5:**551, 614;
   **6:**653; **8:**919, 924; **9:**1113; **12:***1438*;
   **14:**1716
mass production **2:***142*; **14:***1783*
mass spectroscopy **13:**1648–1649
  mass spectrometers **1:***100*; **6:**691;
   **11:***1401*
matches **10:***1230*
matchlocks **6:***724*
mathematics **8:**920–925
  algebra **1:**52–54; **8:***921*, 924
  Archimedes and **1:**102–103
  arithmetic **8:**922, 923
  calculus **3:**265–266; **8:**924–925;
   **10:**1259
  historical developments **8:***920*–922
  logarithms (logs) **3:**263; **8:**921
  Pythagoras and **11:**1387–1388
  *see also* geometry; number systems
matter
  states of **4:**392; **6:**659; **7:**862
  wave nature **11:**1391, 1392
  *see also* atomic theory
Mauchly, John **3:**360
Mauna Kea Observatory **9:***1133*, 1134,
   1135–1136; **12:***1430*; **14:**1762
mauveine **4:***466*
Maxim, Hiram Stevens **1:**37;
   **6:**725–726
Maxwell, James Clerk **4:**508–509;
   **7:**816; **8:**926–927; **10:**1261
Mayans
  number system **9:**1124–1125
  pyramids **1:***104*
Mayer, Adolf **8:**986
Mayr, Ernst **5:**570

Mead, Lake 4:*406*
mean 14:1679
meanders, river 12:1467, 1468
measurement 8:**928–931**
meats
  preservation 5:*622*
  processing 5:619
mechanics 5:626; 10:1259–1260
median 14:1679
medical imaging 8:**932–937**
  angiography 8:935
  computerized axial tomography
    (CAT; CT) scans 8:*934, 939*;
    16:*2033–2034*
  endoscopy 5:*602*; 8:936, *938*
  magnetic resonance imaging (MRI)
    scans and scanners 2:*216*;
    8:*934–935*, 939
  positron emission tomography (PET)
    scans 2:*216*; 7:*801*; 8:*935–937*, 939;
    11:*1375*
  thermography 14:1788, *1789*
  ultrasound 8:*937*; 11:*1344*; 13:*1615*,
    1616; 15:*1871*, 1873
  X-ray images 8:*932*–934, 939;
    14:1729; 16:*2031*, 2032–*2033*
medical sensors 8:941
medical technology 8:**938–945**
  computers 8:944–945
  imaging *see* medical imaging
  medical ethics 8:945
  monitoring equipment 8:939–942
  nanomedicine 9:1082
  treatment 8:942–944
  virtual reality systems
    15:1912–*1913*
  *see also* drugs; surgery
Mediterranean Sea 9:1138
  pollution 15:1810
  Trans-Mediterranean pipeline
    10:1269–1270
meiosis 3:303; 6:*678*
Meissner corpuscles 15:1838
Meitner, Lise 9:1111–1112
melanin 13:1567
melatonin 5:547
melting 2:138; 14:1776
memory 2:220
memory cards, camcorder 3:272
Mendel, Gregor 2:186–187; 5:570;
    6:677, *678*; 8:**946–947**
mendelevium 8:949; 10:1218

Mendeleyev, Dmitry 3:322; 5:541;
    8:**948–949**; 10:*1214*, 1216–1218
  and transition elements 15:1851
meningitis 9:1101
menstruation 12:1452
mental illness 4:443
Mercalli scale 12:1530
mercury, metal 8:**950–951**, 967
  alloys 1:59
  as a superconductor 14:1719
  glowing ions of 7:*794*
  in barometers 2:167–168; 8:951
  in thermometers 8:951; 15:1797
  poisoning 11:1314
Mercury, planet 8:**952–955**; 10:1162;
    13:1604
  missions to 8:*952*, 953, *955*; 13:1627
meridian, prime 8:902
Mersenne Twister 8:*924*
mesas 7:*823*, 824
mesons 2:139; 10:1206, 1207, 1208
mesopause 2:*133*, 134
Mesopotamians
  architecture 2:241
  shipbuilding 13:1551
mesosphere 2:*133*, 134
*Messenger* (space probe) 8:*954*
metabolism 2:179; 5:557; 8:**956–959**
  disorders 8:*959*
  metabolic rate 8:957–958; 9:1127,
    *1132*
metal detectors 1:49, 1:98; 8:*962*, 965
metalloenzymes 7:779
metalloids 13:1540, 1556
metallurgy 8:**966–969**
  powder (sintering) 8:*969*
metals 8:**960–965**
  alkali metals 1:15–16; 8:962–963;
    10:1216
  alkaline earth metals 8:963
  discovery of 8:965
  extraction from ores 8:967–*968*
  metalloids 8:963
  mixtures *see* alloys
  ores 8:*963*, 964–965, *1016*
  properties 8:960–*961*, 968
  reaction with acids 12:1514
  recycling 12:1427
  structure 8:961–962
  transition metals 8:963; 10:*1217*,
    1219; 12:*1513*
  *see also* metallurgy; metalworking

metalworking 8:**970–975**
  *see also* casting; electroplating;
    welding
metamorphosis 8:**976–979**
Meteor Crater, Arizona 1:*119*
meteorites 1:116, *118, 119*; 9:1139
  and dinosaur extinction 4:437
meteoroids 1:116, 118
meteorology 8:**980–985**
  Dalton (John) and 4:402
  radiosondes and 15:1845
  *see also* barometers; weather;
    weather systems
meteors *see* asteroids, comets, and
    meteors
meters, standard 8:930–931
methane 3:*285*; 6:662
  as a greenhouse gas 3:339; 6:710, 711,
    *712*; 11:1317
  bonding of atoms in 15:*1896, 1897*
  discovery 16:1943
  from bacteria 8:987
  in coal mines 3:346; 8:1016–1017
methanol, toxicity 11:1308
methionine 1:71
methyl isocyanate 11:1308
methyl orange 1:15
metronomes 10:*1213*
Métro, Paris 12:1423
Meucci, Antonio 14:1753
mice 10:*1227*
micelles, soap 13:*1581*
Michell, John 2:197
Michelson, Albert 12:1435
microbiology 8:**986–989**
  discovery of microorganisms 8:998
  Pasteur's understanding of
    microorganisms 10:1210, 1211
  *see also* bacteria; fungi kingdom;
    protist kingdom; viruses, biological
microbursts 16:2010
microchips *see* silicon chips
microelectronics 8:**990–995**
  *see also* printed circuits; silicon chips
microlights 1:43
microliths 15:1830
micrometers 8:**996–997**
microphones 10:1265; 13:1618–*1619*
microprocessors 5:*526*; 8:*991*; 12:1479
microscopes 8:987, **998–1001**
  atomic force (AFMs) 8:1001; 9:1081
  electron *see* electron microscopes

optical light 2:*185*; 5:530–531; 8:*999*, 1000, 1001; 10:*1157*

scanning acoustic 8:1001

scanning electron (SEMs) 5:531; 8:*999, 1000–1001*; 9:*1100*

scanning probe 8:1001

scanning tunneling (STMs) 8:987, 1001

specimens and slides 8:1001

underwater 8:1001

microsurgery 5:584; 14:1730

microvilli 14:1751

microwave landing system (MLS) 1:51

microwave radiation 8:**1002–1003**; 13:1644

and communications satellites 3:353–354; 14:1757

and radar 8:1003

and television transmission 8:1003

communications using 8:907, *1002*–1003; 14:1757

microwave ovens 8:*1003*

solar energy and 13:1602

to carry telephone signals 1:*90*

mid-Atlantic ridge 6:694; 11:1295

Miescher, Johann Friedrich 8:986

migration 16:2044

salmon 2:*196*

Miles, G. W. 11:1286

milk and milking 5:*621*

milk of magnesia 1:14

Milky Way galaxy 1:122–123; 6:744; 14:1713; 15:1878

Miller, Stanley 1:*71*; 5:566

milling machines 15:*1834*–1835

mills

tide 15:1810

*see also* windmills and wind pumps

Minamata disease 11:1314

mine, explosive 8:**1004–1007**; 16:1962

mineralogy 6:692

minerals 6:692; 8:**1008–1013**

breaking and cleavage 8:1011

color and streak 8:1011

crystals 8:*1009, 1010*

dietary 9:1127–1128

formation 8:1008

gemstones 8:1013

groups 8:1011–1012

hardness 8:1010

identification 8:1008

in rocks 8:1012–1013

light effects 8:1011

"magical powers" 8:1012

resources 8:1013

weight 8:1010

minesweepers 8:1007; 16:1962

minibrowsers 9:1037

minidiscs 7:832

mining and quarrying 8:**1014–1021**

aluminum 1:*64*, 65

coal 3:*346–349*; 8:*1015*, 1016–1017, *1018*, 1021

copper 3:*375*; 8:1018

diamonds 4:418, *419*

explosives used in 5:581; 8:1015–1016, 1017–1018, *1020*, 1021

gold 6:713, *715*; 8:1019, 1020

history 8:1014–1016

iron 7:*796*

lead 7:836, *837*

quarrying 8:1014, 1019–1020

safety 8:1016–1017

salt 12:1515–1516

sulfur 14:1710

surface mining 8:*1016*, 1017–1019

underground mining 8:*1018*, 1020–1021

underwater mining 8:1018, 1021

Minkowski, Rudolph 9:1107

*Minority Report* (movie) 15:1911

Minton, Thomas 11:1332

Minuteman missiles 9:*1029*

*Mir* (space station) 13:*1622*, 1624, 1634–*1635*

mirages 10:1157; 12:1431

mirrors 7:*845*; 10:1156, 1157; 12:*1430*–1431

concave 10:1157; 12:1430–1431

convex 10:1157; 12:1430

parabolic 13:*1597, 1599*

solar energy using 5:550; 13:*1597, 1599*–1600

virtual images 10:1157

missiles and torpedoes 9:**1028–1033**

air-to-air and air-to-ground missiles 9:1030–1031

antiaircraft missiles 9:*1030*

antiballistic-missile missiles (ABMs) 9:1032

antimissile weapons 9:1032

cruise missiles 6:*719*; 9:*1028*, *1031*–1032

intercontinental ballistic missiles (ICBMs) 9:1028–*1029*

intermediate range ballistic missiles (IRBMs) 9:1030

missiles 6:*719*, 721–*722*; 9:1028; 16:1955–1956, 1959

sea-launched missiles 9:1031

submarine-launched ballistic missiles (SLBMs) 9:1029; 14:1701–*1702*

torpedoes 9:1028, *1032–1033*; 14:*1701*

Mississippian period 6:686

Mississippi River 3:276

mistletoe 10:1197

mites 4:441

red 10:1224

mitochondria 3:*300, 301, 302*; 8:989; 12:1459

mitosis 3:303

mobile communication 9:**1034–1037**

and the Internet 7:*792*–793; 9:*1037*

cellular phones 5:*529*; 7:793; 8:990; 9:*1034*–1037

future 7:793

personal digital assistants 10:1221

videophones 9:1037

*see also* communications satellites

mobile phones *see* cellular phones

mobile telephone switching offices (MTSOs) 9:1034, 1035

Möbius, August 8:922

mode 14:1679

modeling

population 3:266

weather 3:312–313

mohair 5:597

Mohs, Friedrich 8:1010

Mohs' scale 8:1010

molding

ceramics 3:311

plastics 11:*1289*, 1290

molds, for casting 3:292–293

mole 3:316

molecular biology 9:**1038–1039**

molecular weight 2:137

molecules 2:137

valency and 15:1896

moles, on the skin 13:*1567*

mollusks 1:81

monocytes 6:*733*

monomers 11:1320, 1321–1322

monorails 9:**1040–1041**

monosaccharides 3:279–281

monotremes **1:**82
monsoon winds **16:**2008–2009
Montgolfier brothers **2:**162–*163*
Monument Valley **7:***823;* **14:***1776*
Moon **9:1042–1047**
  and eclipses **4:***487–488;* **9:***1044–1045*
  and lunar months **9:**1044
  and tides **15:**1807, 1808, *1809*
  dust **9:**1046
  first television pictures from the
    **14:**1770
  Galileo and the **6:**656
  librations **9:**1044
  missions to **9:**1042, *1043, 1044*
  movements **9:**1043–1044
  origin **9:**1047
  phases **9:**1044
  probes to **13:**1626
  rocks **9:**1046–*1047*
  size **9:**1043
  surface **9:***1042,* 1045–*1047*
  temperature **9:**1043
moons **13:**1606
Moore, Daniel McFarlane **7:**854
Moore, Gordon **3:**366
Moore, Henry **1:***57*
Moore's law **3:**366–367
MOPVE technology **7:**778
moraine **6:**699–700; **7:**824
  end moraine **6:**700
mordanting **4:**466
Morley, Edward **12:**1435
Morse, Samuel **8:**981; **14:**1752–1753
Morse code **14:**1753
mortars **2:**206
mortisers **16:**2021–2022
Morton, William T. G. **4:**410
Mosaic (Web browser) **7:**790
mosquitoes
  and disease **4:***441–442;* **10:***1193,*
    1194–1195, 1197
  studying **16:***2045*
moths
  peppered **5:***570*
  pest control **10:***1229*
  pheromones **10:**1228
motion **9:1048–1051**
  circular **5:**626
  close to the speed of light **5:**628;
    **9:**1051
  Galileo's studies of **6:**655;
    **9:***1049–*1050

linear **9:**1048
Newton's laws of **5:**627–628; **7:**806;
    **9:**1050–1051, 1103; **12:**1489
  rotational **9:**1048
  simple harmonic **9:**1049
  translational **9:**1048
motion-capture technology **1:**87;
    **9:**1056
motion pictures **9:1052–1059**
  film **9:**1053
  history **9:**1052–1053
  movie cameras **9:**1053–*1055*
  projectors **9:**1053, *1058–1059*
  sound track **9:***1057–*1058
  special effects **9:**1055–1057
  *see also* animation
motorcycles **9:1060–1062**
motor racing **2:**147–149
motors
  electric *see* electric motors
  outboard **8:***911–*912
mountains **2:**192–*193;* **7:***820;*
    **9:1063–1066**
  animals **9:**1065–*1066*
  climate **3:***336–337*
  dome **9:**1065
  fault-block mountains **9:***1064,* 1065;
    **12:**1488
  fold mountains **9:***1064*
  formation **7:**822–824; **9:**1063–1065
  habitats **9:***1065*
  height calculated **9:***1064;* **14:***1734*
  railroads **3:**260–261, *350, 351*
  rain shadows **4:**416–417
  rise and fall **9:**1065
  underwater **9:**1065
  volcanic **9:***1064*
mouse, computer **7:***819*
movies *see* motion pictures
Moving Pictures Experts Group
    (MPEG) **4:**429
MP3s **4:**428, *429–431*
MRI *see* magnetic resonance imaging
*MSG-I* satellite **3:***355*
Mudge, Thomas **15:**1822
Mueller, Erwin **8:**1001
mule, spinning **14:**1782; **16:**2026
Müller, Walther **6:**669
multiple independently targetable
    reentry vehicles (MIRVs) **9:**1029
Multiple Mirror Telescope (MMT)
    **14:**1761

multiple sclerosis (MS) **9:**1101
multiplexing **12:**1446
multirole combat aircraft (MRCA)
    **16:**1955
muons **12:**1437
muscular system **9:1067–1072**
  cardiac muscle **9:**1069, *1072*
  muscle performance **9:**1070–1071
  muscle proteins **11:**1368–1369
  skeletal (voluntary; striated) muscles
    **9:***1067, 1068, 1069–*1070
  smooth muscles **9:**1068–1069,
    1071–1072
music, digital audio software
    **4:428–431**
musical instrumental digital interface
    (MIDI) **9:**1080
musical instruments **9:1073–1080**
  brass **2:***226;* **9:***1076,* 1077; **12:**1458
  keyboard **9:**1074, 1078–1079
  percussion **9:***1077–1078*
  science of music **9:**1074
  stringed **9:**1074–1075; **11:**1388;
    **12:***1458*
  synthesizers **9:**1079–*1080*
  wind (woodwind) **9:**1073, 1074,
    *1075–*1077; **12:**1458
Music Teller stations **4:***431*
musk **10:**1229
muskets **6:**724
mutations **6:**679
  and evolution **5:***570*
  causing **1:**29–30
  DNA **4:***455*
  somatic **6:**764
mycelium **6:**648
MYCIN **1:**114
mycoprotein **5:**619
mycorrhizae **6:**649
myelin **2:**216
myelin sheath **9:***1100*
myofibrils **9:***1068,* 1070
myoglobin **1:**79
myopia **5:**583, 584, 585
myosin **11:**1368–1369
myxomatosis **10:**1224

# N

nanotechnology (nanoengineering)
    **5:**554; **8:**994–995; **9:1081–1082**
  nanorobots **8:**995; **9:***1081;* **12:**1482
  nanotubes **8:**1001; **10:***1257*

naphthalene 14:1785
Napier, John 8:921
Napoleon III 1:65
narcolepsy 13:1575
Nasmyth, James 7:872
Natachata (computer program) 1:113
National Radio Astronomy
    Observatory (NRAO) 15:1878
natural gas 5:550; 6:662; 9:1148
  exploration for 6:695–696
  pipelines 10:1266–1267
natural killer cells 6:762
natural selection 2:181, 186; 4:409;
    5:568, 569, 570
Nautilus (submarine) 14:1697
navigation 9:1083–1088
  aircraft 9:1085–1086, 1087–1088
  automobile 2:145; 6:708;
    9:1087–1088; 15:1843
  gyrocompasses and 6:730
  measuring longitude 9:1084–1085;
    15:1816
  navigation satellites 6:705–706, 708;
    9:1086–1087; 12:1522
  ship 9:1083–1088
  spacecraft 9:1088
  submarine 14:1702
  using astrolabes 9:1083–1084
  using cross-staffs and sextants
    9:1084, 1085
  using GPS 9:1087–1088
  using quadrants 9:1084
  using radar 9:1086
  using radio aids 9:1085–1086
  see also compasses; guidance systems
Navstar 6:705–706, 707, 708
Nazca Plate 11:1295
Near Earth Asteroid Rendezvous
    (NEAR) (space probe) 13:1626,
    1630
nearsightedness see myopia
nebulas 9:1089–1091; 14:1675; 15:1878
  bright 9:1089
  dark 9:1089, 1091
  emission nebulas 9:1089–1090, 1091
  planetary 9:1090–1091; 14:1673
  reflection nebulas 9:1090
  supernova remnants and 9:1090,
    1091
  the birthplace of stars 9:1089–1090;
    13:1603; 14:1673, 1675
  needles, manufacture 16:2017, 2018

Neilson, James 2:202
nematodes 10:1193, 1197
neon 7:775
  lights 6:662; 7:774, 775
neoteny 8:976
nephrons 5:571
Neptune 9:1092–1095; 13:1605
  missions to 9:1094–1095; 13:1628,
    1630
  moons 9:1095
neptunium 5:541
Nereid (moon) 9:1095
nervous system 9:1096–1101
  and taste 14:1751
  autonomic (ANS) 9:1096, 1099
  central nervous system (CNS)
    9:1096, 1097–1099
  cranial nerves 9:1099
  disorders 9:1100–1101
  motor nerves 3:303; 9:1099
  nerve cells see neurons
  nerve pathways 2:219–220
  nerves and touch 15:1838
  peripheral (PNS) 9:1096, 1098, 1099
  sensory nerves 9:1099
  somatic (voluntary) 9:1096, 1099
  speed of impulses 9:1099
nets, for fishing 5:611, 612
networks, computer (LANs and
    WANs) 3:364–365
neural networks 1:114–115; 3:367;
    12:1478
neurons (nerve cells) 9:1096, 1098,
    1099, 1100
  brain 2:215, 216
neurotransmitters 3:303; 9:1100
neutrinos 6:717; 10:1201, 1203, 1205,
    1207; 15:1882
neutron activation analysis 11:1403
neutrons 2:136, 139; 5:540; 10:1206,
    1214
  and isotopes 7:800
  and nuclear fission 5:614, 615
  antiparticles of 10:1207
neutrophils 6:733
Newcomen, Thomas 8:1016; 14:1684,
    1685
Newlands, John 10:1216
newspapers, printing 11:1355
Newton, Isaac 9:1102–1103; 10:1260
  and calculus 3:265, 266; 8:922, 924;
    10:1259

and gravity 1:120; 6:716;
    9:1102–1103; 15:1808
and light 7:846; 9:1103; 13:1645
and telescopes 9:1103;
    14:1760–1761
and viscosity 16:1929
laws of motion 5:627–628; 7:806;
    9:1050–1051, 1103; 12:1489
newtons 5:629; 11:1335, 1347
Newton's rings 7:846
Next Generation Space Telescope
    (NGST) 14:1767
niches 4:491
Nicholson, Vanessa-Mae 9:1074
Nicholson, William 4:507
nickel 15:1853
  and the magnetostrictive effect
    15:1872
nickel nitrate 12:1513
nickel silver 2:226
Nicol, William 11:1311
Niépce, Joseph-Nicéphore 10:1236,
    1242–1243
Nipkow, Paul 14:1768
Nipkow discs 14:1769
Nirenberg, Marshall 8:987; 9:1038
nitric acid 12:1513
  production 4:445; 9:1105; 11:1298
nitrocellulose 5:580
nitrogen 6:662; 9:1104–1106
  and "the bends" 10:1178–1179
  compounds of 9:1105–1106
  cycle 9:1106
  fertilizers 5:592–593; 9:1105, 1106
  liquid 4:393; 6:662; 9:1104; 11:1349;
    14:1719
  organic compounds of 9:1106
  production of 9:1104
  uses 9:1104
nitrogenases 7:779
nitrogen trifluoride 9:1105
nitroglycerine 5:579, 580
nitrous oxide 9:1105
  an anesthetic 1:77, 78; 4:410; 6:660
  as a greenhouse gas 3:339
Noble, Alfred 5:579, 580
noble gases see inert gases
nodules, polymetallic 8:1021
noise 13:1616
Nollet, Jean-Antoine 10:1170
northern lights 2:134
Notre Dame cathedral 1:106

novas and supernovas **9:1107–1110**
  novas **9:**1107, 1109; **14:**1676
  supernova remnants **9:**1091,
    1109–*1110*; **14:***1767*; **15:***1882*
  supernovas **1:**121, 123; **9:***1090*, 1091,
    1107–*1109*; **14:**1675, 1676, *1677*;
    **15:**1880
NTSC system **14:**1770, 1771
nuclear magnetic resonance (NMR)
  **7:***893*; **10:***1256*
nuclear reactors **9:1111–1118**
  and transuranic elements **10:**1218
  chain reaction **5:**615; **9:**1111,
    1113–1114; **15:**1884
  design **9:**1114
  electromagnetic pumps and **11:**1386
  fast breeder **15:***1884*
  history of nuclear power **9:**1111–1112
  nuclear fission **9:**1111, 1112–1113;
    **15:**1884
  nuclear fusion **6:**654; **9:***1117–1118*
  nuclear power plants **5:***615*; **9:***1111*,
    1112, *1113*, *1114*, *1115*; **11:**1318,
    *1337*, 1338, *1341*
  safety **9:**1115–*1116*
  types **9:**1114–*1115*; **11:**1339
  waste **9:**1116–*1117*
  *see also* fission, nuclear
nuclear weapons **2:***209*; **9:1119–1122**;
  **10:**1260
  atomic bombs **2:***209*; **5:**614;
    **9:**1112–1113, 1114, *1120*–1121
  hydrogen bombs **2:***209*; **5:**551;
    **9:**1117, 1122
nucleic acids *see* DNA; RNA
nucleons **10:**1208
nucleotides **4:***391*
nucleus, atomic **5:**614; **10:**1206, 1214
  and radioactive decay **11:**1402–1403
  binding force in **10:**1209
  bombarded in particle accelerators
    **10:**1198
  electron shells (orbits) around **5:**540,
    541; **7:**794; **10:**1218–1219; **15:**1852,
    1896–1897
nucleus, cell **3:***301*, 302–303
nuée ardente **16:**1939–1940
numbers, SI prefixes **8:**930, 931
number systems **9:1123–1126**
  bases **9:**1125–1126
  binary **3:**362; **9:**1123, *1126*; **13:***1587*
  decimal **9:**1123–1124

  decimal points **9:**1126
  fractions **9:**1126
  of ancient civilizations **9:**1124–*1125*
  places of digits **9:**1125
  *see also* mathematics
nutrition **9:1127–1132**
  balanced diet **8:***958*; **9:**1127,
    1131–1132
  carbohydrates and **9:**1129
  cereals **9:**1129
  convenience foods **9:**1128
  dairy products **9:**1130
  diets and dieting **9:**1132
  eating disorders and **9:**1132
  fats and **5:***588–589*; **8:***958*;
    **9:**1130–1131
  fiber **9:**1128
  fruit and vegetables **9:**1129; **16:***1930*
  how food is used in the body
    **8:**958–959
  malnutrition **9:**1127, *1131*; **11:***1327*
  meat and fish **9:**1129–1130
  minerals and **9:**1127–1128
  proteins and **1:**70–71; **8:***958*; **9:**1129;
    **11:***1366*, 1367–1368
  sports **13:**1661
  sugars **9:**1130, 1131
  water **9:**1128
  *see also* metabolism; vitamins
nylon **5:**598, *599*; **11:**1288, 1321;
  **14:**1784
nymphs **8:**979
Nyos, Lake **6:***693*

## O

oars **8:**908
Oberon (moon) **15:**1886, 1888
obesity **9:**1127, 1128, 1132
oboes **9:**1077
O'Brien, Willis **1:**86
observatories **9:1133–1136**
obsessive-compulsive disorder
  (OCD) **11:**1376
obstetricians **11:**1343, *1344*
occlusions, warm and cold **16:***1991*
ocean basin **9:***1139*
ocean ridges **9:**1065, 1140, *1143*;
  **11:**1294–1295; **16:***1996*
  mid-Atlantic ridge **6:***694*; **11:**1295
oceans **2:**192; **9:1137–1143**
  and climate **3:**337; **9:**1139
  area, volume, and depth **9:**1137

  creation **9:**1139
  exploitation of **9:**1143
  floor (seabed) **8:**1021; **9:***1139*, 1140
  landforms **7:**825
  life in **2:***183*; **9:***1141*–1142, 1143
  surface temperatures **7:***777*
  *see also* currents; tides
octane numbers **9:**1149
"octaves, law of" **10:**1216
Ohain, Hans von **7:**807
oil
  as a lubricant **7:**876–877; **16:**1929
  grading of motor oil **7:**876
  in paint binder **10:**1181–1182
  linseed **10:**1181
  recycling **12:**1428–1429
  soyabean **10:**1181
  viscosity **7:***863*; **16:**1929
  waste **12:**1426
oil, crude (petroleum) **5:**550
  composition **9:**1144
  formation **9:**1144
  from coal using bacteria **2:**152–153
  geology **9:***1145*
  pipelines **10:***1266*–1267
  spills **2:**152; **11:***1314*; **13:***1583*;
    **14:**1747, *1748*
  world's supply **9:**1145–1146; **14:**1749
  *see also* oil exploration and refining
oil exploration and refining
    **9:1144–1149**
  drilling operations **4:***460–461*; **6:***662*;
    **9:***1144*, *1147*
  exploration **6:***695–696*; **9:***1146*–1147
  history **9:**1145
  petroleum production and refining
    **4:***444*; **9:**1147–*1149*
  *see also* drilling rigs
oil rigs *see* drilling rigs
oil tankers *see* tankers
oil wells, drilling **4:**460–461
olfactometers **16:***2045*
olfactory bulb **13:**1576, 1577
oligosaccharides **3:**281
Omar Khayyam **1:**53
Omega system **9:**1085–1086
Omnirange **9:**1085–1086
onchocerciasis *see* river blindness
Onnes, Heike Kamerlingh **14:**1718
Oort cloud **1:**119; **13:**1606
opal **8:**1010; **13:**1556
opaque substances **10:**1156

Oparin, Aleksandr Ivanovich 5:566
open-hearth process 7:799
operating rooms 14:1727
ophthalmoscopes 5:584
*Opportunity* (robot vehicle) 8:916
optical character recognition (OCR)
    12:1527
optics 10:1156–1159, *1260*
  geometric 10:1159, 1260
  physical 10:1159, 1260
  quantum 10:1159
  the eye and vision 5:*583*
  *see also* fiber optics; light; reflection
    and refraction
optoelectronics 10:1160–1161
orange giants 14:1673
orbit 10:1162–1163
  objects in 6:*718*
orbitals, electron 10:1219; 15:1852
Orbiting Astronomical Observatories
    14:1766
orchestras 9:*1073*
orders 3:333
Ordovician period 6:686
ores 8:*963*, 964–965, *1016*
  extraction of metals from 8:*967–968*
organic chemistry 3:283, 322;
    **10:1164–1167**
organs (instruments) 9:1074
orgasm 12:1451–1452
Orion
  Horsehead Nebula 9:1090
  Orion Nebula 9:*1089*–1090
Ornithischia 4:435–436
ornithopods 4:436
Ørsted, Hans Christian 1:67, 72;
    4:507; 5:522, 587
orthoclase 8:*1009*; 16:1985–1986
orthophotomaps 8:905
Osann, Gottfried 11:1296–1297
oscillating water columns (OWCs)
    16:*1980*, 1981
oscilloscopes 5:533; **10:1168–1169**;
    15:*1848*; 16:*1977*
osmium 8:967; 11:1296; 13:1609
osmosis 10:1170–1172
  osmotic pressure 10:1171
  reverse 10:1171–*1172*
Otis, Elisha 5:543, 544; 13:1569
*OTS2* (orbital test satellite) 3:354
otters, sea 5:625
Otto, Nikolaus 2:141; 7:783

ova (eggs) 12:1449, 1452
ovaries 5:*546*; 12:1449–1450
  hormones 5:548
overfishing 4:489–*490*; 9:1143
ovulation 12:1450
Owen, Richard 4:*433*
oxbow lakes 12:1467, 1469
oxidation and reduction
    **10:1173–1175**
oxidation number 10:1174
oxides, mineral 8:1012
oxygen 10:1176–1179
  abundance 10:1176
  atoms 10:1176
  breathing 10:1178, 1179
  cycle 10:*1178*
  discovery 3:321; 7:835; 10:1177
  from photosynthesis 10:*1176*, 1177,
    1253, 1255
  liquid 4:393; 10:1176, *1178*
  production 10:*1179*
  reactivity 10:1176
  uses 6:661–662; 10:1178–1179
  *see also* ozone
oxytocin 11:1345
ozone 10:1179
  ground-level 3:339
ozone layer 2:134; 10:1179
  development 2:132
  hole and depletion of ozone 2:*135*;
    6:711

**P**
P-51 Mustang (aircraft) 16:*1952*
pacemaker(s)
  artificial 6:732
  natural 6:731–732
pachycephalosaurs 4:436
Pacific Ocean 9:1137
  "ring of fire" 15:1861
  seafloor trenches 9:*1140*, 1141
Pacinian corpuscles 15:1838
packet switching 14:*1758*
Page, Lawrence 7:*791*
pagodas 2:*242*
*pahoehoe* 16:1940
pain 15:1839
paintings, cave 1:99; 3:299; 10:1180
paints 10:1180–1183
  artists' 10:*1180*, 1181, 1182–1183
  lead 7:838; 10:1180
  luminous 7:879

  manufacture 10:1183
  *see also* dyes and dyeing
paleoclimatology 6:691
paleogeography 6:691
paleomagnetism 11:1293
paleontology 6:691
palladium 11:1296
Panama Canal 3:*276*; 14:1747
Panamax vessels 14:1747
pancreas
  as an endocrine gland 5:*546*
  as an exocrine gland 5:575
Pangaea 4:433; 6:686, 690;
    11:1292–1293; 16:1996
Panhard, René 2:141
PANs (personal-area networks) 9:1037
panspermia 5:566
pantographs 12:1425
paper and papermaking
    **10:1184–1189**
  recycling paper 12:1426–1427
Papin, Denis 7:782; 8:909; 14:1684
papyrus 10:*1184*
Paracelsus 8:942
parachutes 10:1190–1192
parallax method 14:1672
paramagnetism 15:1854
paraquat 10:1227
parasitoids 10:1193
parasitology 10:1193–1197
  antiparasitic drugs 10:1196–*1197*
  ectoparasites and endoparasites
    10:1193
  life cycles of parasites 10:1193–1194
  parasite defences 10:1196
  parasitic diseases 10:*1193*,
    1194–1197
  pest-control parasites 10:1197
  plant and fungal parasites 10:*1196*,
    1197, 1275
parathyroid glands 5:*546*, 547
parchment 10:1185
Paré, Ambroise 11:1362
Park, Nick 1:*86–87*
Parkes, Alexander 11:1286
Parkesine 11:1286
Parkinson's disease 2:218; 9:1101
parsecs 14:1672
Parsons, Charles Algernon 6:*665*
Parsons, William 14:1761
Parthenon 1:105
partial pressures, law of 4:403

particle accelerators **2:**139; **5:***629*; **10:1198–1201**
and transuranic elements **10:**1218
circular **10:***1198*, 1199
cyclotrons **10:**1199, *1200*; **14:**1719
insulators **7:***781*
linear **10:**1198–*1199*
Stanford Linear Accelerator (SLAC) **10:***1201, 1207*
superconducting **14:**1719
syncho-cyclotrons **10:**1199
synchrotrons **4:**395–*396*; **10:***1200*–1201; **14:**1719
particle detectors **10:1202–1205**
bubble chambers **10:**1201, *1203–1204, 1206*
cloud chambers **10:**1203
spark chambers **10:**1204–1205
particle physics **10:1206–1209**
antiparticles **10:**1207
cosmic rays and **10:**1207
families of particles **10:**1207–1209
particle detectors **10:**1202–1205
particles for the fundamental forces **5:**629; **10:**1206, 1209
string theory **10:**1209
*see also* particle accelerators
Pascal, Blaise **3:**263, 358; **6:**749, 750
pascals **11:**1347; **15:**1893
Pascal's triangle **14:***1683*
Pasteur, Louis **10:1210–1211**
and fermentation **10:**1210; **16:**2035
and pasteurization **10:**1211
and the silkworm industry **10:**1211
disproves spontaneous generation **5:**565–566
germ theory of disease **7:**866; **8:**938, *986*; **10:**1211
pasteurization **5:**621; **8:***986*; **10:**1211
patch clamping **3:***304*, 305
patio process **13:**1559
PDAs *see* personal digital assistants
Peacekeeper missiles **9:**1029
pea plants, Mendel's experiments **8:***946*–947
peat, humans preserved in **1:**100–101
PEEK (polyetheretherketone) **11:**1291
pellagra **16:**1931
Peltier, Jean **14:**1787
Peltier effect **14:**1786, 1787
Pelton, Lester Allen **6:**756
pelvis **13:***1563*

pendulums **6:**749; **10:1212–1213**; **15:**1816
peneplains **6:**690; **7:**822; **12:**1467
penicillin **5:**591, *617*
discovery **1:**91, *92*; **2:***154*; **5:**617; **8:***942*
side effects **1:**93
*Penicillium* spp.
and antibiotics **1:**91, 93; **2:***154*; **5:***617*
and cheese **2:***153*
penis **12:**1450, 1451, *1452*
Pennsylvanian period **6:**686
pens, ink **16:***2028–2030*
penstocks **6:**755
penumbra **10:**1156
Penzias, Arno **15:***1879*, 1880
pepsin **4:**426; **5:**558; **11:**1369
perceptual noise shaping **4:**430
Peress, Joseph **4:**451
perfumes **10:**1229
periodic table **3:**322; **5:**541; **8:**949; **10:1214–1219**
periods, geological **6:***683*
peristalsis **4:**424, *425*; **9:**1071
Perkin, William **4:***466*
Permian period **6:**686
peroxisomes **3:***301*
personal digital assistants (PDAs) **10:1220–1221**
Peru-Chile Trench **11:**1295
pest control **10:1222–1227**
direct and indirect **10:**1222–1223
pesticides and insecticides **1:**29; **4:**492; **10:***1222, 1223*, 1224–1227; **11:**1312–1313
using parasites **10:**1197
pesticides and insecticides **1:**29; **4:**492; **10:***1222, 1223*, 1224–1227; **11:**1312–1313
pests, cotton **3:***381*
PET *see* positron emission tomography
PETN (pentaerythritol tetranitrate) **5:**580, *581*
petroleum *see* oil, crude
petroleum plants **3:***295*
petrology **6:**692
Petronas Towers, Malaysia **2:***247*; **13:***1569*
pewter **1:**59, 60; **7:***838*; **15:**1825
Pfleumer, Fritz **7:**885
pH **1:**16
phagocytes **6:**762

Phanerozoic eon **6:**685
phenol **7:**866
as an antiseptic **1:**95
phenylalanine **1:***68*, 71
pheromones **10:1228–1229**; **11:***1343*
phloem **10:**1277
phlogiston **3:**321; **7:**834–835
Phobos (moon) **8:**913, *914*
phonographs **4:***494*; **13:**1617–*1618*
phosphates **10:**1231
phosphorescence **7:**879; **10:**1159
phosphorus **10:1230–1231**
in fertilizers **5:***593*–594
photochemical reactions **13:**1598
photoconductive cells **10:**1235
photocopiers **10:1232–1233**
photodiodes (photoemissive cells) **10:**1234, *1235*
photoelectric cells **10:1234–1235**
photoelectric effect **10:**1159; **11:**1390
photoengraving **8:**905
photogrammetry **8:**903
photography **10:1236–1245**
aerial **1:**96; **8:***903*; **14:***1735*
digital **10:1246–1251**
early **10:**1236
films **10:**1236, *1243*, 1244–1245
high-speed **10:**1245
infrared **12:**1448; **14:**1789
light meters **10:***1242*
printing techniques **10:**1245, *1251*
processing films **10:**1242–1245
Schlieren **10:***1245*
silver salts and **10:**1243, 1244; **13:**1560
space **8:**904
used in mapmaking **8:***904*, 905
*see also* cameras
photoluminescence **7:**879, 880
photometry **7:**847–848
photomultipliers **7:**848; **12:**1529
photonics **10:**1160
photons **5:**629; **6:**717; **7:**847; **10:**1159, 1207, 1209; **11:**1390, 1391; **16:**1976–1977
and lasers **7:**827, *828*
gamma-ray **6:**657
X-ray **16:**2031
photosynthesis **2:***178*; **10:1252–1255**, 1274–1275
dark reaction **10:**1255
light reaction **10:**1254

oxygen from **10:***1176*, 1177, 1253, 1255
phototubes (photoemissive cells) **10:**1234, *1235*
phototypesetting **11:**1359
photovoltaic cells **10:**1235
photovoltaic effect **10:**1235
phyla **3:**333
phylloquinone *see* vitamins, vitamin K
physical chemistry **3:**322; **10:1256–1257**
physics **10:1258–1261**
  astrophysics **1:**123–124; **10:**1258
  biophysics **10:**1258–1259
  classical (Newtonian) **10:**1259–1261
  geophysics **6:**692, **693–696**; **10:**1258
  particle **10:1206–1209**
physiology **10:1262–1263**
physiotherapists **13:***1659*
pi (π) **1:**102; **9:**1126
pianos **9:***1078*, 1079
  player **13:**1588
Picard, Jean **4:**505
Piccard, Auguste **14:**1706
pickling **5:**622
picric acid **9:**1106
pie charts **14:**1680
piezoelectricity **4:**398; **10:1264–1265**; **15:**1822
  ceramics **3:**310
pigments **10:***1180–1181*, *1182*, 1183
Pilkington, Alastair **6:**703
pineal gland **5:**547
Pine, Courtney **9:***1076*
Pinel, Philippe **11:**1373
pinions **6:**667
*Pioneer 10* (space probe) **13:**1626, 1629
*Pioneer 11* (space probe) **12:**1524; **13:**1626, 1629
*Pioneer Venus Orbiter* (space probe) **13:**1627
pions **10:**1208
pipelines **10:1266–1271**
  clay pipes **10:**1270–1271
  concrete pipes **10:***1268*, 1271
  history **10:**1266
  laying **10:**1267–1270
  oil and gas **10:***1266*–1267
  pipe manufacture **10:**1270
  plastic pipes **10:***1267*, *1271*
  pumping stations **10:**1267
pistols, automatic **6:**727

pitch (substance), viscosity **16:**1929
pitch (sound) **13:**1613–1614
pitchblende **4:**399
pitot tubes **15:***1902*, 1903
pituitary gland **5:***546*–547, 548
pixels **3:**369; **7:**865
  digital camera **10:**1246, *1247*–1248
placebos **4:**465
placenta **5:***547*; **11:**1343, *1345*, *1346*
placer deposits **6:**713; **8:**1019
plagioclase, in Moon rock **9:**1047
plague, bubonic **4:**440
Planché, Andrew **11:**1331
Planck, Max **2:**205; **10:**1159, **1272–1273**; **11:**1389; **13:**1645–1646
Planck's constant **10:**1273; **11:**1389
planers **16:**2021
planes **15:**1832–1833
planetesimals **13:**1604–1605, 1606
planetoids **1:**117
planets **13:**1604–1605
  atmospheres **2:**134
  formation **7:**812; **9:**1110; **13:**1604–1605
  orbits round the Sun **10:**1162; **13:***1605*
  terrestrial and giant **13:**1603
  *see also* solar system; and *names of individual planets*
Planet X **11:**1302
planing machines **15:**1834
plankton **9:**1142; **16:**2045
plan position indicators (PPIs) **11:**1394, 1395
plant kingdom **10:1274–1277**
  alternation of generations **10:**1275–1276
  asexual reproduction **3:**340–341
  basic features **10:**1274–1275
  binomial classification **7:**861
  biorhythms **2:**195
  breeding **1:**29
  cells **3:***282*, *302*
  communication **2:**212
  desert **4:***416*, 417
  diversity **10:**1276
  fibers from **5:**597
  food chains and **5:**624
  food production *see* photosynthesis
  genetically engineered plants **1:**29–*30*; **2:**210, *211*, 212, *213*; **3:***341*; **6:***676*

  hormones **2:**213
  nonvascular plants **10:***1275*, 1276
  parasitic plants **10:**1197, 1275
  roots causing weathering **16:***1988*
  saprophytic plants **10:**1275
  seed- and nonseed plants **10:**1277
  vascular plants **10:**1276–1277
  water uptake **10:***1254*
  *see also* botany
plaque, dental **4:**411, 413
plasma (in blood) **7:**881
plasma physics **6:**654; **11:1284–1285**; **13:**1609
  hydrogen **9:**1117–*1118*
plasma vapor deposition (PVD) **11:***1285*
plasmids, DNA **1:**29; **3:**341–342, *343*; **6:**674
*Plasmodium* **4:**441–442; **11:***1371*
plastic deformation **4:**497
plastic forming, ceramics **3:**311
plastics **11:1286–1291**
  carbon fibers mixed with **3:**291
  forming processes using **11:***1289*, 1290
  glass-reinforced (GRPs) **11:**1291; **13:***1553*–1554; **15:**1858
  insulating **7:**780; **11:**1290
  pipes **10:***1267*, *1271*
  polymerization **11:**1287
  recycling **11:***1291*; **12:**1428
  silicone **7:**781
  thermoplastics **10:**1271; **11:***1289*
  thermosetting **11:**1289
  waste **12:**1426
  *see also names of individual planets*
plastids **3:**302
plateaus **7:**822, 823
platelets **3:**329; **6:**733
plate tectonics **6:**694; **11:1292–1295**; **16:**1996
  and earthquakes **4:**483–484
  and mountain formation **9:**1063, 1064–1065; **12:**1486
  evidence for **11:**1292, 1293–1294
  mechanisms **11:***1293*
  plates and plate margins **11:***1292*, 1295–1296
  *see also* continental drift
platforms, wave-cut **5:**563; **7:**825
plating *see* electroplating
platinum **11:**1296, *1297*, 1298–*1299*

platinum group metals **11:1296–1299**; 15:1851
Plato **1**:110, 111
play therapy **11**:1374
Pleiades **9**:1090; **14**:1677
Pleistocene epoch **6**:688
  Ice Age **6**:697
*Plongeur* (submarine) **14**:1698
plows **1**:*23, 24*; **11:1300–1301**
Pluto **1**:119, 125; **10**:1162; **11:1302–1305**; **13**:1605
plutonium **5**:541, 551
  and thermoelectric generators **14**:1787
  isotope **7**:801
  nuclear devices using **9**:1120–1121; **15**:1884
plywood boats **13**:1553
pneumatic drills **4**:*472*
pneumatic tools **7**:802
podsols **13**:*1595*
Poincaré, Jules **8**:922
poisons **11:1306–1309**
  toxic wastes **11**:1318–1319
polar deserts **2**:*190*; **4**:*415*
polar easterlies **16**:2008
polar front **16**:2008
polarization **10**:1159; **11:1310–1311**
*Polar Lander* (space probe) **13**:1592
polio
  vaccine (Sabin vaccine) **15**:1890–1891
  virus **15**:1916
pollution **11:1312–1319**
  acid rain **2**:*135*; **3**:339; **5**:*564*; **10**:1178; **11**:*1316, 1318*
  and global warming **6**:*709*
  atmospheric **2**:135; **3**:*286*; **6**:*709*; **11**:*1315*–1316
  climate change and global warming **6**:*709*; **11**:*1317*–1318
  light **11**:1312
  nuclear (radioactive) **5**:551; **9**:1116–*1117*; **11**:1318; **12**:1521
  pesticides as **11**:1312–1313
  sound **11**:1312
  toxic waste **11**:1318–1319
  water **1**:30; **4**:492; **5**:*595*; **11**:*1313*–1315, *1319*; **13**:1583; **14**:*1748*, 1749
  *see also* global warming
polonium **4**:398, 399; **11**:1401, *1402*
polyacrylonitrile (PAN) **3**:290, 291

polycarbonate **11**:1290
polyester **5**:599; **11**:*1288*–1289; **14**:1784
  PVC-coated **2**:247–248
polyetheretherketone (PEEK) **11**:1291
polyethylene (polythene) **10**:1166; **11**:*1287, 1289*, 1320, *1321, 1323*
  pipes **10**:1271
polyethylene terephthalate (PET) **11**:*1288*
polygenes **6**:678
polymerase chain reaction (PCR) **3**:342
polymerization **11:1320–1323**
  addition **11**:1320
  and synthetic fibers **5**:598–599; **11**:1321
  bulk **11**:1322–1323
  condensation **11**:1320
  direct **11**:1320
  emulsion **11**:1323
  of plastics **11**:1287
  suspension **11**:1323
polymers **10**:1165–1166
polypropylene **11**:1288, *1322*
polysaccharides **3**:*279*, 281–*282*
polystyrene **11**:*1287*–1288, 1320
polytetrafluoroethylene (PTFE; Teflon) **7**:780; **11**:1288, *1290*; **12**:1495
polythene *see* polyethylene
polyurethane **11**:1289
polyvinyl chloride (PVC) **11**:1288, *1289*, 1320
  pipes **10**:1271
Popov, Alexsandr **11**:1397
poppies, opium **2**:*212*
population growth **11:1324–1327**
  modeling **3**:266
porcelain **11**:1330–*1332, 1333*
positron emission tomography (PET) scans **2**:216; **7**:*801*; **8**:935–937, 939; **11**:*1375*
positrons **10**:1207; **11**:1403
post-traumatic stress disorder (PTSD) **11**:1375
potassium **1**:16; **8**:962–963
  in fertilizers **5**:594
potassium aluminum sulfate **12**:1514
potassium bicarbonate **5**:604
potassium ferricyanide **12**:1514
potassium hydroxide (caustic potash) **1**:15; **6**:645

potassium nitrate **9**:1105; **12**:1514
potatoes, glowing **2**:212
potentiometers **4**:500–501
  sliding-wire **4**:501
pottery **11:1328–1333**
  dating **1**:100
Poulsen, Valdemar **7**:885
Powell, John Wesley **6**:690
Powell, Lake **12**:*1468*
power **11:1334–1336**
  electrical **11**:1335, *1336*
  *see also* power generation and distribution
power generation and distribution **4**:*500*, 509; **6**:738; **11:1337–1342**
  combined cycle power stations **11**:1338–1339
  fossil-fuel power stations **11**:1338
  hydroelectric power plants **6**:*754, 755*–757; **11**:1337
  nuclear power plants **5**:*615*; **9**:*1111*, 1112, *1113, 1114, 1115*; **11**:*1337*, 1338, *1341*
  power lines **4**:*509*
  solar power stations **13**:*1597*
  steam condensers **15**:1827–1828
  wave power **16:1979–1982**
  wind power **5**:552; **11**:*1339*, 1341; **15**:*1866*; **16**:2011–2014
  *see also* tidal power
power shovels **4**:479
power tools **15**:*1832*, 1833
Precambrian period **6**:*683*, 685
precession **6**:730
precipitation **3**:345; **16**:1967–1968
  *see also* rain and rainfall; snow and frost
precipitation, chemical, and sewage treatment **13**:1546–1547
pregnancy and birth **11:1343–1346**; **12**:1452
  birthing process **11**:1345–*1346*
  fetal heart-rate monitoring **8**:940–941
  the placenta **5**:*547*; **11**:1343, *1345, 1346*
  *see also* reproductive system
premedication **1**:77, 78
preservatives, food **5**:623
pressure **11:1347–1349**
  absolute **11**:1349
  atmospheric **6**:660; **11**:*1347*–1348

differential **11:**1349
  gauge **11:**1349
  osmotic **10:**1171
  static and dynamic **15:**1902
pressure gauges **11:**1348–*1349*
pressurized water reactors (PWRs)
  **9:***1114*; **11:**1339
prickly pears **10:**1227
prick test **1:**56
Priestly, Joseph **3:**321; **10:**1177
prime meridian **8:**902
printed circuits **11:1350–1351**
  printed circuit boards (PCBs)
    **8:**990, *991, 994*
  *see also* silicon chips
printing **11:1352–1359**
  computers and **11:***1358, 1359*
  dye-sublimation **10:***1251*; **14:***1696*
  early presses **11:***1354*
  gravure **11:**1358–1359
  Gutenberg and **11:**1353
  Linotype **11:***1356*
  lithography **11:**1356–1358
  Monotype **11:**1356
  moveable type **11:**1353
  photographs **10:**1245, *1251*
  phototypesetting **11:**1359
  stereotyping **11:***1355*–1356
  typesetting **11:**1354–1355
  woodblock **11:***1352*–*1353*
prions, and CJD **9:**1100–*1101*
prisms **6:***749*; **7:***844*, 845; **9:**1103;
  **13:**1645
  raindrops as **10:***1156*; **12:**1420
probability **14:**1680–1681
Prochorov, A. M. **7:**827
progesterone **5:**548; **11:**1343, 1344
projections, map **8:**904–905
projectors, motion-picture **9:**1053,
  *1058–1059*
prokaryotes **8:**987; **11:**1370
prolactin **5:**547
propellers **1:**41; **8:***910–911*;
  **11:1360–1361**
  aircraft **1:**41; **11:***1361*
  ships' **8:***910–911*; **11:**1360–1361
propulsors, electrical **8:***910*
prostaglandins **2:**213; **11:**1345
prostate gland **5:**577
  cancer **5:***577*
prosthetics **11:1362–1365**
  hip replacements **11:***1363*; **15:***1828*

proteins **1:**68–69; **3:**302; **11:1366–1369**
  complement **6:**762
  dietary **1:**70–71; **8:**958; **9:**1129;
    **11:**1367–1368
  enzymes as **5:**557
  formed from amino acids **1:**69–*70*;
    **8:**959
  genetically engineered **6:**673–674
  iron-sulfur **7:**779
  structural **11:**1366
  structure of **11:***1367*
  synthesis **1:**70; **2:**179; **4:**454–455;
    **6:**680
  transport **11:**1366
  *see also* amino acids
protist kingdom **11:1370–1372**
  and diseases **4:**441–442; **11:***1371*
protons **2:**136; **5:**540; **10:**1206, 1214
  and antiprotons **10:***1209*
  and electrical charge **4:**504
  collisions **2:***136*
protozoans **11:**1370
Proxima Centauri **15:**1878
Prozac **11:***1376*
psychiatry **11:1373–1376**
psychoanalysis **11:**1374
psychology **11:1377–1380**
  cognitive **11:**1378–1379
  Gestalt **11:**1378
  sports **13:**1661
psychotherapy **11:**1373, *1374*
pterosaurs **4:**436
PTFE *see* polytetrafluoroethylene
Ptolemy **15:**1877
ptyalin **5:**558
puffer fish **11:**1309
pulleys **11:1381–1382**
pulsars **1:**122; **14:**1676, 1677
  and time measurement **15:**1824
pulse-jets **7:**810
pulse rate **2:**194
pumice **12:**1484
pumps **11:1383–1386**
  centrifugal **11:**1385–*1386*
  electromagnetic **11:**1386
  jet **11:**1386
  peristaltic **11:**1385
  positive displacement **11:***1383,*
    1384–*1385*
  reciprocating **11:**1385
  rotary **11:**1384, *1385*; **15:**1893
  screw **8:**910; **11:**1383–1384

steam **8:**1016
  vapor diffusion pumps **15:**1893–*1894*
  wind pumps **16:***2013*, 2014
pupae **8:**978–979
pupil **5:**582
Purkinje cells **2:***215*
purse seines **4:***490*
purse seining **5:**611
putrefaction **5:**591
PVC *see* polyvinyl chloride
pyramids
  Egyptian **1:**105; **2:***240*, 241; **8:**1019;
    **13:**1568; **14:**1733
  Mayan **1:***104*
  ziggurats **1:**105; **13:**1568
pyrethroids **10:**1225
pyridoxine **16:**1932
pyrite **8:***1013*
pyroclasts **16:**1938
pyrolysis **3:**290
pyruvic acid **8:**957
Pythagoras **8:**921; **11:1387–1388**

## Q

quadrants **9:**1084
quanta **2:**205; **7:**846–847; **10:***1273*;
  **11:***1390*; **13:**1645–1646
quantum entanglement **10:**1273
quantum theory **7:**846–847; **9:**1051;
  **10:**1273; **11:1389–1392**
  Compton effect **11:**1390–1391
  Einstein and the photoelectric effect
    **11:**1389–1390
  Planck and **2:**205; **10:**1272–1273;
    **11:**1389; **13:**1645–1646
  quantum mechanics **11:**1391–1392
  uncertainty principle **11:**1392
  wave nature of electrons **11:***1389,*
    1392
  wave nature of matter **11:**1391, 1392
  wave-particle duality of light **11:**1391
quarks **10:**1208–1209
quarrying **8:**1014, 1019–1020
quartz **8:***1008, 1009*; **16:**1984
  a piezoelectric crystal **13:**1557;
    **15:**1817, 1822, 1871
  in quartz watches and clocks
    **10:***1264*; **15:**1817
  specific gravity **8:**1010
quasars **1:**124; **15:**1878, 1879
Quaternary period **6:**688
Quorn **5:**619

# R

rabbits, myxomatosis **10:**1224
rabies **9:**1101; **10:***1211*; **15:**1916
Rabi, Isidor **15:**1822
raccoons **5:**625
racing
  motorcycles **9:**1062
  motor racing **2:**147–149
  race car tires **12:**1500
rack-and-pinion system **3:***350, 351*
rackets
  squash and badminton **13:**1655
  tennis **13:**1652, *1654*
radar **11:1393–1396**
  airfield-control **1:**50
  antennas **11:**1394, *1395*
  displays **11:**1395
  Doppler **11:**1396
  ground-penetrating **1:**98; **6:**695;
    **11:**1396
  microwaves and **8:**1003
  tracking **11:**1395
  two-way **11:**1396
  use in archaeology **1:**97, 98
  use in astronomy **9:**1135; **11:***1396*
  use in navigation systems **9:**1086
  use in weather-detection **8:**982
radiation **7:**795
  Hawking **2:**199
  in nuclear power stations
    **11:**1339–1340
  *see also* radioactivity
radiation (heat) **6:***735, 738*
radiation therapy *see* radiotherapy
radio **11:1397–1400**
  amplitude modulation (AM) **1:**89,
    90; **11:***1398*, 1399–1400
  antennas and **1:**89, 90; **11:**1298–1299,
    1394, 1400
  astronomy **1:**124–*125*; **9:**1134–1135;
    **14:**1763–*1765*
  broadcasting **2:***234–235*;
    **11:**1397–*1398*, 1399
  carrier waves **11:***1398*, 1399, 1400
  digital **11:**1399, 1400
  frequency modulation (FM) **1:**89, 90;
    **11:***1398*, 1400
  Marconi and **8:**906–*907*; **11:**1397
  modulation **11:***1398*, 1399
  ranges (bands) **8:**1002; **11:**1400
  speed of waves **11:**1394, 1399
  stations **1:**90

tuning receivers **12:**1458
use in aircraft-landing systems **1:**51
use in MRI scans **8:**935
use in navigation systems
  **9:**1085–1086
use in remote control **12:***1441*–1442,
  1446
use in transmitting television
  **14:**1770–1771
waves **1:**89–90; **11:**1399; **13:**1644
*see also* microwave radiation; radar
radioactivity **5:**541, 614;
  **11:1401–1403**; **15:**1883
  alpha decay **11:**1402
  and gamma rays **6:**657
  beta decay **11:**1402–1403
  carbon-14 isotope **3:**287–288
  dating rocks using **6:**684, 690, 691
  detection **6:***669–670*; **10:**1205
  gamma ray emission **11:**1403
  natural **6:**670
  radioactive and nuclear waste **5:**551;
    **9:**1116–*1117*; **11:**1318
  work of Becquerel **3:**322; **4:**399;
    **10:**1261; **11:**1401
  work of Marie and Pierre Curie
    **4:**399; **11:**1401, *1402*
  work of Rutherford **12:**1502
  *see also* carbon dating; nuclear
    reactors
radiocarbon dating *see* carbon dating
radio data systems (RDSs) **15:**1843
radioisotopes **7:**800–*801*; **11:**1403
radiolarians **11:**1372
radiology **8:**932–937
  interventional **8:**943
radiosondes (weather balloons)
  **8:**982, *983;* **15:**1845
radiotherapy **6:***658;* **7:**801; **8:**943;
  **11:1404–1405**; **16:**1933, 2024
radium **4:**398, 399; **11:**1401, *1402*
radius and ulna **13:**1564
radon **2:**248; **7:**775; **12:**1502
*Rafflesia* **10:**1197, 1275
rafts, used for water power **16:***1982*
railroad systems **12:1412–1417**
  cable railroads **3:***260–261*
  car brakes **2:**222, 223
  cog railroads
  elevated **12:***1422*
  light **12:**1422–*1423*
  marshaling yards **12:**1416–*1417*

monorails **9:1040–1041**
signaling and traffic control
  **12:**1414–*1416*
transcontinental **12:**1413, *1414*
rain and rainfall **3:**344; **12:1418–1419**;
  **16:**1966
  acid rain **2:***135;* **3:**339; **5:***564;* **10:**1178;
    **11:***1316, 1318*
  and erosion **5:**559–560
  and weathering **16:***1984*, 1986, *1987*,
    1988
  areas with highest and lowest **4:**474
  how raindrops form **12:**1418–1419;
    **13:**1578
  kinds **12:**1419
  rainfall distribution **12:**1419
  water cycle and **12:**1418
rainbows **10:***1156*; **12:1420–1421**
rain forests, tropical **2:***180;* **16:**2045
  slash and burn agriculture **4:***489*
rain gauges **8:**980–981
rain shadows **4:**416–417
rallying **2:**149
ramjets **7:**809
ramp metering, for traffic control
  **15:**1842
rams, hydraulic **11:**1386
Ramsay, William **7:***775*
Rance River, tidal power **6:**757;
  **15:***1803*, 1804, 1810
random-access memory (RAM)
  **3:**264, 362, 363
Ransome, Robert **11:**1301
rapid transit systems **12:1422–1425**
  light railways **12:**1422–1423
  monorails **9:1040–1041**
  subway systems **12:**1423–*1424, 1425*
  trains used in **12:**1425
  trams **14:***1692*, 1694
  trolleybuses **12:**1422; **14:***1691*, 1692
  *see also* streetcars and buses
rare gases *see* inert gases
rashes, skin **1:**56
Rayleigh, Lord **7:***775*; **10:**1260
rayon **5:**598; **14:**1784
RDAs (recommended daily
  allowances) **9:**1131–1132
RDSs (radio data systems) **15:**1843
RDX (cyclonite) **5:**580, *581*
read-only memory (ROM) **3:**264, 362
Reber, Grote **14:**1763
rechargeable batteries **2:**172

records
  land-speed **2:**147
  vinyl **13:**1618, *1619*
recycling **1:***67*; **12:1426–1429**
  glass **12:**1427–*1428, 1429*
  plastics **11:***1291*; **12:**1428
  silver **13:**1560
red giants **1:**121; **9:**1109; **14:**1675
Redi, Francesco **5:**565
redox reactions **2:**200; **10:**1174, 1175
redshift **4:**457; **14:**1674
red tides **9:**1142
reduction *see* oxidation and reduction
reflection and refraction **10:***1260*;
    **12:1430–1431**
  double refraction **8:**1011
  of sound **13:**1614–1615
  reflection **7:***845*; **10:**1156–1157;
    **12:**1430–1431; **13:**1614
  refraction **6:***749*; **7:***845*;
    **10:**1157–1158; **12:**1420, *1431*;
    **13:**1614–1615, 1645
  total internal reflection **5:**600;
    **10:**1158
reflexes **2:**220; **9:***1097*–1099
refraction *see* reflection and refraction
refractive index **7:**845; **10:**1158
refrigeration **5:***622*; **6:**661;
    **12:1432–1434**
  *see also* air-conditioning
Reinitzer, Friedrich **7:**865
rejuvenation **12:**1467, 1468
relative atomic mass (RAM) **3:**315, 316
relative density *see* specific gravity
relativity **12:1435–1438**
  general theory of **3:**266; **4:**496; **6:**718;
    **12:**1438
  special theory of **4:**495–496; **8:**955;
    **12:**1436–1438
relays **12:1439–1440**
reluctance **12:**1454; **15:**1847
remote control **12:1441–1446**, *1481*
  Remotely Operated Vehicles
    (ROVs) **14:***1706*
remote handling **12:**1443–1444
Remotely Operated Vehicles (ROVs)
    **14:***1706*
remote sensors **12:1447–1448**
  animal tracking **12:***1447*; **16:**2045
  geological **12:**1448
  in archaeology **12:**1448
  military **12:**1447–1448

Renaissance **1:**107
Reno, Jesse W. **5:**543
reproduction
  asexual **1:**81; **3:**340–341; **12:**1452
  sexual **1:**81; **12:**1449
reproductive system **12:1449–1452**
  female **12:**1449–*1450*
  male **12:***1450–1451*
  *see also* pregnancy and birth
reptiles **1:**82
reservoirs **12:**1470; **16:**1971, *1973*
  and hydroelectric power **6:***755*
resins
  epoxy **1:**18
  vinyl **1:**18
resistance **12:1453–1454**
  air **5:**637
  electrical **4:**503; **7:**780–781; **12:***1453,
    1455*; **14:**1717–1718; **15:**1800
  friction and **12:**1454
  magnetic (reluctance) **12:**1453–1454
resistivity **7:**780–781
  meters **1:**97
resistors **4:**503; **12:1455–1456**
resonance **12:1457–1458**
respiration **10:***1177*, 1178;
    **12:**1459–1461
  aerobic **9:**1070
  anaerobic **9:**1070
  cellular **8:**956–957
respirators **12:***1464*
respiratory system **12:1459–1464**
restriction fragment length
    polymorphisms (RFLPs) **1:**29
retina **5:***582*
retinol *see* vitamins, vitamin A
retrosynthetic analysis **10:**1166–1167
revolvers **6:***726*–727
Reynaud, Émile **1:**84
rheostats **4:**501
Rhesus factor **6:**734
Rhind, Alexander Henry **8:**920
rhodium **5:***536*; **11:**1296, 1297
rhodopsin **2:**213; **3:**304
riboflavin **16:**1932
ribonucleic acid *see* RNA
ribosomes **3:***301, 302*; **4:**454; **9:**1082
Rice, Chester W. **13:**1640
Richter, C. F. **4:**486
Richter scale **4:**486; **12:**1530
rickets **2:**179; **15:**1876; **16:***1933*
ridges, ocean *see* ocean ridges

Riemann, Georg Bernhard **8:**923
rifles **6:**724
  assault **6:**726
  cartridge **6:**725
rigidity modulus (shear modulus)
    **4:**498
rills **5:**561
rime **13:**1579
Ring Nebula **1:***121*; **9:**1090, *1091*
"ring of fire" **15:**1861
Riva-Rocci, Scipione **8:**940
river blindness (onchocerciasis) **4:**442;
    **10:**1194, 1195–1196
rivers and lakes **2:**192; **12:1465–1470**
  creation of landforms and landscapes
    **7:**824–825; **12:**1467–1468
  erosion by rivers **5:**561–562;
    **12:**1465–1466, 1467–1468
  lakes **2:**192; **6:**700; **12:**1467,
    1468–*1469*
  river deltas **7:***824*; **12:***1467*
  stages of rivers **12:**1465–1467
RNA (ribonucleic acid) **3:**303
  and protein synthesis **4:**454–455;
    **9:**1039
  viral **15:**1914, 1915
roads and road construction
    **12:1471–1476**; **15:**1840
  *see also* traffic control
road trains **15:**1857
Robert, M. N. **2:**163
Robert, Nicholas-Louis **10:**1185
Robodoc **14:**1731
robotics **1:**112–113, *114, 115*;
    **12:1477–1482**; **14:***1708*
  and virtual reality systems **15:**1912
  for surgery **12:***1480*; **14:***1729*, 1731
  metalworkers **8:**974, 975
  nanobots (nanorobots) **8:**995; **9:***1081*;
    **12:**1482
  remote-controlled robots **12:***1444*
  *see also* artificial intelligence
Rochelle salt **15:**1871
roches moutonnées **6:**699
rock **12:1483–1488**
  ages **6:**683–684, 690
  igneous **6:**689; **8:**1012; **12:**1483–1484,
    1488
  index (zone) fossils in **6:**684, *685*, 690
  magnetism **7:**893
  metamorphic **8:**1013; **12:***1486*
  quarrying **8:***1019*–1020

rock (*continued*)
  radioactive dating **6:**684, 690, 691
  rock cycle **12:**1486–*1487*
  samples **6:**692
  sedimentary **6:**689; **7:**820, 825;
    **8:**1012–1013; **12:***1484*–1486
  strata **6:***690*; **12:**1485
  structures and landscape
    **12:**1487–1488
  weathering **5:**559; **16:***1984–1988*
rock arches **7:**824
*Rocket* (locomotive) **7:***870*, 871
rockets **2:**160; **7:**806; **12:**1489–1492
  hybrid **12:***1490*
  propellants **10:**1179; **12:***1490,
    1491*–*1492*
rock flour **6:**699–700
rodents, teeth **4:**411
roller coasters **12:**1493–1496
rolling metal **8:***972–973*
Romans, ancient
  agriculture **1:**24
  architecture **1:**106
  brickmaking **2:**243
  bridges **2:**230, *231*
  buildings **2:**240–241
  calendar **15:**1815
  firefighting **5:**606
  locks (security) **7:**869
  mortar **2:**244
  numerals **9:**1124, *1125*
  pipes **10:**1266
  roads **12:**1471
röntgenoluminescence **7:**880
Röntgen, Wilhelm **8:**932, 939; **16:**2031
root canal therapy **4:**412
ROSAT (satellite) **1:**125; **9:**1136
rotameter flow gauges **15:***1903*
rotoscoping **9:**1056–1057
routers **16:**2021
rubber **4:***498*; **12:**1497–1500
  latex **3:***378*; **12:***1497*, 1498–1499
  neoprene and nitrile **12:**1499
  polyurethane **12:***1499*
  SBR **12:**1499
  silicone **7:**781
  synthetic **1:**18; **12:**1499
rubella **11:**1343
rubidium **1:**15–16; **8:**962–963
rubisco **10:**1255
ruby **8:**1013; **15:**1854
Rudbeck, Olof, the Younger **7:**860

Ruffini corpuscles **15:**1838, *1839*
rumble strips **10:***1268*, 1271
rust **3:***377*; **7:**797; **10:***1174*, 1175;
  **16:**1984, 1985
ruthenium **11:**1296–1297
Rutherford, Ernest **2:***138*, 205; **3:**322;
  **6:**657; **12:**1501–1502
  and atomic structure **2:***139*;
    **5:**539–540; **10:**1206
rutile **15:**1829
RXTE (satellite) **9:**1136

S

*Saccharomyces cerevisiae* **16:**2035
safes and vaults **12:**1503–1506
  *see also* locks (security)
saffron yellow **10:**1180
Sahara Desert **4:***414*, 417; **7:**821
sailing **8:**908; **12:**1507–1512
Sainte-Claire Deville, Henri **1:**65
St. Helens, Mount **9:***1138*–1139
Salford transverse oscillators **15:***1804*
salivary glands **5:**575–576
salmon **2:**196
salt (sodium chloride) **3:**323; **5:**539
  crystals **4:***394*; **10:**1264, *1265*
  electrolysis of **5:**520, 521
  in solution **16:**1966
  production **12:**1515–1516
  reaction with hydrochloric acid
    **12:**1514
salt domes **9:***1145*
Salter's duck **16:***1981*, 1982
Salter, Stephen **16:**1982
salt pans **4:***394*
saltpeter (potassium nitrate) **9:**1105
salts, chemical **12:**1513–1514
  simple, double, and complex **12:**1514
salvarsan **5:**616; **8:**942
Salyut space stations **13:**1621,
  1622–1623
San Andreas Fault **4:**484, 486; **11:***1295*;
  **12:***1530*
sand **16:**1984
  glass manufacture from **6:**701
sandblasting **1:**12, *13*
sanders **1:***12*; **16:***2021*, 2022
sandstone **6:***689*; **8:**1013, 1019;
  **12:***1484*, 1485
San Francisco
  earthquakes **4:**484, *485*
  street cable cars **3:***261*

saponification **13:**1581
sapphire **8:**1013
saprophytes **6:**649
*saqiyas* **11:**1383
satellites **12:**1517–1522; **13:**1621
  astronomical **9:**1135, 1136; **12:**1522;
    **14:**1713
  communications *see* communications
    satellites
  first artificial **12:**1518
  images of Earth from **6:***681*; **12:***1522*
  launched **12:**1519
  life times **12:**1519–1520
  navigation **6:**705–706, *708*;
    **9:**1086–1087; **12:**1522
  orbits **10:**1162–1163; **12:**1517–1518,
    *1519*
  satellite television **2:**237, 252–*253*;
    **3:**352; **14:**1775
  solar power (SPSs) **13:**1602
  spy **12:**1522
  subsystems **12:**1520–1521
  telemetry links to **12:**1446
  used in mapmaking **8:***904*
  use in archaeology **1:**96, 97
  weather **3:**354–355; **8:***980*, 981;
    **10:**1163; **12:**1522
  *see also* space laboratories
Saturn **1:***122*; **12:**1523–1526; **13:**1604
  Huygens and **6:**749
  missions to **12:***1524, 1525, 1526*;
    **13:***1628*, 1629, 1629–1630
  moons **12:***1526*; **13:***1606, 1625*
  rings **8:***927*; **12:**1524–1526
Saurischia **4:**434–435
sauropods **4:***435*
Savery, Thomas **8:**1016; **14:**1684
sawmills **15:***1813*
saws **15:***1831*, 1832
  band saws and jigsaws **16:**2021
  circular (table) **16:**2019–*2020*, 2021
  radial **16:**2020
Sax, Antoine-Joseph (Adolph) **9:**1077
saxophones **9:***1076*, 1077
scabies **4:**441
scales *see* balances and weighing
  machines
scandium **8:**949, 963
  electron structure **15:**1852
scanners, image **12:**1527–1529
  *see also* photocopiers
scapula **13:**1564

Schawlow, Arthur **7**:827
Scheele, Carl Wilhelm **9**:1104
schistosomiasis (bilharzia) **10**:1196
schizophrenia **11**:*1375*
Schmidt, Bernard **10**:1244
Schöffer, Peter **11**:1353
Schönbein, Christian Friedrich **11**:1286
Schott, Otto **8**:999–1000
Schrödinger, Erwin **11**:*1391*, 1392
Schrödinger equation **11**:1392
Schulze, Johann Heinrich **10**:1242
Schwarzschild, Karl **2**:*197*
Schwarzschild radius **2**:*199*
scissors **7**:*842*
sclera **5**:582
SCOOT (split-cycle-and-off-set-optimizing technique) **15**:1841–1842
scramjets **1**:45; **7**:810
scrapers, motor **4**:481
screwdrivers **15**:*1830*, 1832
scuba diving **4**:*446*, *447*, 448–449
Scud missiles **9**:1030
scum **7**:795
scurvy **2**:179; **16**:1931
sea anemones **10**:1276
seabed (ocean floor) **9**:*1139*, 1140
  mineral wealth **8**:1021; **9**:*1144*
  polymetallic nodules **8**:1021
Seaborg, Glenn Theodore **5**:540
Sea Fighter **16**:*1962*
seafloor (ocean) spreading **7**:893; **11**:1295
sea levels, rising **6**:712; **11**:1317
seamounts **9**:1140
seaplanes **1**:*44*
search engines, Internet **7**:790, *791*, 792
seas **9**:1137–1138
seasons **4**:*476*, *477*, 478
sea stacks and sea arches **7**:825
seat belts, car **2**:146–147
sea urchins **5**:625
sea walls **5**:564
seawater **16**:1966
  desalination **16**:*1972*
seaweeds **9**:1141
sebaceous glands **5**:575, 576; **9**:1072; **13**:*1566*
Sedna **1**:125
Seebeck, Thomas J. **14**:1786
Seebeck effect **14**:1786–1787

Seeberger, Charles D. **5**:543
seed drills **1**:26
seeds **10**:1277
seiches **12**:1468
Seikan Tunnel **15**:1865
seining, purse **5**:611
seismology **4**:486; **6**:*692*, 693–694, *695*; **12**:**1530–1533**
  seismic surveying **5**:581; **6**:695–696; **9**:*1146*; **12**:1532
  seismic waves **12**:1531–1532
  seismographs **10**:1213; **12**:1532–*1533*
  *see also* earthquakes
*Seismosaurus* **4**:434
selection, natural *see* natural selection
selenium **8**:963
Semantic Web **7**:793
semen **12**:1451, *1452*
semicircular canals **4**:471
semiconductors **5**:528; **12**:1453, 1455; **13**:**1540–1543**
  doped **13**:*1541*; **15**:1848
  in digital cameras **10**:1246–1247
  in silicon chips **13**:1543
  in thyristors **13**:1543
  in transistors **13**:*1542*–1543; **15**:1848
  junctions **13**:*1541*–1542
  lasers made from **13**:*1543*
  LEDs **13**:1543
  *n*-type and *p*-type **13**:*1541*; **15**:1848
  pure **13**:1540–*1541*
Semtex **5**:580, *581*
Senefelder, Aloys **11**:1357
senses
  biorhytms and **2**:194–195
  *see also* ears and hearing; smell; taste; touch; vision
sensors
  medical **8**:941
  remote *see* remote sensors
  robotic **12**:1480–1481
separators **3**:307
septic tanks **13**:1549
seracs **6**:698
serotonin **1**:71; **11**:1376
servomechanisms **13**:**1544–1545**; **15**:1800
servomotors **13**:1545
sewage treatment **13**:**1546–1549**
sextants **9**:1084, *1085*
Seysenegg, Erich von **8**:947
shadows **10**:1156

*shadufs* **11**:1383
shales **12**:1485
shapers **15**:1834; **16**:2021
shear forces **4**:498
shear modulus (rigidity modulus) **4**:498
sheep
  breeding **1**:25–26
  mountain **9**:1066
  shearing **16**:2024
shells *see* bombs and shells
ships and shipbuilding **13**:**1550–1555**
  autopilots **13**:1545
  boatbuilding **13**:*1551*–1554
  bulk carriers **13**:1555
  container ships **13**:*1555*
  cruise ships **13**:*1550*
  drill ships **9**:1147
  dry cargo vessels **13**:1555
  gyrocompasses **6**:730
  gyrostabilizers **6**:730
  lay-barges **10**:*1269*–1270
  propulsion *see* marine propulsion
  ship navigation **9**:*1083*–1088
  sonar **13**:1611–*1612*
  speedboats **13**:*1554*
  stability **13**:1550–1551
  steamships **8**:*908*
  tankers **13**:1555; **14**:**1746–1749**
  warships **16**:**1957–1962**
  *see also* hovercraft; hydrofoils; sailing
shock absorbers **14**:1736, *1737*
Shockley, William **3**:360; **5**:527; **13**:1542; **14**:1768; **15**:1849
shockwaves
  earthquake **4**:486
  from supersonic flight **14**:1722–1723
shooting stars (meteors) **1**:116, *117*, 118
Shortt, William **15**:1822
shotguns **6**:727
shrapnel **2**:206
*Shrek* (movie) **1**:*83*
shrews **5**:*624*
shrublands **2**:191
Shuttle Radar Topography Mission (SRTM) **8**:*904*
"sick building syndrome" **2**:248
Sickdhar, Radhanath **9**:1064
sickle-cell anemia **3**:331; **4**:443, *455*
siderite **8**:964
Sidewinder missiles **9**:1031

Sidgier, Henry **16:**1963–1964
Siebe, Augustus **4:**446
Siemens, William **7:**799
Sikorsky, Igor **6:***742*
silencers **6:**727
silica (silicon dioxide) **13:**1556–*1557*
silicates **8:**1011; **13:**1556
silicon **8:**963; **13:1556–1557**
  as a semiconductor **13:**1540–*1541*,
    1556
silicon carbide (carborundum) **3:**310;
    **4:**397; **16:**2038
silicon chips (integrated circuits;
    microchips) **3:**359, *360*, 362; **5:***526*,
    *527*; **8:***990*, 991–994; **11:**1350–1351;
    **13:**1557
  future uses of **8:**995
  identity implants **8:**995
  in calculators **3:**264
  in televisions **14:**1774
  production of **7:**778; **8:**991–992;
    **13:***1540*, 1556
  switches in **14:***1739*
  transistors in **8:**991
silicone plastics **7:**781
silicone rubber **7:**781
silicones **13:**1557
silk **5:**596, 597; **14:**1780, 1781, 1782
silkworms **10:**1211
siltstone **12:**1485
Silurian period **6:**686
silver **8:**967; **13:1558–1560**
  alloys **1:**59; **13:**1560
  ores **8:**1013
  plate **13:**1560
  sterling **13:**1560
  tarnish **10:**1175
silver bromide **10:**1243, 1244; **13:**1560
silver chloride **13:**1560
silver nitrate **1:**95; **10:**1242; **13:**1559
silver sulfide **13:**1558, 1560
Simpson, James Young **1:**77
SIM (subscriber identification
    module) cards **9:**1036
singularities **2:***199*
sink holes **7:**825
sinoatrial node **6:**731–732
sintering **8:***969*
Sirius **15:**1878, 1879, *1880*
SI (*Système International*) units **8:**931;
    **11:***1335*
  prefixes **8:**930, 931

skeletal system **13:1561–1564**
skiing **13:***1579*
skin **13:1565–1567**
  and touch **15:**1838, *1839*
  burn treatment **13:**1567
  color **13:**1567
  excretion through **5:**574
  hairs **13:***1566*, 1567
  natural immunity and **6:**762, *763*
  rashes **1:***56*
skulls **13:***1562*
  fossil **13:***1563*
*Skylab* space station **13:***1622*
skyscrapers **1:**109; **2:**246–*247*; **6:**708;
    **13:1568–1571**
  *see also* building techniques
Skysweeper guns **9:**1030
SLAC (Stanford Linear Accelerator)
    **10:***1201*, *1207*
slate **8:**1019
sleep and dreams **11:***1380*;
    **13:1572–1575**
  dreams **13:**1574–1575
  stages of sleep **13:**1572–1574
sleeping pills **13:**1575
sleeping sickness **4:**442; **10:**1194;
    **11:**1371
sleet **3:**345; **12:**1419; **13:**1578
slides (transparencies) **10:***1244*, 1245
slime molds **11:**1372
smallpox **6:**676; **15:***1914*, 1916
  vaccination **7:***804–805*; **10:**1211;
    **15:***1889*–1890, 1891–1892
smart technology **8:**990
  bombs **2:**209; **6:***721*
  shells **2:**207
smell **13:1576–1577**
  *see also* pheromones
smelting **1:**59–60; **2:**200; **8:**966
Smith, William **6:**689–*690*
smog **3:**339; **11:***1315*
smoke alarms (detectors) **5:***606*;
    **15:***1850*
smokejacks **6:**665
smoking, food **5:**622
smoking, tobacco **3:***331*; **11:***1309*
  effect on the lungs **12:***1462*
SN 1987A (supernova) **9:**1110
snakes **1:**82
  venom **11:***1306*, 1307
Snell, Willebrord **10:**1158
Snell's law **10:**1158

snow and frost **13:1578–1579**
  frost **13:**1579
  hailstones **13:**1579
  snow **3:**345; **12:**1419; **13:**1578, *1579*;
    **16:***1990*
soaps and detergents **13:1580–1583**
  and surface tension **13:**1580; **14:**1724
  hard water and **7:**795
  soap flakes **13:**1582
  soap manufacture **13:**1580–1581
  soap powder **13:**1582
  synthetic detergents **13:**1582–1583
Soddy, Frederick **12:**1502
sodium **1:**15; **8:**962–963; **13:1584–1586**
  ions **7:**794; **13:**1585
  liquid **13:**1599
  making pure sodium **13:**1586
  properties **13:**1585–1586
  reactions, general **13:**1584–1585
  reaction with air **13:***1584*
  reaction with chlorine **10:**1219;
    **13:**1585
  reaction with water **3:***317*
  sodium-vapor discharge lamps
    **7:**855
  storage **13:***1584*
  tarnishing **13:**1584
  uses **7:**855; **13:***1585*, 1586
sodium acetate **12:**1514
sodium bicarbonate **3:**323; **4:**425;
    **12:**1514
sodium carbonate **12:**1514
sodium chlorate **10:**1227
sodium chloride *see* salt
sodium dioxide **13:**1584
sodium hydroxide (caustic soda) **1:**15;
    **5:**521; **10:**1187; **12:**1513
sodium monosulfite **10:**1188
sodium nitrate **9:**1105
sodium sulfate **10:**1187
sodium thiosulfate **10:**1244
software **3:**365; **13:1587–1592**
  antivirus **16:***1926*–1927
  bugs **13:**1590, 1592
  computer programs **3:**361, 362;
    **13:**1588, *1589*–1591
  graphical user interface (GUI) **3:***365*;
    **7:**819; **13:***1591*
  software engineering **13:**1591–1592
  voice-recognition **16:***1935*
  word-processing programs **16:**1935,
    2030

soil **13**:1593–1596
  and climate **13**:1594–1596
  core samples **13**:*1593*
  electrical resistance **1**:97
  erosion **5**:560–561, *563*; **13**:*1595*
  fertility **13**:1594
  horizons **13**:1593–*1594*
  *see also* weathering
Solar and Heliospheric Observatory
  (SOHO) **14**:1713
solar energy **13**:**1597–1602**
  solar panels **5**:*552*; **13**:*1597–1598*
  solar ponds **13**:1601–1602
  solar-powered vehicles **1**:*62*; **13**:1600,
  *1601*
  solar power generators **14**:*1786*
  solar power satellites (SPSs) **13**:1602
  solar water heaters **13**:1597–1598,
  1601
  using mirrors **5**:550; **13**:*1597,
  1599–1600*
  using solar (photoelectric) cells
  **5**:550; **10**:*1234*, 1235; **13**:*1602*, 1625
solar system **13**:**1603–1606**
  origin **13**:1603–1605
  other solar systems **13**:1606
  planets revolve around the Sun
  **3**:*373*; **13**:*1605*
  *see also* asteroids, comets, and
  meteors; planets; Sun; and *names of
  individual planets*
solar wind **11**:1285; **13**:1605–1606;
  **14**:1715
solder **1**:59; **7**:838; **15**:1825
solenoids **5**:*523*; **7**:*891*–892;
  **13**:**1607–1608**
solids **2**:138; **13**:**1609–1610**
  and pressure **11**:*1348*
solstices **4**:478; **14**:1712
sonar **10**:1265; **13**:**1611–1612**
  torpedoes and **9**:1032, 1033
sonic booms **1**:20; **14**:1722
Sopwith F1 Camel **16**:*1951*
Sörensen, Sören **1**:16
Soulé, Samuel **7**:817
sound **4**:470, 472; **13**:**1613–1616**;
  **16**:1976
  and sonar **13**:1611
  and the Doppler effect **4**:456–*457*;
  **13**:1615
  decibels **4**:*472*; **13**:1616
  noise **13**:*1616*

speed of **13**:*1611*–1612, 1613;
  **14**:1721–1722
  ultrasound *see* ultrasonics
  waves **13**:*1614*–1615
  *see also* ears and hearing
sound barrier **14**:1721
sound recording **13**:**1617–1620**
  digital **13**:1620
  Edison's phonograph **4**:*494*;
  **13**:1617–*1618*
  microphones **10**:1265;
  **13**:1618–*1619*
  records **13**:1618
  using tape **13**:1620
  *see also* CDs (compact discs);
  speakers
Southern Ocean **9**:1137
spacecraft
  navigation **9**:1088; **13**:1545
  telemetry links to **12**:1446
  *see also* space probes
SPACEHAB laboratory **13**:*1623, 1634*
Spacelab **13**:1623–*1624*
space laboratories **12**:1520;
  **13**:**1621–1624**
  International Space Station **10**:*1163*;
  **13**:*1621*, 1624, *1637*
  *Mir* **13**:*1622*, 1624, 1634–*1635*
  Salyut space stations **13**:1621,
  1622–1623
  *Skylab* **13**:*1622*
  SPACEHAB **13**:*1623, 1634*
  Spacelab **13**:1623–*1624*
  space shuttles and **13**:1624,
  1634–*1635*
space probes **1**:125; **13**:**1625–1630**
  powered **13**:1625; **14**:*1787*
  telemetry links to **12**:1446
  *see also names of individual planets*
space shuttles **11**:1336; **12**:*1489*, 1491;
  **13**:**1631–1636**
  and satellites **12**:1519, *1520*
  tiles on **3**:308, *309*; **13**:*1557*, *1636*
space stations *see* space laboratories
space suits **13**:**1637–1639**
space-time **15**:1818
  curved by mass **12**:*1436*, 1438
Space Transportation Systems (STSs)
  *see* space shuttles
Spandex **14**:1784
spark chambers **10**:1204–1205
spark plugs **3**:*309*; **11**:1299

Sparrow missiles **9**:1031
speakers (loudspeakers) **5**:*525*;
  **13**:*1614*, 1619, **1640–1641**;
  **15**:*1845*
  moving-coil **13**:*1641*
  ribbon **13**:1641
species **3**:333
  cryptic **2**:181
  definition **2**:181
  endangered *see* endangered species
  formation **2**:181–182
  number on Earth **2**:181
specific gravity (relative density)
  **1**:102; **13**:**1642–1643**
spectacles **5**:584–*585*
spectrograms, speech **16**:1934–1935
spectroscopy **10**:1256; **13**:**1644–1649**
  absorption and emission spectra
  **13**:1646
  and compounds **13**:1646–1647
  and light emitted by stars **13**:*1648*;
  **14**:1674
  mass spectroscopy **13**:1648
  spectrographs **13**:1645, 1647–1648
  spectrometers **13**:*1645, 1646*, 1647
  spectrophotometers **13**:1647, 1648
  spectroscopes **7**:844; **13**:*1647*;
  **14**:1674, 1716
  ultraviolet **15**:1876
  *see also* nuclear magnetic resonance
speech **13**:1617, **1650–1651**;
  **16**:1934
  speech problems **16**:1937
  speech therapists **16**:*1936*
  synthesized **16**:*1934*, 1935, *1937*
  *see also* voice analysis
speed **5**:626
speedboats **13**:*1554*
speed cameras **15**:*1842*
speed increasers **6**:667
speed limits, on roads **12**:1476
speed reducers **6**:667
Spemann, Hans **3**:341
sperm cells **3**:*305*; **12**:1449, 1450,
  *1451*, *1452*
sperrylite **11**:1297
sphalerite **16**:2037, *2038*
sphygmomanometers **6**:*734*;
  **8**:939–*940*
spillways **6**:*757*
spinal cord **9**:1097–1099
spine **13**:*1562*, 1564

spinning **14:**1781, 1782, 1784;
   **16:**2023, *2025*
   spinning jenny **14:**1782;
      **16:**2025–2026
   spinning mule **14:**1782; **16:**2026
spirit levels **14:***1733*
Spitzer Space Telescope **14:**1766
split-cycle-and-off-set-optimizing
   technique (SCOOT)
   **15:**1841–1842
Spode, Josiah **11:**1332
spoilers **1:**41–42
spokeshaves **15:**1833
spontaneous generation **5:**565
spores, fungal **6:**648
sporophytes **10:**1275, 1276
sports equipment **13:1652–1658**
   athletics **13:***1656*–1657
   badminton **13:**1655
   baseball **13:***1657*–1658
   football **13:***1658*
   golf **13:**1655–1656
   ice hockey **13:**1658
   squash **13:**1655
   tennis **13:**1652, *1654–1655*
sports science **13:1659–1661**
spread-spectrum frequency hopping
   **9:**1037
springs **14:1668–1669**, 1736
   air **14:**1669, 1736–1737
   coil **14:**1736, *1737*
   extension **14:**1668
   leaf **14:**1668–*1669*, 1736
   torsion-bar **14:***1737*
springs (water) **16:**1970
sprinklers, water **1:**59
*Sputnik 1* (satellite) **12:**1518
SQUIDS (superconducting quantum
   interference devices) **14:**1719
SR-N1 (hovercraft) **6:***746*, 747
stacks **7:**824
   sea **5:**563
stalactites and stalagmites **3:***297*;
   **16:***1969, 1985*, 1986
stammering **16:**1937
Stanford Linear Accelerator (SLAC)
   **10:***1201, 1207*
Stanhope, Charles **11:**1354
Stanley, Francis Edgar **14:**1687
Stanley, Freelan Oscar **14:**1687
*Staphylococcus aureus*, division **2:***155*
starch **3:***279*, 281–282

stars **1:**121; **14:1670–1677**
   and black holes **2:**198, 199; **12:***1438*;
      **14:**1676
   and navigation **9:**1083–1084, 1088
   binary **1:**122; **2:**199; **6:**744; **9:**1109;
      **14:**1676–1677
   brightness **1:**122; **15:**1878
   closest to Earth **14:**1672; **15:**1878
   clusters **14:**1677
   constellations **1:***120*, 121;
      **14:**1670–1671
   created in nebulas **9:**1089–1090;
      **14:***1673*
   distances from Earth **1:**122;
      **14:**1672, 1674
   evolution of lives **1:**121–122;
      **9:**1089–1091, 1107–1110; **14:***1673*,
      1675–1676; **15:***1882*
   fate **14:**1673
   formation **9:**1089–1090; **13:**1603;
      **14:***1673*, 1675
   life time **14:**1672
   locating **14:**1671
   magnitude (brightness) **9:**1110;
      **14:**1672–1674
   main sequence **14:**1674
   mass **14:**1672, 1674
   moving **14:**1671–1672, *1674*
   multiple **14:**1677
   neutron stars **1:**121–122; **9:**1091,
      1108–1109; **14:**1675–1676
   new **1:**123
   nuclear fusion in **1:**121; **9:**1117
   oldest **15:**1880
   pulsars **1:**122; **14:**1676, 1677;
      **15:**1824
   radiation from **1:**121
   spectral classes **14:**1674
   speed of travel **14:**1674
   temperature **14:**1672, 1674
   traveling toward/away from Earth
      **4:**457
   variable (Cepheids) **14:**1676; **15:**1880
   *see also* galaxies; novas and
      supernovas; Sun
Starstreak missiles **9:**1029
statics **10:**1260
statistics **14:1678–1683**
Staudinger, Hermann **11:**1287
stealth technology
   aircraft **1:**44; **16:***1958*
   ships **16:**1962

steam **6:**737
steam engines **1:**26; **2:**140; **7:**870;
   **8:**909–910; **14:1684–1688**
   boilers **14:**1686, 1688
   compound **14:**1687–1688
   double-acting **14:**1686, *1687*
   governors **13:**1544–*1545*
   single-acting **14:***1686*
   steam locomotives **7:***870*–873, 874;
      **14:***1686*, 1687, 1688
   *see also* turbines, steam
steel *see* iron and steel
stegosaurs **4:**435
stem cells **3:**343; **8:**945
Stephenson, George **7:**871; **8:**1016
Stephenson, Robert **7:***870*, 871; **14:***1686*
stereotyping **11:***1355*–1356
sterilization (microbial) **7:**866–867;
   **15:***1875*, 1876
stethoscopes **8:**939, *940*
Stevens, John **7:**871; **12:**1412
stills **4:**444–*445*
Stinger missiles **9:***1030*
Stirling engines **14:1689–1690**
Stirling, Robert **14:**1689
stock-car racing **2:**149
STOL aircraft **1:**44
   *see also* V/STOL aircraft
stomach **4:**424–426, 427
stomata **10:***1253, 1254*–1255
stopwatches **15:***1822*
Stradivari, Antonio **9:**1075
strain **4:**498
Strassman, Fritz **9:**1111–1112
stratigraphic sections **6:***690*
stratigraphy **6:**691
stratopause **2:***133*, 134
stratosphere **2:***133*, 134; **11:***1398*;
   **15:***1801*
streamlines **9:***1051*
streetcars and buses **14:1691–1694**
   buses **14:**1693–*1694*
   cable cars **3:***261*; **14:**1691, *1693*
   streetcars **12:**1422; **14:**1691–*1692*,
      1694
   trams **14:***1692*, 1694
   trolleybuses **12:**1422; **14:***1691*, 1692
streetlights **7:**855; **12:***1476*; **15:**1824
streptomycin **1:**91
stress **4:**498
   shear **4:**498
Stringfellow, John **1:**37

strokes **3:**330, 331; **4:**443; **16:**1937
strong nuclear force **5:**629; **10:**1209
strontium **8:**963; **11:**1403
Strowger, Almon **14:**1755
Struve, Wilhelm von **8:**997
stuttering **16:**1937
subatomic particles **2:**136, 139
  detection *see* particle detectors
  in particle accelerators **10:**1198–1201
  muons **12:**1437
  *see also* particle physics
subduction **9:**1063; **11:**1295
subduction zones, volcanoes at
    **16:**1941
sublimation **6:**662; **13:***1609*;
    **14:***1695–1696*
submachine guns **6:**726
submarines **14:1697–1702**
  breathing underwater **14:**1699
  diving and surfacing **14:**1698, *1699*
  earliest **14:***1697*
  engines **14:**1698
  navigation **14:**1702
  nuclear-powered **14:**1698, 1702
  propulsion **8:**910
  steering **13:**1545; **14:**1699, *1700*
  the hull **14:**1699–1700
  weapons **9:***1032–1033*; **14:**1700–*1702*
submersibles **14:1703–1708**
  bathyscaphes **14:***1704*–1706
  bathyspheres **14:***1703–1704*
  diving bells **4:**449, 450–451
  propulsion **14:**1708
  uses **14:**1706–*1708*
  *see also* submarines
subphyla **3:**333
Subroc missiles **9:**1031
subscriber identification module
    (SIM) cards **9:**1036
subspecies **2:**181; **3:**333
substations, electricity **11:***1340*, 1342;
    **15:***1846*
subway systems **12:**1423–*1424*
  trains **12:***1425*
sucrose **3:**281
Suez Canal **3:***273*, 276; **14:**1746–1747
sugar **3:**281, *282*
  processing **5:***620*
sulfadiazine **13:**1559
sulfate minerals **8:**1012
sulfide minerals **8:**1012
sulfur **14:1709–1710**

sulfuric acid **1:**14, 15
  molecules **2:**138
Sulston, John **6:***680*
Sumerians, writing **11:***1352*
Sun **6:***652*; **14:**1672, **1711–1716**
  and eclipses **4:***487–488*; **14:**1715
  and tides **15:**1807, 1808, *1809*
  atmosphere **14:**1715–1716
  distance **14:**1711
  elements in **14:***1716*
  heat from the **6:***738*
  magnitude (brightness) **14:**1673
  mass **14:**1711, 1715
  motion **14:**1712–1713
  nuclear fusion in **1:**121; **5:**613; **6:***652*;
      **14:***1714*, 1716
  observing the **14:***1712*, 1713
  prominences and flares **13:***1603*;
      **14:***1714*, 1715
  radiative and convective zones
      **14:***1713*
  solar radiation **14:***1712*;
      **15:**1874–1875
  solar spectrum **14:***1716*
  sunlight **7:***843*; **14:***1711*
  sunspots **14:**1714
  surface **14:***1676*, 1713–1715
  temperature **14:**1713, 1715
  *see also* solar energy
sundials **15:**1816, 1819
sunspots **14:**1714
supercharging **4:**422–423
supercomputers **3:***363*, 364
superconducting quantum interference
    devices (SQUIDS) **14:**1719
superconductivity **4:**393; **7:**778, *779*;
    **12:**1453; **14:1717–1720**
  superconductor types **14:**1719–1720
superfinishing **8:**974
supergiants **14:**1673, 1674, 1675
supernovas *see* novas and supernovas
supersonic flight **1:***20*, 45;
    **14:1721–1723**
  scramjets **1:**45
surface mounting **11:***1350*
surface tension **7:**863; **13:**1580;
    **14:1724–1725**
surfactants **13:**1580–1581
surgery **8:**943–944; **13:***1580*;
    **14:1726–1731**
  and stitches **14:**1728
  antiseptic **1:**94; **7:**866–867; **14:**1727

aseptic **14:**1727
cryosurgery **4:**393
holography and **7:**829
laser **5:**584; **7:**828, *829*; **8:**945; **14:**1729
microsurgery **5:**584; **14:**1730
minimal access (MAS; keyhole)
    **8:***938*; **13:***1661*; **14:***1728*, 1730
operating rooms **14:***1727*
orthopedic **14:**1731
surgeons **14:**1728–1729
surgical instruments **14:**1727–*1728*
telesurgery **12:***1480*
using robotics **12:***1480*; **14:***1729*, 1731
*see also* anesthetics; transplants
Surtsey **16:**1941
surveying **14:1732–1735**
  and mapmaking **8:***901*, 903
  geodetic **14:**1732
  plane **14:**1732
  seismic **5:**581; **6:**695–696; **9:***1146*;
      **12:**1532
  using triangulation **14:**1732–1733
  using trilateration **14:**1732
suspension **14:1736–1737**
  automobile **2:**144; **14:**1736–*1737*
  bicycle **2:**177
  hydropneumatic **14:**1742
Sutton Hoo **1:**97
Swammerdam, Jan **8:**998
swamp buggies **1:**75
Swan, Joseph **5:**598; **7:**854
sweat **5:***575*, 576, 577; **13:**1567
sweat glands **5:**576; **9:**1072
Swinton, A. A. Campbell **14:**1768
switchers, for fiber-optic systems **4:**397
switches **14:1738–1739**
  mercury **15:**1799–1800
  solenoids and **13:***1608*
  time **15:**1823–1824
Sydney Harbor Bridge **2:**233
symbiosis **10:**1193, 1276
  mycorrhizae and **6:**649
  *see also* parasitology
symbols, chemical **3:**314, 315, 323
Symington, William **8:**909
synapses **9:**1100
syncho-cyclotrons **10:**1199
synchrotrons **4:**395–*396*;
    **10:***1200*–1201; **14:**1719
synclines **6:**692; **12:**1488
synesthesia **13:**1577
syphilis, treatment **5:**616

testosterone, drugs similar to **10:***1166*
Teton Dam, Idaho **4:**405–406
tetracycline **1:**92
tetrahertz scanners **10:**1161
tetrodotoxin **11:**1309
textiles **14:1780–1785**
  dyes **4:**466–469; **14:***1781*
  finishing treatments **14:**1785
  "intelligent" fabrics **14:**1784
  uses in industry **14:**1783
  *see also* cotton; fiber; silk; wool
textured vegetable protein (TVP) **5:**619
thalamus **2:**218
Thales of Miletus **5:**538; **8:**921
Thames Flood Barrier **4:**406, 407;
  **12:***1470*
thaumotropes **9:***1053*
theodolites **8:***901*; **14:**1733, *1734*, 1735
Theophrastus **2:**185
therapods **4:**434–435
Thera (Santorini), volcanic explosion
  **16:**1939
thermal imaging **7:**777; **10:***1161*
thermionic emission **5:**532
thermocouples **11:**1299; **14:**1787;
  **15:**1798
thermoelectricity **14:1786–1787**
thermography **7:***776*; **8:**933;
  **14:1788–1789**; **15:**1798
  *see also* infrared radiation
thermomechanical generators **14:**1690
thermometers **15:1796–1798**
  bimetallic strip **15:**1798
  bulb **8:**980; **15:***1796*, 1797
  digital **15:***1797*
  electrical **15:**1798
  liquid crystals used in **7:***864*
  liquid-in-glass **15:**1796
  maximum-minimum **15:**1797–1798
  mercury **8:**951; **15:**1797
  strip **15:***1798*
  tympanic (infrared) **15:**1798
  *see also* thermocouples
thermopause **2:***133*
thermoplastics **10:**1271; **11:***1289*
thermoresistors (thermistors)
  **15:**1798
thermos (vacuum) flasks **15:**1895
thermosphere (ionosphere) **2:***133*, 134;
  **7:**795; **8:**1002–1003; **11:***1398*
thermostats **12:**1432, 1440;
  **15:1799–1800**

thiamine **16:**1932
Thomson, J. J. **2:**139, 204–205; **5:**539;
  **10:**1206; **12:**1501
Thomson, Robert William **12:**1500
Thomson effect **14:**1787
thorium **4:**399
Thor missiles **9:**1029
Three Gorges Dam **4:***407*
threonine **1:**71
thrombin **6:***733*
thrust **1:**41
*Thrust SSC* (jet-powered car) **2:**147
thunderstorms **15:1801–1802**;
  **16:***1989*
  lightning **4:***504*; **7:856–857**;
    **15:**1801–*1802*
  thunder **7:**856
thymine **9:**1039
thymus **6:**765
thyristors **13:**1543; **14:1738–1739**
thyroglobulin **11:**1369
thyroid gland **2:**195; **5:***546*, 547
thyrotropin **5:**548
Tibetan Plateau **11:**1295
tibia and fibula **13:**1564
tidal flooding **12:***1470*
tidal power **5:**552; **6:**757; **9:**1143;
  **15:1803–1806**, 1810
tides **9:**1043, 1138; **15:**1804,
  **1807–1810**
  high and low **15:**1807, *1808*
  spring and neap **15:**1808, *1809*
  *see also* tidal power
TIFF files **10:**1248, *1249*
Tilghman, Benjamin **10:**1185
tiles, ceramic **3:**308, *309*, 311
till **6:**700
tillite **12:**1484
tiltmeters **16:**1941
timber industry **15:1811–1814**
time **15:1815–1818**
  measures of **8:**931; **9:**1124
  sidereal and solar **15:**1816
  theory of relativity and **12:**1437;
    **15:**1818
  time zones **15:**1817–*1818*
  *see also* calendars; timekeeping
    devices
timekeeping devices **15:**1816–1817,
  **1819–1824**
  atomic clocks **6:**706; **8:**931; **15:***1817*,
    1822–1823, *1824*

chronometers **15:***1816*, *1820*–1821
clepsydras (water clocks) **15:**1816,
  1819
digital watches **7:**865; **15:**1822
electrical clocks and watches
  **15:***1821*, 1822
event timers **15:***1823*, 1824
hourglasses **15:***1815*, 1816, 1819
mechanical clocks and watches
  **15:***1819*–1822
pendulum clocks **10:***1212*, 1213;
  **15:**1816, 1820
quartz clocks and watches **10:***1264*;
  **15:**1817, 1822
stopwatches **15:***1822*
sundials (shadow clocks) **15:**1816,
  1819
time switches **15:**1823–1824
tin **15:1825–1826**
  alloys **15:**1825
  block **15:**1826
tin chloride **15:**1826
tin oxides **15:**1826
tinplate **15:**1825
tires **12:**1497, *1500*; **14:**1736
  bicycle **2:**176
  racing car **2:**148
Titania (moon) **15:**1886, 1888
*Titanic* (ship) **14:**1708
titanium **15:1827–1829**
  alloys **11:**1363; **15:**1827
  production **15:***1829*
  uses **15:***1827–1828*
titanium dioxide **10:**1180, *1181*;
  **15:**1829
titanium oxide **15:**1827
titanium tetrachloride **15:**1829
Titan missiles **9:**1029
TNT (trinitrotoluene) **5:**580;
  **9:**1106
tocopherol *see* vitamins, vitamin E
tokamaks **6:**654; **9:**1117–*1118*
  Tokamak Fusion Test Reactor
    **11:**1285
Tomahawk missiles **9:***1028*,
  1031–1032
tomatoes, genetically engineered
  **2:**210; **6:**675
Tombaugh, Clyde **11:***1302*
*Tom Thumb* (locomotive) **12:**1412
tongue, taste buds **14:**1750–*1751*
tonsils **7:**884

tools and tool manufacture **15:**1830–1835
  *see also* woodworking
toothpaste **1:**13
topaz **8:***1009*
topography **7:**821
torches
  burning **7:**853
  oxyacetylene **10:**1178
tornadoes **15:**1836–1837; **16:***1994*
  *see also* cyclones (hurricanes; typhoons)
torpedoes **9:**1028, *1032–1033*; **14:***1701*
torques **5:**626; **6:**729
Torricelli, Evangelista **2:***167*; **11:**1348
Torricellian vacuum **2:**167
torrs **15:**1893
touch **15:**1838–1839
  plants' sense of **2:**210–212
touch-screen technology **10:***1220*, 1221
tourmaline **8:**1011
towers **13:***1571*
Towneley, Richard **8:**996
Townes, Charles H. **7:**826, 827
Townshend, Charles **1:**25
trachea **12:**1461–1462
tracked air-cushion vehicles **9:**1041
traffic control **12:**1476; **15:**1840–1843
  speed limits **12:**1476
trains
  automatic **12:**1425
  brakes **2:**222–223, 224; **12:**1425
  bullet **7:***874*, 875
  electric **12:**1425
  maglev **7:***858*, 859, *875*; **9:**1041; **10:***1261*; **14:***1718*
  rapid-transport-system **12:**1425
  *see also* locomotives
trams **14:***1692*, 1694
transcendental numbers **9:**1126
transducers **10:**1265; **13:**1640; **15:**1844–1845
  capacitative **15:**1845
  electrostrictive **15:**1872
  inductive **15:**1845
  magnetostrictive **15:**1871–1872
  micromechanical friction **15:***1844*
  piezoelectric **15:**1871
  potentiometric **15:**1844–1845
  strain-gauge **2:**158; **15:**1845
  ultrasound **8:**937; **15:**1871–1872
  *see also* microphones; speakers

transformers **6:**672, 756–757; **7:***772*, 773; **11:**1337–1338, *1340*, 1342; **15:**1846–1847
  early **7:**772
  flyback **14:**1779
transgenic organisms **1:**29; **6:**675–676
transistors **5:**527–528, 533; **8:**990, 994; **14:**1768; **15:**1848–1850
  field effect (FETs) **13:**1543; **15:**1850
  in microchips **8:**991
  insulated-gate field effect (IGFETs) **15:**1850
  invention **3:**360; **5:**527; **13:**1542; **14:**1768; **15:**1849
  junction (bipolar) **13:**1542; **15:**1849–1850
  junction-gate field effect (JFETs) **13:***1542*, 1543; **15:**1850
  light-emitting **10:**1161
  semiconductors **15:**1848–1849
transition elements **15:**1851–1854
transits **14:**1734
translucent substances **10:**1156
transmutation **5:**541
transparent substances **10:**1156
transpiration **16:**1969
transplants **8:**943–944; **14:**1730–1731
  bone **4:**413
  heart **3:**331; **14:**1730
  kidney **5:**574; **14:***1731*
  lung **14:**1731
Transrapid system **7:**859
transuranic elements **5:**541; **10:**1218
TRANSYT system **15:**1841
Trapezium **9:**1089–1090
travelators **5:**545
trawling, stern **5:**612
tree rings, to date objects **1:**99–100
trees
  felling **15:***1812*
  hardwood **15:**1811, 1812
  softwood **15:***1811*–1812
trenches, ocean **4:**484; **9:***1140*; **11:**1294
  Mariana Trench **9:**1141
Trésaguet, Pierre-Marie-Jérôme **12:**1471–1472
Trevithick, Richard **7:**870; **8:**1016; **14:**1686–1687
triacetate **5:**599
"triads, law of" **10:**1215
triangulation **8:**928–929

Triassic period **6:**687
*Triceratops* **4:***436*
Trident missiles **9:**1029; **14:***1702*
*Trieste* (submersible) **14:**1706
trilobites **6:***685*
trinitrotoluene (TNT) **5:**580; **9:**1106
triodes **5:**527, 533; **11:**1398
triple point of water **14:**1777
tritium **5:**552; **6:**652, *653*, 760
  and nuclear fusion **9:**1117, 1118, 1122
Triton (moon) **9:***1095*
Trojan horses **3:**366
Trojans (computer viruses) **16:**1925
trolleybuses **12:**1422; **14:***1691*, 1692
trombones **9:**1077
*Troodon* **4:**435
trophic levels **5:**625
tropopause **2:***133*; **16:**2007
troposphere **2:**132–*133*; **3:**345; **11:***1398*
trucks **15:**1855–1858
  brakes **2:**222, 224; **15:***1856*
  forklift **5:**634–635
truffles **6:***649*
Truman, Harry S. **2:***234*
trumpets **9:**1077
tryptophan **1:**71
Tschermak von Seysenegg, Erich **6:**677
Tsiolkovsky, Konstantin Eduardovich **12:**1490
tsunamis **15:**1808, **1859–1861**
Tsvet, Mikhail **3:**324
Tube, London **12:**1423, 1424
Tull, Jethro **1:**26
tumbling **8:**973
tumors
  detected using thermography **14:**1788
  *see also* cancer
tundra **2:**189–190; **13:**1595
tungsten **15:***1852*
tuning forks **13:***1613*
tunneling **12:**1424; **15:**1862–1865
turbines **15:**1866–1869
  gas *see* gas turbines
  hydraulic **5:**518; **6:**755–756
  impulse **6:**755–756; **15:**1867
  reactor **6:**756
  steam **5:**518; **6:**738; **8:**910; **14:***1688*; **15:***1867, 1868–1869*

Straflo **15:***1805*, 1806
water **6:**755–756; **15:**1803, *1805*, 1806,
  1866–1868
wind **5:**518; **11:***1339*; **15:***1866*;
  **16:***2014*
*Turbinia* (ship) **8:**910
turbochargers **4:**422–423;
  **15:***1857–1858*
turbulence, air **1:**22
Turing, Alan **1:**113; **3:**359
Turing test **1:**113
turntables, record **13:***1620*
turquoise **8:***1009*
Turri, Peregrino **7:**817
Tusi, Nasir ad-Din at- **8:**921
tweeters **13:**1641
twins, identical **3:***340*; **6:***677*
twisters *see* tornadoes
typesetting **11:**1354–1355
typewriters *see* keyboards and
  typewriters
typhoons *see* cyclones (hurricanes;
  typhoons)
*Tyrannosaurus rex* **4:**434
tyrosine **1:**71

**U**
UGSs (unattended ground sensors)
  **12:**1448
UHT process **5:**621
Ulloa, Antonio de **11:**1296
ultracentrifuges **3:***307*
ultrafiltration **10:**1172
ultralights **1:**43
ultrasonics **15:***1870–1873*
  for drilling **15:***1873*
  for welding **15:***1873*; **16:**2002
  medical uses **8:***937*; **11:***1344*;
    **13:***1615*, 1616; **15:***1871*, 1873
  to clean materials **15:**1873
  to test materials **15:***1872*, 1873
  ultrasound **8:**937; **13:**1616;
    **15:***1870*–1871
  undersea **15:**1873
ultraviolet **7:**844; **13:**1644;
  **15:1874–1876**
  and fluorescence **15:**1875
  observatories and **9:**1136
  uses **15:***1875–1876*
umbra **10:**1156
Umbriel (moon) **15:**1888
uncertainty principle **11:**1392

unified field theory **4:**496
Union Carbide disaster **11:***1308*
United States
  inland waterways **3:**276
  roads and road building
    **12:**1472–*1473*
  time zones **15:**1817–*1818*
Universal Product Code (UPC) **2:**165
Universal Resource Locators (URLs)
  **7:**790
universe **15:1877–1882**
  age **15:**1879, 1880
  background (fireball) radiation
    **15:***1879*, 1880–1881
  big bang and **1:**123; **2:**198; **5:***538*;
    **12:**1438; **15:***1877, 1879*
  death of **15:**1881–1882
  early understanding of **1:**120;
    **3:**372–373; **15:***1877–1878*
  expanding **1:**123; **4:**457;
    **15:**1879–1880
  inflation **15:**1881
  measuring distances in **15:**1880
  missing mass in **15:**1882
  open or closed **15:**1881
  oscillating **15:**1881
  scale of **15:**1878–1879
  steady-state theory **15:**1881
  *see also* black holes; nebulas;
    novas and supernovas; solar
    system; stars; Sun
uraninite **15:***1883*
uranium **5:**540; **11:**1401; **12:***1502*;
  **15:1883–1884**
  and nuclear fission **5:**551, 613,
    *614–615*; **9:**1113, 1114, 1119–1120;
    **11:**1339; **15:**1884
  and the atomic bomb **5:**614;
    **9:**1120, 1121
  enriched **9:**1121; **15:**1884
  fuel rods **10:***1219*
  half life **5:**615; **7:**801
  isotopes **5:**614, 615; **7:**801; **9:**1114,
    1119–1120; **15:**1884
  ores and mining **15:**1883
  prospecting for **6:**670
  refining **15:**1884
uranium hydroxide **15:***1883*
uranium oxide **15:***1883*, 1884
Uranus **13:**1605; **15:1885–1888**
  discovery **6:***744*; **15:**1885
  effect of Neptune on **9:**1092–1093

magnetic field **15:**1888
moons **15:***1886*, 1888
rings **15:***1887–1888*
tilting axis **15:**1887
urea **10:**1164
ureters **5:***571*
urethra **12:**1450–1451
Urey, Harold **1:***71*; **5:**566
Ussher, James **4:**473; **6:**689
uterus **11:**1344–1345, 1346

**V**
V-1 missiles **9:**1028, 1031
V-2 rockets **12:***1491*
V22 Osprey (aircraft) **16:**1961
V838 Monocerotis **9:***1107*
vaccinations **15:1889–1892**, 1917
  bioengineered vaccines **6:**676
  Jenner and **7:**805; **15:**1889–1890
  Pasteur and **10:***1211*
  smallpox **7:***804–805*; **10:**1211;
    **15:***1889*–1890, 1891–1892
vacuoles **3:***302*
vacuum **15:1893–1895**
  heat in a **6:**738
  vacuum coating **15:**1894–1895
  vacuum cleaners **15:***1893*, 1895
  vacuum drying, salt **12:**1516
  vacuum (thermos) flasks **15:**1895
  vacuum tubes (thermionic valves)
    **5:**526, 527, 533
    diodes **5:**527, *533*
    triodes **5:**527, 533; **11:**1398
vagina **12:**1450
valence **5:**541; **10:**1216, 1219;
  **15:1896–1897**
valleys
  hanging **6:**699
  rift **7:**824; **12:**1488
  U-shaped **6:**699; **7:***821*, 824
  V-shaped **6:**699; **7:**824
valves **15:1898–1899**
  artificial heart-valves **15:***1899*
  balance **15:**1898
  check **15:**1899
  demand **4:***448*, 449
  gate **15:***1898*, 1899
  globe **15:**1899
  hydraulic **6:**753
  internal combustion engine
    **15:**1899
  lift **15:**1898

valves (*continued*)
  needle **15**:1899
  slide **15**:1899
  steam **15**:1899
  stop **15**:1898–1899
  thermionic *see* vacuum tubes
vanadium **8**:963
Van Allen belts **11**:1285
Van de Graaf generators **4**:*506*
vapor **15**:*1900*–1901
vaporization **4**:444
vapor pressure **15**:**1900–1901**
variables **8**:925
varnish **10**:1181
*Vasa* (ship) **1**:101
vas deferens **12**:1450
vaults **12**:*1504, 1506*
vegetables
  in the diet **9**:1129
  processing **5**:618
vegetarians **9**:1130
veins **3**:*326*–327, *328*
  pulmonary vein **12**:*1460*
vellum **10**:1185
velociraptors **4**:434–*435*
velocity **5**:626
  terminal **6**:718; **16**:1929
  vector nature **9**:*1050*
ventilators **8**:942, *945*
venturi effect **15**:**1902–1903**
Venturi, Giovanni **15**:1902
Venus **13**:1604; **15**:**1904–1907**
  atmosphere **15**:1904–1907
  atmospheric temperature **14**:1777
  missions to **1**:125; **13**:1627; **15**:*1905*
  phases of **15**:1904
  rotation **15**:1905
  surface **11**:*1396*; **13**:*1605*; **15**:*1904, 1906, 1907*
*Venus 7* (space probe) **13**:1626
Verrazano Narrows Bridge **2**:233
vertebrae **13**:*1562*, 1564
vertebrates **1**:80, 82
very high frequency omnidirectional radio (VOR) **9**:1086
Very Large Array (VLA) **1**:*89*; **14**:*1764*, 1765
very large-scale integration (VLSI) **8**:991
Very Large Telescope (VLT) **1**:124
Very Large Telescope Interferometer (VLTI) **9**:*1135*

Very Long Baseline Array (VLBA) **9**:1135
very long baseline interferometry (VLBI) **14**:1765
Vesalius, Andreas **2**:185; **8**:938
Vesuvius, Mount **16**:1941
vibrations **12**:1457
vibratory systems **12**:1457
videophones **9**:1037; **15**:**1908–1909**
video recording **14**:1774
  videocassette recorders (VCRs) **7**:887
  videocassettes **7**:*887*
  videotape recorders (VTRs) **7**:887
Vidie, Lucien **2**:168
*Viking 1* (space probe) **13**:1626, 1628
*Viking 2* (space probe) **13**:1628
Villard, Paul **6**:657; **11**:1403
villi **4**:*426*; **7**:*882*
violins **9**:*1074*, 1075; **12**:*1458*
virtual reality (VR) **3**:*367*; **15**:**1910–1913**
viruses, biological **8**:989; **15**:**1914–1917**
  and disease **4**:440–441; **6**:765
  classification **3**:*335*
  discovery **8**:986
  DNA **4**:440–441; **15**:1914–1915
  grown in the laboratory **15**:1917
  influenza **6**:765; **15**:*1890*, 1915, 1916
  multiplication of **15**:1915–1916
  rabies **10**:*1211*
  spread **15**:*1916*
  structure and shapes **15**:*1915*
  types **15**:*1915*
  *see also* AIDS
viruses, computer **3**:366; **16**:**1924–1927**
viscometers **16**:1928–1929
viscosity **7**:*863*; **12**:1454; **16**:**1928–1929**
  coefficient of **16**:1929
vision
  color **5**:582; **7**:*848*
  ion channels in **3**:304
  persistence of **14**:1773
vitamins **9**:1127, 1129; **16**:**1930–1933**
  vitamin A (retinol) **9**:1129, 1130; **16**:1930, 1931, 1932, 1933
  vitamin B **9**:1129, 1130; **16**:1930–1931, 1932, 2036
  vitamin C (ascorbic acid) **1**:*14*; **9**:1127, 1129; **16**:*1931*, 1932, 1933
  vitamin D (calciferol) **14**:*1712*; **15**:1876; **16**:1931, 1932, *1933*
  vitamin E (tocopherol) **16**:1931, 1932

vitamin K (phylloquinone) **9**:1129; **16**:1932
VO2 max **13**:*1660*–1661
voice analysis **16**:**1934–1937**
volcanic bombs **16**:1938
volcanoes **6**:*691*; **7**:822–823; **11**:*1294*; **16**:**1938–1941**
  active **16**:*1938*–1939
  causing tsunamis **15**:1860
  cinder cones **16**:*1939*
  composite **16**:*1939*
  eruptions **16**:1939–1940
  eruptions predicted **16**:1941
  extinct **16**:1938
  fissure **16**:*1939*
  intermediate **16**:1940–1941
  quiet **16**:*1939*, 1940
  shield **16**:*1939*, 1940
  why volcanoes occur **16**:1941
Volta, Alessandro **2**:169–*170*; **4**:506; **10**:1260; **14**:1752; **16**:**1942–1943**
voltage **4**:502
  ratios **15**:1847–1848
  SI number prefixes **8**:930
voltaic pile **2**:169–*170*; **16**:*1943*
voltmeters **4**:*499*, 500
volts **16**:1942, 1943
"Vomit Comet" **16**:1998
vomiting **9**:1071
von Braun, Wernher **12**:1490–1491
von Patera process **13**:1559
Voyager space probes **6**:*656*; **13**:1626, *1627*, 1629–1630
  data about Uranus and its moons **15**:*1885, 1886*, 1887–*1888*
  to Neptune **9**:*1094–1095*; **13**:*1628*, 1630
  to Saturn and its moons **12**:*1524, 1525, 1526*; **13**:*1628*, 1629
Vries, Hugo de **6**:677; **8**:947
V/STOL aircraft **7**:*808*; **16**:**1944–1947**, 1958, 1960
VTOL aircraft **1**:44–45
Vulcan, search for **8**:955
vulcanization **12**:1497, *1498*, 1499
vulcanology **6**:692

**W**

wadis (arroyos) **4**:414
Walcott, Charles **6**:685
Wallace, Alfred Russel **2**:186; **4**:409; **5**:569

Walters, W. Grey **1:**113
Wankel, Felix **7:**787; **16:***1948*
Wankel engines (rotary engines)
  **7:**787; **8:**912; **14:**1685–1686;
  **16:1948–1949**
WAP (wireless application protocol)
  **9:**1036
warfarin **10:**1224
warplanes **16:1951–1956**
  against ships **16:**1957–1958
warships **16:1957–1962**
  nuclear-powered **16:***1960*, 1961
washboards, on boats **13:**1551
washers **15:**1898
washing machines **16:1963–1964**
wasps **2:**212; **8:***1001*
  as parasitoids **10:**1193
  gall **10:**1194
waste **11:**1312
  disposal **11:**1319
  factory **11:**1314
  radioactive (nuclear) **5:**551;
    **9:**1116–*1117*; **11:**1318
  toxic **11:**1318–1319
watches *see* timekeeping devices
water **16:1965–1966**
  boiling point **4:**393; **6:**737
  chemical bonds **15:***1897*
  electrolysis of **5:***520*
  freezing point **4:**393; **16:**1965
  freshwater from seawater **4:**445;
    **10:**1171, *1172*
  hard **7:**795; **16:**1966, 1973
  molecules **2:**138; **16:**1965–1966
  properties **16:**1965
  required by the body **9:**1128;
    **16:***1965*, 1967
  softening **7:**795; **16:**1973
  solubility **16:**1965–1966
  states of **4:**392
  testing **7:***837*
  treatment plants **16:***1971*
  triple point **14:**1777
  vapor **15:***1900*; **16:**1967, 1968
  *see also* water cycle; water supply
water cycle **4:**492; **12:**1418;
  **16:1967–1970**
  waterfalls **16:***1967*
water frames **14:**1782; **16:**2026
waterjets **8:**911, *912*
Waterman, Lewis E. **16:**2028
waterspouts **15:**1837

water supply **16:1971–1974**
  *see also* sewage treatment
water table **16:**1970
water towers **16:**1971
water wheels **15:**1866; **16:***2003*
Watson, James *see* Crick, Francis, and
  James Watson
Watson, John Broadus **11:**1378
Watson-Watt, Robert **11:**1393–1394
Watt, James **8:**1016; **11:**1336; **13:**1544;
  **14:**1685–1686
watt-hour meters **4:**501
watts **5:**550; **11:**1335; **12:**1455
wave-cut platforms **7:**825
wave motion **16:1975–1978**
  amplitude **15:**1870; **16:**1975
  period **16:**1975
  transverse and longitudinal **16:***1976*
  velocity **16:**1976
  wave frequency **15:**1870;
    **16:**1975–1976
  wavelength **15:**1870; **16:**1975
  *see also* diffraction; interference
wave power **16:1979–1982**
waves, ocean **9:***1137*; **16:***1975*, 1976
  and coastal erosion **5:**562, 563
  providing energy **5:**552
  tidal *see* tsunamis
  wave power **16:1979–1982**
weakly interacting massive particles
  (WIMPS) **15:**1882
weak nuclear force **5:**629; **10:**1208,
  1209
weather **16:1989–1990**
  global warming and **6:**711, 712
  *see also* climate; clouds; weather
    systems
weather forecasting **8:**981, *982*
  chaos theory and **3:**312–313
  *see also* meteorology
weathering **5:***559–561*; **12:**1487;
  **16:1983–1988**
  biological **16:***1988*
  chemical **16:***1984*–1987
  mechanical **16:***1987*–1988
  *see also* erosion
weather stations **8:**980, *983*
weather systems **16:1989–1994**
  air masses **16:**1990, 1991
  anticyclones **16:**1993–1994
  cyclones (depressions) **12:**1419, 1470;
    **16:**1992–1993

  destructive *see* cyclones (hurricanes;
    typhoons)
  fronts **12:**1419; **16:**1990–1991,
    1992–1993
  *see also* meteorology
Weaver, Warren **9:**1038
weaving **14:**1780–1781, 1782; **16:**2026
Web cams **7:**789
Wedgwood, Thomas **10:**1242
weeds, control **10:***1224*, 1226–1227
Wegener, Alfred **6:**690; **11:**1292–1293;
  **15:**1853; **16:1995–1996**
weighing machines *see* balances and
  weighing machines
weight *see* mass and weight
weight, personal **14:***1681*–1682
weightlessness **6:***717*; **8:**918–*919*;
  **12:***1435*; **16:1997–1998**
welding **16:1999–2002**
  arc **11:**1285; **16:**1999–*2000*
  electron-beam **16:**2001
  explosion **16:**2002
  friction **16:**2002
  gas **16:**1999
  laser **16:**2001–*2002*
  plasma **16:***2000*–2001
  resistance **16:**2002
  using ultrasonics **15:**1873; **16:**2002
Wells, Horace **4:**410
Welsbach, Carl Auer, Count of
  **7:**853
Wenner-Gren, Axel L. **9:**1040
Wertheimer, Max **11:**1378
westerlies **16:**2008
West Nile virus **10:**1197
wetas **9:**1066
wetlands **2:***192*
wet oil **9:**1148
wetting agents **14:**1725
whales, humpback **9:***1142*
wheat, genetically engineered **2:**210,
  *213*
Wheatstone, Charles **14:**1752, 1753
wheat take-all **6:***676*
Wheeler, John **2:**198
wheel-locks **6:**724
wheels **16:2003–2004**
  bicycle **2:**176
white dwarfs **1:**121; **9:**1091, 1109;
  **14:**1673, 1675, 1716
Whitehead, Robert **9:**1032
white holes **2:**199

Whitelaw, James 15:1866
Whitney, Eli 1:26; 3:380–381; 5:596
Whittle, Frank 1:39; 7:806–807
wide-area networks (WANs)
    3:364–365
Wilkins, Maurice 4:391, 454
Wilkinson, John 2:202
Wilmut, Ian 3:342
Wilson, Edward O. 2:181
Wilson, Robert 15:1879, 1880
WIMPS (weakly interacting massive
    particles) 15:1882
winches and windlasses
    16:2005–2006
wind 16:1990, 2007–2010
    anabatic winds 16:2009
    Beaufort scale 16:2009, 2010
    chinook winds 16:2009, 2010
    jet streams 16:1991, 2010
    katabatic winds 16:2009
    monsoon winds 16:2008–2009
    patterns 3:337
    trade winds 16:2007–2008
    weathering by 5:559; 16:1987
    wind power 5:552; 11:1339, 1341;
        15:1866; 16:2011–2014
windlasses 16:2005, 2006
windmills and wind pumps
    16:2011–2014
    windmills 13:1544; 15:1866;
        16:2011–2014
    wind pumps 16:2013, 2014
    wind turbines 5:518; 11:1339;
        15:1866; 16:2014
windows, stained-glass 6:703–704
wind shear 16:2010
windsurfing 12:1506
wind tunnels 1:21–22; 16:2010
wings 1:19, 22, 40, 41
    supersonic 14:1723
wingsails 12:1512
wire and cable 16:2015–2018
wire guidance systems 9:1029, 1033
wireless application protocol (WAP)
    9:1036
woad 10:1180
Wöhler, Friedrich 1:67; 10:1164
Wollaston, William 11:1296
wood
    building with 2:242–243
    paper made from wood pulp 10:1185,
        1186–1187

wood tin 15:1826
woodworking 16:2019–2022
woofers 13:1641
wool 5:596–597; 14:1780;
    16:2023–2026
    see also spinning
Woolworth Building 13:1569
work, measuring 11:1335
World Meteorological Organization
    8:983
World Ocean Circulation Experiment
    8:985
World Product Code (WPC) 2:166
World War I (1914–1918)
    aircraft 1:38–39; 16:1951–1953
    naval battles 16:1957
    tanks 14:1740, 1744
World War II (1939–1945)
    aircraft 1:39; 16:1953, 1957–1958
    amphibious vehicles 1:74, 75
    ships 16:1957, 1958
    submarines 14:1698, 1701
    tanks 14:1740
World Wide Web 7:789–790
wormholes 2:199
worms (computer viruses) 16:1925
    Code Red 16:1926
wounds, treatment 1:95
W particles 10:1208, 1209
Wright, Orville and Wilbur 1:36, 37
writing
    cuneiform 1:53; 11:1352; 16:2027
    hieroglyphic 16:2027–2028
writing tools 16:2027–2030
    ink pens 16:2028–2030
    keyboards and typewriters
        7:817–819; 16:2030
    word processors 16:1935, 2030
Wundt, Wilhelm 11:1378

X
X-29 (aircraft) 16:1953, 1956
xenon 7:774, 775
xerography 10:1232
X-rays 13:1644; 16:2031–2034
    and radiation therapy 8:943
    computerized axial tomography
        (CAT; CT) scans 8:934, 939;
        16:2033–2034
    dental 16:2033
    discovery 8:932; 16:2031
    images of Egyptian mummies 15:1913

industrial uses 16:2034
in medicine 8:932–934, 939; 14:1729;
    16:2031, 2032–2033
making X-ray pictures 16:2032
observed from space 9:1136
production 16:2031–2032
radiotherapy and 11:1404; 16:2034
security X-ray machines 1:49
X-ray crystallography 4:394, 395–396;
    16:2034
X-ray diffraction 4:454; 10:1256
xylem 10:1254, 1277

Y
Yablonovitch, Eli 10:1161
yachts 12:1508, 1511
Yale, Linus 7:868, 869
Yeager, Chuck 1:45
years 4:475
yeasts 5:590; 8:988–989; 11:1372;
    16:2035–2036
    and beer making 5:591
    and bread making 2:227, 228; 5:590
    and wine making 5:590; 16:2036
yellow fever 10:1193; 16:2045
Yersinia pestis 4:440
Young, Thomas 16:1978
Young's modulus 4:498

Z
Zeiss, Carl 8:999
Zeya Dam 4:405
ziggurats 1:105; 13:1568
zinc 16:2037–2039
    alloys see brass
    reaction with hydrochloric acid
        3:318; 12:1514
zinc chloride 12:1514
zinc oxide 16:2037, 2038, 2039
zinc sulfide 16:2037, 2039
zirconium boride 3:310
zoetropes 1:84; 9:1052
zoo 16:2040–2043
zoology 16:2044–2045
    see also animal kingdom; evolution;
        parasitology; zoo
zooplankton 16:2045
zooxanthellae 3:339; 9:1141
Z particles 10:1204, 1208, 1209
Zwicky, Fritz 9:1107, 1109
Zworykin, Vladimir 14:1768
zygote 12:1452